The Philosophy of Rawls

A Collection of Essays

Series Editors

Henry S. Richardson
Georgetown University

Paul J. Weithman
University of Notre Dame

A GARLAND SERIES
READINGS IN PHILOSOPHY
ROBERT NOZICK, *ADVISOR*
HARVARD UNIVERSITY

Contents of the Series

1. Development and Main Outlines of Rawls's Theory of Justice
2. The Two Principles and Their Justification
3. Opponents and Implications of *A Theory of Justice*
4. Moral Psychology and Community
5. Reasonable Pluralism

Reasonable Pluralism

Edited with an introduction by

Paul J. Weithman
University of Notre Dame

GARLAND PUBLISHING, INC.
A MEMBER OF THE TAYLOR & FRANCIS GROUP
New York & London
1999

Library of Congress Cataloging-in-Publication Data

Reasonable pluralism / edited with an introduction by Paul J.
Weithman.
      p.   cm. — (The philosophy of Rawls ; 5)
    "A Garland series, readings in philosophy."
    Includes bibliographical references.
    ISBN 0-8153-2929-6 (alk. paper)
    1. Rawls, John, 1921—Contributions in political science.
2. Pluralism (Social sciences) I. Weithman, Paul J., 1959–.
II. Series.

JC251.R32 R43 1999
320'.092—dc21
                                        99-048466

Printed on acid-free, 250-year-life paper
Manufactured in the United States of America

Contents

vii   Series Introduction

ix   Volume Introduction

NEUTRALITY

1   Liberalism, Autonomy, and the Politics of Neutral Concern
Joseph Raz

33   Liberal Individualism and Liberal Neutrality
Will Kymlicka

OVERLAPPING CONSENSUS AND REASONABLE PLURALISM

56   Moral Pluralism and Political Consensus
Joshua Cohen

78   Disagreements About Justice
Jeremy Waldron

94   The Appeal of Political Liberalism
Samuel Scheffler

113   Justice and the Aims of Political Philosophy
Kurt Baier

POLITICAL PHILOSOPHY WITHOUT METAPHYSICS

133   Facing Diversity: The Case of Epistemic Abstinence
Joseph Raz

177   Should Political Philosophy Be Done Without Metaphysics?
Jean Hampton

201   The Priority of Democracy to Philosophy
Richard Rorty

223   Liberalism and the Political Character of Political Philosophy
Paul Weithman

PUBLIC REASON

247   On Public Reason
Kent Greenawalt

269   Contexts of the Political Role of Religion:
Civil Society and Culture
David Hollenbach

RAWLS AND HABERMAS

295   Toward a Critical Theory of Justice
Iris M. Young

320   Kantian Constructivism and Reconstructivism:
Rawls and Habermas in Dialogue
Thomas McCarthy

341   Reconciliation Through the Public Use of Reason:
Remarks on John Rawls's Political Liberalism
Jürgen Habermas

365   Acknowledgments

Series Introduction

John Rawls is the pre-eminent political philosopher of our time. His 1971 masterpiece, *A Theory of Justice*, permanently changed the landscape of moral and political theory, revitalizing the normative study of social issues and taking stands about justice, ethics, rationality, and philosophical method that continue to draw followers and critics today. His *Political Liberalism* (rev. ed., 1996) squarely faced the fundamental challenges posed by cultural, religious, and philosophical pluralism. It should be no surprise, then, that turn-of-the-century searches of the periodical indices in philosophy, economics, law, the humanities, and related fields turn up almost three thousand articles devoted to a critical discussion of Rawls's theory. In these Volumes we reprint a wide-ranging selection of the most influential and insightful articles on Rawls.

While it was impossible, even in a collection of this size, to reprint all of the important material, the selection here should provide the student and scholar with a route into all of the significant controversies that have surrounded Rawls's theories since he first began enunciating them in the nineteen-fifties — issues that the Introductions to each Volume of this series delineate. Eight criteria guided our selection. First, these volumes form part of a series devoted to *secondary* literature. We reprint no articles by Rawls: most of these have just appeared together for the first time in his *Collected Papers*.[1] Second, we reprint only self-contained articles published in English, rather than selections from books or articles in other languages. Third, the articles reprinted here are all *about* Rawls's view, as opposed to being original reflections inspired by Rawls's work. Fourth, we aimed for a broad coverage of controversies and of the main features of Rawls's theory that they surround. Since the Volumes are organized in terms of these controversies, we include very few overall assessments or book reviews. Some central elements of Rawls's theory, while relatively novel and well-articulated, have not been controversial enough to draw critical fire in the secondary literature. The Volume Introductions mention many of these features. Fifth, we aimed to include the most influential articles that have appeared. In identifying these, we used a systematic search of the citation indices to supplement our own judgment. Naturally, we also took special notice of pieces cited by Rawls himself. Sixth, we sought to reprint articles by a large number of authors representing the widest possible range of points of view. In some cases, this meant refraining from reprinting a certain article because its author was already well represented in the selections. Seventh, we have sought to exhibit through our selections the broadly interdisciplinary influence of Rawls's writings. We have included articles by political theorists, economists, lawyers, religious thinkers, and social scientists as well as by philosophers. Eighth, we have favored including articles that are now relatively hard to find. For this reason, with the exception of H.L.A. Hart's exceptionally influential essay, we refrained from including any of the fine articles that were reprinted in Norman Daniels's 1975 collection, *Reading Rawls*,[2] which the reader interested in the early reception of Rawls's views should consult.

Utilizing all of these selection criteria did not leave us without painful choices. The secondary literature on Rawls is so deep that another set of five volumes could cover all the main issues with a completely non-overlapping set of fine articles. Some articles unfortunately had to be cut because of their sheer length: dropping one of them allowed us to include two or three others. Others, more arbitrarily, fell victim to the high permissions costs set by their initial publishers. We particularly regret that it proved impossible to find a short enough, self-contained essay by Robert Nozick that would have represented his trenchant libertarian critique of Rawls. While we do include (in Vol. 3) some of the secondary literature that responds to and picks up on Nozick's influential arguments, one should consult Nozick's *Anarchy, State, and Utopia* (1974) to appreciate their richness, subtlety, and power.[3]

The five volumes are arranged in roughly chronological order. The first volume includes articles on Rawls's early statements of his view and on its central contractarian ideas. Volume 2 covers the two principles of justice as fairness and Rawls's most general ideas about their justification. Volume 3 focuses on the concrete implications of Rawls's view and on the debates between Rawls and his utilitarian, perfectionist, libertarian, conservative, radical, and feminist critics. Volume 4 treats of Rawls's moral psychology and his attempt to accommodate the value of community. Volume 5, on Rawls's most recent work, is entitled "Reasonable Pluralism."

The serious student of Rawls's initial impact is greatly assisted by *John Rawls and His Critics: An Annotated Bibliography*, put together by J.H. Wellbank, Denis Snook, and David T. Mason, which catalogues and provides abstracts for most of the secondary literature in English prior to 1982.[4] While this work was of great help with that earlier period, completing the onerous task of collecting and sorting through the voluminous secondary literature, which has since continued to balloon, would not have been possible without the able and thorough research assistance of Rachael Yocum. We are grateful to the Dean of Georgetown College and to the Graduate School of Georgetown University for their generosity in supporting this research assistance.

Henry S. Richardson

Paul J. Weithman

Notes

[1] John Rawls, *Collected Papers*, ed. Samuel Freeman (Cambridge, Mass.: Harvard University Press, 1999).

[2] Norman Daniels, ed., *Reading Rawls* (N.Y.: Basic Books, 1975).

[3] Robert Nozick, *Anarchy, State, and Utopia* (N.Y.: Basic Books, 1974).

[4] J.H. Wellbank, Denis Snook, and David T. Mason, *John Rawls and His Critics: An Annotated Bibliography* (New York: Garland, 1982).

Volume Introduction

Rawls's stated aim in *A Theory of Justice* is to develop a conception of justice that can serve as an "appropriate moral basis of a democratic society".[1] That conception is to provide society's "public charter" (*TJ*, p. 131): its publicly known and mutually acknowledged basis for settling conflicting claims. The societies to which Rawls's work is addressed are characterized by what he calls "the fact of pluralism": their citizens adhere to views of the good life that are in practice irreconcilable. Rawls says that a deeper appreciation of this fact was what moved him to recast the arguments of *TJ* (*PL*, p. xix). The argument in *TJ* that justice as fairness would generate its own support once it was accepted as a public charter presupposed, he indicates, that all citizens in a well-ordered society would come to share the liberal view of the good described in part III of *TJ*. This presupposition, he now acknowledges, was "unrealistic" (*PL*, p. xix).[2] A well-ordered society under realistic circumstances will contain many views of the good with which justice as fairness must be shown congruent. The argument that justice as fairness could generate its own support therefore had to be recast. This, Rawls notes, sent reverberations throughout justice as fairness and led to a new presentation of the theory as a whole. Rawls indicated what form that presentation would take in a series of papers published in the 1980s.[3] The new presentation was systematically laid out and defended in *Political Liberalism*.

The new presentation of justice as fairness in *PL* shows the famous political turn of Rawls's later work. In *PL* as in *TJ*, Rawls takes his task to be that of elaborating a conception of justice that can serve as a mutually acceptable public charter. He came more fully to appreciate that deriving justice as fairness from controversial positions in moral philosophy and metaphysics, including controversial liberal views of the good, would stand in the way of its acceptability. He therefore presents justice as fairness as standing free of all views of the good life and the nature of persons. Justice as fairness, he says in *PL*, is political rather than metaphysical at its base. It is elaborated from fundamental ideas latent in the political culture of liberal democracies (*PL*, pp. 13–15), ideas whose deeper philosophical vindication he does not provide. Justice as fairness is also political rather than metaphysical in its pretensions. To avoid long-standing controversy on the nature of truth as it applies to philosophical positions, Rawls says that the object of the overlapping consensus should not be presented as true. Instead Rawls claims only that justice as fairness is the most reasonable conception for a democratic society characterized by the fact of pluralism. The assertion that it is true is an "extra step" which citizens may, if they like, take from their own points of view (*PL*, p. 153). For Rawls himself to claim truth for justice as fairness would be "unnecessary and may interfere with the practical aim of finding an agreed public basis for justification" (*PL*, p. 153). As is clear from his reliance on ideas found in political culture and his refusal to claim truth, the political turn in Rawls's later work led him to a much more modest conception of political philosophy. The papers in this volume examine the political turn in Rawls's work, its implications for political philosophy, and the ideas in *TJ* which seem to anticipate it.

To see what ideas in *TJ* anticipate the political turn, it is helpful to see how Rawls's own description of his reasons for taking it can mislead. While his increasing appreciation of the fact of pluralism may have led him to recast the arguments of *TJ*, part III, that fact is essential to the arguments of *TJ*, part I. There pluralism about religious and philosophical views is numbered among the circumstances of justice (*TJ*, p. 127). Parties in the original position know they must adopt a conception suitable for a pluralistic society. Furthermore, the fact of pluralism is one of Rawls's reasons for imposing the veil of ignorance on the parties. By keeping them ignorant of their own views of the good life, the veil effectively prevents them from adopting a conception founded on one of those views. When Rawls wrote *TJ*, he may have thought that once justice as fairness was publicly accepted in a well-ordered society, it would encourage citizens to converge on a liberal view of the good. He also recognized from the outset that because of the pluralism that characterizes modern democracies, conceptions of justice explicitly premised on a view of the good life would not be acceptable as a public charter in the first place. Thus what Rawls realized after the publication of *TJ* was not that a conception of justice for a pluralistic society should not be based on a controversial view of the good. That he knew already. What he came to appreciate is that a liberal view of the good is controversial.

TJ's insistence on both the fact of pluralism and the requirement that a conception of justice be capable of serving as a public charter have led some philosophers to think that justice as fairness aspires to *neutrality* among the views the good citizens actually or potentially embrace. Rawls's commitment to neutrality is said to become greater as his response to Hart deepened his appreciation of the social role of justice. In the first of his two articles reprinted here, Joseph Raz claims to find a commitment to neutrality in the "Dewey Lectures." As Raz notes, there are different ways in which a conception of justice can be neutral. It might be "passively neutral," neutral in the sense that it does not have the consequence of favoring one conception of the good life over another. It could be "actively neutral," in that it affects all conceptions of the good to some degree, but affects all equally. It could be "neutral in its purposes," in that it forbids government to act for the purpose of promoting any conception of the good. This points to a second way in which a conception can be actively neutral: it could permit government to promote some conception of the good, but only in order to bring about some form of equality among adherents of all conceptions. Raz takes Rawls to be committed to this last version of neutrality. He then argues that pluralism does not require neutrality of the sort to which he thinks Rawls is committed. Will Kymlicka begins his article by contesting Raz's interpretation. He argues that Rawls is committed, not to the second sort of active neutrality, but to neutrality of purposes. This commitment is consistent with government action's advancing some ways of life over others. The most pressing question, for Kymlicka, is whether Rawlsian liberalism is systematically likely to advance ways of life that are objectionably individualistic. The charge of excessive individualism has dogged Rawls since the publication of *TJ* (see the introduction to Volume 4). Kymlicka argues, however, that the charge is ultimately without merit.

It should not be surprising that commentators have asked what form of neutrality Rawls endorses. Discussions of neutrality bulked large in political philosophy in the late 1980s and early 1990s.[4] It is natural that contributors to those discussions would try to locate Rawls's work within them. Yet Rawls himself is chary of the term 'neutral' and reluctant to apply it to his own view (see *PL*, p. 191). He thinks that a workable conception of justice that is publicly acknowledged will, over time, shape citizens' moral attitudes and considered moral judgments. It may not shape them in the way Rawls thought when he wrote part III of *TJ*. Even so, the effect of a public conception of justice on citizens' attitudes is a fact of social learning which explains how conceptions of justice generate their own support; encouraging citizens to live up to the ideals of citizenship is part of the social role of justice (cf. *PL*, p. 213). The conformity of basic institutions to justice is fairness is bound to have some implications for the conceptions of the good that citizens of a well-ordered society pursue. Therefore an appreciation of the social role of justice does not imply a commitment to neutrality. It implies that the question of whether justice as fairness is neutral among conceptions of the good is too imprecisely stated to be of interest. The really interesting question, Rawls would say, is how it is possible for a conception of justice to shape citizens' moral attitudes and judgments so that they support it for the right reasons, even while they are deeply divided in many of their moral views (*PL*, p. xx).

The answer Rawls gives in *PL* is that this is possible because it is possible for justice as fairness to be the object of what he calls "an overlapping consensus." It is possible, that is, for adherents of incompatible conceptions of the good to endorse justice as fairness as their society's public charter, each from her own point of view. For Rawls's purposes, the possibility of an overlapping consensus may be sufficient; perhaps he need not show that such a consensus is probable or likely (see the introduction to Volume 4). Still, it will not do to assert that such a consensus is possible because it is not logically *im*possible.[5] Some political phenomena that are not logically impossible – that the whole world will be voluntarily united under the rule of the first person born in a given year, for example — are nonetheless so highly unlikely as to be of no interest to political philosophy. An overlapping consensus must be possible in some more robust sense of the term.

Rawls does not distinguish various ways in which an overlapping consensus can be possible. What he seems to have in mind is that an overlapping consensus is possible in the sense that it is neither *psychologically* nor *politically* impossible. To show that an overlapping consensus is possible in this sense, Rawls draws on reasonable laws of moral psychology and reasonable conjectures about political sociology to explain how an overlapping consensus might develop among the adherents of various conceptions of the good in a society whose public culture is already imbued with democratic ideas (*PL*, pp. 158–68). The problem with this explanation is that it is highly *im*plausible that all conceptions of the good, even in a just democratic regime, would or even could participate in an overlapping consensus on justice as fairness. It seems certain that there will always be some outliers. One way to deal with the outliers would be to alter the contents of justice as fairness in whatever way is necessary to secure their support. This coalition-building around justice as fairness is clearly unacceptable, for the alterations they demand may be unjust. The altered conception could then hardly purport to be acceptable as a public conception of justice. What Rawls needs is a non-ad hoc way to distinguish conceptions which could participate in an overlapping consensus on justice as fairness from those which could not, and an argument that it is legitimate to focus exclusively on the former when establishing the possibility of such a consensus.

By distinguishing the pluralism of conceptions of the good from reasonable pluralism in the article reprinted here, Joshua Cohen provides Rawls the conceptual machinery he needs to do just that. He therefore provides Rawls the tools he needs to fill a potentially fatal gap in his argument (cf. *PL*, p. 36, note 37). Cohen shows that an overlapping consensus is not a brokered compromise among all conceptions of the good, tailored to win over the outliers. Instead, he argues, the possibility of an overlapping consensus is established by showing that justice as fairness could be supported by the adherents of reasonable conceptions.

The papers that immediately follow Cohen's in this volume raise questions about the significance of showing that an overlapping consensus is possible in the way that Rawls can show it to be if Cohen is right. Jeremy Waldron remarks that Rawls has established only the "theoretical possibility" of an overlapping consensus on justice as fairness. The possibility is merely a theoretical one because its realization, though not politically impossible, is still politically implausible. It depends, Waldron claims, upon society-wide agreement on a conception of justice. The possibility of such a consensus is no less remote than agreement on a conception of the good. Indeed it so remote, he concludes, that Rawls's work after his political turn is of little help in theorizing about the political problems pluralistic democracies actually face. Whether or not this point undermines the conclusions Rawls wants to draw, Waldron would say, it shows how much political philosophy remains to be done even after Rawls's work has been assimilated. Samuel Scheffler, too, argues that an overlapping consensus is politically implausible. He thinks this problem is exacerbated by the conditions Rawls himself imposes upon an overlapping consensus, including the conditions that participants to the consensus must acknowledge justice as fairness as free-standing, and as reasonable rather than true. Kurt Baier argues that the problem Rawls sets himself can be answered without appeal to an overlapping consensus. He maintains that the United States, at least, enjoys a stable consensus on the constitution. It is not clear that an overlapping consensus would be more stable or more desirable. Finally, he says, the American constitutional consensus is supported by consensus on underlying moral principles and values. There is therefore no need for the sharp distinction between moral and political philosophy to which Rawls is led by his political turn.

In the second of his articles in this volume, Joseph Raz refers to Rawls's refusal to assert the truth of justice as fairness as "epistemic abstinence." He contends that Rawls is mistaken to suppose he can put forward a conception of justice without at the same time claiming that it is true. Raz says here that Rawls is driven to epistemic abstinence by the same considerations that he earlier claimed drove Rawls to a "politics of neutral concern": a view of the social role of justice and, more specifically, a view of what consensus on a conception of justice contributes to social stability. He concludes his treatment of Rawls by echoing a note sounded in the articles by Waldron and Baier in this volume and in the piece by Haldane in Volume 4. Actual societies achieve stability without achieving an overlapping consensus. The task of political philosophy should not be either to establish the possibility of such a consensus or to identify the conditions under which that possibility could be realized. The self-conception of political philosophy should not be derived from the modest role it would have to play if an overlapping consensus is to be secured. Instead, political philosophy should examine and critique existing institutions in light of all that can be learned from moral philosophy.

What Raz calls Rawls's "epistemic abstinence" is but one tenet of the more embracing methodological credo Rawls calls the "method of avoidance."[6] It requires that he not only avoid claiming truth for justice as fairness, but also, as we have seen, that he avoid taking positions on contentious questions outside political philosophy. This enables him to satisfy the practical political aims of political philosophy by framing a conception of justice that can be accepted by citizens regardless of their metaphysical views. In doing this, Rawls thinks, he is merely taking the lessons of the modern period one step further. The Reformation required the states of early modern Europe to secure political consensus among citizens of diverse religious views. This led to the gradual adoption of religious toleration (PL, p. xxvi). The conditions of the contemporary world, Rawls thinks, require modern liberal democratic states to secure political consensus among citizens of diverse metaphysical views. This leads systematic political reflection to the method of avoidance, Rawls says, for to adopt this method is simply to apply the principle of toleration to philosophy itself (PL, p. 10).

In her article in this volume, Jean Hampton draws inspiration from Thomas Hobbes, an early modern political theorist whose response to the Reformation was hardly one of avoidance. She takes Rawls's practical aim to be the Hobbesian one of achieving "peace and stability at the lowest political cost." She joins Raz in vigorously criticizing the practical conception of political philosophy and argues that philosophers should seek the real truth about justice. Answering the rhetorical question which gives her article its title, Hampton concludes that political philosophy cannot be done without metaphysics. Where Raz and Hampton try to block Rawls's political turn, Richard Rorty applauds it. He thinks Rawls has drawn the right lesson from the history of religious tolerance and so responds accurately to the naturalistic temper of the societies he addresses. Rorty claims that after two centuries of toleration citizens in the western democracies have grown accustomed to thinking that religion is of no political significance.[7] Similarly, after two centuries of democratic practice citizens of those societies have grown increasingly accustomed to thinking that metaphysics may be of no political significance either. When they are fully accustomed to this idea the need for a deep, philosophical legitimation of a conception of justice "may gradually cease to be felt." Rorty thinks Rawls provides a conception of justice appropriate for a society that has lost the desire for deeper legitimation. The citizens of a well-ordered society, he conjectures, will think that justification proceeding from ideas and practices of their public culture will be justification enough.

Paul Weithman contends that Rorty draws the wrong lesson from the history of toleration. Examination of how the Catholic church came to accept religious toleration shows, Weithman argues, that the work of political philosophy can be divided between what he calls "political theory" and "comprehensive public philosophy." The task of the former is to articulate political principles like the principle of toleration, and to give them a prima facie justification by appealing to their place in political practice and culture. The task of the latter is to justify those principles more fully to adherents of various religious and philosophical views like Catholicism or Kantianism, drawing on their metaphysical commitments to do so if necessary. This division of labor, Weithman argues, corresponds to a distinction implicit in Rawls's earlier work and more explicit later. He can be read as restricting himself to political theory, but as recognizing the need for comprehensive public philosophy (cf. *PL*, p. 386). If this reading is correct, then Rawls's conceptions of justification and of political philosophy are both more complex and less obviously anti-metaphysical than either Rorty or Hampton recognizes.

Justice as fairness is appropriate to regulate the basic structure of a democratic society, Rawls thinks, because it can be publicly acknowledged by reasonable and rational citizens. A conception of justice fully plays its social role by encouraging citizens to live up to an ideal of reasonable and rational persons who govern themselves. For this, citizens' public knowledge that their institutions conform to an acceptable conception is not enough. They must also know that at least the most fundamental political issues, the issues that bear most directly on the development and exercise of their moral powers, are settled on grounds they could accept as reasonable and rational. This requires, Rawls thinks, that these political questions must be settled on the basis of values, ideals and principles drawn from the conception of justice with which their basic institutions conform. As we have seen, Rawls thinks that a conception of justice is an acceptable public charter only if it is capable of being presented as "free-standing" and independent of controversial claims about the good. Therefore if citizens are to govern themselves as reasonable and rational, at least the most fundamental political questions must be settled by appeal to conceptions of justice without reliance on these controversial claims. This is how the public is to reason about fundamental questions, both as a collective body of citizens and through their representatives. Rawls writes:

> political liberalism says: our exercise of power is fully proper only when it is exercised in accordance with a constitution the essentials of which all citizens as free and equal can reasonably be expected to endorse in light of their common human reason. This is the liberal principle of legitimacy. To this it adds that all questions arising in the legislature that concern or border on constitutional essentials, or basic questions of justice, should also be settled, so far as possible, by principles and ideals that can be similarly endorsed. Only a political conception of justice that all citizens might reasonably be expected to endorse can serve as the basis of public reason and justification. (*PL*, p. 137)

Rawls adds that what holds of the public as a collective body of citizens holds of citizens singly in their public deliberations. They too must be ready and able to reason about fundamental questions in the requisite terms. After reiterating the liberal principle of legitimacy he says:

since the exercise of power itself must be legitimate, the ideal of citizenship imposes a moral, not a legal, duty — the duty of civility — to be able to explain to one another on those fundamental questions how the principles and policies they advocate and vote for can be supported by the political values of public reason. (*PL*, p. 217)

Some philosophers have argued that this asks too much of citizens who, it is said, should be allowed to defend their political positions on any grounds.[8] In some of his latest work, Rawls has modified and qualified the treatment of public reason he defended in the first edition of *PL*.[9] This volume reprints two of the most searching examinations of that treatment. Kent Greenawalt seizes on Rawls's claim that it is most important to honor the requirements of public reason in settling the most fundamental political questions. He suggests that there is no principled way to distinguish the questions that are most fundamental from those that are not. Since the requirement that citizens honor public reason when settling all political questions would clearly be too strong, Rawls lacks a principled basis for a distinction essential to his treatment of public reason. In an essay Rawls later cited[10], David Hollenbach seizes on Rawls's claim that the requirements of public reason apply only to citizens' public deliberations. This, he notes, presupposes a distinction between deliberations that take place in the public forum and those that take place in what Rawls calls "the background culture" of civil society (*PL*, p. 14). Noting that deliberations in civil society affect the terms of debate in the public forum and vice versa, Hollenbach queries whether this distinction is the right one to draw or whether some other distinction would more accurately capture our considered judgments about where standards of public reason do and do not apply.

One of the most important exchanges in recent philosophical literature is that between Rawls and the great German political philosopher and social theorist Jürgen Habermas. Rawls's "Reply to Habermas" is the last essay in the paperback edition of *PL*. It is fitting that Habermas's probing essay on Rawls appears as the last piece in this volume, hence as the last piece in this set of volumes devoted to Rawls's work. It is preceded by two articles which illuminate the connection between Rawls's work and Habermas's. Iris Marion Young begins her essay by noting that for the liberal tradition, the most basic questions of justice are distributive. Thus Rawls takes as the most basic question that of how the basic structure of society should distribute primary goods (*TJ*, p. 7). Young contends that this way of posing questions about justice leaves unexamined a more fundamental question: that of whether power relationships in a society are just or oppressive. She argues that an account of justice which relies on Habermas's ideal speech situation rather than on Rawls's original position would have the appropriate focus. In another essay published before the Rawls-Habermas exchange, Thomas McCarthy notes that philosophical conversations about similarities and differences between the two thinkers is just beginning, both in the English-speaking world and on the continent. Though McCarthy's sympathies are clearly with Habermas, he has a deep knowledge of both and Rawls thanks him for his help in his own article on Habermas (*PL*, p. 372). McCarthy draws on that knowledge to indicate what he thinks is the most promising direction these conversations might take.

Paul J. Weithman

Notes

[1] John Rawls, *A Theory of Justice* (Harvard University Press, 1971), p. viii. References to this work will hereafter be given parenthetically in the body of the text, with the title abbreviated '*TJ*.'

[2] John Rawls, *Political Liberalism* (Columbia University Press, 1996), p. xix. References to this work will hereafter be given parenthetically in the body of the text, with the title abbreviated '*PL*.'

[3] See especially John Rawls, "Justice as Fairness: Political not Metaphysical," *Philosophy and Public Affairs* 14 (1985): 223–51; also "The Idea of an Overlapping Consensus," *Oxford Journal of Legal Studies* 7 (1987): 1–26.

[4] The discussions resulted in the publication of some very fine collections. See, for example, *Liberal Neutrality* (Routledge, 1989), ed. Goodin and Reeve; also *Liberalism and the Good* (Routledge, 1990), ed. Douglass, Mara and Richardson.

[5] For a discussion of this sense of 'possibility' and related modal notions, see Alvin Plantinga, *The Nature of Necessity* (Oxford University Press, 1974), pp. 1–9.

[6] Rawls, "Justice as Fairness: Political not Metaphysical," p. 231.

[7] See also Richard Rorty, "Religion as Conversation-Stopper" *Common Knowledge* 3 (1994): 2.

[8] Philip Quinn, "Political Liberalisms and Their Exclusions of the Religious," *Proceedings and Addresses of the American Philosophical Association* 69 (1995): 35–56; also Nicholas Wolterstorff, "The Role of Religion in Decision and Discussion of Political Issues," in Robert Audi and Nicholas Wolterstorff, *Religion in the Public Square* (Rowman and Littlefield, 1997), pp. 67–120.

[9] See the "Introduction to the Paperback Edition," *PL*, pp. l-lvii; also John Rawls, "The Idea of Public Reason Revisited," *The University of Chicago Law Review* 64 (1997): 765–807.

[10] Rawls, "Public Reason Revisited," p. 785, note 52.

Liberalism, Autonomy, and the Politics of Neutral Concern

JOSEPH RAZ

1. LIBERALISM AND RESTRAINT

By definition, a liberal is a person who believes in liberty."[1] But not surprisingly liberals differ in the reasons for their belief in liberty and in the way they translate it into political doctrine and action. Three traditions dominate liberal political thought, and though they are often combined they can be treated separately. The first regards liberty as protected by a presumption favoring it. If the presumption means no more than that any curtailment of liberty by political action requires justification, then it is a presumption of rationality and not of liberty. All action requires rational justification.[2] Liberal doctrine reflects the specific importance of liberty in political contexts. Some writers interpret the presumption of liberty as requiring a particularly weighty reason to justify any restriction of liberty. But is there any reason to subject any political action that restricts liberty to this onerous requirement? The difficulty is not only that some liberties are worthless. It is primarily that while sometimes restricting one's liberty in some respects increases one's liberty overall, no one has yet satisfactorily explained the basis and limits of comparative judgments of overall liberty.

A second liberal tradition focuses on absolute or near absolute rights to some basic liberties, such as freedom of conscience and expression, as the complete defense of liberty. But such doctrines distort the value of liberty by regarding it as (near) absolute in certain areas of conduct and as non-existent in others. They also overvalue formal liberties while disregarding their actual worth to individuals, which usually depends on those peoples' relative success in other spheres of life.[3]

A third liberal tradition pins its defense of liberty on the adoption of some principle of political restraint. These are principles which claim that certain reasons which can justify private action are out of bounds in politics and cannot be used to justify some political actions. By doing so, they protect the liberty of individuals.

1

But unlike doctrines of basic liberties which limit the power of the state by declaring that certain areas of conduct are outside its authority (except perhaps in an emergency), principles of political restraint, as here understood, deny the appropriateness of certain reasons as grounds for political action, or for certain kinds of political action. Therefore, acceptance of principles of restraint may affect one's judgment of all and any political actions, not only of those that intrude into certain privileged areas. In practice they may, of course, protect from governmental interference some areas of conduct more than others.

A principle is a principle of restraint if, and only if, the reasons deemed inappropriate for political action are good reasons. No restraint is entailed by an argument purporting to show that certain reasons are invalid and therefore not to be heeded at all. Principles of restraint are based on arguments designed to establish that reasons of certain kinds, though generally valid, should not, because of the nature of (some) political actors or actions, count as reasons for some or any political actions.

Whereas Locke fathered the basic liberties brand of liberalism, Mill dominates the liberal tradition expressing itself in principles of restraint. Many liberals regard their belief in liberty as essentially expressed in the harm (to others) principle:

> That principle is, that the sole end for which mankind are warranted, individually or collectively, in interfering with the liberty of action of any of their number, is self-protection. That the only purpose for which power can be rightfully exercised over any member of a civilized community, against his will, is to prevent harm to others[4]

Mill's principle has sometimes been misinterpreted, by supporters and opponents alike, as stating an absolute right to noninterference in "private" actions. That is, it has been twisted to fit the basic liberties tradition by attributing to Mill a belief in a sphere of action that does not affect others (except by being disliked or judged offensive or immoral) and by interpreting the harm principle as stating that others should not intrude into this sphere of private action. But Mill does not presuppose such a private sphere, nor, if it exists, is the harm principle concerned only with it. The point is well explained by C. L. Ten:

> It is not essential to Mill's position that there should be an area of conduct which must always remain completely free from intervention. The absoluteness of Mill's barrier against intervention, or the 'theoretical limit' he sets to the power of the state and society to exercise coercion, is of a different kind. There are certain reasons for intervention in the conduct of individuals which must always be ruled out as irrelevant. Even when intervention is justified in a particular case it is on the basis of certain reasons rather than others. [5]

In other words the harm principle is a principle of restraint. In recent years several other principles of restraint have attracted much attention which, because of their fundamental similarities, I shall regard as so many manifestations of a doctrine of neutral political concern. "A state or government that claims . . .[the citizen's] allegiance (as other individuals do not), writes Robert Nozick, "there-

2

fore scrupulously must be *neutral* between its citizens."[6] Writers of an egalitarian liberal persuasion often join libertarian liberals in applauding the same sentiments, different though their interpretation of them usually is.

The doctrine of political neutrality claims that (some) political actions should be neutral regarding ideals of the good life, that implementation or promotion of ideals of the good life is, though worthy in itself, not a legitimate ground for (some) political actions. Such a doctrine is a doctrine of restraint since (as understood here) it advocates neutrality between valid and invalid ideals of the good alike. It demands not only that the promotion of unacceptable ideals should not be the ground for (some) political actions, but also that the promotion of acceptable, correct, desirable ideals should be equally shunned.

When principles of neutral political concern are used to provide the foundation of a political theory, they can be regarded as attempts to capture the core sense of the liberal ethos. Not all the supporters of the various principles of neutral political concern advance them as interpretations of liberalism, but their nature and the culture that produces them endow them with such a character. This essay criticizes some versions of the doctrine of neutral political concern and claims that such plausibility as they appear to possess derives from a conception of the good which values autonomy. Autonomy, however, requires pluralism but not neutrality.

Sections 2 and 3 examine the meaning of political neutrality and conclude that no political theory can be neutral. Yet a political theory can strive to be as neutral as is possible. Therefore, the rest of the essay examines and criticizes some arguments in favor of neutrality.

2. FORMS OF NEUTRALITY

Nozick in the quotation given above writes of neutrality between individuals. I referred to neutrality between ideals of the good. The two ideas are closely related. Discrimination between individuals consists in making it easier for some than for others to realize their ideals of the good. But it is important to distinguish between two principles of political neutrality:

A. Neutrality concerning each individual's chances of implementing the ideal of the good he or she happens to have.
B. Neutrality as in A but also regarding the likelihood that an individual will adopt one conception of the good rather than another.

B is the more radical principle, and in the absence of any special reason to prefer A, and given that the writers supporting neutrality say little that bears on the issue, I will assume that the doctrine of neutrality advocates neutrality as in B.

It is important to realize what is involved in talking of *principles* of neutrality. "To be neutral . . . is to do one's best to help or to hinder the various parties concerned in an equal degree."[7] This is the primary sense of neutrality which I will call principled neutrality. In this sense one is neutral only if one can affect the fortunes of the parties and if one helps or hinders them to an equal degree and one does so because one believes that there are reasons for so acting which essentially depend on the fact that the action has an equal effect on the fortunes of the parties. One secondary sense of neutrality regards persons as neutral if they can affect the fortunes of the parties, and if they affect the fortunes of all parties equally regardless of their reasons for so doing. When "neutral" is used in this sense, I refer to it as by-product neutrality, for here neutrality may well be an accidental by-product of the agent's action and not its intended outcome.

Principles of neutrality state that there are reasons to be neutral. They are satisfied by any behavior that affects the fortunes of the parties in equal degree (by-product neutrality). They are followed by people acting neutrally in a principled way, i.e., because they believe that there is a reason not to help or hinder one side more than the other. Our interest is in political theories that require neutrality, i.e., that are followed by acting neutrally in a principled way. Some theories may be such that behavior that follows them is also neutral as a by-product. But those are of no special interest from our point of view.

Neutrality is sometimes conceived as being necessarily at least prima facie desirable. If so, the principles of neutral concern are at least prima facie valid. But the definition of neutrality adopted above is not committed to such a view, which is rooted in the confused notion that to act neutrally is to act fairly. Montefiore gives a familiar example:

> two children may each appeal to their father to intervene . . . in some dispute between them. Their father may know that if he simply 'refuses to intervene' the older one, stronger and more resourceful, is bound to come out on top. . . . In other words, the decision to remain neutral, according to the terms of our present definition, would amount to a decision to allow the naturally strong child to prevail. But this may look like a very odd form of neutrality to the weaker child.[8]

One should, however, reject this objection. Even if (and I do not accept this at all) neutrality could only be justified as a means to a fair contest, it should not be identified with action securing a fair contest. An attorney representing a client before a court helps to make the trial fair, but the attorney is not neutral. All that the example shows is that there are circumstances in which it is unfair to act neutrally, where there are not even prima facie reasons to be neutral. The example is of a case where the father should not, not where he cannot, remain neutral. The question of the justification of neutral political concern invites moral and political argument and cannot be settled by the inherent appeal of neutrality as such.

Supporters of the doctrine of neutral political concern may differ on many issues. But all of them endorse one or the other of the principles of political neutrality mentioned above and seek to implement it by some variant of the following principles of restraint which limit the political use of ideals of the good.

1. No political action may be undertaken or justified on the ground that it promotes an ideal of the good nor on the ground that it enables individuals to pursue an ideal of the good.
2. No political action may be undertaken or justified on the ground that it promotes an ideal of the good except in order to secure for all persons an

equal ability to pursue in their lives and promote in their societies any ideal of the good through nonpolitical action.

3. No political action may be undertaken or justified on the ground that it promotes an ideal of the good except in order to secure for all persons an equal ability to pursue in their lives and promote in their societies any ideal of the good, and to enable them to do so by political means.

The first principle seeks to achieve political neutrality by excluding any regard for ideals of the good from all political justifications. The second and third principles are less extreme. The second allows regard to be paid to ideals of the good in designing the legal-political framework for political institutions, but only to the extent that it requires such institutional arrangements as are necessary to ensure that all persons have an equal ability to promote in their own lives or in their societies any ideals of the good of their choice, provided pursuit of ideals is confined to nonpolitical action. The third principle resembles the second in requiring political institutions to ensure that individuals have an equal ability to pursue the good, but it also allows them to do so by political action. Therefore, the principle seeks to guarantee the neutrality of the constitution but not the neutrality of all political action according to the constitution.

Robert Nozick and libertarian liberals are committed to a version of the first principle. John Rawls and egalitarian liberals accept a principle not unlike the third. Rawls's theory differs from it in requiring equal ability to pursue an idea of the good only insofar as that ability depends on the principle of equal liberty. For the rest, the difference principle allows deviations from equal distribution of the means to pursue the good where the worst-off group will benefit from them. Finally, Rawls is only to a limited extent concerned with correcting inequalities in the ability to promote the good which are due to one's natural endowments.

The doctrine of neutral *political* concern claims that the difference between political and other actions is morally significant. It thus presupposes a distinction between these two spheres of activity. I will avoid a lengthy discussion of this controversial topic. Political action is here taken to be any action of a political institution and any individual action designed to affect the existence, constitution, powers, or actions of political institutions.[9] The state and its organs are the primary but not necessarily the only political institutions. The principles that should guide political action can be referred to as political morality. The doctrine of neutral political concern claims that political morality is a distinct part of morality in that certain valid reasons are inappropriate as grounds for (some) political actions. It further claims that principles of restraint of the kind it favors are at least partly justified by the fact that compliance with them secures political neutrality and that political neutrality is a prerequisite of justice.

3. THE IMPOSSIBILITY OF STRICT POLITICAL NEUTRALITY

It has been argued that neutral political concern is impossible. This section examines the objection, first as addressed to libertarian principles seeking to achieve neutrality by excluding ideals from politics, and then as an objection to the possibility of egalitarian liberal neutrality which principles such as 2 or 3 strive to achieve.

Some arguments challenge not so much the possibility of political neutrality as the very possibility of neutrality under any circumstances. Not helping differs from hindering. Neutrality is concerned only with the degree to which the parties are helped or hindered. This may lead some to suppose that any attribution or commendation of neutrality assumes that whereas one is morally responsible (i.e., accountable) for what one does, one is not morally responsible for what one does not do, or some similar distinction. Those who reject this view may conclude that neutrality is impossible. The conclusion is, however, unwarranted. No such assumption underlies attributions of neutrality. Commendations of neutrality, while consistent with such a view, do not depend on it. They may be defended simply because in certain circumstances not helping is to be preferred to helping. It is true that affirmative talk of neutrality presupposes a distinction between not helping and hindering, but it does not presuppose that this distinction is always of moral significance (neutrality is not always defensible); nor does it assume that the distinction can always be drawn: Neutrality is possible in some cases, but it may be impossible in others.[10]

A second argument designed to show that neutrality is impossible claims that whether or not a person acts neutrally depends on the base line relative to which his or her behavior is judged, and that there are always different base lines leading to conflicting judgments and no rational grounds to prefer one to the others. Imagine that the Reds are fighting the Blues. We have no commercial or other relations with the Blues, but we supply the Reds with essential food which helps them maintain their war effort. If we want to be neutral, should we continue normal supplies to the Reds or should they be discontinued? If we continue supplying the Reds, we will be helping them more than the Blues. If we discontinue supplies, we will be hindering the Reds more than the Blues. (I am assuming that even if similar supplies to the Blues will help them, continuing not to help them is not hindering them.) It may be said that this is just one of the cases where it is impossible to be neutral. Without confusing not helping and hindering, such cases cannot be multiplied. They form a special class where, in the circumstances of the case, not helping is hindering. But the case invites a more radical rebuttal. In it two standards of neutrality conflict. The basic idea is simple. Neutrality is neutrality between parties in relation to some issue regarding which the success of one sets the other back. Various aspects of the parties' life, resources, and activities will be helpful to them in the conflict, but many of these are resources and activities that they will have possessed or engaged in or wished to possess or to engage in in any case, even if they did not take part in the contest. Some of the activities and resources are such that the parties do or wish to engage in them or to possess them only because of the conflict. We could therefore distinguish between comprehensive and narrow neutrality. Comprehensive neutrality consists in helping and hindering the parties in equal degree in all matters relevant to the conflict between them. Narrow neutrality consists in helping and hindering them to an equal degree in those activities and regarding those resources that they would wish neither to engage in nor to acquire but for the conflict.

'Neutrality' is used in ordinary discourse to indicate sometimes narrow and sometimes comprehensive neutrality. Sometimes various intermediate courses of conduct are seen as required by neutrality. This reflects the fact that several kinds of considerations may lead to different and incompatible policies all of which are commonly regarded as policies of neutrality, because all of them demonstrate an evenhanded treatment of the parties either by not helping one more than the other, or by not helping one more than the other to take special measures to improve his position in the conflict, and so on. The difference between military equipment and food supplies illustrates the point. To be comprehensively neutral one should supply the Reds in our example neither with arms nor with food. But one is narrowly neutral even if one provides the Reds with normal food supplies. Arms on the other hand are needed specifically for military use, and continued supply of arms to one side is incompatible with neutrality.[11]

With these general objections out of the way we can face the charge that political neutrality is impossible. The charge against libertarian liberals is that the political actions their theory allows, by means of its property laws and its contract laws, result in a distribution of the means to realize conceptions of the good which is unequal and differs from what it might otherwise be.

Nozick's reply to this objection is:

> Not every enforcement of a prohibition which differentially benefits people makes the state non-neutral. . . . Would a prohibition against rape be non-neutral? It would, by hypothesis, differentially benefit people; but for potential rapists to complain that the prohibition was non-neutral between the sexes . . . would be absurd. There is an *independent* reason for prohibiting rape. . . . That a prohibition thus independently justifiable works out to affect different people differently is no reason to condemn it as non-neutral, provided it was instituted or continues for (something like) the reasons which justify it . . . similarly with the prohibitions and enforcements of the minimal state.[12]

How convincing is this answer? It looks as if Nozick is claiming that to act neutrally is to act on adequate reasons. This is clearly wrong. Nozick may claim on grounds similar to those he invokes above that the state is impartial. One acts impartially if one acts on adequate reasons in matters concerning the interests of others where one's own preference or interests are unaffected or, if they are affected, while disregarding them. Nozick's state having no interests or preferences of its own is indeed impartial if his theory is sound. Yet, just like a judge convicting a rapist, so too Nozick's state may be impartial—but it is not neutral.

Could Nozick claim that even though his state is not comprehensively neutral it is narrowly neutral? The conflict in which the state is supposed to be neutral is about the ability of people to choose and successfully pursue conceptions of the

7

good (and these include ideals of the good society or world). It is, therefore, a comprehensive conflict. There is nothing outside it which can be useful for it but is not specifically necessary for it. The whole of life is, so to speak, involved in the pursuit of the good life. Can one be narrowly neutral in a comprehensive conflict?

Not if one believes that ultimate moral principles are all teleological humanistic principles. These regard the consequences of one's action on the well-being of people as the ultimate grounds for the evaluation of action and therefore leave no possibility of distinguishing between narrow and comprehensive neutrality in comprehensive conflicts. Nor are deontological theories any more neutral. These prohibit coercion by the state on grounds that do not depend on the consequences of such state action. Nevertheless, if the permitted coercion by the state causes more harm to some than to others, the state cannot be comprehensively neutral. But is it at least narrowly neutral on the ground, invoked by Nozick, that its action is *not intended* to favor some more than others? The answer must be negative. Neutrality does not depend on intention. One may fail to act neutrally while trying to do so. What matters is that the libertarian deontologist fashions the state to favor those whose conception of the good includes not coercing others in the circumstances where coercion is prohibited by the law. Their conception of the good is in part realized by the state. Others who disagree with it may be unable to realize their conception of the good in the libertarian state. In this way as well as in causing unequal economic distribution the libertarian state is neutral neither narrowly nor comprehensively.

A similar argument was used by T. Nagel to show that Rawls's theory is not neutral either:

> It is a fundamental feature of Rawls' conception of the fairness of the original position that it should not permit the choice of principles of justice to depend on a particular conception of the good over which the parties may differ.
>
> The construction does not, I think, accomplish this, and there are reasons to believe that it cannot be successfully carried out. Any hypothetical choice situation which requires agreement among the parties will have to impose strong restrictions on the grounds of choice, and these restrictions can be justified only in terms of a conception of the good. It is one of those cases in which there is no neutrality to be had, because neutrality needs as much justification as any other position. (pp. 8-9)[13]

The specific point Nagel is making is that there is no way of justifying the conditions of choice in the original position except from the point of view of a certain ideal of the good. But later on he makes it clear that this is so, at least in part, because the supposedly inevitable outcome of that choice is not really neutral:

> The original position seems to presuppose not just a neutral theory of the good, but a liberal, individualistic conception according to which the best that can be wished for someone is the unimpeded pursuit of his own path, provided it does not interfere with the rights of others. The view is persua-

sively developed in the later portions of the book but without a sense of its controversial character.

Among different life plans of this general type the construction is neutral. But given that many conceptions of the good do not fit into the individualistic pattern, how can this be described as a fair choice situation for principles of justice? (p. 10)

One should be careful not to misinterpret this point. Rawls often writes of indivuals' conceptions of the good as if they are their views of the good life for themselves. But he is also aware that they may be conceptions of the good life for people generally and for society as a whole. Individuals may use their primary goods to promote nonindividualistic conceptions of the good. To use Nagel's own words, individuals may use their primary goods to implement

> views that hold a good life to be readily achievable only in certain well-defined types of social structure, or only in a society that works concertedly for the realization of certain higher human capacities and the suppression of baser ones, or only given certain types of economic relations among men. (p. 9)

The individualistic bias that Rawls is accused of by Nagel is not that he rules out such conceptions but that he is not neutral regarding them because he makes their successful pursuit more difficult than that of individualistic conceptions of the good. Nagel's reason for alleging the existence of the bias is that "the primary goods are not equally valuable in pursuit of all conceptions of the good" (p. 9). They serve individualistic conceptions well enough, but "they are less useful in implementing" nonindividualistic conceptions. This point is valid. Rawls is surprisingly brief and inexplicit on this issue. He seems to take assessment of wealth to be unproblematic.[14] If some market mechanism, actual or hypothetical, is assumed, the value of primary goods is the function of supply and demand where the demand is partly determined by the usefulness of the goods in the implementation of those conceptions of the goods which are actually pursued in that society and by the number of those pursuing different conceptions. Relative to any such evaluation of primary goods some conceptions of the good will be harder to implement, i.e., will require more primary goods to realize, than others. These need not be nonindividualist conceptions. All conceptions involving the cultivation and satisfaction of the so-called expensive tastes are harder to satisfy, and the Rawlsian theory can be said to discriminate against them. Nonindividualist conceptions are likely to be among the expensive tastes since their realization depends on the cooperation of others, and they will take some convincing to come round to the agent's point of view. This consideration merely points to the fact that the very restrictions imposed on societies by the Rawlsian principles of justice make the implementation of some conceptions of the good more difficult and their pursuit by individuals less attractive than that of others. Furthermore, the implementation of some conceptions of the good is incompatible with the principles of justice and is ruled out altogether.

Neutrality, however, can be a matter of degree. One can deviate from complete neutrality to a greater or lesser degree. Rawls may be able to defend his theory by pointing out that, having committed himself to a principle of neutrality, he designed the veil of ignorance to guarantee the greatest degree of neutrality possible. It is not a fault of his theory that it does not achieve the impossible. Given the impossibility of neutral political concern, one must strive to realize as much of it as possible, and this is what the veil of ignorance guarantees.

No such second line of defense is available to Nozick. He is committed to a principle of neutrality. But in fact at no stage in the construction of his theory does he rely on any principle of neutrality. Neither the egalitarian nor the libertarian principles of restraint which limit ideals in politics (explained on pp. 92-3) are neutral. But unlike the egalitarian one, which is a principle of neutrality for it seeks to maximize it; the libertarian principle is not a principle of neutrality at all.

Defenders of Rawls's theory might also find the second line of defense a problematic resting place. Should one not make sure that the sound, valid conceptions of the good are tolerated by the maximally neutral state? Should not one prefer a less neutral state to a more neutral one if it turns out that the latter rules out all or even some of the sound ideals of the good? But such considerations bring evaluation of different conceptions of the good into the foundation of the theory of the right.

4. POLITICAL WELFARISM

Brian Barry identifies the doctrine of neutral concern as one important strand in liberalism:

> Classical liberalism had other strands besides this one no doubt, but one was certainly the idea that the state is an instrument for satisfying the wants that men happen to have rather than a means of making good men (e.g. cultivating desirable wants or dispositions in its citizens).[15]

Barry, therefore, defines liberalism, for the purpose of his argument, as the view that ideal-regarding principles should not be used for prescribing the conduct of political actors. The definition identifies liberalism with the endorsement of a particular version of the doctrine of neutrality by its use of Barry's previous distinction between want- and ideal-regarding principles:

> Want-regarding principles . . . are principles which take as given the wants which people happen to have and concentrate attention entirely on the extent to which a certain policy will alter the overall amount of want-satisfaction or on the way in which the policy will affect the distribution among people of opportunities for satisfying wants. (p. 38)

I will regard the second half of the definition as referring to the distribution of actual satisfaction of desires rather than to the distribution of opportunites, though these may be an indicator of actual satisfaction: "in order to evaluate the desirability of a state of affairs according to such principles, all the information we need is the amount and/or distribution among persons of want-satisfaction" (*ibid.*). Any nonwant-regarding principle is ideal-regarding. Want-regarding theories are, therefore, instances of what Sen calls 'welfarism', i.e., the view that "the goodness of a state of affairs depends ultimately on the set of individual utilities in that state."[16]

Not all welfarist theories are based on a principle of restraint. According to some, want-regarding considerations are the only ones relevant for the evaluation of any action. On this view, which I will call moral welfarism, there are no valid ideal-regarding principles and therefore to advocate excluding them from political action is not to advocate restraint. Only those theorists who accept ideal-regarding principles for determining the desirability of at least some states of affairs and yet rely exclusively on want-regarding principles in evaluating or advocating political action subscribe to the liberal precept as described by Barry above, i.e., that it is not the business of the state to promote the goodness of individuals. It should confine itself to the satisfaction of their desires. I shall dub 'political welfarism' the kind of welfarist political theories that admit the validity of some ideal-regarding principles but which confine their force to nonpolitical actions.

Political welfarism owes part of its popularity to the widespread confusion between it and two quite distinct ideas. One is its confusion with moral welfarism; since moral welfarists do not accept the validity of any ideal-regarding principles, they are not advocating restraint when they object to reliance on ideal-regarding principles. This simple point is often lost sight of by, for example, some moral welfarists who object to the proscription of so-called deviant sexual practices or of marijuana. They sometimes appeal to principles denying the state's right to enforce "private morality," whereas what they mean is the denial of the state's right to enforce the wrong morality. It is all too convenient for moral welfarists to assume the mantle of political welfarists since these will serve their purpose just as well. But though their *political* results may be identical, the two doctrines represent radically different views of both morality and politics.

The other confusion is the belief that a commitment to representative government commits one to political welfarism. "Does not representative government mean an equal chance for all to have their goals supported by the state? And is not that the meaning of political welfarism?" The answer to both questions is negative. The principles of representative government guarantee some measure of control by the population over those in authority. They do not entail a commitment by the democratically constituted authorities to act on welfarist considerations alone.

With these clarifications behind us, we can turn to an evaluation of political welfarism. Want-satisfaction can be supported as a good in itself or as a means to some other good. Suppose a political welfarist holds want-satisfaction to be a good in itself. He is then committed to the view that some intrinsic goods (want-satisfaction) may, while others (ideals in Barry's sense) may not, be pursued politically. He is committed, that is, to the view that certain means (political ones) may be used in pursuit of some goals but not of others. I shall take it for granted that, while possibly there are some ideals that cannot be promoted by political means and others that cannot be efficiently so promoted, it is not the case that no ideals can be efficiently pursued by political means. Such considerations cannot therefore be used to support a total ban on ideals from politics. After all, our hypothetical theorist is not proposing to ban the satisfaction of wants as a ground of political action, even though there are wants the satisfaction of which cannot, and others which cannot efficiently, be pursued by political means.

Are there grounds to believe that it is wrong to pursue politically any intrinsic goods other than the satisfaction of wants? It follows from the conclusion of the last section, that political welfarism is not neutral between ideals of the good since it clearly favors moral welfarism above all other moral views. But neutral or not, the main problem is to find any reason for supporting politically some elements of a conception of the good and not others that are admitted to be valid and valuable. I know of no attempts to answer the question which neither reduce themselves to an endorsement of moral welfarism nor rely on the false claim that one cannot promote ideals politically.

The difficulties with political welfarism, however, go deeper. Belief in ideal-regarding principles undermines the plausibility of regarding want-satisfaction as a good in itself. People pursue goals and hold desires for reasons. They believe that the objects of their desires or their pursuits are valuable. This reason-dependent character of goals and desires entails that any person who has a goal or a desire believes, if he has a minimal understanding of their nature, that if he came to believe that there were no reasons to pursue the goal or the desire, he would no longer have them. Notice that belief in an appropriate reason is here merely made a necessary condition for the having of a goal or a desire. It is not assumed that one desires whatever one sees a reason for or whatever one holds to be valuable.[17]

A further consequence of the reason-dependent character of desires is that agents do not wish their desires satisfied if their belief in the existence of a reason for their desires is unfounded. One does not wish to have the medicine one desires to have if it does not have the medical properties that one believes to be the only reason for having it. People who wish the state to subsidize the arts do not wish it to do so if such subsidies will not help the development or propagation of the arts which they believe to be the only reason to subsidize them. One way in which 'wishing' is weaker than 'desiring' is that it is very close to 'believing that there is an undefeated reason for'.[18] Not wishing that what one desires shall happen if one's belief in a reason for it is mistaken is no more than an acknowledgment of the reason-based character of desire. The desire is not itself a reason; it is merely an endorsement of a reason independent of it.[19] The point of this argument is that one does not wish one's desire satisfied if one's reason for the desire is mistaken even if one continues, through ignorance, to entertain the desire. One does not wish merely not to have mistaken desires; one also does not wish to have them satisfied. It is primarily the craving conception of desires that obscures this point by making the disappointment at a failure to satisfy one's desire appear like the suffering caused by a frustrated craving. In fact, the disappointment may be little more than belief that something for which there is a reason failed to happen. Where the fate of the desire largely depends on the personal performance of the agent, its failure is accompanied by disappointment at one's own incompetence, lack of good fortune, lack of support from others for one's plans, etc., and these do often constitute valid reasons for preventing the relevant kind of frustration. But it is enough to consider a desire to see one's party win the election (which leads one to vote for it) to see that not all desires lead to such reactions when frustrated.

If the observations on the reason-dependent character of desires are correct, even if they apply to some nontrivial categories of desire only, then it would appear that want-satisfaction as such cannot be an intrinsic good. Those who deny the validity of all ideal-regarding principles may perhaps resist this conclusion. They may argue that it is based on the common existence of a second-order desire not to have one's false desires satisfied. They may proceed to claim that these second-order desires presuppose that some of the ideal-regarding reasons are valid reasons. They may concede that almost all persons believe in some ideal-regarding principles and have a second-order desire that their false ideal-based desires need not be satisfied. This second-order desire, however, relates to local mistakes, i.e., to mistakes concerning which ideal-regarding principles are valid, and to their consequences given the facts of the case. It does not apply to a case of a global mistake, i.e., where the mistake is a failure to see that *no* ideal-regarding principles are valid. If this is so, if people are guilty of the global mistake, then there is no reason to respect their second-order desire or rather it does not apply in such circumstances. I do not wish to endorse this argument, but for the purpose of the present point we need not evaluate it. Suffice it to say that it is not available to political welfarists, for they accept the validity of some ideal-regarding principles.

It may be objected that all I have argued for is that people's desires are not their own reasons for pursuing the object of those desires. This need not mean that they are not reasons for others, who ought to help them. But the only reason for satisfying other people's desires is to help them, i.e., help them get what is good for them or what they want. The preceding argument shows that people do not wish their false desires satisfied, and that though in certain circumstances it is good for them to have them satisfied, this is by no means always the case. Hence want-satisfaction *qua* want-satisfaction is not a good in itself, at least not if there are valid ideal-regarding principles.

Many who feel tempted by political welfarism are influenced by a picture that depends on viewing want-satisfaction as instrumentally valued (whatever its intrinsic value may be). Even if the preceding argument is wrong, even if want-satisfaction is an intrinsic good, it is possible that it is its instrumental and not its intrinsic value which accounts for the view that want-regarding principles may, while ideal-regarding ones may not, guide political action.

The picture I mentioned is that of live and let live. People's lives are their own affairs. They may be moral or immoral, admirable or demeaning, and so on, but even when immoral they are none of the state's business, none of anyone's business except those whose lives they are. All that politics is concerned with is providing people with the means to pursue their own lives, i.e., with helping them satisfy their wants and realize their goals. The state should therefore act on welfarist grounds alone and shun all ideal-regarding principles. Attractive though this simplified picture is, it is riddled with ambiguities and difficulties the solving of which transforms it in a radical way. One of these issues will be taken up now. Others will occupy us for the rest of this essay.

The live-and-let-live picture is ambiguous on the relevance of personal goals. Is it the state's duty to try and maximize their satisfaction, i.e., to make sure that people do succeed in leading the lives they have chosen, or should it make opportunities available to them that will enable them to try and lead the lives they have chosen?

The first interpretation is open to an objection analogous to the one above. One does not help people to lead the life they want to have by satisfying their false desires. People do not want to have a life based on falsehood. The second interpretation requires the state while being maximally neutral between conceptions of the good to provide individuals with the means of pursuing their ideals of the good. But satisfying people's wants is not to be equated with providing them with the means of pursuing their ideals. Satisfying false wants concerning the means to one's ideals will not help in realizing them, and some useful means may not be wanted since the person does not realize their usefulness or fails to form rational plans concerning them.

The live-and-let-live picture leads us away from political welfarism and toward the suggestion — not to be further explored in this essay — that the state's concern is with the provision of adequate opportunities for individuals to pursue their own ideals of the good.[26] One presupposition of this view will preoccupy us later in the essay. If the live-and-let-live picture is interpreted as requiring the state to provide opportunities for individuals to pursue their own conception of the good, this could be because of the intrinsic value of autonomy, i.e., because a person's life is not a good life unless that person chose to have it or at least some of its main features. Does autonomy require political neutrality? I will return to this question later in the essay.

5. NEUTRALITY AND THE SOCIAL ROLE OF JUSTICE

Since in the original position no one knows his own moral ideals, his own conception of the good, Rawls concludes that no perfectionist standards will be adopted in it. The principles of justice adopted in the original position are neutral between different conceptions of the good. To vindicate Rawls's position, one requires convincing reasons first for excluding moral and religious beliefs from the information available behind the veil of ignorance, and second for accepting that neutral or maximally neutral principles will be chosen in these circumstances. A Theory of Justice contains hardly an explicit argument for the exclusion of moral and religious beliefs from the original position. Such argument as there is turns on the need to secure unanimity, the need to have, in the original position, one viewpoint which can be the "standpoint of one person selected at random" which excludes bargaining and guarantees unanimity. Therefore, only noncontroversial information can be available. Otherwise there will be different standpoints defined by different informational bases, and it will be impossible to guarantee agreement. The obvious reply to this argument is that we need a reason to accept a decision reached behind *this* veil of ignorance, and the claim that no decision would be reached behind a differently constructed veil of ignorance is not such a reason except if it has already been shown, as it has not in fact, that we are bound by the results of one or the other veil of ignorance.

The argument showing that no moral ideal of the good will be chosen as a principle of justice in the original position is the argument that Rawls uses for rejecting what he calls "perfectionist" principles:

> For while the persons in the original position take no interest in one another's interests, they know that they have (or may have) certain moral and religious interests and other cultural ends which they cannot put in jeopardy. Moreover, they are assumed to be committed to different conceptions of the good and they think that they are entitled to press their claims on one another to further their separate aims. The parties do not share a conception of the good by reference to which the fruition of their powers or even the satisfaction of their desires can be evaluated. They do not have an agreed criterion of perfection that can be used as a principle for choosing between institutions. To acknowledge any such standard would be, in effect, to accept a principle that might lead to a lesser religious or other liberty, if not to a loss of freedom altogether to advance many of one's spiritual ends. If the standard of excellence is reasonably clear, the parties have no way of knowing that their claims may not fall before the higher social goal of maximizing perfection. Thus it seems that the only understanding that the persons in the original position can reach is that everyone should have the greatest equal liberty consistent with a similar liberty for others. They cannot risk their freedom by authorizing a standard of value to define what is to be maximized by a teleological principle of justice. (pp. 327-28)

Rawls, however, claims more than this argument establishes. He claims not only that the parties to the original position will avoid choosing any particular perfectionist principle as a constituent of their doctrine of justice, but that they will not even accept a doctrine of justice including an agreed process for determining which perfectionist principle should be incorporated in a doctrine of justice. Given their concern that only a well-founded ideal of the good, and not any ideal one believes in, should be implemented, and given the general knowledge of human fallibility, it is not really surprising that the original position does not yield a commitment to any particular ideal. But it may yield an agreement to establish a constitutional framework most likely to lead to the pursuit of the best-founded ideal, given the information available at any given time.[21] Ignorance of one's particular moral beliefs will not exclude this possibility, since the parties in the original position know that they have moral ideals. They accept in other words "a natural duty" to pursue the best-founded moral ideal. This argument presupposes that moral ideals

15

are based on rational considerations, and Rawls is anxious not to deny this: "in making this argument," he says, referring to the passage quoted above, "I have not contended that the criteria of excellence lack a rational basis in everyday life" (p. 328). An agreement on a method for choosing between perfectionist principles cannot be ruled out on the grounds that the methods of evaluating different ideals are themselves subject to evaluative controversy. They are not more controversial nor more evaluative then some of the psychological facts available to the parties, such as the Aristotelean principle and the considerations concerning self-respect on which the priority of liberty is based (cf. sections 65, 67, and 82). Nor has Rawls provided any argument to show that they are.

In his Dewey lectures Rawls regards the exclusion of beliefs about ideals of the good from the original position as part of an exclusion of all controversial information and forms of reasoning. Moral and religious disagreements are seen as endemic to a democratic society, and the validity of the Rawlsian conception of justice is limited to such a society.[22] The justification for excluding controversial truths from the original position lies in the social role of justice, which is "to enable all members of society to make mutually acceptable to one another their shared institutions and basic arrangements, by citing what are publicly recognized as sufficient reasons."[23] The interest of subjecting one's society and one's life to such principles of justice is assumed to be everyone's highest interest.[24]

It is of the utmost importance that the Rawlsian method of argument requiring unanimity behind a veil of ignorance not be defended on the ground that otherwise the resulting principles would not be fair because unanimity is a condition of fairness or by any other moral argument. Rather, the reason must be that principles not generated by the Rawlsian method will fail to fulfill the social role of a doctrine of justice.

> The essential point is that a conception of justice fulfills its social role provided that citizens equally conscientious and sharing roughly the same beliefs find that, by affirming the framework of deliberation set up by it, they are normally led to a sufficient convergence of opinion. Thus a conception of justice is framed to meet the practical requirements of social life and to yield a public basis in the light of which citizens can justify to one another their common institutions. Such a conception need be only precise enough to achieve this result.[25]

Even if one accepts this view of the social role of a doctrine of justice, and gives it the priority Rawls assigns to it, his conclusions are not supported by his arguments for at least three reasons:
First, even though different people differ in their conception of the good, it does not follow that in a given culture (and Rawls's theory claims validity only within our culture) there are no common elements in their varying conceptions of the good. Such common elements need not be eliminated by the veil of ignorance since their presence does not jeopardize the social role of the doctrine of justice. Second, in particular it is possible that there is a wide measure of agreement con-

cerning the modes of reasoning by which ideals of the good are to be evaluated. *Third*, and most important, is Rawls's blindness to the possibility that the social role of a doctrine of justice may be met by consensus concerning the second best, given that an ideal constitution is not feasible. Rawls assumes without argument that that social role can be fulfilled only by a perfect doctrine of justice, i.e., one which establishes a perfect government for this actual society. But there is no reason why the doctrine of justice actually reflected by the constitutional arrangements of a state may not be reached as a result of people realizing that their different ideals of the good, each leading to different doctrines of justice, cannot be implemented because of the widespread disagreement in society concerning their value. Each will then agree, as a second best, to a doctrine of justice to which all or nearly all members of society could agree (as a second best) if they argue rationally each from his or her different conception of the good provided they are united in ranking the need for a public conception of justice very highly in their order of priorities.

Such a doctrine of justice, which is likely to differ from Rawls's principles of justice, will fulfill the social role he assigns to the doctrine of justice but will be agreed upon by a process of reasoning quite different from his. *First*, different ideals of the good, far from being excluded from the argument for the doctrine of justice, will form the starting points of this argument. *Second*, and as a result, supporters of different conceptions of the good will follow different routes in arguing for the doctrine of justice. There will be a unanimity in the conclusion but (given the different starting points) no unanimity on the route to it. *Third*, the common feature of most routes will be the reliance on a rational reconstruction of a process of bargaining by which the common overriding goal to reach an agreement leads the parties to compromise by accepting a less than perfect doctrine as the optimally realizable second best.

Given the assumption of the overriding goal to reach agreement, there is no reason to think that such a compromise will not be reached. The assumption of this overriding goal is the very same one that Rawls makes and cannot do without. The resulting compromise will be fair by Rawls's own standards, in that each one of the parties conforms, while bargaining, to the principles of his or her morality. By the moral standards of some of the bargainers the claims of some of the others may be immoral. But this does not undermine the fairness of the outcome of the bargaining as long as all acknowledge the Rawlsian assumption of the overriding goal of achieving a common agreement concerning a doctrine of justice. This overriding goal entails that the best constitutional arrangements each person can reach while acting in conformity with his or her own moral ideals are morally valid, and since the commonly agreed upon arrangements are so regarded by everyone, they are morally binding on all. Given that their subject matter is that of a theory of justice, they are a morally valid (if second best) theory of justice.

For reasons I cannot fully explain here, but which are fairly obvious, this procedure of bargaining may in some societies lead to the endorsement of highly wicked principles as that society's doctrine of justice. This should be regarded as a *reductio ad absurdum* of the presupposition of Rawls's theory of justice, and especially the assumption of the overriding goal to reach a doctrine of justice around which there is rational unanimity. I am not advocating the bargaining procedure delineated above. My purpose is merely to show that, though it is a perfectionist procedure, it is not ruled out by Rawls's explicit arguments against perfectionism; and to suggest that the assumption that he relies upon against perfectionism leads to strongly counterintuitive results.

6. TREATING PEOPLE AS ENDS

There are only individual people, different individual people with their own individual lives. Using one of these people for the benefit of others, uses him and benefits others. Nothing more. What happens is that something is done to him for the sake of others. Talk of an overall social good covers this up. (Intentionally?) To use a person in this way does not sufficiently respect and take account of the fact that he is a separate person, that his is the only life he has. *He* does not get some overbalancing good from his sacrifice, and no one is entitled to force this upon him—least of all a state or government that claims his allegiance (as other individuals do not) and that therefore scrupulously must be *neutral* between its citizens.[26]

These words of Nozick echo the Kantian injunction always to treat people also as ends in themselves and not only as means. Nowhere again does he use the state's claim to allegiance as a reason for political neutrality. His argument amounts to an interpretation of the Kantian imperative. Nozick's interpretation relies on the notion of a side constraint which is an agent-relative agency reason of an absolute or near absolute force. Let me explain.[27]

Some reasons for action are based on the value of the outcome of those actions. Let us call these 'outcome reasons'. The reason for bringing injured people to hospital is (barring special circumstances) an outcome reason. So acting will secure their health which since it is a valued outcome is also a reason for bringing it about. Some reasons, however, are based on the value of a particular (class of) agent(s) performing a certain action (including the bringing about by those agents of a certain outcome). I will call these agency reasons. Parents have both an outcome and an agency reason to show concern for the welfare of their children. The outcome reason is satisfied by parents employing teachers and child minders. The agency reason is satisfied only if parents personally involve themselves in the affairs of their children. Some reasons are reasons for everyone. Everyone has reason to respect the rights of others, for example. Such reasons are agent-neutral. Other reasons are reasons for some people and not for others. Those are agent-relative reasons. A person who made a promise has an agent-relative reason to keep it. Both agency and outcome reasons can be either agent-neutral or agent-relative.

The Kantian imperative is explicable only in terms of agency reasons. The requirement is that people should personally treat people as ends, not that they should secure that people shall prosper. But the imperative is open to an agent-neutral interpretation. Each person may be thought to have a reason to help, or even make, others treat people as ends. It may be thought that the Kantian imperative is indifferent in a choice between treating others as ends oneself or treating them as means where doing so will make them treat others as ends, and where but for that action they would not have done so (for example, coercing a person not to coerce another).

Nozick rejects this interpretation of the Kantian imperative. He regards it as imposing a side constraint, and side constraints are agent-relative reasons of absolute or near absolute weight. It cannot be defeated by any other consideration or can only be defeated by a small number of enumerated considerations. Nozick explains:

> The issue of whether a side-constraint view can be put in the form of the goal without-side-constraint view is a tricky one. One might think, for example, that each person could distinguish in his goal between *his* violating rights and someone else's doing it. Give the former infinite (negative) weight in his goal, and no amount of stopping others from violating rights can outweigh his violating someone's rights.[28]

Broadly speaking, Nozick believes in an agent-relative agency reason against imposing sacrifices on individuals against their will. In fact Nozick does not regard the prohibition as absolute and exceptionless as one would expect if it is to be an interpretation of the Kantian imperative. He allows for imposing sacrifices on people, even if there are no counterbalancing benefits for them (even though they are separate people and their lives are the only lives they have) in cases of self-defense. Moreover, Nozick goes a long way beyond self-defense by sanctioning the use of force by an organization not created by consent, if it could have been created by consent through the Invisible Hand mechanism. Perhaps an even more significant exception to the Nozickian version of the Kantian imperative is his principle of compensation that allows coercing some to reduce risks for others provided the former are adequately compensated.[29] In fact, on occasion Nozick seems to suggest that imposing a sacrifice on a person does not offend against his version of the Kantian principle so long as he is compensated by receiving a counterbalancing good. So long as he is a net beneficiary from a transaction, could not one say that he was not treated merely as a means? Is it not true in such a case that his separateness and the fact that his life is the only one he has have been respected? And if so, can one not regard a whole series of mutually dependent transactions from some of which he stands to lose and from others to gain as one transaction since none will take place if the others do not? Such a series will be allowed if the initial expected balance of benefits and sacrifices is positive. The condition is met in many states, even in many illiberal states. Some people are perhaps net losers, but the initial expected balance may still be favorable to all.

These questions are genuine questions. They point to gaps in Nozick's argument and to ambiguities in his position which, if resolved in some ways, lead to conclusions far removed from the spirit of *Anarchy, State, and Utopia*, though consistent with a certain interpretation of its premises.

Does the Kantian imperative in Nozick's interpretation lead to a principle of political neutrality or of the exclusion of ideals from politics? Not without further and independent moral assumptions (which Nozick does not defend). The crucial question is whether coercion to comply with moral duties is consistent with the Kantian imperative as interpreted by Nozick. Nozick's view about self-defense suggests that it is but that the duties not to infringe or put at risk others' rights are the only moral duties there are. This pushes the question one step back. What rights do people have? Do they, e.g., have a right that other members of their community contribute to the life of the community? Nozick's answer is uncertain. He appears to deny the existence of such rights but in principle excludes the justification of a theory of rights from the book. It has been pointed out that it is this love of moral deserts which accounts for most of the more significant conclusions of *Anarchy, State, and Utopia*.[30] What is clear is that it is not the Kantian imperative, nor Nozick's interpretation of it, which lead to the moral deserts, and that there is nothing in them to require either neutral political concern or the exclusion of ideals from politics. If individuals have moral duties to contribute to other persons and to promote certain ideals, then they are not being treated as means by being made to live up to them.

7. COERCION AND AUTONOMY

Nozick appears to claim that it is because the state acts through coercion that it has to be neutral. It is unobjectionable to win over another's clients in order to benefit oneself, but one may not coerce them not to trade with another. Mill too regards the use of coercion as the reason for restraining the state by the harm principle. Is there anything about coercion or its political use to justify principles of restraint or of neutrality?

Coercion is an evaluative term. While it has a fixed descriptive core, its meaning cannot be fully explained without noting the moral significance of coercion. I will adopt the following definition of coercion.[31]

P coerces Q into not doing act A only if

A.   (1) P communicates to Q that he intends to bring about or have brought about some consequence, C, if Q does A.

(2) P makes this communication intending Q to believe that he does so in order to get Q not to do A.

(3) That C will happen is, for Q, a reason of great weight for not doing A.

(4) Q believes that it is likely that P will bring about C if Q does A and that C would leave him worse off, having done A, than if he did not do A and P did not bring about C.

(5) Q does not do A.

(6) Part of Q's reason for not doing A is to avoid (or to lessen) the likelihood of C by making it less likely that P will bring it about.

B.   P's actions which conform to the conditions set out in A are prima facie wrong.

C.   The fact that Q acted under those circumstances is a reason for not blaming him for not doing A.

Only a communication meeting conditions A1-4 is a coercive threat. This definition is not an accurate explanation of the meaning of the expression in English for it disregards some of its uses. It concentrates on coercion by threats since this is the form of coercion relevant to political theory.[32] The definition's first, descriptive, part sets only necessary conditions for the application of the term. One's list of sufficient conditions as well as one's view of how evil must the threatened consequence be to count as a coercive threat depends on one's view of the evaluative significance of coercion. Conditions B and C are deliberately weak for there is no general agreement in the linguistic community as to the precise evaluative significance of coercion. By some, or sometimes, it is held to render the coerced not responsible in the sense that the action is only nominally theirs, whereas in fact the coerced are being controlled by another in a way akin to physical compulsion. By others, or at other times, coercion is held to be no more than a mitigating circumstance. Whichever view one takes, it is not to be justified on linguistic or conceptual grounds but by the soundness of the moral theory of which it is a part.

I will briefly sketch, but will not be able here to elaborate or defend, a view of coercion based on assigning it the following evaluative role:

B1.   By issuing a coercive threat to another person one invades his autonomy.

C1.   The fact that a person acted under coercion is either a justification or a complete excuse for his action.

These principles state the evaluative significance of coercion regarding the acts of the coercer and the coerced respectively. They enable one to draw on one's views about autonomy and excuses for determining what kinds of threats are (provided they meet conditions A1-4) coercive ones.

The following considerations begin to outline the motivation for these two principles. The descriptive meaning of coercion (conditions A1-6) is enough to explain some of the reasons for limiting coercion. Coercive threats differ from offers, for example, in that the former reduce the options available to the person to whom they are addressed whereas offers never worsen and often improve them.[33] Therefore, coercive threats are likely by themselves to change a person's situation significantly to the worse. Furthermore, it is normally more difficult to get people to act against their interests by making them an offer than by coercively threatening them (assuming that making the offers and the coercive threats are equally easy). Finally, though coercion is sometimes meant to benefit the coerced person, we are only too familiar with the danger of exaggerating the degree to which people's well-being can be promoted in flat contradiction of their formed judgment and preferences. While offers may be made in order to induce people to act against their long-term interests, they are in normal circumstances the best judges of that. Our concern is raised only if the person receiving an offer lacks the ability or knowledge to assess

21

it or if there are reasons to regard the bargaining situation as unfair or inefficient. None of these considerations, however, explain why coercion is more suspect than other methods of encouraging people to act in ways deemed to be socially beneficial by making the alternatives less attractive. Their main thrust is to cast doubt on the justification of widespread use of paternalistic coercion. Even in this area the differences between coercion and other paternalistic methods which these considerations reveal are merely in probabilities.

I will regard two common views about coercion as providing the clue to its normative significance. It is commonly said of the coerced that they were forced to do the coerced act and that they acted against their will. Such statements may appear paradoxical since the coerced prefer to comply with the threat and avoid the penalty. The coerced may regret the circumstances they are in, but so do many people who face hard unpleasant choices. This does not make us say that they acted against their will. Nor would it always justify saying that they were forced to act as they did. They had, as do the coerced, a genuine choice. The explanation lies in the character of the choice. Certain choices are forced or dictated choices. Certain choices (not necessarily the same) are made against one's will. I propose to identify the relevant choices by their normative consequences. This proposal is not to be justified as a piece of ordinary language analysis but on the grounds that while conforming to the core meaning of coercion it fruitfully ties it to sound moral principles.

A person is forced to act in a certain way if (1) he regrets the fact that he is in the circumstances he believes himself to be in and which are his reasons for acting as he does and (2) his action is justified or excused. The coerced person is forced to act as he did. Hence his action is either justified or excused. It is justified if the reasons for it, including the threat of harm if it is not undertaken, outweigh the reasons against it, including the fact that undertaking it amounts to submitting to coercion which violates the agent's autonomy (as will be explained below). Not all forced actions are justified. A person may be forced to act immorally as when a shipwrecked sea captain abandons many passengers to certain death in order to save the life of his only child.

Whether or not such action is excusable depends on further moral views the reasons for which have little to do with coercion. But since one's choice of excusing principles affects one's willingness to acknowledge that people were coerced to act as they did, let me put forward a principle that I regard as reasonable, namely, that persons are excused where they acted in order to preserve the life they have or have embarked upon, provided only that their life is neither immoral nor not worth having.

Let the conditions necessary to enable a person to have the life he or she has or has set upon be called personal needs. Choices are dictated by personal needs if all but one nontrivial option will sacrifice a personal need and will make impossible the continuation of the life the agent has.[34] Personal needs are not necessarily the needs of survival. They are more like the needs for having a worthwhile life. For example, life may not be worthwhile, may not be morally possible, for parents who have betrayed their child. Therefore, persons threatened with the death of their child if they do not obey are, for those holding such a view, faced with a choice dictated by personal needs: Disobedience to the order of the child's kidnapper will make life morally impossible, will make the parents' life not worth living. Personal needs are, however, what is necessary to have the life one has or has set upon. Concert pianists may lose the life they have if their fingers are broken. A choice in which the pianist has only one option to avoid his or her fingers being broken is dictated by personal needs, even though the pianist is able to make a new life as a business consultant.[35]

Much more can and need be said to make the notion of a personal need clearer, though nothing can make it precise enough to avoid difficult questions concerning many of its applications to particular cases. For present purposes, however, further elaboration is not required. My aim is merely to tie the notion of 'coercion' to a view about excuses. Let me repeat, however, that a choice is dictated by personal need only if the need is neither to preserve a wicked life nor one not worth living. Hitler cannot be excused by claiming that he had to continue as he started or he would not have been able to pursue the life he had embarked upon.

In light of all this, how serious need a threat be to be a coercive one? If it would justify a coerced action, its seriousness depends on the reasons against that action. If those are not very weighty, the threat need not be as serious as a threat to a personal need. It need only be of great weight to meet the linguistic convention concerning 'coercion' (condition $A3$ in the definition given above). A nonjustifying threat, however, is a coercive one only if it excuses and it does so only if it is serious enough to create a choice dictated by personal needs.

Persons may be forced to act in a certain way by circumstances that are nobody's making, or they may be forced by another's action which created the circumstances that forced them to act as they did. They are forced by another person only if they are forced by that person's action which was undertaken in order to force them to act as they did. One person may force another by changing the circumstances facing that other person's choice or by credibly threatening to do so if the other does not act in a certain way. Such forcing threats are coercive threats, and those who are forced by them are coerced to act as they did.

A person who forces another to act in a certain way, and therefore one who coerces another, makes him act against his will. He subjects the will of another to his own and thereby invades that person's autonomy. Let me explain. An autonomous agent or a person is one who has the capacity to be or to become significantly autonomous at least to a minimal degree. Significant autonomy is a matter of degree. A person may be more or less autonomous. (Significantly) autonomous persons are those who can shape their life and determine its course. They are not merely rational agents who can choose between options after evaluating relevant information, but agents who can in addition adopt personal projects, develop relationships, and accept commitments to causes, through which their personal integrity and sense of dignity and self-respect are made concrete. In a word, significantly autonomous agents are part creators of their own moral world. Persons who are

23

part creators of their own moral world have a commitment to projects, relationships, and causes which affects the kind of life that is for them worth living. It is not that they may not sacrifice projects or causes they are committed to for good reasons, but rather that there are certain kinds of actions vis à vis their commitments which amount to betrayal, compromise their integrity, sacrifice their self-respect, and in extreme cases render their life, i.e., the life they made for themselves, worthless or even impossible (in a moral sense).

Much of the writing on autonomy focuses on an agent's ability to form informed and effective judgments as a condition of autonomy. There can be no doubt of their importance. But there are two more aspects to autonomy as (part) authorship of one's life. One is relational: an autonomous person is not subjected to the will of another. The other aspect of autonomy concerns the quality of the options open to agents: Their choices must not be dictated by personal needs. One is a part author of one's world only if in creating it one is not merely serving the will of another. Forcing persons, and therefore coercing them, to act invades their autonomy because, first, the person who forces others directly intends them to conform to his will. Subjecting others to his will is either his end or his means to it. And, second, the coercer aims at and succeeds in forcing others by restriciting their options.

All coercion invades autonomy by subjecting the will of the coerced. Coercive threats which create a choice dictated by personal needs, and most serious cases of coercion by the state are of this kind, invade autonomy by offending against the third aspect of autonomy as well. The autonomous agent is one who is not always struggling to maintain the minimum conditions of a worthwhile life. The more one's choices are dictated by personal needs, the less autonomous one becomes. Of course natural conditions may also force people to make choices determined by the need to secure the necessities of a worthwhile life. And it would be wrong to think that every such condition is in any way regrettable. Autonomy is possible only within a framework of constraints. The completely autonomous person is an impossibility. The ideal of the perfect existentialist with no fixed biological and social nature who creates himself as he goes along is an incoherent dream. An autonomous personality can only develop and flourish against a background of biological and social constraints which fix some of its human needs. Some choices are inevitably determined by those needs. Yet, harsh natural conditions can reduce the degree of autonomy of a person to a bare minimum just as effectively as systematic coercive intervention. Moreover, noncoercive interferences with a person's life and fortunes may also reduce his or her autonomy in the same way as coercive interventions do. The only differences are that *all* coercive interventions invade autonomy and they do so intentionally, whereas only *some* noncoercive interventions do so and usually as a by-product of their intended results. They are *not* direct assaults on the autonomy of persons.

Inasmuch as the liberal concern to limit coercion is a concern for the autonomy of persons, the liberal will also be anxious to secure natural and social conditions which enable individuals to develop an autonomous life. The liberal will seek to control the physical environment and to regulate the noncoercive effects that one person's acts have over others in order to secure an environment suitable for autonomous life. In pursuing such goals the liberal may be willing to use coercion. Autonomy is after all a matter of degree. A single act of coercion of a not too serious nature makes little difference to a person's ability to lead an autonomous life. Of course coercion invades autonomy not only in its consequences but also in its intention. As such, it normally is an insult to the persons's autonomy. He or she is being treated as a nonautonomous agent, an animal, a baby, or an imbecile. Often coercion is wrong primarily because it is an affront or an insult and not so much because of its more tangible consequences which may not be very grave. In this respect, however, there is a significant difference between coercion by an ideal liberal state and coercion from most other sources. Since individuals are guaranteed adequate rights of political participation in the liberal state and since such a state is guided by a public morality expressing concern for individual autonomy, its coercive measures do not express an insult to the autonomy of individuals. It is common knowledge that they are motivated not by lack of respect to individual autonomy but by concern for it. After all, coercion can be genuinely to the good of the coerced and can even be sought by them. These considerations do not, however, affect the liberal concern to limit coercion in a nonideal state.

8. LIBERALISM, AUTONOMY, AND PLURALISM

The previous section raised the question whether the state's reliance on coercion requires political neutrality. It ended with the conclusion that the special liberal concern with coercion is a result of a belief in the value of autonomy. Does valuing autonomy require political neutrality? Does it require limiting the use of ideals in politics? Rawls's Kantian constructivist approach to ethics suggests an argument for political neutrality which is in part independent of the one criticized above and which turns on autonomy:

> Kant held, I believe, that a person is acting autonomously when the principles of his action are chosen by him as the most adequate possible expression of his nature as a free and equal rational being. The principles he acts upon are not adopted because of his social position or natural endowments, or in view of the particular kind of society in which he lives or the specific things that he happens to want. To act on such principles is to act heteronomously. Now the veil of ignorance deprives the persons in the original position of the knowledge that would enable them to choose heteronomous principles.[36]

Rawls applies the Kantian insight only to the choice of the principles of justice. But it seems that if it is valid for that purpose, it must be valid for morality generally. In *A Theory of Justice* Rawls does not use the Kantian insight as an argument for the acceptability of his theory. He merely points out that his theory is consistent with it. But in "Kantian Constructivism in Moral Theory" the Kantian insight is used to defend his theory against various criticisms by providing it with an epistemological foundation. Applied to moral considerations generally, the Kantian insight yields a new argument for excluding the parties' moral and religious beliefs behind the veil of ignorance. While not explicitly using this argument, Rawls comes close to doing so in saying that

> the parties in the original position do not agree on what the moral facts are, as if there already were such facts. It is not that, being situated impartially, they have a clear and undistorted view of a prior and independent moral order. Rather (for constructivism), there is no such order, and therefore no such facts apart from the procedure of construction as a whole; the facts are identified by the principles that result.[37]

In developing the Kantian insight along Rawlsian lines, several points must be borne in mind. *First*, the fundamental idea which enjoys universal validity is that morality is the free expression of a person's rational nature. The claim that principles chosen in the original position express this nature depends on a certain conception of the person which is among the deep common presuppositions of our culture but no more.[38] *Second*, Rawls is anxious to make clear that the choice of principles because they express human nature "is not a so-called 'radical' choice: that is, a choice not based on reasons. . . . The notion of radical choice . . . finds no place in justice as fairness."[39] Furthermore: "The ideals of the person and of social cooperation . . . are not ideals that, at some moment in life, citizens are said simply to choose. One is to imagine that, for the most part, they find on examination that they hold these ideals, that they have taken them in part from the culture of their society."[40] The conception of morality as an expression of the rational nature of people is consistent with the view that people's nature is socially determined, thus rendering the concrete manifestation of morality equally socially determined. *Third*, Rawls's conception of the person does not lead to unanimity of moral views.

Given this conception of morality, it is evident that the parties to the original position know nothing of their moral beliefs. They are not excluded, as is knowledge of the particular circumstances of each participant's life, in order to ensure that choice in the original position represents people's rational nature. They are in fact not excluded at all. The parties to the original position have no knowledge of their moral beliefs because they have as yet no moral beliefs and because whatever moral beliefs they should have depends on the outcome of their deliberations in the original position and cannot affect it. Thus extending the Kantian insight beyond political morality to morality as a whole explains the elimination of moral beliefs and ideals of the good from behind the veil of ignorance. But this argument by itself does not justify political neutrality. The argument for neutrality still rests on the further assumption that it is in people's highest interest to adopt principles fulfilling the social role of justice, and Rawls shows neither that this assumption follows from the Kantian insight nor that it leads to neutral political concern. The counterargument of section 5 above still holds good.

This reconstruction of Rawls's argument for the doctrine of neutral political concern attempts to found it on the notion of autonomy through the notion of moral self-determination. The intuitive idea behind it seems to be this: since morality is an expression of one's rational nature, it is essentially self-determined. Given the social determination of the concept of a person and the absence of unanimity in the outcome of moral deliberation, the only proper course seems to be to endorse constitutional arrangements neutral between conceptions of the good in order to enable all individuals to develop and pursue their own conception of the good. Since no conception of the good which expresses the rational nature of the person upholding it is better than any other, the constitutional arrangements should be neutral between them. The role of the state is to enable all persons to express their nature and pursue their own autonomously conceived conception of the good and plan of life.

As noted, this intuitive idea relies on a plausible-looking but unfounded belief in the acceptance of a need for unanimously approved principles of justice as everyone's highest interest. This is enough to reject it. Furthermore, this way of expressing the intuitive idea is unlikely to gain Rawls's approval. It advocates not neutral political concern as a principle of restraint but neutrality between those conceptions of the good which greatly value an autonomous development of one's life in accordance with one's rational nature. It is in fact not a doctrine of neutrality but of moral pluralism. Since moral pluralism is often thought to necessitate neutral political concern, I will conclude with a brief and tentative sketch of an argument purporting to show that valuing autonomy leads to moral pluralism, which in turn supports a conception of liberalism based on the harm principle and not on the doctrine of neutrality.

Persons enjoy significant autonomy to the degree that their choices are not entirely dictated by an effort to secure their basic needs. Such persons develop relationships with other creatures, and commit themselves to projects, plans, and causes. A moral theory prizes autonomy if it assesses a person's life not merely by the value of the person's relationships, plan of life, and commitments, but also by the degree to which they were chosen and developed autonomously. Such a theory is committed to moral pluralism, that is, to the view that there are many worthwhile and valuable relationships, commitments, and plans of life which are mutually incompatible, so that autonomous people can and should choose between them.[41] This presupposes a controversial view which cannot be properly explained, let alone defended, here. A choice between the morally correct and the morally wrong is like a choice dictated by the necessity to secure personal needs. It is a dictated choice and not one that exercises significant autonomy. The chooser may not, of course, know the right option from the wrong one. This, however, does not alter the situation; what matters is that the chooser regards his or her choice as a choice between the morally right and the morally wrong. Significant autonomy is exercised when a choice is perceived to be one between morally acceptable options, though since the choice itself often creates a commitment it may render the rejected option morally unacceptable in the future. (Think, for example, of a decision to marry a certain person.)

Valuing autonomy and accepting moral pluralism does not, however, entail that forms of life are good because they are chosen. On the contrary, they are chosen because they are thought to be good. Choice is possible only where there is belief in a reason for choosing as one does. People may choose between what they conceive to be equally valuable options or between incommensurate options. They may choose one option even though they believe that its alternative is supported by better reasons. They cannot, however, choose where they see no reason at all for the choice they make; and in all but exceptional cases that will include a reason for the chosen action. Given that a significantly autonomous choice is not determined by the agent's personal needs, the reasons that make it attractive have to do with the value of the chosen option or its contribution to a valuable way of life.

Since significant autonomy presupposes a choice of ways of life among morally worthwhile possibilities, it requires that the state should make worthwhile options available and accessible to individuals. It is not required to protect or to avoid discouraging morally unacceptable options. Moral pluralism does not require tolerating the morally wrong. It does not demand neutrality between good and bad. But whereas the state may take noncoercive action to encourage people to pursue worthwhile forms of life by creating an environment conducive to such a choice and whereas it may discourage the pursuit of morally unacceptable ways of life by trying to uproot the conditions that make them appealing, it should not use coercive measures to stop autonomous persons from engaging in morally unacceptable activities unless they are also harmful to others. Only action that denies others their fair opportunities to pursue the kind of valuable life they may prefer is harmful to them. The state's concern for autonomy entitles it in principle to use coercion to stop harm to others. Its task is to ensure that they have fair opportunities for autonomous life. It may coercively invade the autonomy of some to protect the autonomy of others. It may not invade their autonomy for other reasons.

The arguments that elaborate and support these final remarks must await another occasion. The aim of this programmatic essay was merely to show that the arguments commonly adduced in favor of the doctrine of neutral political concern do not bear the weight of their conclusion. Where they touch fundamental beliefs embedded in our culture, they rest on concern for autonomy and therefore also for pluralism. These, when coupled with a moral outlook asserting responsibilities toward others, which is equally deeply embedded in it, lead to affirming the social and political responsibility of creating a social framework ensuring that individuals have fair opportunities for a worthwhile autonomous life. The fundamental moral affirmation of autonomy and pluralism is itself an aspect of an ideal of the good and leads to a conception of the political based on toleration but not on neutrality.[42]

Notes

1. "Liberalism" by M. Cranston in *Encyclopaedia of Philosophy*, ed. P. Edwards (New York, 1967).

2. It is a mistake to think that a presumption of rationality requires reasons only for political changes and therefore differs from the presumption of liberty, being, unlike the latter, a

conservative presumption sanctioning the status quo. Two questions have to be kept distinct. The justification of existing political arrangements is one thing. Justifying a change in existing arrangements is another. Rationality decrees that political arrangements are justified only if supported by reasons. It has conservative implications only in requiring separate reasons for changing them. But surely the presumption of liberty interpreted as above must allow that un-justified existing curtailments of liberty should be changed only if there are—and not always will there be—additional arguments showing that changing them will not do more harm than good. This weak presumption of liberty does not therefore avoid the conservative tendency of the requirements of rationality. This article is concerned with arguments about the justifiabil-ity of political arrangements, and not specifically with the conditions that make changes to ex-isting arrangements justifiable.

3. An entrenched bill of rights may, of course, be recommended by theories belonging to the other liberal traditions for countries in certain circumstances. My comment in the text ap-plies to rights of the common kind. Some rights (e.g., rights against discrimination) introduce principles of restraint of the kind discussed in this article.

4. J. S. Mill, *On Liberty*, Everyman ed. (London, 1979), p. 72.

5. C. L. Ten, *Mill on Liberty* (Oxford, 1980), p. 40. See also Ruth Gavison, "The Enforce-ment of Morals and the Status of the Principle of Liberty, " *IYYVN* 27 (1976/7):274-94 (in Hebrew).

6. R. Nozick, *Anarchy, State, and Utopia* (New York, 1974), p. 33. Italics in the original.

7. A. Montefiore in *Neutrality and Impartiality*, ed. A. Montefiore (Cambridge, 1975), p.5.

8. *Ibid.*, p. 7.

9. In a wider sense. appropriate for other contexts, individuals' acts are political insofar as (1) they are likely to affect political institutions or their actions, or(2) they are designed to or are conventionally regarded as expressions of views or positions in matters of political morality.

10. Montefiore may have wished to avoid the problem by defining neutrality as requiring help or hindrance to an equal degree rather than as the absence of help or hindrance. I do not be-lieve, however, that this enables one to dispense with the distinction between not helping and hindering. Consider a country that has no commercial or other relations with either of two war-ring parties. This was true of Uruguay in relation to the war between Somalia and Ethiopia a few years ago. It may nevertheless be true that such a country may have been able to establish links with either party. Would we say that Uruguay was not neutral unless the help that it could have and did not give Ethiopia was equal to the help that it could have and did not give Somalia? This will not be the case if, for example, Uruguay could have supplied the parties with a com-modity that, though useful to both, was in short supply in one country but not in the other. Should we then say that Uruguay is not neutral unless it starts providing the country suffering from the shortage in that commodity? If by not helping it Uruguay is hindering it, then this conclusion is forced on us. But according to the common understanding of neutrality, Uruguay would have been nonneutral if in the circumstances described it would have started supplying one of the parties with militarily useful materials after the outbreak of the war. It follows that the distinction between helping and not hindering is crucial to an understanding of neutrality, as is the distinction between hindering and not helping.

11. Several points require further argument. First, some arms are necessary for police action, some may be solicited and supplied in anticipation of a different possible conflict. This may show that unequal supply of arms can be compatible with narrow (though clearly not with comprehensive) neutrality. Second, some feel that no supply of arms to the combatants, how-ever evenhanded, is compatible with neutrality. My response is, in brief, that no-supply is not more neutral than evenhanded supply. If it is thought to be preferable, this is for reasons having nothing to do with neutrality, such as a desire to bring the war to a speedy end or not to allow people to profit from wars. Third, my example assumed that we are regular suppliers of food to the Reds. This assures us that the continued supply is of normal quantities required anyway, but it also makes discontinuation of supply a positive harm rather than a refusal to help. Thus a person who has no regular trading relations with the parties can provide the Reds with their

ordinary requirements of food while remaining narrowly neutral or refuse to sell them anything that improves their position and be comprehensively neutral. We, being their regular suppliers, do not have the option of action that neither helps nor hinders. Finally, it may be claimed that real neutrality is comprehensive neutrality, narrow neutrality being compromised neutrality which is sometimes all that is possible. My point is merely that even if this is so, the fact remains that narrow neutrality is often all that is meant by 'neutrality.'

12. Nozick, *Anarchy, State, and Utopia*, pp. 272-73.

13. T. Nagel, "Rawls on Justice," *Philosophical Review* 82 (1973): 220-34, reprinted in *Reading Rawls*, ed. D. Daniels (Oxford, 1975), to which all page references refer.

14. J. Rawls, *A Theory of Justice* (Oxford, 1971), pp. 93-94.

15. B. Barry, *Political Argument* (London, 1965), p. 66. All page references to Barry are to this book. Barry has some effective critical arguments against liberalism thus understood which I shall not repeat here.

16. A. Sen, "Utilitarianism and Welfarism," *Journal of Philosophy* 78 (1979): 463.

17. The point deserves a more detailed defense than is possible here. Let me note in brief that I am not supposing that deliberation on the nature of the reasons always accompanies the formation of desires nor that one always gives oneself an explicit account of such reasons. Akratic agents believe that the reason for their akratic behavior is defeated by other reasons, but akratic action is undertaken for some reason that they believe in. Unconscious desires depend on conscious ones and are essentially redescriptions of them in ways that the agent may not use in accounting for his or her reasons for them.

18. On the other hand wishing is stronger than desiring in being an overall judgment of the merits of the wished for. whereas a desire need be based on a partial evaluation of the desired only.

19. Sometimes the fact that persons have desires changes their situation in a special way — the desires may acquire the character of a craving, i.e., they may as it were escape their control and dominate them quite independently of their beliefs about the appropriateness of the desires (though, except in extreme pathological cases, the agents will continue to believe that they desire for a reason). In such cases they may acquire a new reason to satisfy their desires, i.e., to liberate themselves from their hold. But even in such cases it is not merely the fact that they desire that is their reason for wishing the desires to be satisfied. They may, e.g., be wrong in thinking that satisfying the desires is the best way to terminate their irrational craving and, unless they are akratic, they will wish the desires not to be satisfied if this is the case.

20. Barry distinguishes between private-oriented and public-oriented wants. The first are those whose satisfaction "materially impinges" only upon the life of the person whose desires they are, or upon his or her family. Public-oriented wants are ones whose satisfaction affects a larger group. (pp. 12-13; see also p. 63). Barry notes that public-oriented wants reflect people's ideals concerning the state of society and objects to giving them any weight as wants. They should be weighed according to the value of the ideals they express. My argument earlier in this section accords with this line of thought inasmuch as want-satisfaction is considered to be possibly of intrinsic value. But if the state's goal is to provide people with opportunities to pursue their own conception of the good, then public-oriented wants should count as well, though, as we have just seen, not in the sense that the state should strive to satisfy them, but in that it should provide opportunities for their pursuit as well as for the pursuit of private-oriented wants.

21. This point raises a wider issue of some importance to the evaluation of Rawls's procedure. Should one assume that the parties take notice in the original position of their own fallibility, and agree on constitutional arrangements that will be self-correcting if it turns out that the fundamental beliefs concerning human nature, on which their substantive principles of justice are based, turn out to be wrong, or not? One might think that they need not. We could always engage in the Rawlsian form of argument and apply it to the new information once it becomes available. This seems to be the way Rawls treats the problem (though he is sensitive to fallibility concerning applied principles (see pp. 195-97). But quite apart from the

fact that by this one assumes that in the original position the parties discount a general fact of human nature, namely its fallibility, this procedure will sanction nonadaptable constitutions—a highly counterintuitive conclusion.

22. Rawls, "Kantian Constructivism in Moral Theory," *Journal of Philosophy* 77 (1980): 540-42.

23. *Ibid.*, p. 517 and cf. p. 561.

24. *Ibid.*, p. 525.

25. *Ibid.*, p. 561.

26. Nozick, *Anarchy, State, and Utopia*, p. 33.

27. The explanation is adapted from the distinctions drawn by D. Parfit in "Is Common-Sense Morality Self-Defeating," *Journal of Philosophy* 70 (1979):533.

28. Nozick, *Anarchy, State, and Utopia*, p. 29n. He regards such reformulations as inadequate but does not explain why.

29. *Ibid.*, pp. 78ff.

30. Cf., for example, H. L. A. Hart, "Between Utility and Rights," in *The Idea of Freedom*, ed. A. Ryan (Oxford, 1979), p. 77.

31. The first part of the definition is a modification of Nozick's in "Coercion" in *Philosophy, Politics, and Society*, ed. P. Laslett, W. G. Runciman, and Q. Skinner, 4th series (Oxford, 1972), pp. 104-6.

32. In "Threats, Offers, Law, Opinion, and Liberty" *American Philosophical Quarterly* 14 (1977): 257; at p. 265 P. Day mentions six coercive modes of influence: (1) forcing, (2) threatening, (3) extreme intimidation, (4) extreme temptation, (5) extreme domination, (6) extreme provocation.

33. An offer creates an option its receiver may not have had before. It does not deprive the receiver of any options. A credible threat deprives the threatened person of the option of not acting as he or she is told to act and not suffering the threatened consequence. No new desirable options are created for the person. The traveler stopped by a highwayman gains the option of resisting a robber. But such an option is not a desirable one, i.e., it is one that people in normal circumstances would prefer not to have. A threatened consequence may be one that will happen anyway independently of the threat. If the threatened person knows of this, the threat is rendered ineffective, so that such cases will be rare or can be disregarded here. It is sometimes assumed that a person making an offer intends it to be taken up and that an offer gives an advantage or benefit. Neither are universally true. The person making the offer may be indifferent as to whether it will be accepted. (Consider a polite offer to give a lift home to a person met at a party.). An offer is more like a conditional promise: I undertake to do it if you want me to.

34. The reference to nontrivial options is needed since trivial options are always available. One can hand the money more or less slowly to the gunman who threatens, "Your money or your life."

35. Whether or not an act is justified is an objective question, depending on how things were or could have reasonably been believed to be, rather than on the agent's beliefs. And this is true of moral as well as of other beliefs. The principle that personal needs excuse is similarly an objective one. Although to a degree persons make the life they have, what life they have made for themselves and whether this choice is dictated by personal need is an objective question. This is not to deny that other excusing principles may excuse those who erroneously believe that they are forced to act as they do. My only point is that they are neither forced nor coerced to take this action.

36. Rawls, *A Theory of Justice*, p. 252.

37. Rawls, "Kantian Constructivism in Moral Theory," p. 568.

38. Cf., *ibid.*, p. 520. It seems to me that Rawls is ambiguous on the crucial issue of whether the reflective equilibrium argument supports the fundamental Kantian insight or presupposes it—I assume here that there is a sense in which the latter is the case though the full story is more complex and cannot be explored here.

39. *Ibid.*, p. 568.

40. *Ibid.*, pp. 568-69.

41. This in essence is Nagel's conclusion of his criticism of Rawls's claim that his theory is neutral: Nagel, *Rawls on Justice*, p. 10.

42. I am grateful to J. Waldron, H. Oberdiek, H. Steiner, P. M. S. Hacker, and to members of the All Souls moral and political philosophy discussion group for comments on an earlier version of this paper. I have also benefited from conversations with P. Day and H. L. A. Hart on coercion, threats, and offers.

Liberal Individualism and Liberal Neutrality*

Will Kymlicka

A distinctive feature of contemporary liberal theory is its emphasis on "neutrality"—the view that the state should not reward or penalize particular conceptions of the good life but, rather, should provide a neutral framework within which different and potentially conflicting conceptions of the good can be pursued. Liberal neutrality has been criticized from many angles, but I will be concerned here only with the connection critics draw between neutrality and individualism, particularly in the context of Rawls's theory of justice. One of the most persistent criticisms of Rawls's theory is that it is excessively individualistic, neglecting the way that individual values are formed in social contexts and pursued through communal attachments. I will distinguish three different ways that critics have attempted to connect neutrality and individualism and argue that all rest on misinterpretations of Rawls's theory. However, there are important aspects of the relationship between individual values and social contexts which Rawls does not discuss, and I hope to show that the dispute over liberal neutrality would be more fruitful if both sides moved away from general questions of "individualism" toward more specific questions about the relationship between state, society, and culture in liberal democracies.

DEFINING LIBERAL NEUTRALITY

What sort of neutrality is present, or aspired to, in Rawls's theory? Raz distinguishes two principles which he believes are present, and inadequately distinguished, in liberal writings on neutrality. One, which Raz calls "neutral political concern," requires that the state seek to help or hinder different life-plans to an equal degree—that is, government action should have neutral consequences. The other, which Raz calls the "exclusion of ideals," allows that government action may help some ways of life more than others but denies that government should act in order to help some ways of life over others. The state does not take a stand on which ways of life are most worth living, and the desire to help one way of life over another

* I would like to thank G. A. Cohen, Sue Donaldson, Les Green, Amy Gutmann, Dave Knott, and Arthur Ripstein for helpful comments on an earlier draft.

Ethics 99 (July 1989): 883–905

is precluded as a justification of government action. The first requires neutrality in the consequences of government policy; the second requires neutrality in the justification of government policy. I will call these two conceptions consequential and justificatory neutrality, respectively.

Which conception does Rawls defend? Raz argues that Rawls endorses consequential neutrality,[1] and some of Rawls's formulations are undoubtedly consistent with that interpretation. But there are two basic tenets of Rawls's theory which show that he could not have endorsed consequential neutrality. First, respect for civil liberties will necessarily have nonneutral consequences. Freedom of speech and association allow different groups to pursue and advertise their way of life. But not all ways of life are equally valuable, and some will have difficulty attracting or maintaining adherents. Since individuals are free to choose between competing visions of the good life, civil liberties have nonneutral consequences—they create a marketplace of ideas, as it were, and how well a way of life does in this market depends on the kinds of goods it can offer to prospective adherents. Hence, under conditions of freedom, satisfying and valuable ways of life will tend to drive out those which are worthless and unsatisfying.

Rawls endorses such a cultural marketplace, despite its nonneutral consequences. Moreover, the prospect that trivial and degrading ways of life fare less well in free competition is not something he regrets or views as an unfortunate side effect. On the contrary, the liberal tradition has always endorsed civil liberties precisely because they make it possible "that the worth of different modes of life should be proved practically."[2]

Consequential neutrality is also inconsistent with Rawls's explanation of the role of "primary goods." They are supposed to be employable in the pursuit of diverse conceptions of the good. But not all ways of life have the same costs, and so an equal distribution of resources will have nonneutral consequences. Those who choose expensive ways of life— valuing leisure over work, or champagne over beer—will get less welfare out of an equal bundle of resources than will people with more modest tastes. This is unlike an equality of welfare scheme, in which those with expensive tastes would be subsidized by others in order to achieve equality of welfare. On an equality of welfare scheme, resources would be unequally distributed so that every way of life is equally helped, no matter how expensive—those who wish beer get enough money for beer, those who wish champagne get enough money for champagne.

Rawls favors equality of resources, despite its nonneutral consequences and, indeed, because it prohibits excess demands on resources by those with expensive desires:

> It is not by itself an objection to the use of primary goods that it does not accommodate those with expensive tastes. One must argue

1. Joseph Raz, *The Morality of Freedom* (Oxford: Oxford University Press, 1986), p. 117.

2. J. S. Mill, *On Liberty*, ed. David Spitz (New York: Norton, 1975), p. 54.

in addition that it is unreasonable, if not unjust, to hold people responsible for their preferences and to require them to make out as best they can. But to argue this seems to presuppose that citizens' preferences are beyond their control as propensities or cravings which simply happen. Citizens seem to be regarded as passive carriers of desires. The use of primary goods, however, relies on a capacity to assume responsibility for our ends. This capacity is part of the moral power to form, to revise, and rationally to pursue a conception of the good. . . . In any particular situation, then, those with less expensive tastes have presumably adjusted their likes and dislikes over the course of their lives to the income and wealth they could reasonably expect; and it is regarded as unfair that they now should have less in order to spare others from the consequences of their lack of foresight or self-discipline.[3]

Since individuals are responsible for forming "their aims and ambitions in the light of what they can reasonably expect," they recognize that "the weight of their claims is not given by the strength or intensity of their wants and desires."[4] Those people who have developed expensive tastes in disregard of what they can reasonably expect have no claim to be subsidized by others, no matter how strongly felt those desires are.[5]

So the two fundamental components of liberal justice—respect for liberty and fairness in the distribution of material resources—both preclude consequential neutrality. However ambiguous his terminology is, Rawls has to be interpreted as endorsing justificatory neutrality.[6] As

3. John Rawls, "Social Unity and Primary Goods," in *Utilitarianism and Beyond*, ed. Amartya Sen and Bernard Williams (Cambridge: Cambridge University Press, 1982), pp. 168–69; see also Rawls, "Fairness to Goodness," *Philosophical Review* 84 (1975): 553.

4. John Rawls, "Kantian Constructivism in Moral Theory: The Dewey Lectures 1980," *Journal of Philosophy* 77 (1980): 545.

5. This principle of responsibility is also central to Dworkin's equality of resources scheme: the cost to others of the resources we claim should "figure in each person's sense of what is rightly his and in each person's judgment of what life he should lead, given that command of justice" (Ronald Dworkin, "What Is Equality? Part 2," *Philosophy and Public Affairs* 10 [1981]: 289). Indeed, Dworkin's scheme does a better job than Rawls's difference principle of distinguishing the costs that people are responsible for from the costs that are an unchosen part of people's circumstances. Some people argue that an accurate assessment of individual responsibility requires going beyond either primary goods or equality of resources to "equal opportunity for welfare" (Richard Arneson, "Equality and Equal Opportunity for Welfare," *Philosophical Studies* 55 [1989]: 79–95), or "equal access to advantage" (G. A. Cohen, "On the Currency of Egalitarian Justice," *Ethics*, in this issue). While these critiques of Rawls's account of primary goods are important, they are not moves away from justificatory neutrality.

6. Although I cannot argue the point here, I believe that the other major statements of liberal neutrality must similarly be interpreted as endorsing justificatory neutrality— e.g., Bruce Ackerman, *Social Justice in the Liberal State* (New Haven, Conn.: Yale University Press, 1980), pp. 11, 61; Charles Larmore, *Patterns of Moral Complexity* (Cambridge: Cambridge University Press, 1987), chap. 3, esp. pp. 44–47; Ronald Dworkin, "Liberalism," in *Public and Private Morality*, ed. Stuart Hampshire (Cambridge: Cambridge University Press, 1978), p. 127, and *A Matter of Principle* (London: Harvard University Press, 1985), p. 222; Robert Nozick, *Anarchy, State and Utopia* (New York: Basic, 1974), pp. 272–73 (for an extended exegetical discussion of these passages, see David Knott, *Liberalism and the Justice of Neutral*

Rawls puts it, government is neutral between different conceptions of the good, "not in the sense that there is an agreed public measure of intrinsic value or satisfaction with respect to which all these conceptions come out equal, but in the sense that they are not evaluated at all from a social standpoint."[7] The state does not justify its actions by reference to some public ranking of the intrinsic value of different ways of life, for there is no public ranking to refer to. This kind of neutrality is consistent with the legitimate nonneutral consequences of cultural competition and individual responsibility. Indeed, and I'll return to this point, one might think that good ways of life are most likely to establish their greater worth, and individuals are most likely to accept responsibility for the costs of their choices, when the state is constrained by justificatory neutrality—that is, when individuals cannot "use the coercive apparatus of the state to win for themselves a greater liberty or larger distributive share on the grounds that their activities are of more intrinsic value."[8]

NEUTRALITY AND POSSESSIVE INDIVIDUALISM

I now want to consider three versions of the claim that liberal neutrality, as envisioned by Rawls, is excessively individualistic. The first version, advanced separately by Schwartz and Nagel shortly after the publication of *A Theory of Justice*, focuses on the content of people's aims and ambitions. Rawls claims that a state which gives each individual the largest possible share of resources and liberties to pursue their disparate ends, consistent with the claim of others to an equal share, lives up to the requirements of justificatory neutrality. But, according to Schwartz and Nagel, this presupposes a kind of possessive individualist theory of human motivation. It suggests that what people want in life is to maximize their share of social resources (rather than promote the good of others), and indeed to maximize their material good (rather than promote their spiritual or emotional well-being). Such a theory of motivation may suit the self-

Political Concern [D.Phil. thesis, Oxford University, 1989], chap. 2.) Hence, I will be using "liberal neutrality" and "justificatory neutrality" interchangeably. It is quite possible that 'neutrality' is not the best word to describe the policy at issue. Rawls himself has avoided the term until recently because of its multiple and often misleading meanings—e.g., neutrality in its everyday usage usually implies neutral consequences (John Rawls, "The Priority of Right and Ideas of the Good," *Philosophy and Public Affairs* 17 [1988]: 260, 265; cf. Raz, chap. 5). He has instead used the term "priority of the right over the good." But that too has multiple and misleading meanings, since it is used by Rawls to describe both the affirming of neutrality over perfectionism, and the affirming of deontology over teleology. These issues need to be kept distinct, and neither, viewed on its own, is usefully called a matter of the "priority of the right"; see my "Rawls on Teleology and Deontology," *Philosophy and Public Affairs* 17 (1988): 173–190, for a critique of Rawls's usage of "priority of the right." Given the absence of any obviously superior alternative, I will continue to use the term "neutrality."

   7. Rawls, "Social Unity," p. 172; cf. Rawls, *A Theory of Justice* (London: Oxford University Press, 1971), p. 94.
   8. Rawls, *Theory of Justice*, p. 329.

seeking and materialistic culture of contemporary capitalist cultures, but it penalizes those who value other ends. "Consider a socialist somewhat in the lines of the early Marx. This individual believes that a good life must rest on self-realization through labor . . . and that a person is morally harmed by the possession of more than a certain minimal amount of wealth."[9] Such a socialist will claim "that his good is furthered by just enough wealth so that he is decently fed, housed, and clothed" and that

> he would be harmed by living in a society based on a preference for a greater rather than a lesser amount of wealth. He could say that living in such a society he would devote valuable time to thinking about material wealth and trying to decide whether or not to avoid the temptation of attempting to acquire more possessions. . . . In addition, the socialist could claim that a system based on a preference for a greater amount of wealth would be against his interest since it would prevent him from forming strong ties of affection with other human beings. He could claim that, in such a system, people would tend to be more interested in wealth than in other people.[10]

Now this might seem at first glance to be attacking the idea of consequential neutrality, since Schwartz emphasizes that not all ways of life will fare equally well in a Rawlsian society. But the objection is not simply that communal ways of life will fare less well. After all, they might fare badly, not because primary goods are less useful for communal ways of life, but simply because most people choose not to use them for that purpose. Rather, the claim is that primary goods (beyond a certain point) are only useful for individualistic ends, and so Rawls's demand that society aim to increase the share of primary goods available to individuals reflects a decision that individualistic ways of life should be promoted at the expense of nonindividualistic ways of life, a decision which violates justificatory neutrality. The problem is not simply that communal ways of life do less well but, rather, that the reason they do less well is that Rawls's account of primary goods is arbitrarily and unfairly biased against them, since that account is based on (nonneutral) assumptions about people's individualistic aims.[11]

But this critique misinterprets Rawls's justification for the importance of primary goods.[12] Rawls does not assume anything like a possessive

---

9. Adina Schwartz, "Moral Neutrality and Primary Goods," *Ethics* 83 (1973): 302.

10. Ibid., p. 304; cf. Jurgen Habermas, *Communication and the Evolution of Society*, trans. Thomas McCarthy (Boston: Beacon, 1979), pp. 198–99.

11. Thomas Nagel, "Rawls on Justice," *Philosophical Review* 82 (1973): 228–29.

12. Both Schwartz and Nagel use the issue of individualistic conceptions of the good to make broader claims about Rawls's theoretical project. According to Schwartz, this issue is one example of the way in which Rawls invokes more than "minimalist" assumptions about reason and morality; according to Nagel, this issue is one example of the way in which Rawls exaggerates the relationship between impartiality and choice under ignorance. Both of these broader claims could be true even if, as I will argue, the particular example they cite is misconceived.

individualist theory of motivation. On the contrary, one of the things that people can do, and indeed are expected to do, with their resources and liberties is to join or create meaningful associations and attachments, including spiritual and emotional ones. Schwartz claims that material resources (above a certain minimum) are not useful in the pursuit of nonmaterialistic ends, and so Rawls's primary goods scheme is biased against the socialist who sees the good life as self-realization through labor and views material wealth as positively harmful. But Schwartz's discussion here is far too quick. The socialist needs resources in order to pursue a life of self-realizing labor—she needs access to land or other raw materials and to the technology which enables work to be creative and variable rather than merely onerous and repetitive. Someone who only has enough wealth to be decently clothed has no way to ensure that her labor is self-realizing, since the conditions under which she works will be determined by the exigencies of nature or by the aims of those who own the land and tools. Even if she wishes to live in harmony with nature and use only simple tools and techniques (perhaps the socialist is converted to deep ecology), she must still have control over resources. The desire to keep an ecological habitat in its natural condition requires restrictions on the way other people use not only the immediate habitat but also the surrounding land, air, and water. These nonindividualistic and nonmaterialistic ways of life require that substantial amounts of social resources be set aside for their purposes. It is entirely wrong to suppose that the less materialistic someone is, the less of an interest she has in Rawls's primary goods.[13]

Indeed, it is difficult to imagine a viable way of life which is genuinely harmed by, or even indifferent to, increases in the availability of material resources. One would not need resources if there was nothing in one's life which could go better or worse, nothing which would count as success

---

13. Schwartz's claim that material resources are harmful depends, I think, on confusing equality of resources with equality of income. People should be free to decide how and when their labor, or the fruits of their labor, will be sold in the economic marketplace, and many valuable ways of life will seek partial or total exclusion from it. People will not sacrifice all their leisure, or accept the degradation of their work conditions, in return for additional income, and some people put leisure and quality of work well above income in their scale of priorities. But this emphasis on values other than income, far from conflicting with a desire for resources, requires access to resources. We all want to do things, or produce things, which are not marketable, but these activities require resources which other people desire for conflicting purposes. The socialist prefers developing her personal skills, and the monk prefers celebrating God, to selling goods and services in the market. But the socialist and monk require land and other resources to pursue their nonmaterialist ends. One way to legitimately acquire those resources is to spend part of one's time acquiring income through the provision of goods and services others desire. But the more one desires to pursue nonmarketable activities, and to avoid income-producing activities, then the more dependent one is on acquiring resources through one's claim to a fair division of society's wealth. The groups which are least interested in earning income for a materialistic life-style are precisely the groups which are most dependent on their fair share of society's wealth.

or failure in the pursuit of one's goals. But so long as there are things that matter in one's life, things that are worth defending and promoting, then there will be threats to the promotion of those values. Resources help one to exercise some control over the social and natural environment, and hence control the direction and consequences of those environments for the pursuit of one's values.

There may be some ways of life which are not aided by increased amounts of Rawls's primary goods. Rawls cites the case of religious lifestyles which include a vow of personal poverty, although that too may be a little quick. Monks committed to personal asceticism often belong to monastic orders that have large land holdings, revenues from which help pay for the land, buildings, and maintenance of their community and which are used in promoting their good works. Moreover, the vow of poverty is often understood as a renunciation of their legitimate entitlements under a theory of fairness, not, as Schwartz and Nagel require, a renunciation of things which they think should not be part of a legitimate theory of fairness. In any event, such examples do not show that access to primary goods harms these ways of life, or favors individualistic and materialistic ways of life.[14]

Rawls's emphasis on what individuals are entitled to may seem misplaced for people who deploy their resources in group relations and activities. But a theory of individual entitlement is required, even for communally oriented people, because it teaches each person what is available for the pursuit of their attachments. As Dworkin says, "We are free to make decisions [about our attachments] with respect to the resources that are properly assigned to us in the first instance, though not, of course, to dispose in this way of resources that have been assigned, or rather are properly assignable, to others. Equality enters our plans by teaching us what is available to us, to deploy in accordance with our attachments and other concerns."[15] Rawls invokes a standard of individual entitlement, not because of an individualistic theory of motivation, but because of his principle of individual responsibility. If people are to be legitimately held responsible for any expensive aims and attachments they may have, then there must be a standard of individual entitlement in the light of which they can adjust those aims.

This requirement of justice holds just as much for communally oriented people as for materialistic people. Communally oriented socialists can have expensive desires. The Marxian socialist wants a piece of land on which to labor cooperatively so as to "humanize" the natural world.[16] But the naturalist wants the same land left unhumanized, and the monk

---

14. Rawls, *Theory of Justice*, pp. 142–43.

15. Ronald Dworkin, "In Defense of Equality," *Social Philosophy and Policy* 1 (1983): 31.

16. Karl Marx, *Economic and Philosophical Manuscripts* (London: Lawrence & Wishart, 1977), pp. 306–9.

wants it for sacred purposes, to build a community that will honor God. Each of these aims has costs for other people, who must forgo their aims with respect to that land. It is naive to expect that the desired land will automatically be available for one's preferred purposes, and it is selfish to demand that it be automatically available. The test of what is properly available for the pursuit of these ends is given by the difference principle. The naturalist may want more resources set aside than is allotted him under the difference principle, but he is responsible for adjusting his claims to the rightful claims of others, and to demand excess resources for his naturalist aims would be just as unfair as it would be for a materialistic person to demand excess resources in order to purchase consumer goods. The nonindividualistic content of their aims does not excuse socialists or naturalists from taking into account the legitimate claims of others.

Schwartz and Nagel might accept that we should take into account the cost of our choices for other people but claim that the problem with Rawls's theory is that the costs are assessed in a biased way, since a Rawlsian society produces people whose basic preference is for more wealth. Costs would be assessed differently in a society that is designed to produce socialist individuals: the socialist's desire for land would not be as costly, since fewer people would have conflicting desires.

But while it is true that Rawls's theory makes the costs of a particular choice dependent on the extent to which other people's aims coincide or conflict, that does not show that the primary goods scheme is biased against communal ways of life. For the extent to which other people share one's ends will depend on the judgments the others freely make when considering the various ways of life available to them. If socialists are unable to convince others of the worth of that way of life, then it will be difficult to acquire the resources necessary to start up a socialist community. On the other hand, if materialists are unable to convince people of the value of a high income and a consumer life-style, then they will have difficulty attracting people to choose income over leisure, or monotonous but productive labor over enjoyable but less productive labor. These are indeed problems which materialists have faced when promoting consumerism in various cultures, and Marx predicted that they will reoccur when people can acquire a decent standard of living in a shortened workday. Rawlsian neutrality does not prejudge the relative value of self-realizing labor and consumer goods, and the relative difficulty of pursuing these different ways of life is determined by the choices the members of a given society freely make at a given moment. Schwartz and Nagel do not explain how socialists are disadvantaged by this arrangement, or why their choices should be subsidized regardless of how costly they are for others, and regardless of how attractive the members of a society find that way of life. As Rawls says, communal ends that cannot flourish under this arrangement should not "be upheld by the coercive apparatus of the state. If socially collective communitarian aims could survive in no other way, why should we regret their demise, and consider the original position unfair and biased against them?"[17]

Schwartz and Nagel note that socialists are disadvantaged by Rawlsian neutrality in contrast to a society which is designed to produce as many socialists as possible. But every way of life would do better in a society designed to ensure that no one had conflicting preferences. That does not establish a legitimate grievance, since no one has the right that other people be socialized so as to best fit one's own way of life (other people are not resources to be distributed or molded so as to promote one's ends). Fairness for the adherents of different ways of life requires that people be guaranteed a fair share of resources to pursue their way of life, and the freedom to seek out new adherents. It does not require that each way of life be guaranteed a certain number of adherents, and indeed fairness precludes treating people as resources to be distributed or molded so that each way of life fares equally well. The question is whether socialists are disadvantaged by Rawls's scheme with respect to the things which they have a legitimate claim to—that is, resources and liberties, but not other people's preferences—and Schwartz and Nagel do not establish this.[18]

One respect in which communally oriented people may be disadvantaged is that they must coordinate the deployment of resources distributed to individuals, and this coordination involves costs and effort that individualistic people avoid. Communally oriented people would prefer that resources be distributed directly to groups and then allow individualistic people to withdraw their resources from the group (this would involve costs for individualistic people that communally oriented people avoid). This problem would be solved if there were mechanisms for communally oriented people to receive benefits communally and for individualistic people to receive benefits individually. And this is indeed what Rawls endorses. He proposes that one branch of the state be organized so as to facilitate such coordination.[19] Rawls would not object if various

---

17. Rawls, "Fairness to Goodness," p. 551. Rawls has recently retracted the claim that there is no reason to regret the loss of life-styles which cannot sustain themselves in a free society. As he rightly says, these ways of life may well have had considerable value. An aristocratic life-style may have value, even if would-be aristocrats cannot find people in a free society who are willing to be their subordinates. But while the loss of aristocratic life-styles may be a cause for legitimate regret, it is not a cause for legitimate grievance, for it is not the product of arbitrary biases (Rawls, "Priority of Right," pp. 266–67). See also Dworkin's explanation of the fairness of liberal neutrality in "What Is Equality? Part 3: The Place of Liberty," *Iowa Law Review* 73 (1987): 1–54, where he notes that neutrality "allows each person's social requirements—the social setting he claims he needs in order successfully to pursue his chosen way of life—to be tested by asking how far these requirements can be satisfied within an egalitarian structure that measures their cost to others" (p. 31).

18. Rawls, "Priority of Right," pp. 265–66.

19. Rawls, *Theory of Justice*, pp. 282–84. This passage refers only to the exchange branch of government, but the same reasoning seems equally applicable to distribution (p. 280).

marital and cultural groups pay taxes, and receive benefits, collectively, where the members have so agreed.

It is true that any collective provision of benefits requires the ongoing consent of individuals. But this requirement reflects Rawls's commitment to autonomy, not any commitment to individualistic aims. According to the "ideal of the person" underlying Rawls's theory, individuals "do not regard themselves as inevitably bound to, or identical with, the pursuit of any particular complex of fundamental interests that they may have at any given moment."[20] People are capable not simply of pursuing their given ends, but also of reflecting on the value of those ends, considering alternatives, and revising even their most deeply held beliefs about what is worthwhile in life:

> As free persons, citizens recognize one another as having the moral power to have a conception of the good. This means that they do not view themselves as inevitably tied to the pursuit of the particular conception of the good and its final ends which they espouse at any given time. Instead, as citizens, they are regarded as, in general, capable of revising and changing this conception on reasonable and rational grounds. Thus it is held to be permissible for citizens to stand apart from conceptions of the good and to survey and assess their various final ends.[21]

According to Rawls, this ability for autonomous choice is one of our two fundamental moral powers, and respect for autonomy requires that individuals retain the right to opt out of any particular communal practice (and corresponding communal provision of benefits). Hence Rawls's two principles of justice are designed to ensure that individuals can "stand apart" from their current ends—the liberties and resources distributed by Rawls's two principles do not preempt or penalize the attempt by individuals to form and revise their conceptions of the good, or to acquire the information needed to make those judgments rationally and intelligently. Since individuals can come to question their ends, they must have access to resources which are flexible, which can be translated into the goods and services appropriate for other ways of life, including, of course, other communal ways of life.[22]

---

20. John Rawls, "Reply to Alexander and Musgrave," *Quarterly Journal of Economics* 88 (1974): 641.

21. Rawls, "Kantian Constructivism," p. 544.

22. This feature of Rawls's theory is discussed in Allen Buchanan, "Revisability and Rational Choice," *Canadian Journal of Philosophy* 5 (1975): 395–408; and Dworkin, "In Defense of Equality," pp. 24–30. Rawls's view of the self as able to stand apart from its ends has been vigorously criticized by communitarians—e.g., Alasdair MacIntyre, *After Virtue: A Study in Moral Theory* (London: Duckworth, 1981), chap. 15; Michael Sandel, *Liberalism and the Limits of Justice* (Cambridge: Cambridge University Press, 1982), pp. 150–65. They argue that this view of the self as "unencumbered" by social attachments is at odds with our "deepest self-understandings." I believe the communitarians are simply wrong here (see my "Liberalism and Communitarianism," *Canadian Journal of Philosophy*

Rawls's commitment to the importance of primary goods, therefore, is not evidence of possessive individualism, but rather of two distinct ideas: (*a*) our way of life should reflect our autonomous choice, and so the resources available to us must be flexible; and (*b*) we are responsible for the costs of our choices, and hence there must be some standard which teaches us what is available to us to use in accordance with our attachments. Neither of these is primarily concerned with the content of people's ends. Rather they concern the relationship between the individual and her ends—an individual's ends are not fixed or imposed by others but, rather, are the objects of her autonomous and responsible choice.

NEUTRALITY AND ATOMISTIC INDIVIDUALISM

The second and third versions of the claim that neutrality is excessively individualistic accept Rawls's emphasis on the capacity for autonomous choice. But autonomous choices are only possible in certain contexts, and these two objections claim that liberal neutrality is incapable of ensuring the existence and flourishing of that context. While both objections attribute this failure of neutrality to a certain kind of atomistic individualism, they locate the failure in different places—the second objection centers on the need for a shared cultural structure that provides individuals with meaningful options, and the third centers on the need for shared forums in which to evaluate these options.

Neutrality and a Pluralist Culture

The second objection claims that liberal neutrality is incapable of guaranteeing the existence of a pluralistic culture which provides people with the range of options necessary for meaningful individual choice. Autonomy requires pluralism, but "any collective attempt by a liberal state to protect pluralism would itself be in breach of liberal principles of justice. The state is not entitled to interfere in the movement of the cultural market place except, of course, to ensure that each individual has a just share of available necessary means to exercise his or her moral powers. The welfare or demise of particular conceptions of the good and, therefore, the welfare or demise of social unions of a particular character is not the business of the state."[23] The state is not allowed to protect pluralism, yet if the cultural marketplace proceeds on its own it will eventually undermine the cultural structure which supports pluralism. Neutrality may ensure

---

18 [1988]: 181–203), but Rawls himself wishes to remain agnostic on the question of whether our self-understandings are or are not bound to any particular complex of ends. He now argues that people can accept his account of the self for the purposes of determining our public rights and responsibilities, without necessarily accepting it as an accurate portrayal of our deepest self-understandings (John Rawls, "Justice as Fairness: Political not Metaphysical," *Philosophy and Public Affairs* 14 [1985]: 240–44; cf. "Kantian Constructivism," p. 545). I raise some questions about the possibility and/or desirability of this agnosticism in *Liberalism, Community, and Culture* (Oxford: Oxford University Press, 1989), pp. 58–61.

23. Wesley Cragg, "Two Concepts of Community," *Dialogue* 25 (1986): 47.

that government does not denigrate a way of life that some individuals think is worthy of support, but "whatever else can be said about this argument one point is decisive. Supporting valuable ways of life is a social rather than an individual matter . . . perfectionist ideals require public action for their viability. Anti-perfectionism in practice would lead not merely to a political stand-off from support for valuable conceptions of the good. It would undermine the chances of survival of many cherished aspects of our culture."[24] The problem, then, is not that liberal neutrality fails to achieve its aim of genuine neutrality (as the possessive individualism objection claimed) but, rather, that neutrality undermines the very conditions in which it is a worthwhile aim.

Liberal neutrality is therefore self-defeating. There seem to be two possible ways out of this dilemma. One is to deny that the value of autonomous choice depends on a viable and flourishing culture. This is the "atomist" route which accepts "the utterly facile moral psychology of traditional empiricism,"[25] according to which an individual's capacity for meaningful choice is self-sufficient outside of society and culture. This route is inadequate, since our dependence on the cultural structure for worthwhile ways of life is undeniable, and few if any liberals have ever been "concerned purely with individual choices . . . to the neglect of the matrix in which such choices can be open or closed, rich or meagre."[26]

The second response is to accept that meaningful autonomous choice requires a viable culture but insist that good ways of life will sustain themselves in the cultural marketplace without state assistance.[27] But this too is an inadequate response. In conditions of freedom, people are able to assess and recognize the worth of good ways of life and will support them. But the interests people have in a good way of life, and the forms of support they will voluntarily provide, do not necessarily involve sustaining its existence for future generations. My interest in a valuable social practice may be best promoted by depleting the resources which the practice requires to survive beyond my lifetime. Even if the cultural marketplace can be relied on to ensure that existing people can identify valuable ways of life, there is no reason to assume that it can be relied on to ensure that future people have a valuable range of options.

So let us grant Raz's argument that state support may be needed to ensure the survival of an adequate range of options for those who have not yet formed their aims in life. Why does that require rejecting neutrality?

24. Raz, *Morality of Freedom*, p. 162.
25. Charles Taylor, *Philosophy and the Human Sciences: Philosophical Papers* (Cambridge: Cambridge University Press, 1985), vol. 2, p. 197.
26. Ibid., p. 207. See, e.g., Rawls, *Theory of Justice*, pp. 563–64; Dworkin, *A Matter of Principle*, pp. 220–24.
27. Rawls, *Theory of Justice*, pp. 331–32; Jeremy Waldron, "Autonomy and Perfectionism in Raz's *Morality of Freedom*," *University of Southern California Law Review* 62 (1989), in press; Robert Nozick, "Commentary on 'Art as a Public Good,'" *Art and the Law* 9 (1985): 162–64.

Consider two possible cultural policies. In the first case, the government ensures an adequate range of options by providing tax credits to individuals who make culture-supporting contributions in accordance with their personal perfectionist ideals. The state acts to ensure that there is an adequate range of options, but the evaluation of these options occurs in civil society, outside the coercive apparatus of the state.[28] In the second case, the evaluation of different conceptions of the good becomes a political question, and the government intervenes, not simply to ensure an adequate range of options, but to promote particular options. Now Raz's argument simply does not address this choice. What is "decisive" in Raz's argument is that one or the other of these policies must be implemented, but he has not given a decisive reason, or any reason at all, to prefer one policy over the other.

A perfectionist state might hope to improve the quality of people's options by encouraging the replacement of less valuable options by more valuable ones. But it is worth repeating that liberal neutrality also hopes to improve the range of options, and the cultural marketplace is valued because it helps good ways of life displace bad. Each side aims to secure and improve the range of options from which individuals make their autonomous choices. What they disagree on is where perfectionist values and arguments should be invoked. Are good ways of life more likely to establish their greater worth when they are evaluated in the cultural marketplace of civil society, or when the preferability of different ways of life is made a matter of political advocacy and state action? Hence the dispute should perhaps be seen as a choice, not between perfectionism and neutrality, but between social perfectionism and state perfectionism—for the flip side of state neutrality is support for the role of perfectionist ideals and arguments in civil society.[29]

---

28. This is endorsed by Dworkin in *A Matter of Principle,* chap. 11. This use of tax credits would only be fair if the distribution of resources in society was in fact just. Indeed, it might not be fair even if the difference principle was honored, since it gives disproportionate power in shaping cultural development to those who are endowed with (undeserved) natural talents, as they are likely to have more disposable income. I assume there are ways to ensure that this operates fairly while still leaving the evaluation of cultural options outside the political sphere. For a discussion of the problem of fairness in influence over culture, in the context of the neutrality/perfectionist debate, see Amy Gutmann, *Democratic Education* (Princeton, N.J.: Princeton University Press, 1987), chap. 9, esp. pp. 263–64.

29. Failure to recognize this undermines Beiner's argument against liberal neutrality, which he concludes by saying: "Even if the state is or tries to be neutral (which likely proves impossible), in any case the wider social order in which the individual is nourished *is not.* Liberal 'neutralism' is therefore a mirage. It is hard to see why the *state* is constrained to be neutral (whatever that might mean) if social life as a whole is and must be, however much denied by liberals, strongly partial towards a particular way of life" (Ronald Beiner, "What's Wrong with Liberalism?" in *Law and Community,* ed. Leslie Green and Alan Hutchinson [Toronto: Carswell, in press]). This is entirely off target. The best reason for state neutrality is precisely that social life is nonneutral, that people can and do make discriminations among competing ways of life in their social life, affirming some and rejecting others, without using the state apparatus. If individuals are unable to make these judgments in

Neutrality and Collective Deliberations

The third and final objection accepts that liberal neutrality recognizes
the necessity of having a secure cultural structure. But it claims that a
different sort of atomistic individualism is found in the liberal account
of how cultural options should be evaluated. The liberal preference for
the cultural marketplace over the state as the appropriate arena for
evaluating different life-styles stems from an individualistic belief that
judgments about the good should be made by isolated individuals, whose
autonomy is ensured by protecting them from social pressures. Liberals
think that autonomy is promoted when judgments about the good are
taken out of the political realm. But in reality individual judgments
require the sharing of experiences and the give and take of collective
deliberations. Individual judgments about the good always depend on,
and flow from, the collective evaluation of shared practices. They become
a matter of purely subjective and arbitrary whim if they are cut off from
collective deliberations:

> Self-fulfillment and even the working out of personal identity and
> a sense of orientation in the world depend upon a communal en-
> terprise. This shared process is the civic life, and its root is involvement
> with others: other generations, other sorts of persons whose dif-
> ferences are significant because they contribute to the whole upon
> which our particular sense of self depends. Thus mutual interde-
> pendency is the foundational notion of citizenship . . . outside a
> linguistic community of shared practices, there would be biological
> *homo sapiens* as logical abstraction, but there could not be human
> beings. This is the meaning of the Greek and medieval dictum that
> the political community is ontologically *prior* to the individual. The
> polis is, literally, that which makes man, as human being, possible.[30]

Or, as Crowley puts it, state perfectionism is "an affirmation of the notion
that men living in a community of shared experiences and language is
the only context in which the individual and society can discover and
test their values through the essentially political activities of discussion,
criticism, example, and emulation. It is through the existence of organised
public spaces, in which men offer and test ideas against one another . . .
that men come to understand a part of who they are."[31] The state should
be the proper arena in which to formulate and pursue our visions of the

---

social life, then state perfectionism might be the appropriate way to enable people to
discriminate among different conceptions of the good (although it is unclear how moving
from the cultural marketplace to the state would remove the disability). So the argument
for state neutrality presupposes, rather than denies, social nonneutrality.

30. William Sullivan, *Reconstructing Public Philosophy* (Berkeley: University of California
Press, 1982), pp. 158, 173.

31. Brian Lee Crowley, *The Self, the Individual, and the Community: Liberalism in the
Political Thought of F. A. Hayek and Sidney and Beatrice Webb* (Oxford: Oxford University
Press, 1987), p. 282; see also Beiner, *Political Judgment* (London: Methuen, 1983), p. 152.

good, because the good for individuals requires collective interaction and inquiry—it cannot be pursued, or even known, presocially.

But this misconstrues the sense in which Rawls claims that the evaluation of ways of life should not be a public concern. Liberal neutrality does not restrict the scope of perfectionist ideals in the collective activities of individuals and groups. Perfectionist ideals, although excluded from a liberal state, "have an important place in human affairs" and, hence, an important place in a liberal society.[32] Collective activity and shared experiences concerning the good are at the heart of the "free internal life of the various communities of interests in which persons and groups seek to achieve, in modes of social union consistent with equal liberty, the ends and excellences to which they are drawn."[33] Rawls's argument for the priority of liberty is grounded in the importance of this "free social union with others."[34] He simply denies that "the coercive apparatus of the state" is an appropriate forum for those deliberations and experiences: "While justice as fairness allows that in a well-ordered society the values of excellence are recognized, the human perfections are to be pursued within the limits of the principle of free association. . . . [Persons] do not use the coercive apparatus of the state to win for themselves a greater liberty or larger distributive shares on the grounds that their activities are of more intrinsic value."[35]

Unfortunately, civic republicans, who make this objection most frequently, rarely distinguish between collective activities and political activities. It is of course true that participation in shared linguistic and cultural practices is what enables individuals to make intelligent decisions about the good life. But why should such participation be organized in and through the state, rather than through the free association of individuals? It is true that we should "create opportunities for men to give voice to what they have discovered about themselves and the world and to persuade others of its worth."[36] But a liberal society does create opportunities for people to express and develop these social aspects of individual deliberation. After all, freedom of assembly, association, and speech are fundamental *liberal* rights. The opportunities for collective inquiry simply occur within and between groups and associations below the level of the state—friends and family, in the first instance, but also churches, cultural associations, professional groups and trade unions, universities, and the mass media. These are some of the "organized public spaces of appearance" and "communication communities" of a liberal society.[37] Liberals do not deny that "the public display of character and judgment and the exchange

32. Rawls, *Theory of Justice*, p. 543.
33. Ibid.
34. Ibid.
35. Ibid., pp. 328–29.
36. Crowley, p. 295.
37. Ibid., pp. 7, 239.

of experience and insight" are needed to make intelligent judgments about the good, or to show others that I "hold [my] notion of the good responsibly."[38] Indeed, these claims fit comfortably in many liberal discussions of the value of free speech and association.[39] What the liberal denies is that I should have to give such an account of myself *to the state.*

A similar failure to confront the distinctive role of the state weakens radical critiques of liberalism, like that of Habermas. Habermas, in his earlier writings at least, wants the evaluation of different ways of life to be a political question, but unlike communitarians and civic republicans, he does not hope or expect that this political deliberation will serve to promote people's embeddedness in existing practices.[40] Indeed, he thinks that political deliberation is required precisely because in its absence people will tend to accept existing practices as givens and thereby perpetuate the false needs and false consciousness which accompany those historical practices.[41] Only when existing ways of life are "the objects of discursive will-formation" can people's understanding of the good be free of deception. Rawls's view of distributive justice does not demand the scrutiny of these practices and, hence, does not recognize the emancipatory interest people have in escaping false needs and ideological distortions.

But why should the evaluation of people's conceptions of the good be tied to their claims on resources, and hence to the state apparatus? Communities smaller than the entire political society, groups and associations of various sizes, might be more appropriate forums for those forms of discursive will formation which involve evaluating the good and interpreting one's genuine needs. While Habermas rejects the communitarian tendency to uncritically endorse existing social practices as the basis for political deliberations about the good, he shares their tendency to assume that anything which is not politically deliberated is thereby left to an individual will incapable of rational judgment.

So the liberal commitment to state neutrality does not manifest abstract individualism either in regard to the importance of a shared cultural

---

38. Ibid., p. 287.

39. See, e.g., Thomas Scanlon, "Freedom of Expression and Categories of Expression," in *Pornography and Censorship*, ed. David Copp and Susan Wendell (Buffalo, N.Y.: Prometheus, 1983), pp. 141–47; Loren Lomasky, *Persons, Rights, and the Moral Community* (Oxford: Oxford University Press, 1987), p. 111.

40. Habermas seems to endorse this position when he says that the need for a "discursive desolidification of the (largely externally controlled or traditionally fixed) interpretation of our needs" is the heart of his disagreement with Rawls (Habermas, *Communication and the Evolution of Society*, pp. 198–99). However, he now rejects the idea of politically evaluating people's conceptions of the good (Jürgen Habermas, "Questions and Counterquestions," in *Habermas and Modernity*, ed. Richard Bernstein [Cambridge, Mass.: MIT Press, 1985], pp. 214–16). For discussion of the (apparent) shift, see Seyla Benhabib, *Critique, Norm, and Utopia* (New York: Columbia University Press, 1986), chap. 8; and Nanette Funk, "Habermas and the Social Goods," *Social Text* 18 (1988): 29–31.

41. Habermas, *Communication and the Evolution of Society*, pp. 198–99; Benhabib, pp. 312–14.

context for meaningful individual options, or in regard to the importance of the sharing of experiences and arguments for meaningful individual evaluation of those options. Liberal neutrality does not deny these shared social requirements of individual autonomy but, rather, provides an interpretation of them.

EVALUATING THE NEUTRALITY DEBATE

I have argued that liberal neutrality is not excessively individualistic, either in terms of the way it conceives the content of people's ends, or in the way that people evaluate and pursue those ends. Of course neutrality may be indefensible for other reasons. Neutrality requires a certain faith in the operation of nonstate forums and processes for individual judgment and cultural development, and a distrust of the operation of state forums and processes for evaluating the good. Nothing I have said so far shows that this optimism and distrust are warranted. Indeed, just as critics of neutrality have failed to defend their faith in political forums and procedures, so liberals have failed to defend their faith in nonstate forums and procedures. The crucial claims have not been adequately defended by either side.

In fact, it is hard to avoid the conclusion that each side in the neutrality debate has failed to learn the important lesson taught by the other side. Despite centuries of liberal insistence on the importance of the distinction between society and the state, communitarians still seem to assume that whatever is properly social must become the province of the political. They have not confronted the liberal worry that the all-embracing authority and coercive means which characterize the state make it a particularly inappropriate forum for the sort of genuinely shared deliberation and commitment that they desire. Despite centuries of communitarian insistence on the historically fragile and contingent nature of our culture, and the need to consider the conditions under which a free culture can arise and sustain itself, liberals still tend to take the existence of a tolerant and diverse culture for granted, as something which naturally arises and sustains itself, the ongoing existence of which is therefore simply assumed in a theory of justice. Hegel was right to insist that a culture of freedom is a historical achievement, and liberals need to explain why the cultural marketplace does not threaten that achievement either by failing to connect people in a strong enough way to their communal practices (as communitarians fear), or conversely, by failing to detach people in a strong enough way from the expectations of existing practices and ideologies (as Habermas fears). A culture of freedom requires a mix of both exposure and connection to existing practices, and also distance and dissent from them. Liberal neutrality may provide that mix, but that is not obviously true, and it may be true only in some times and places. So both sides need to give us a more comprehensive comparison of the opportunities and dangers present in state and nonstate forums and procedures for evaluating the good.

While both sides have something to learn from the other, that is not to say that the truth is somewhere in between the two. I cannot provide here the sort of systematic comparison of the empirical operation of state and nonstate forums and procedures that is required for a proper defense of neutrality, but I want to suggest a few reasons why state perfectionism would have undesirable consequences for our society. I will assume, for the moment, that the public ranking of the value of different ways of life which a perfectionist state appeals to would be arrived at through the collective political deliberation of citizens, rather than through the secret or unilateral decisions of political elites.

What are the consequences of having a collectively determined ranking of the value of different conceptions of the good? One consequence is that more is at stake when people publicly formulate and defend their conception of the good. If people do not advance persuasive arguments for their conception of the good, then a perfectionist state may take action which will make their way of life harder to maintain. In a liberal society with a neutral state, on the other hand, people who cannot persuade others of the value of their way of life will lose out in the competition with other conceptions of the good being advanced in the cultural marketplace, but they will not face adverse state action.

Why is that an undesirable consequence? In principle, it is not undesirable—it may simply intensify the patterns of cultural development, since the pros and cons of different ways of life might be revealed more quickly under the threat of state action than would occur in the cultural marketplace, where people are sometimes reluctant to confront opposing values and arguments. However, I believe that state perfectionism would in fact serve to distort the free evaluation of ways of life, to rigidify the dominant ways of life, whatever their intrinsic merits, and to unfairly exclude the values and aspirations of marginalized and disadvantaged groups within the community.

First, state perfectionism raises the prospect of a dictatorship of the articulate and would unavoidably penalize those individuals who are inarticulate. But being articulate, in our society, is not simply an individual variable. There are many culturally disadvantaged groups whose beliefs and aspirations are not understood by the majority. Recent immigrants are an obvious example whose disadvantage is partly unavoidable. But there are also groups which have been deliberately excluded from the mainstream of American society, and whose cultural disadvantage reflects prejudice and insensitivity. The dominant cultural practices of our community were defined by one section of the population—that is, the male members of the upper classes of the white race—and were defined so as to exclude and denigrate the values of subordinate groups. Members of these excluded groups—women, blacks, Hispanics—have been unable to get recognition for their values from the cultural mainstream and have developed (or retained) subcultures for the expression of these values, subcultures whose norms, by necessity, are incommensurable with those of the mainstream. It is unfair to ask them to defend the value of their way of life by reference to cultural standards and norms that were defined by and for others. Even where these historical factors are absent, the majority is likely to use state perfectionism to block valuable social change that threatens their preferred cultural practices. This cultural conservatism need not be malicious—the majority may simply not see the value of cultural change, partly due to incomprehension, partly from fear of change.

State perfectionism would also affect the kinds of arguments given. Minority groups whose values conflict with those of the majority often put a high value on the integrity of their practices and aim at gaining adherents from within the majority slowly, one by one. But where there is state perfectionism, the minority must immediately aim at persuading the majority, and so they will describe their practices in such a way as to be most palatable to the majority, even if that misdescribes the real meaning and value of the practice, which often arose precisely in opposition to dominant practices. There would be an inevitable tendency for minorities to describe and debate conceptions of the good in terms of dominant values, which then reinforces the cultural conservatism of the dominant group itself.

In these and other ways, the threats and inducements of coercive power would distort rather than improve the process of individual judgment and cultural development. Some of these problems also arise in the cultural marketplace (i.e., penalizing the inarticulate, social prejudice). Insensitivity and prejudice will be problems no matter which model we choose, since both models reward those groups who can make their way of life attractive to the mainstream. But state perfectionism intensifies these problems, since it dictates to minority groups when and how they will interact with majority norms, and it dictates a time and place—political deliberation over state policy—in which minorities are most vulnerable. State neutrality, on the other hand, gives culturally disadvantaged groups a greater ability to choose the time and place in which they will confront majority sensitivities and to choose an audience with whom they are most comfortable. There will always be an imbalance in the interaction between culturally dominant and subordinate groups. State neutrality ensures that the culturally subordinate group has as many options as possible concerning that interaction, and that the costs of that imbalance for the subordinate groups are minimized. State perfectionism, I think, does just the opposite.

Some of these problems could be avoided if the public ranking of ways of life was determined by political elites, insulated from popular debate and prejudice. Indeed, an enlightened and insulated political elite could use state perfectionist policies to promote the aims and values of culturally disadvantaged groups. Just as the Supreme Court is supposed to be more able to protect the rights of disadvantaged groups because of its insulation from political pressures, so an insulated political elite may be able to give a fairer hearing to minority values than they get in the cultural marketplace. But this raises troubling questions about accountability and the danger of abuse (after all, if majority groups are insensitive to minority aspirations, why won't they elect leaders who are similarly insensitive?). And, in any event, why shouldn't the aim of the political elite be to counteract the biases of the cultural marketplace, which affect the public evaluation of all minority values, rather than deciding for themselves which minority values are worth promoting? Using state power to counteract biases against minority values may be legitimate, not because of a general principle of perfectionism, but because of a general principle of redressing biases against disadvantaged groups.

These are some of the reasons why liberals distrust state perfectionism for our society.[42] Communitarians are right to insist that we examine the history and structure of a particular culture, but it is remarkable how little communitarians themselves undertake such an examination of our culture. They wish to use the ends and practices of our cultural tradition as the basis for a politics of the common good, but they do not mention that these practices were historically defined by a small segment of the population, nor do they discuss how that exclusionary history would affect the politicization of debates about the value of different ways of life. If we look at the history of our society, surely liberal neutrality has the great advantage of its potential inclusiveness, its denial that marginalized and subordinate groups must fit into the historical practices, the "way of life," which have been defined by the dominant groups. Forcing subordinate groups to defend their ways of life, under threat or promise of coercive power, is inherently exclusive. Communitarians simply ignore this danger and the cultural history which makes it so difficult to avoid.[43]

42. There are other reasons for opposing state perfectionism. I have been discussing the difficulty of finding acceptable procedures for formulating a public ranking of different ways of life. There are also difficulties about how the state should go about promoting its preferred ways of life, once those are identified. Even if the state can be relied on to come up with an accurate ranking and can get people to pursue the right ways of life, it may not be able to get people to pursue them *for the right reasons*. Someone who acts in a certain way in order to avoid state punishment, or to gain state subsidies, is not guided by an understanding of the genuine value of the activity (Waldron; Lomasky, pp. 253–54). This criticism is important and precludes various coercive and manipulative forms of perfectionism, but it does not preclude short-term state intervention designed to introduce people to valuable ways of life. One way to get people to pursue something for the right reasons is to get them to pursue it for the wrong reasons and hope they will then see its true value. This is not inherently unacceptable, and it occurs often enough in the cultural marketplace. Hence a comprehensive defense of neutrality may need to focus on a prior stage of state perfectionism—i.e., the problems involved in formulating a public ranking of conceptions of the good.

43. On the exclusionary tendencies of communitarianism, see Amy Gutmann, "Communitarian Critics of Liberalism," *Philosophy and Public Affairs* 14 (1985): 318–22; Don Herzog, "Some Questions for Republicans," *Political Theory* 14 (1986): 481–90; H. Hirsch, "The Threnody of Liberalism: Constitutional Liberty and the Renewal of Community," *Political Theory* 14 (1986): 435–38; Nancy Rosenblum, *Another Liberalism: Romanticism and the Reconstruction of Liberal Thought* (Cambridge, Mass.: Harvard University Press, 1987), pp. 178–81.

While liberalism need not be committed to neutrality in all times and places, the relationship between the culture and the state in our society makes neutrality particularly appropriate for us. However, certain features of that relationship also make neutrality particularly difficult to implement. I have discussed different ways a neutral state might protect and promote its culture. But if we look at actual states and actual cultures, we will quickly notice that most liberal democracies contain more than one cultural community. Most countries contain many cultures, like the French, English, and aboriginal cultures in Canada. When we say that the cultural context can be enriched or diminished, whose culture are we discussing? Whose language should be used in the schools and courts and media? If immigration policy should give consideration to the consequences of immigration on the cultural structure, as most liberals have agreed, then shouldn't we accept demands by Francophones in Quebec, or the Inuit in Northern Canada, to have some control over immigration into their cultural communities? What does liberal neutrality require when the state contains more than one culture?

The dominant view among contemporary liberals, to which Rawls apparently subscribes, is that liberalism requires the "absence, even prohibition, of any legal or governmental recognition of racial, religious, language or [cultural] groups as corporate entities with a standing in the legal or governmental process, and a prohibition of the use of ethnic criteria of any type for discriminatory purposes, or conversely for special or favored treatment."[44] But this view, which achieved its current prominence during the American struggle against racial segregation, has only limited applicability. Once we recognize the importance of the cultural structure and accept that there is a positive duty on the state to protect the cultural conditions which allow for autonomous choice, then cultural membership does have political salience. Respect for the autonomy of the members of minority cultures requires respect for their cultural structure, and that in turn may require special linguistic, educational, and even political rights for minority cultures. Indeed, there are a number of circumstances in which liberal theories of equality should recognize the special status of minority cultures (as prewar liberal theories often did).[45] The attempt to answer questions about the rights of cultural communities with the formula of color-blind laws applying to persons of all races and cultures is hopelessly inadequate once we look at the diversity of cultural membership which exists in contemporary liberal

44. Milton Gordon, "Toward a General Theory of Racial and Ethnic Group Relations," in *Ethnicity: Theory and Experience*, ed. Nathan Glazer and Daniel Moynihan (Cambridge, Mass.: Harvard University Press, 1975), p. 105.

45. Minority rights were a common feature of prewar liberalism, both in theory (e.g., L. T. Hobhouse, *Social Evolution and Political Theory* [New York: Columbia University Press, 1928], pp. 146–47) and practice (e.g., the League of Nations). I attempt to provide a liberal theory of the rights of minority cultures in "Liberalism, Individualism, and Minority Rights," in *Law and Community*, ed. Leslie Green and Alan Hutchinson (Toronto: Carswell, 1989), and *Liberalism, Community, and Culture*, chaps. 7–10.

democracies.[46] However, the alternatives have rarely been considered in contemporary liberal writings, which are dominated (often unconsciously) by the model of the nation-state.[47]

CONCLUSION

The real issue concerning neutrality is not individualism: nothing in Rawls's insistence on state neutrality is inconsistent with recognizing the importance of the social world to the development, deliberation, and pursuit of individuals' values. It is commonly alleged that liberals fail to recognize that people are naturally social or communal beings. Liberals supposedly think that society rests on an artificial social contract, and that a coercive state apparatus is needed to keep naturally asocial people together in society. But there is a sense in which the opposite is true— liberals believe that people naturally form and join social relations and forums in which they come to understand and pursue the good. The state is not needed to provide that communal context and is likely to distort the normal processes of collective deliberations and cultural development. It is communitarians who seem to think that individuals will drift into anomic and detached isolation without the state actively bringing them together to collectively evaluate and pursue the good.[48]

---

46. Even in a genuine "nation-state," there are questions about how to deal with immigrants from other cultures. Liberals have historically disagreed over the extent to which respect for the autonomy of existing members of the polity requires restrictions on immigration which might damage the cultural structure. They have also disagreed over the extent to which respect for the autonomy of immigrants requires encouraging or compelling their assimilation to the cultural structure of the new country. Again, the requirements of liberal neutrality are not at all obvious.

47. The assumption that the political community is culturally homogeneous is clear in a number of passages in Rawls and Dworkin—e.g., John Rawls, "The Basic Structure as Subject," in *Values and Morals*, ed. Alvin Goldman and Jaegwon Kim (Dordrecht: Reidel, 1978), p. 55, and "On the Idea of Free Public Reason" (1988, photocopy), p. 8; Dworkin, *A Matter of Principle*, pp. 230–33. While revising that assumption would affect the conclusions they go on to draw about the distribution of rights and responsibilities, Rawls and Dworkin never discuss what changes would be required in culturally plural countries. Indeed, they do not seem to recognize that any changes would be required. For a criticism of Rawls's inattention to cultural pluralism, see Vernon Van Dyke, "Justice as Fairness: For Groups?" *American Political Science Review* 69 (1975): 607–14.

48. For example, Crowley says that politics makes possible "a context within which our own self-understandings *may* be articulated and compared with others" (p. 290; my emphasis). But it would be more accurate to say, as he indeed goes on to say, that "politics both *makes* us test dialogically the adequacy of our present self-awareness and makes us aware of other dimensions articulated by other people" (p. 290; my emphasis). Since Crowley never discusses this shift, it seems that he believes that individuals are only able to deliberate collectively when they are made to do so. A similar belief may explain why Sullivan thinks that state perfectionism is needed to ensure that no one is "cut off" from collective deliberations (Sullivan, p. 158). Since people in a liberal society are only cut off from the associations and forums of civil society if they cut themselves off, state perfectionism is needed only if one is assuming that uncoerced people will choose not to participate in collective deliberations. Liberals make the opposite assumption that uncoerced individuals

The question is not whether individuals' values and autonomy need to be situated in social relations but whether the relevant relations are necessarily or desirably political ones. This should be the real issue in debates over neutrality, and settling that issue requires a closer examination of the relationship between society, culture, and the state than either defenders or critics have so far provided.

---

will tend to form and join collective associations, and participate in collective deliberations (the suggestion that nonpolitical activity is inherently solitary is also present in Sandel's claim that under communitarian politics "we can know a good in common that we cannot know alone" [Sandel, p. 183]).

Moral pluralism and
political consensus

JOSHUA COHEN

The idea of normative consensus plays a central role in John Rawls's theory of justice.[1] In a well-ordered society, he says, "everyone has a similar sense of justice and in this respect a well-ordered society is homogeneous."[2] But is a consensus on fundamental norms of justice a realistic and attractive prospect for a morally pluralistic society?[3]

Rawls says little about this question in *A Theory of Justice*. Although he is closely attentive there to the diversity of interests and of conceptions of good among citizens in a well-ordered society, he is generally inattentive to the pluralism of moral conceptions that can be expected when expressive and associative liberties are protected. As a consequence, he does not consider the possibility that this pluralism might either exclude consensus on justice altogether or throw its value into question by turning it into mere compromise. Moreover, since the argument in *A Theory of Justice* that justice as fairness is a realistic conception – in particular, the case for the stability of a just society – depends on the idea that a just society features a consensus on principles of justice, the inattention to moral pluralism renders the force of that argument uncertain. So justice as fairness may be, after all, unrealistic and utopian.[4]

To address these concerns and show that the case for justice as fairness can be restated under more realistic assumptions, Rawls recently introduced the idea of an *overlapping consensus* and, corresponding to this idea, a condition on the acceptability of a conception of justice that I refer to as the "pluralistic consensus test." A society features an *overlapping consensus* on norms of justice if and only if it is a morally pluralistic society with a consensus on norms of justice in which citizens holding the different moralities that win adherents and persist over time in the society each support the consensual norms as the correct account of justice. Norms of justice satisfy the *pluralistic consensus test* if and only if those norms could provide the focus of an overlapping consensus in a society regulated by those norms and operating under favorable conditions.[5] A conception of justice that would not be so supported by

at least some of the moral doctrines that persist within a society regulated by it, and so could not be the focus of an overlapping consensus, fails to meet the pluralistic consensus test and is, to this extent,
unreasonable.[6]

Why unreasonable? Why (if at all) should requirements of justice be
realistic? "Because ought implies can" will not do as an answer, because
the question concerns justice, not what ought to be done, all things
considered. Judgments about what ought to be done, all things considered, must, of course, be sensitive to all sorts of practical matters, since
issues of practicality plainly are among the things to be considered. The
question is what sorts of constraints on realizability are constitutive of
ideal justice. And in matters of justice, realism is an uncertain good. By
accepting the "demands" of realism, we may be led to build an accommodation to unhappy, grim, and even hideous facts of political life into
the foundations of political justification and into fundamental principles
of justice themselves.

Focusing this general concern about the demands of realism on the
pluralistic consensus test, one might say that in aiming for a conception
of justice that could realistically be supported by a pluralistic consensus
one in fact undercuts the attraction of the conception that results.
Consider the following elaboration of this objection:

The pluralistic consensus test asks us to evaluate a conception of justice in part
by asking whether we can realistically expect the conception to be supported as
the correct account of justice by the diverse moralities in a well-ordered society.
But why should we be concerned with such support? In fact, requiring it forces
an accommodation to power at the foundations of a theory of justice – to the
power of those who believe the false and spurn the good. Accommodation to
power is commonly prudent and often recommended by our all-things-
considered judgments about the application of moral ideals to the facts of life.
We give money to the thief who threatens our life; we let the rich get richer if
that is what's needed to get them to invest; we pay the lion's share of the surplus
to the greedy if that is necessary to motivate them to use their talents for the
common good (at least in the first case we don't call it "justice"). And we often
frame our political arguments and proposals to win broad acceptance, if that is
what we must do to keep those who don't believe the true and love the good
from making life worse for those of us who do. But adjustments designed to
build support do not define ideal justice. To suppose otherwise would be to
permit the facts of power to fix the content of the fundamental requirements of
justice, thus undercutting their attraction as basic requirements. Philosophers,
above all, should resist the confusion of justice with accommodation and a
moral ideal with a consensus on principles that accommodate the power of
thieves, pirates, and benighted souls. Because if philosophers are not good for
that, then just what are they good for?[7]

Responding to this objection, Rawls argues that consensus on justice is both a realistic and an attractive prospect for a morally pluralistic society, and that subjecting conceptions of justice to the pluralistic consensus test is not tantamount to substituting mere compromise for genuine moral consensus and through that substitution advancing an account of justice that is "political in the wrong way" (p. 234).[8]

I agree with Rawls's main contentions, and my aim here is to explore the problem itself, to discuss some surrounding issues, and to clarify the grounds of agreement. After some initial points of clarification, I offer a generic statement of the problem of moral consensus and pluralism. Then I discuss some historical background, linking the problem of pluralism, realism, and moral consensus to a line of argument extending from Rousseau through Hegel to Marx. Next I discuss and criticize one source of concern about imposing constraints of realism and in particular the pluralistic consensus test on a conception of justice – that the constraint of realism undermines a substantively egalitarian conception of justice. Although this discussion does not address the concern about pluralism and realism in its most generic form, I include it because I suspect that the energy surrounding the debate about pluralism and political consensus derives importantly from alleged implications of the debate for matters of equality. Finally, I argue in more general terms that the pluralistic consensus condition does not fall prey to the objection I have sketched here. The argument turns on understanding what Rawls calls "the fact of pluralism" (p. 235) in a certain way. In particular, I distinguish the fact of pluralism from the fact of reasonable pluralism and, drawing on this distinction, I suggest that in aiming to find a conception of justice that meets the pluralistic consensus test, we are not simply adjusting ideals to the facts of life and to moral pluralism as one such fact. Instead we are acknowledging the scope of practical reason. Put otherwise, in aiming to find a conception of justice that meets the pluralistic consensus test we are not accommodating justice to an unfavorable condition of human life, since, as the idea of reasonable pluralism shows, we ought not to count moral pluralism itself among the unfavorable conditions.

The place of consensus

Before getting to these issues, I need to clarify one remark I made earlier. I said that a conception of justice that fails to meet the pluralistic consensus test is, *to this extent*, unreasonable. The phrase "to this extent" is meant to indicate the place of the pluralistic consensus test in an account of justice and in particular its role in the two-stage strategy of argument that Rawls sketches in "The Domain of the Political."

Rawls emphasizes that the idea of an overlapping consensus and the pluralistic consensus test come into play at the second stage of a two-part argument for a conception of justice. The aim of the first stage is, roughly, to show that the content of a conception is attractive – that it organizes a set of fundamental political values in a plausible way. The aim of the second stage is to determine whether a conception of justice that is in other respects attractive is also realistic – in particular, that it is stable. Showing that it is stable consists in part in showing that it satisfies the pluralistic consensus test: that different people, brought up within and attracted to different traditions of moral thought might each affirm the conception as the correct account of justice.

But how, more precisely, are we to understand the relationship between the results of the first stage and the argument at the second? What would follow if there were problems at the second stage? Three possibilities suggest themselves: (1) It is *necessary* that the correct account of justice satisfy the pluralistic consensus test; (2) satisfying the test is not necessary though it does provide *some support* for a conception of justice; or (3) satisfying the test is a *desideratum* that has *no bearing on the correctness* of an account of justice. In case (3), the pluralistic consensus test might be interpreted as a condition on the all-things-considered reasonableness of a conception of justice or perhaps as a test of the *legitimacy* of the exercise of state power, not as a condition on the justice of the institutions through which that power is exercised. On this interpretation if the best understanding of justice failed to satisfy the pluralistic consensus test even under favorable conditions, we ought to conclude that there is an unhappy divergence between justice and legitimacy – that even under the best conditions we can realistically hope for it will be illegitimate to secure justice – but not that we should revise our conception of justice.

Interpretation (3) may be suggested by Rawls's emphasis (p. 234) on the importance of separating the two stages of argument, and so distinguishing questions of justice from issues about the course of the world. But it is, in fact, ruled out by the description of the conclusions of the first stage as "provisionally on hand" (p. 246) and the remark that the argument is "not complete" until the case for stability has been presented (p. 245, n. 27). I am not sure which of the other two views Rawls means to endorse. But for the purposes of this essay, I will assume that (2) is right, that satisfying the pluralistic consensus condition does count in favor of the correctness of a conception of justice, and that while failure to meet it is not a sufficient reason for rejecting a conception, it would provide some reason to modify a view to bring it into conformity with that test.

Consensus and moral pluralism

Pluralism takes a variety of forms, and so there are correspondingly a variety of ways that it might raise troubles for consensus and social unity. To state the specific problem of pluralism and consensus that I will be considering here, I first need to fix some terminology. Following Rawls, then, I will say that a "well-ordered society" is a society in which it is common knowledge that the members share an understanding of justice and a willingness to act on that understanding. A well-ordered society, that is, features a restricted but important moral consensus. The moral consensus is restricted in that it extends only to certain basic constitutional values and principles and norms of distributive justice, and not to all aspects of the conduct of life. Despite this limitation, the consensus that defines a well-ordered society is a genuinely *moral* consensus. For the norms and ideals on which there is consensus play a reason-giving and authoritative role in the deliberation and choices of individual citizens.[9]

At the same time, a well-ordered society may be morally pluralistic in that members may have conflicting views about the fundamental norms and ideals that ought to guide conduct in life more generally. In a morally pluralistic society, the members hold different theories about what is valuable and worth doing. Thus understood, moral pluralism is to be distinguished both from cultural pluralism – the existence of groups of people within a single society who share distinct histories and ways of life, and a common identity as members of a group – and from organizational pluralism – the existence of a plurality of organized groups pursuing distinctive interests or ideals. These forms of pluralism are distinct phenomena, and less plausibly understood as a matter of people holding different theories. So the discussion here of moral pluralism and consensus is limited and does not naturally translate into an account of consensus and either cultural or organizational pluralism.

Moving now from terminology to substance: a moral consensus on political fundamentals is a fundamental good for at least three reasons. First, for any conception of justice, the likelihood that social order will stably conform to the conception is increased by the existence of a moral consensus on it.[10]

Second, the existence of a moral consensus supports a variety of specific values of considerable importance. It increases social trust and harmony, supports social peace, reduces the complexity of decision making, encourages a willingness to cooperate and so reduces the costs of monitoring and enforcement, and – assuming the consensus is reflected in public debate and decisions – reduces alienation from public choices because citizens embrace the norms and ideals that guide those choices.

Third, a consensus on norms of justice provides a way to reconcile the ideal of an association whose members are self-governing with an acknowledgment of the central role of social and political arrangements in shaping the self-conceptions of citizens, constraining their actions, channeling their choices, and determining the outcomes of those choices.[11] For when a consensus on norms and values underlies and explains collective decisions, citizens whose lives are governed by those decisions might nonetheless be said to be self-governing because each endorses the considerations that produce the decisions as genuinely moral reasons and affirms their implementation.[12]

But not just any consensus is attractive, as is indicated by reflection on these reasons themselves. If, for example, a moral consensus is attractive because it provides a way to make the ideal of free association consistent with the unavoidable chains of political connection, then the consensus must be a free moral consensus and not simply a form of enforced homogeneity. A free consensus is a consensus arrived at under conditions that ensure the possibility of individual reflection and public deliberation – conditions in which, for instance, expressive and associative liberties are protected.

It is at just this point that a minimal condition of realism appears to undermine either the possibility of consensus or at least its attractions as an ideal. For the assurance of expressive and associative liberties – an assurance that is necessary if the consensus is to be free and attractive – will also produce moral, religious, and philosophical pluralism.[13] But can a genuine moral consensus survive this "fact of pluralism" (p. 235)? Or does an insistence on consensus under conditions of pluralism in effect turn political philosophy into a search for a political compromise among people who disagree?

Historical excursus

These concerns about the pluralistic consensus condition ought to have a familiar ring. Earlier I mentioned the problem of reconciling self-government with the chains of political connection. Rousseau identified this problem, and thought it could be solved if social order were regulated by a consensual understanding of the common good – a "general will." Rousseau's solution is commonly rejected on the ground that it is inattentive to differences among people and to the diversity of human interests and ideals. In the face of that diversity, according to the objection, consensus on the common good can only be achieved through the unattractive combination of a sectarian conception of virtue and, for those who do not share that conception, enforced subordination and homogeneity in the name of freedom.

Hegel's response to Rousseau was more complex. He agreed that freedom could be reconciled with the chains of political connection, and applauded the notion of a general will as the way to achieve that reconciliation.[14] But he also appreciated the force of the critique of Rousseau that I just sketched. His conclusion was that it was necessary to reformulate the classical ideal of a political community organized around a moral consensus in light of the modern distinction between the unity of political society and the diversity of civil society. This distinction shapes Hegel's own political conception in three important ways:

1. He endorsed a fundamental distinction between civic diversity and political unity, associating that distinction with the differentiation between two spheres of social life. While the civil sphere would feature a diversity of aims and ideals and a range of individual and group activities organized around those aims and ideals, the political sphere would be organized around a set of values that both claim authority over individual concerns and are alleged to lie within the diverse aspirations of civil life and to provide their common ground.[15]

2. His distinction between political unity and civic diversity is associated with an acceptance of substantially inegalitarian forms of civic diversity,[16] as though an acceptance of that distinction and of a social sphere in which people pursue diverse aims itself brings inegalitarian implications in its wake.

3. Concerned to affirm the unity of the state in the face of the tendencies to social fragmentation that might follow from civic diversity, he defended a strong, highly centralized, executive-dominated constitutional monarchy, featuring a corporatist form of representation and special political rights for the landed class.

At least since Marx, critics of Hegel have objected that some or all of these gestures at reinterpreting the ideal of political unity in the face of civic diversity represent unwanted accommodations to de facto power in the formulation of basic political ideals. Marx, for example, objected to all three.[17] Putting Hegel's favored form of state to the side, these allegations of "accommodation" raise two questions that are relevant for our purposes here.

First, does the reformulation of the ideal of consensual political unity with an eye to respecting the diversity of civil society itself represent an objectionable accommodation? Do we find unacceptable accommodation in Hegel's reformulation of the ideal of political society to accommodate the diversity of aspirations characteristic of civil society or in Rawls's broadly parallel idea that a reasonable conception of justice should be supportable by an overlapping consensus?

Second, does the affirmation of moral diversity lead to an accommodation of social and economic privilege? *A Theory of Justice* defended an egalitarian liberalism that departed from Hegel's accommodation to inegalitarian forms of civic diversity. Does this egalitarianism survive the gesture at realism reflected in the pluralistic consensus condition? Put otherwise: The pluralistic consensus condition presumably restricts the content of norms of justice in some way. More demanding norms are less plausibly the object of agreement than less demanding norms. So does the importance of accommodating moral diversity lead to a thinner conception of justice that lacks the critical egalitarian dimension of Rawls's earlier position?

Because an affirmative answer to the second question would fuel an affirmative answer to the first, I will begin with diversity and equality.

The case of equality

A number of commentators on Rawls's recent work have noted that the many reformulations of his views about political justification have not yet been matched by similar revisions in the substance of the theory. My impression[18] is that lots of people now think that Rawls's recent discussions of political justification – with their emphasis on the importance of realism, on the practical nature of political philosophy, and on the associated idea of an overlapping consensus – do require a shift in the substance of his theory of justice, and in particular a shift in an inegalitarian direction.[19]

The reasoning goes something like this: "Rawls recognizes the utopianism of his earlier conception of a well-ordered society. So he now recommends that political justification proceed by identifying the common ground among the diverse moralities and conceptions of justice in our own society. But if we follow that recommendation, we will certainly not find support for the specifically egalitarian aspects of *Theory of Justice*, since there is (to put it mildly) considerable contemporary controversy about egalitarian political views."

This account of the idea of an overlapping consensus, with its emphasis on locating common ground among current political views, is mistaken in several ways. Once we see where it goes wrong we shall see as well that the concern for realism expressed in the pluralistic consensus test has none of the alleged implications. To make this case, I will begin with a sketch of the egalitarian content of the theory and the strategy of argument for it, and then proceed to a discussion of the objection.

The egalitarian content of *A Theory of Justice* is encapsulated in three requirements: the fair value of political liberty, fair equality of opportunity, and the maximin criterion of distributive equity. These three conditions, which are meant to sever the distribution of advantage from social background and natural difference, represent substantively egalitarian interpretations of more formal and less controversial norms of equal liberty, equal opportunity, and the common good.[20] A contention common to egalitarian liberal political conceptions generally, and advanced in *A Theory of Justice* in particular, is that we are led to these substantively egalitarian interpretations by considering the justification of the more formal and less controversial political norms.

The basic strategy of argument for this contention is familiar, and proceeds by *bootstrapping*. Thus, associated with the more formal requirements of equal liberties and assurances of opportunity is a conception of the properties of human beings that are important for the purposes of political justification. That conception of persons supposes that the relevant features are not race, color, cultural creed, sex, religion, and the like. The relevant features are certain potentialities (moral powers) – for example, the capacity to govern one's conduct and to revise one's aspirations – rather than the determinate form in which those potentialities are realized. The rationale for the protection of liberties and formal opportunity, for example, lies in part in the importance of assuring favorable conditions for the realization of the basic potentialities. But – and here is the where the bootstrapping comes in – once we acknowledge the need for favorable conditions for realizing the basic potentialities, we are naturally led from the more formal to the more substantively egalitarian requirements since the latter more fully elaborate the range of favorable conditions.

With this quick sketch as background, I can now state more precisely the concern already noted about the idea of an overlapping consensus. The intuitive objection was that the need to confine fundamental political justification to considerations that lie on common ground would undercut the egalitarian components and result in an unacceptable accommodation to power in the formulation of principles. Is this right? Does the requirement of proceeding on common ground deprive us of the argumentative resources necessary for the bootstrapping argument for an egalitarian form of liberalism?

Common ground

To see why the answer is no, it is important to note first that the bootstrap argument for the egalitarian view is itself meant to proceed on common ground shared by different moral conceptions in a well-ordered society governed by it. That may seem puzzling, since the conception of potentialities as morally fundamental may strike some as peculiarly Kantian. But the contention of the argument (which I am not evaluating here) is that those ideas will seem attractive for the purposes of political argument to anyone who considers how best to defend the liberties, formal norms of equal opportunity, and the requirement that public powers be exercised for the common good.[21]

Noting this draws attention to a first feature of the notion of an overlapping consensus that is important in assessing the objection. What lies in the intersection of different moral conceptions is not simply a set of policies or a system of norms within which political conflict and competition proceed.[22] Nor is it simply a determinate set of moral principles. Instead, the consensus extends to a view of persons, of the importance of fairness and other political values, of what counts as an advantage, and of which practices are paradigmatically evil (e.g., slavery, religious intolerance, and racial discrimination). In short, what lies at the intersection of different views is a (restricted) terrain on which moral and political argument can be conducted, and not simply a fixed and determinate set of substantive points of political agreement.

To show, then, that an egalitarian conception of justice meets the pluralistic consensus test, one needs to show that the bootstrap argument succeeds and that the terrain on which that argument proceeds could itself be the focus of an overlapping consensus in a society governed by it. One need not deny the obvious fact of disagreement on egalitarian political ideals or the only slightly less obvious fact that such disagreement is likely to persist even under favorable conditions.

Contemporary support

When the case for an egalitarian conception of justice is understood as a bootstrap argument and the common ground is understood in the way that I just sketched, it is not so obvious that an appeal to a wide range of *contemporary* political views will fail to support the substantively egalitarian aspects of the conception. For we do not require de facto agreement on substantively egalitarian norms, but only that the reasoning supporting those norms proceed on common ground. That is, we require that the egalitarian features represent a reasonable extension of what people do agree to – that they "extend the range of some existing consensus" by bringing the best justification of certain fundamental points of agreement to bear on unsettled and controversial matters.[23] That contention is not so implausible, because – as I noted earlier – the bootstrap argument for the egalitarian ideals proceeds principally by reference to points of agreement about the value of the liberties and certain formal requirements of equality.

Role of overlapping consensus

While the contention that the resources for defending an egalitarian political conception are implicit in current understandings may not, then, be entirely implausible, it should *not* be *identified* with the thesis that an egalitarian liberal political conception can meet the pluralistic consensus test. That test does not require that we rummage through the political culture searching for underlying points of agreement among the views featured in it.[24] Rummaging may serve an important function, and I will say a word about it below. But the pluralistic consensus test does not itself command a search for de facto points of agreement at all, and so the failure to find any would not undercut the force of an egalitarian conception of justice.

Instead it formulates a test on the reasonableness of a political conception that is in other respects attractive. The test is this: Consider a proposed conception of justice in operation, and then consider whether the principles, ideals, and terms of argument that figure in it provide moral reasons within the views that could be expected to arise among those who live in a society governed by it. Bringing this to bear on the issue of egalitarian liberalism, then, we are to imagine a society regulated by such a conception and existing across several generations. In such a society, we can reasonably expect moral diversity. We also can expect widespread agreement on the fundamental value of the liberties and on at least formal understandings of equality. But then, if there is such agreement and if the bootstrap argument has any force, the diverse moral understandings would each still have the resources necessary for supporting the substantively egalitarian conception as the correct conception of justice.

I have, of course, not tried to defend the bootstrap argument here. Instead, I have only argued that the pluralistic consensus test does not undercut the force (whatever its magnitude may be) of that argument. The *acknowledgment of diversity* underscored by the notion of an overlapping consensus does not undercut the *critique of privilege* contained in the egalitarian aspects of egalitarian liberalism.

Contemporary support, again

I have been emphasizing that the pluralistic consensus test does not itself require a search for implicit points of agreement in current moral views. Nonetheless the existence of such points might have a certain indirect relevance to justification. For, given that the deliberative liberties now receive some protection, it seems implausible to suppose that the full range of existing moral views simply represent accommodations to current and historical injustices, and would not continue to have some hold under just conditions. So it would be surprising if we could not already find the resources available in current moral understandings for defending a view of justice that we would also be able to defend under more favorable conditions. And if the pluralistic consensus test is acceptable, then there is also some rationale for taking current points of agreement seriously.

But it must be emphasized that when we understand the rationale for an examination of current points of agreement this way, we are not letting anything about justification turn on the mere fact of current consensus. In fact, it is never the case – not in the gesture to current understandings of value, and not in the requirement of overlapping consensus – that de facto agreement itself plays a role in justification.

With this last point I have begun to tread on the issues of the next section and so shall move directly to them.

Realism and reason

Now we come to the first of the issues about accommodation that I noted earlier: Does the pluralistic consensus test represent an unwanted accommodation to power? I begin my discussion of this question with some distinctions that will play an essential role in my (negative) answer.

Reasonable pluralism

Rawls refers to the fact that the deliberative liberties produce diversity as "the fact of pluralism." I think that this terminology may be misleading because "fact" puts the emphasis in the wrong place.[25] To explain why, I need first to introduce the idea of reasonable pluralism.[26]

The idea of reasonable pluralism is that there are distinct understandings of value, each of which is fully reasonable (pp. 235–8). An understanding of value is fully reasonable just in case its adherents are stably disposed to affirm it as they acquire new information and subject it to

67

critical reflection.[27] The contention that there are a plurality of such understandings is suggested by the absence of convergence in reflection on issues of value, which leaves disagreements, for example, about the value of choice, welfare, and self-actualization; about the value of contemplative and practical lives; about the value of devotions to friends and lovers as distinct from more diffuse concerns about abstract others; and about the values of poetic expression and political engagement.

What we ought to suppose about the truth of our beliefs about any subject matter, evaluative or otherwise, in the face of such an apparently "irresoluble rivalry" of reasonable alternative views is an open philosophical question.[28] But among the rationally acceptable answers to that question is that it is permissible, even with full awareness of the fact of reflective divergence, to take the *sectarian* route of affirming one's own view, that is, believing it as a matter of faith. And since believing is believing true, a rationally permissible (though not mandatory) response to an apparently irresoluble rivalry of evaluative conceptions is to affirm that one's own view contains the whole truth, while the truths in other views are simply the subsets of those views that intersect with one's own. This being one of the options, and the option that creates the most trouble for the pluralistic consensus test, I will frame the rest of my discussion so that it is consistent with it.

These remarks about reasonable pluralism suggest two different ways to understand the fact of pluralism:

The simple fact of pluralism: The protection of the deliberative liberties will result in moral pluralism.

The fact of reasonable pluralism: The protection of the deliberative liberties will result in moral pluralism, and some of the moral conceptions will fall within the set of fully reasonable conceptions.

The reasonable pluralism interpretation does make a factual claim. The asserted fact, however, is not simply that the protection of deliberative liberties will result in a plurality of conceptions of value but, further, that a number of those conceptions will be reasonable, and permissibly taken by their adherents to be true.

The reasonable pluralism explanation

Consider now a conception of justice that we wish to subject to the pluralistic consensus test. We imagine a society regulated by that conception and in which the condition of reasonable pluralism obtains. The pluralistic consensus test requires that the values and principles used to authorize the exercise of power by the state must be restricted to those that are compelling to the different reasonable moral views adhered to in the society. Consider some people – call them "us" (or "we") – who hold one such view, and think that others believe what is false about the domain of value. Should we think that the pluralistic consensus test, which prevents us from relying on the whole truth in authorizing the use of power, is simply an accommodation to the de facto power of those others? It depends, and what it depends on is clarified by the distinction between simple and reasonable pluralism.

Suppose that we are impressed by the lack of reflective convergence in understandings of value, that we acknowledge the idea of reasonable pluralism, and at the same time embrace (not unreasonably) the sectarian view that our moral views are true. Because these are consistent positions, our sectarianism does not require that we condemn as unreasonable everyone who believes what we take to be false. And this provides a rationale for formulating a conception of justice that is confined to considerations that they take to be moral reasons as well.

In particular, when we restrict ourselves in political argument to the subset of moral considerations that others who have reasonable views accept as well, we are doing three things. First, we are advancing considerations that we take to be genuine moral reasons; the adherents of each of the views that supports the overlapping consensus hold that *nothing but the truth* lies in the overlapping consensus.

Second, in restricting ourselves to a subset of the true moral reasons – appealing to nothing but the truth, though not to the whole truth – we are not simply acknowledging that those who believe the false and spurn the good have the power to make their voices heard, or to make our lives miserable if we fail to heed those voices. Instead, we are acknowledging that their views are not unreasonable, even if they do believe what is false. In short, we are moved not by their power, but by an acknowledgment that they are reasonable.

Third, we are taking cognizance of a peculiarity in insisting on the whole (sectarian) truth in the face of our acknowledgment of the idea of reasonable pluralism. For suppose we acknowledge it, and affirm the divergence of moralities under reflection. Then we must see that if we were to appeal to the whole truth, that appeal would be, from the standpoint of others who we take to be reasonable, indistinguishable from simply appealing to what we believe. But we already acknowledge that the mere appeal to what we believe carries no force in justification.[29]

Suppose, for example, we believe that welfare is the sole ultimate good, and we understand that view to imply that choice is not an independent final value. In the course of political argument, we affirm:

69

"It is true that welfare is the sole ultimate good." Now others ought not to suppose that what we *mean* is equally well captured by "We believe that welfare is the sole ultimate good." The indistinguishability at issue is not semantical. The point, rather, is that if others accept the idea of reasonable pluralism, then they notice what we also notice, namely, that what lies between our taking our views to be reasonable (about which there may be no disagreement) and our taking them to be true (about which there is disagreement) is not a further reason, but simply our (rationally permissible) belief in those views. Because there is nothing else that lies in between, an appeal to the whole truth will seem indistinguishable from an appeal to what we believe.

The simple-fact explanation

Following the reasonable pluralism interpretation, then, when we restrict ourselves to common ground in face of the fact of diversity, we are acknowledging that reason does not mandate a single moral view and then are refraining from imposing ourselves on others who are prepared to be reasonable. This account of whom we need to accommodate turns on our willingness to acknowledge that some people with whom we fundamentally disagree are not unreasonable. That is why we are not simply accommodating principles to power when we are concerned to ensure that the conception of justice is acceptable to them as well. This explanation of the pluralistic consensus test might be clarified by contrasting it with another explanation, which is suggested by some of Rawls's remarks, but which is not persuasive.

As I indicated at the outset, Rawls emphasizes the importance of realism in the formulation of reasonable ideals. And he suggests that when we confine ourselves to considerations that are reasons for others as well, we are simply adjusting to certain general facts about the social world. Here the emphasis is on the need to be realistic, to find common ground because disagreement is a basic fact of life under free conditions.

To see why this explanation of the need to accommodate diversity is not right, notice that it is a plausible general fact that there will always be people with unreasonable views. But the fact that there are some people with unreasonable views does not require that we *adjust our conception of justice* so that it can be supported by an overlapping consensus that will appeal to them. While we need to take the fact of disagreement into account in some way in deciding what to do, the pluralistic consensus condition is certainly not the only way to do that and is not mandated by the recognition that there are and will always be such people. Furthermore, if we did embrace the requirement that a conception of justice be able to bring everyone on board – that it restrict itself to reasons embraced by all understandings of value – then it is hard to see what the response would be to the objection that the requirement of an overlapping consensus simply forces an accommodation to power.

The problem with this explanation is that it makes too much of the de facto diversity highlighted in the simple-fact interpretation. The first explanation – which draws essentially on the idea of reasonable pluralism – does not deny the relevance of the fact that under conditions of deliberative liberty there will be diversity. But the response to that fact is not undiscriminating, and in particular is controlled by the distinction between reasonable and unreasonable understandings of value.

Ensuring that a conception of justice fits the fact of diversity under conditions of deliberative liberty is not, then, an unacceptable accommodation to power. But the reason that it is acceptable is not because diversity is a fact of life, as the simple-fact interpretation of pluralism states, and because adjustment to general and unalterable facts of social life is always to be distinguished from accommodation to power. Instead, that adjustment is reasonable because some forms of diversity are the natural consequence of the free exercise of practical reason. Once we agree that they are, we will not be inclined to count moral diversity among the unfavorable facts of human life, nor to confuse a concern to find a conception of justice consistent with it with a willingness to compromise justice in the face of the course of the world.

Exclusion

Answering the charge of unwarranted accommodation, then, commits us to the view that we need not accommodate the unreasonable. Indeed, given the explanation for this view, if we did accommodate the unreasonable in the formulation of fundamental principles, then we would be unacceptably adjusting principles to de facto power.

But this brings me to a different concern about power and political consensus: that the promise of consensus is associated with the practice of arbitrary exclusion. In view of the problem of securing general agreement on anything, claims to speak on behalf of all of the reasonable depend, it will be argued, on drawing arbitrary boundaries around the community of the reasonable.[30] So the charge is that any appeal to the ideal of consensus in fact rests on the power to exclude, exercised in this case through the pretense of discovering that some people are unreasonable.

In the case at hand, the exclusion is of a special kind. It does not amount to a deprivation of liberties or of what are conventionally

71

understood to be the advantages of social cooperation. Instead, exclusion lies in the fact that the arguments used to justify the exercise of power depend on norms, values, and ideals that are rejected by some people whose views will as a consequence not belong to an overlapping consensus. Although this does not violate the ideal of consensus, which requires that justification proceed by reference to reasons located on the common ground occupied by all who are prepared to listen to reason, it is exclusion all the same. And it is of a troublesome form. Its implication is that some people will reject the values, ideals, principles, and norms that serve, at the most fundamental level, to justify the exercise of power over them.

These are extremely important and complicated matters, not least because the charge of unreasonableness is commonly a ponderous way to express simple disagreement, or, in the distinctively American political idiom, a thinly disguised signal that one's opponents are poor, or female, or black. But as important as these issues are, I must be very brief here, and intend my comments only as a way to mark out certain issues for further examination and to introduce some doubts about the alleged arbitrariness of characterizations of views as unreasonable.

Consider, then, some views that might end up being excluded in this way, in particular those that would deny the protection of liberties on the basis of the doctrine that "outside the church there is no salvation." Rawls discusses this case, and states that it is "unreasonable" to use public powers to enforce this doctrine. I agree. But it is important to distinguish two ways that such enforcement might be unreasonable. Distinguishing them will help illustrate what is involved in exclusion on the grounds of unreasonableness.

The first case is presented by a "rationalist fundamentalist." This is the person who denies the idea of reasonable pluralism, affirming instead that it lies within the competence of reason to know that salvation is the supreme value, that there is a single path to salvation, that there is no salvation among the damned, and therefore that liberty of conscience is to be condemned. This is not a common view, if only because it claims for reason territory usually reserved for faith.[31] But if someone were to advance it, then one ought to say that they are simply mistaken. Even if these views are all rationally permissible, reason surely does not mandate them, and in insisting that it does they are not acknowledging the facts.

This response will not do in the second case. These are the nonrationalist fundamentalists who accept the limited competence of reason, but deny that reason is controlling in the authorization to use power. By contrast with the rationalist fundamentalists, they agree that an appreciation of the value of salvation and of the conditions for achieving it fall outside the competence of reason, and that grasping the truth about the proper conduct of life depends on faith. But they affirm that truths accessible only through faith are sufficient to authorize the legitimate exercise of power. What is important is that they are *truths*, and not the mode of access to them available for finite human creatures. Faced with nonrationalist fundamentalists, it will not do to state the case for the idea of reasonable pluralism; they know that case, celebrate the limited competence of reason as a guide in human affairs, and lament the self-imposed disabilities of those who insist on proceeding within its narrow compass.

Still, what they are prepared to do is to impose on those who are outside the faith in a way that – so far as those others can tell – is indistinguishable from the concededly irrational practice of imposing in the name of their beliefs. To resist such imposition is not simply to affirm a disagreement with the nonrationalist fundamentalist. Instead, it is to complain about this fundamental form of unreasonableness. And finding them unreasonable in this way is sufficient to show that the exclusion is not arbitrary.

Conclusions

I noted earlier that the problems addressed in Rawls's essay – the reasonableness of the ideal of a consensual order and of the pluralistic consensus condition – echo a set of concerns familiar from Hegel's political philosophy and critical discussion of it. Returning now to these concerns, what conclusions about them can we draw from the discussion here?

First, in *A Theory of Justice* Rawls proposed a formulation of the distinction between political and civil society and a conception of justice that was meant to accommodate that distinction without carrying the inegalitarian implications that some have thought intrinsic to it. Whatever the merits of that earlier defense of egalitarian liberalism, the pluralistic consensus condition does nothing to weaken it.

Second, Hegel thought that an account of the ideal of a consensual polity suited to modern conditions needed to accommodate the diversity of values and attachments characteristic of civil society.[32] While Hegel emphasized that the universal–particular distinction and its institutionalization in the separation of civil and political spheres is a distinguishing feature of modern societies, he did not suppose it to be simply a brute fact about post-Reformation Europe. Instead, his rationalism led him to suppose that this peculiarity represented a historically situated discovery about the operation of practical reason. In accommodating the diversity institutionalized in civil society, then, political philosophy was not simply accommodating the bare fact that people differ in aims and aspirations. Instead, it was acknowledging the diverse promptings of practical reason itself, even as it sought to find within that diversity the seeds of the set of common values underlying political society.[33] In short, some form of civil–political society distinction is an unavoidable aspect of any attractive ideal, once we see the scope and competence of practical reason. In a Hegelian *Doppelsatz*: We need to accommodate the ideal to the real because the real manifests the ideal.

Rawls's talk about the fact of pluralism, the role of the Reformation in prompting acknowledgment of that fact, and the need for an overlapping consensus can be taken in this same spirit. If we accept the idea of reasonable pluralism, then moral diversity is not simply a bare fact, even a bare general fact about human nature, but, rather, indicates something about the operation and powers of practical reason. With this account of diversity, we have a response to the contention that accommodating different understandings of value in the formulation of basic moral principles for the political domain is tantamount to supposing that justice commands that we turn our money over to thieves. The response is that we are accommodating basic principles not to the reality of power but, rather, to the way that social reality reveals the powers of practical reason.[34]

Notes

1 This essay began as comments on an unpublished paper by John Rawls on "A Reasonably Realistic Idea of a Well-ordered Society." I have rewritten it to address Rawls's "The Domain of the Political and Overlapping Consensus," originally published in *New York University Law Review* 64, no. 2 (May 1989): 233–55, and reprinted in this volume.

2 John Rawls, *A Theory of Justice* (Cambridge, Mass.: Harvard University Press, 1971), p. 263.

3 Rawls is concerned with forms of diversity that extend beyond the domain of morality, for example, to religious and philosophical matters. Nothing turns on the limitation that I adopt here.

4 The ideal of consensus may, of course, be unrealistic in other ways as well.

5 I return to the issue of favorable conditions later.

6 I explain the point of the phrase "to this extent" later.

7 The objection extrapolates on some points made by Jerry Cohen in a conversation about Rawls's difference principle.

8 All references to "The Domain of the Political" are included parenthetically within the text. Page numbers refer to the *New York University Law Review* edition cited in note 1.

9 I identify moral reasons by their functional role in individual deliberation and choice, not their content. There may be content restrictions as well, but I think that the functional role characterization captures a central aspect of ordinary usage and in any case suffices for my purposes here.

10 See Rawls's "third general fact," p. 235.

11 See Jean-Jacques Rousseau, *On the Social Contract*, trans. Judith R. Masters (New York: St. Martin's, 1978), Book 1, chap. 6.

12 We also need to add that everyone believes with good reason that the decisions express the values.

13 This is what Rawls calls the "first general fact." See pp. 234–5.

14 Hegel's discussion of Rousseau in the *History of Philosophy* are more balanced than his critical remarks in the *Philosophy of Right*. Compare *Lectures on the History of Philosophy*, vol. 3, trans. Elizabeth Haldane (New York: Humanities Press, 1968) with *Philosophy of Right*, trans. T. M. Knox (Oxford: Clarendon Press, 1952), pp. 156–7.

15 See *Philosophy of Right*, paragraph 261, where Hegel says that the state is both an "external necessity" with respect to the family and civil society, and "the end immanent within them."

16 Hegel did acknowledge the need to regulate property in the name of the general welfare, and to avoid certain extreme cases of poverty (see *Philosophy of Right*, paragraphs 234–48). But his view does not appear to countenance the regulation of economic activity with an eye to ensuring that the final distribution of resources is not determined by differences of social background and natural ability.

17 See his "On the Jewish Question," in *Marx-Engels Reader*, second edition, ed. Robert Tucker (New York: Norton, 1978), pp. 26–46; *Critique of Hegel's Philosophy of Right*, trans. Joseph O'Malley (Cambridge: Cambridge University Press, 1970).

18 This impression was confirmed by conversations at the conference at which I presented the first draft of these comments. See also the concerns about the "abstraction, vagueness, and conservativism" of Rawls's later work expressed in Thomas Pogge's *Realizing Rawls* (Ithaca, N.Y.: Cornell University Press, 1989), p. 4.

19 See, for example, John Gray, "Contractarian Method, Private Property, and Market Economy," in *Markets and Justice, Nomos XXIII*, eds. John W. Chapman and J. Roland Pennock (New York: New York University Press, 1989), pp. 13–58; and William Galston, "Pluralism and Social Unity," *Ethics* (July 1989): 711.

20 See *Theory of Justice*, p. 65.

21 The attribution to Kant in particular of the idea that abstract human potentialities are morally fundamental is also off the mark historically. That idea plays a central role in Rousseau's view, and is also suggested in Locke's theory of natural law. The variations on this general theme are complex, as is the evolution of the idea; fortunately these details are not relevant here.

22 Robert Dahl, for example, emphasizes the importance of "underlying consensus on policy" and on the basic rules of political competition in *A Preface*

to Democratic Theory (Chicago: University of Chicago Press, 1956), pp. 75–84, 132.

23 See *Theory of Justice*, p. 582. For elaboration of this strategy, see my "Democratic Equality and the Difference Principle," *Ethics* (July 1989): 727–51.

24 See John Rawls, "The Priority of the Right and Ideas of the Good," *Philosophy and Public Affairs* 17, no. 4 (Fall 1988): 275–6.

25 One reason for referring to a *fact* of pluralism is to distinguish the view that we need to accommodate the diversity of values that follows on the protection of the liberties from the view that that diversity should be accommodated because it is a good thing in itself. Nothing that I say is meant to challenge the propriety of this usage.

26 My discussion of reasonable pluralism is in agreement with Rawls's account of the "burdens of reason" (pp. 235–8). The point of the discussion is largely to indicate the special importance of those burdens, as distinct from the four other general facts that Rawls discusses (pp. 234–5), in explaining the pluralistic consensus test and in responding to objections to it.

27 I take this formulation from Mark Johnston.

28 See, for example, W.V.O. Quine, *Pursuit of Truth* (Cambridge, Mass.: Harvard University Press, 1990), pp. 98–101, from whom I take the phrase "irresoluble rivalry," and the term "sectarian" as it is used in the next sentence.

29 For elaboration of this point, see Thomas Nagel, "Moral Conflict and Political Legitimacy," *Philosophy and Public Affairs* 16, no. 3 (Summer 1987): 215–40. Joseph Raz has criticized Nagel's point, suggesting that it rests on an untenable distinction between the position of the speaker who advances a justification, and the listener to whom it is addressed. See his "Facing Diversity: The Case of Epistemic Abstinence," *Philosophy and Public Affairs* 19, no. 1 (Winter 1990): 37–9. I am not persuaded by Raz's contention. He is right that the positions of speaker and listener are parallel. But taking up the point of view of the person to whom a justification is addressed is simply a heuristic for understanding the limited force of an argument that appeals to the whole truth. So far from undermining Nagel's point, the parallelism is essential to drawing the right conclusions from the use of the heuristic.

30 I am indebted to Uday Mehta for many discussions of these issues. For discussion of a variety of different strategies of exclusion, see his "Liberal Strategies of Exclusion," *Politics and Society* 18, no. 4 (December 1990): 427–54.

31 It is an analog to "creation science," operating in the domain of salvation. The proper response is the same in both cases.

32 I am not confident that Hegel held the view I attribute to him in this paragraph. It does fit with and make sense out of various pieces of his view, including his account of the relationship between civil society and the state, his conception of the role of reason in history, and his views about the

rationality of modern social arrangements. But he does not state it anywhere in the way that I put it here. If I am wrong in thinking that he held it, nothing else in the article would need to change.

33 See *Philosophy of Right*, paragraph 261.

34 I thank Michael Hardimon, John Rawls, Tim Scanlon, and Judith Thomson for very helpful comments on earlier drafts of this essay.

DISAGREEMENTS ABOUT JUSTICE

BY

JEREMY WALDRON

I.

What is the relation between philosophical disagreement about the good and disagreements about justice in a pluralistic society? By "philosophical disagreements about the good," I mean differences between various views about ultimate value, various conceptions of the nature and meaning of life. I include, most prominently, religious disagreements, but also disagreements among various secular conceptions of the good. What is the relation between differences of these kinds and the disagreements we have in politics (and in political philosophy) concerning the fundamental principles of justice?

Here are a couple of models, a couple of ways of thinking about the relation between disagreements of the two kinds:

(1)   In the first model, each conception of the good is associated with or generates a particular vision of the just society. Catholics, for example, have a particular conception of the good, and for many that conception issues in a particular vision of law and justice, expounded (say) in the jurisprudence of Thomas Aquinas. Muslims proclaim a comprehensive religious vision, and this generates for them a particular vision of the well-ordered society, a conception of law and justice which they refer to as *Shari'a.* Also, on this model, someone who holds a secular view of human needs may develop a conception of justice which corresponds to that view; his convictions about justice may be expected to differ somewhat from convictions of justice held by people who base them on different visions of human fulfilment. Disagreement about justice is what disagreement about the good amounts to in the social and political sphere.

Pacific Philosophical Quarterly 75 (1994) 372–387   0031-5621/94/0200-0000
© 1994 University of Southern California. Published by
Blackwell Publishers, 108 Cowley Road, Oxford OX4 1JF, UK and
238 Main Street, Cambridge, MA 02142, USA.

(2)   In the second model, particular theories of justice are not seen as tied to or generated by particular conceptions of the good. Instead, they stand apart from competing religious and philosophical conceptions. They present themselves as solutions to the various problems which disagreement about the good generates in society. Conceptions of justice, on this second model, are viewed as rival attempts to specify a quite separate set of principles for the basic structure of a society whose members disagree about the good. The rivalry between competing conceptions of justice is seen as independent of (and cutting across) the rivalry between competing conceptions of the good. Thus among Catholics there are socialists and libertarians, who, although they agree about ultimate values, disagree fundamentally about the principles that should govern the economic structure of a modern plural society. In the debate about justice, a Catholic socialist may have more in common with someone who is a Marxist-Leninist and thus an atheist, than he has with a fellow Catholic who is politically conservative. The disagreement between socialist Catholics and politically conservative Catholics—or between socialists and political conservatives generally—is motivated quite separately, on the second model, from disagreements about the good.

Which (if either) of these models is implied or assumed in the arguments of John Rawls's book *Political Liberalism*? The answer seems obvious: the second model is the one that corresponds to Rawls's view of the matter.

The answer *seems* obvious, in part because Rawls explicitly rejects the first model as a way of characterizing his own theory, justice as fairness (JAF). JAF is not the upshot of any particular conception of the good; it is presented as a "free-standing" conception (p. 12),[1] intended to represent the terms of an "overlapping consensus" among the many ethical and religious conceptions that compete for adherents in society. And Rawls presents this not only as a claim about JAF; he maintains that *any* view of the kind he is defending must reject the first model as a way of specifying the agenda for discussions of justice.

[T]he problem of political liberalism is: How is it possible that there may exist over time a stable and just society of free and equal citizens profoundly divided by reasonable though incompatible religious, philosophical, and moral doctrines? This is a problem of political justice, not a problem about the highest good. (p. xxv)

Thus Rawls's approach to justice seems to fit the second model inasmuch as it defines a task or an agenda in whose performance people may be at odds in a way that (as I said) cuts cross the disagreements which they have about the good.

II.

On the other hand, fitting Rawls's account into the second model presupposes that he actually contemplates disagreements about justice in a well-ordered society. In fact, it is not at all clear that he does.

I mean that last statement to be as tentative as it sounds. Rawls of course does not deny that people disagree about what justice requires.[2] But he does not say much about these disagreements in his own discussion. Compared with what he says about ethical, religious, and philosophical disagreements, Rawls's treatment of disagreements about justice is really quite insignificant.

To see this, imagine the following way in which the second of our models could be defended. One might offer an explanation of people's disagreements about justice that differed from the explanation one offered of their disagreements about the good. The dissonance between these explanations would then yield a prediction that the two types of disagreement could be expected to cut across one another.

Now Rawls devotes a lot of attention to the etiology of disagreement in society. He asks:

Why does not our conscientious attempt to reason with one another lead to reasonable agreement? It seems to do so in natural science, at least in the long run. (p. 55)

Rawls uses the phrase "the burdens of judgment" as a way of articulating his answer to this question. The burdens of judgment are "the many hazards involved in the correct (and conscientious) exercise of our powers of reason and judgment in the ordinary course of political life" (p. 56). For example, he says that, on any plausible account, human life engages multiple values and it is natural that people will disagree about how to balance or prioritize them. Also, on any plausible account, people's respective positions, perspectives and experiences in life will give them different bases from which to make these delicate judgments. These differences of experience and position combine with the evident complexity of the issues being addressed, meaning that reasonable persons may disagree not openly about what the world is like but about the relevance and weight to be accorded the various facts and insights that they have at their disposal. Together factors like these make disagreement in good faith not only possible but predictable.

Different conceptions of the world can reasonably be elaborated from different standpoints and diversity arises in part from our distinct perspectives. It is unrealistic ... to suppose that all our differences are rooted solely in ignorance and perversity, or else in the rivalries for power, status, or economic gain. (p. 58)

Thus, Rawls concludes, "many of our most important judgments are made under conditions where it is not to be expected that conscientious persons with full powers of reason, even after free discussion, will arrive at the same conclusion" (p. 58).

This account, as it stands, could characterize political as well as ethical and religious disagreements; it could characterize differences about justice as well as differences about the good.[3] However, Rawls quickly orients the burdens-of-judgment argument purely in the direction of disagreements about the good. "The evident consequence of the burdens of judgment," he says, "is that reasonable persons do not all affirm the same comprehensive doctrine" (p. 60). Nowhere, as far as I can tell, does he infer the equally evident conclusion that reasonable persons cannot be expected to agree about the proper balance to be assigned in social life to their respective comprehensive conceptions. Nowhere does he infer that reasonable people might be expected to disagree fundamentally about the basic terms and principles of their association.[4]

One of the things Rawls takes from the burdens-of-judgment argument is that "a public and shared basis of justification that applies to comprehensive doctrines is lacking in the public culture of a democratic society" (p. 61). This provides positive evidence for attributing to Rawls the belief that issues of justice are *not* subject to the burdens of judgment. The argument to that effect goes as follows.

According to Rawls, issues of justice are to be dealt with on the basis of public reason: "As far as possible, the knowledge and ways of reasoning that ground our affirming the principles of justice ... are to rest on the plain truths now widely accepted, or available, to citizens generally" (p. 225). To apply the burdens-of-judgment idea in this area would suggest that some of the reasons which people appeal to in articulating their views about justice are not, and cannot be, widely shared in this sense. Thus, if he is to sustain the idea of public reason as a basis for argument about justice, Rawls must deny that the burdens of judgment affect such argumentation. If the burdens of judgment preclude the use of public reason in a given area, it would seem to follow that the burdens of judgment do not apply in areas where the idea of public reason is appropriate.[5]

This leaves us with the rather uncongenial conclusion that there is no such thing as reasonable disagreement in politics. The burdens of judgment explain how reasonable disagreement is possible. But the ideal of public reason seems to presuppose that the burdens of judgment do not apply to the issues that are under discussion in politics.

III.

I am reluctant to attribute this conclusion to Rawls. Surely, there would be no need for public reason if there were *not* disagreement about justice. If they did not disagree about justice, what would people have to reason or argue (or vote) about in a democratic society? If, however, there *is* disagreement about justice, and people make proper use of public reason to articulate and resolve it, it would seem churlish to deny that such disagreement was—initially, at any rate—reasonable.

As far as I can tell, Rawls says that the idea of public reason is incompatible at most with the existence of reasonable disagreement about *the fundamentals* of justice. It is not incompatible with reasonable disagreement about the way details are worked out.

Accepting the idea of public reason and its principle of legitimacy emphatically does not mean ... accepting a particular liberal conception of justice down to the last detail of the principles defining its content. We may differ about these principles and still agree in accepting a conception's more general features. (p. 226)

But while he denies that the specific content of JAF is definitive of public reason, he is unabashed about offering the general principles of JAF— "the values expressed by the principles and guidelines that would be agreed on in the original position" (p. 227)—as a criterion of whether political argument is being conducted in accordance with the idea of public reason or not.

We should pause to consider how remarkable this view is. In the world we know, people disagree radically about justice. Their disagreement is not just about details but about fundamentals. There are places where Rawls acknowledges this diversity. He says near the beginning of *Political Liberalism* that "[w]e turn to political philosophy when our shared political understandings ... break down" (p. 44). Still, in the passages we have been discussing, his view seems to be that these differences are to be aired and debated only within the medium of "principles and guidelines ... agreed on in the original position" (p. 227). In fact, there is barely more than a handful of academic political philosophers who accept the original position idea as Rawls expounds it or his view of the principles and guidelines that would be accepted therein. It seems odd to select this extraordinarily controversial conception as the basis of one's view of public reason, i.e. as the basis of one's normative view about the terms in which citizens properly conduct and attempt to resolve their disagreements with one another about justice. More abstractly, it is surely a mistake to identify the norms framing the public debate about justice with values and principles which are constitutive (even if only *broadly* constitutive, let alone constitutive in detail) of a particular position in that debate.

In the passage we have been discussing, Rawls acknowledges the controversial nature of his suggestion about the content of the criterion which determines whether people are arguing in accordance with the ideal of public reason or not.

> Many will prefer another criterion ... It is inevitable and often desirable that citizens have different views as to the most appropriate political conception; for the public political culture is bound to contain different fundamental ideas that can be developed in different ways. (p. 227)

Quite so. Why, then, in the face of such controversy select one of the participants as the criterion to set the terms in which the controversy will subsequently be conducted? Rawls's answer is: "An orderly contest between [different fundamental political ideas] over time is a reliable way to find out which one, if any, is most reasonable" (p. 227).

As I understand it, the idea is as follows. *Ex ante*, there may be many apparently reasonable approaches to justice, Rawls's approach among them. A process of argument must therefore take place in political philosophy to sort out which one, if any, is acceptable as a fundamental conception for a well-ordered society. Part of what we are trying to sort out in that argument, is which one of the competing approaches to justice would be acceptable as a basis for public reason.[6] If we come up with an answer, then we can say *ex post* that the other views are unreasonable, because they have failed as candidates for criterion of public reason. *Ex ante*, we *can* talk about reasonable disagreement concerning political fundamentals; but having settled on a view about fundamentals we are no longer in a position to talk in that way. *Ex post*, the only reasonable disagreements that remain are disagreements about the working out of the details of the conception that the first phase of argument has yielded.

I believe this is Rawls's position. I hope he will show me that it is not. For it seems to be open to a serious objection.

IV.

Before I outline that objection,[7] let me back up a little. The view I have just been unravelling is not very different from the line which Rawls took in chapter four of *A Theory of Justice*.[8] There he noted—quite properly— that "the question whether legislation is just or unjust, especially in connection with economic and social polices, is commonly subject to reasonable differences of opinion."[9] The existence of such disagreement necessitates constitutional procedures (such as voting) that enable decisions to be taken and carried out even when the members of the society are divided as to what the decisions should be. Now of course people disagree also about these procedural arrangements. Thus, Rawls says, the public-minded citizen addressing the justice of his society's structure faces questions of two kinds:

First of all, he must judge the justice of legislation and social policies. But he also knows that his opinions will not always coincide with those of others, since men's judgments and beliefs are likely to differ especially when their interests are engaged. Therefore secondly, a citizen must decide which constitutional arrangements are just for reconciling conflicting opinions of justice. We may think of the political process as a machine which makes social decisions when the views of representatives and their constituents are fed into it. A citizen will regard some ways of designing this machine as more just than others. So a complete conception of justice is not only able to assess laws and policies but it can also rank procedures for selecting which political opinion is to be enacted into law.[10]

How and on what basis are proposals about political procedure to be evaluated? Rawls's answer in *A Theory of Justice* is that people "are to choose the most effective just constitution, the constitution that ... is best calculated to lead to just and effective legislation."[11] Of course, we cannot guarantee that the results of any procedure will be just: "Clearly any feasible political procedure may yield an unjust outcome."[12] At best, the situation is one of imperfect procedural justice. The task is to find a constitution that will maximize the prospect that legislative decisions will be good ones.

But how can citizens agree on issues of constitutional choice given that they disagree about the telos of such choice. A libertarian will seek procedures that maximize the prospect of legislation that is just by his own free market standards, while a social democrat will seek procedures that maximize the prospects for legislation embodying collective and egalitarian concern. This indicates to Rawls that disagreements about justice must be dealt with first, before issues of constitutional design are even addressed. Thus what he says about constitutional choice, i.e. about the choice of legislative process, is predicated on the assumption that we *already* know and *already* agree about the basic principles of social justice.

In framing a just constitution I assume that the two principles of justice already chosen define an independent standard of the desired outcome. If there is no such standard, the problem of constitutional design is not well posed, for this decision is made by running through the feasible just constitutions (given, say, by enumeration on the basis of social theory) looking for the one that in the existing circumstances will most probably result in effective and just social arrangements.[13]

Rawls concedes that people do have "reasonable differences of opinion" about whether legislation is just; but he characterizes those as disagreements about how to apply Rawlsian principles in a complex world, not disagreements about which principles to apply. Thus the approach in *A Theory of Justice* is almost exactly the same as that in *Political Liberalism*, where Rawls suggests that political differences are to be played out in a medium of public reason that not only accommodates, but is defined in terms of, "principles and guidelines that would be agreed to in the original position" (p. 227). Both books assume that there will come a point at which reasonable politics can presuppose that participants are agreed, at least at a general level, about which principles of justice they are to apply.

V.

Suppose, for a moment, that we buy this. Obviously, it would be a mistake to infer anything from it for the problems about politics, procedure and constitutional choice that *we* face—we, in the real world where people do not at all agree about the fundamentals of justice. To think—as *we* have to, in the real world—about the politics of a society whose members differ radically and in principle about what justice requires is—in Rawls's terms—to move from ideal (or strict compliance) theory to non-ideal (partial compliance) theory.[14] Both books are about "a well-ordered society"—"a society in which everyone accepts, and knows that everyone else accepts, the very same principles of justice" (p. 35). The application of their arguments to a society like ours, in which people do not accept, nor do they think of themselves as accepting, the same principles of justice—a society whose politics is dedicated quite explicitly to grappling with fundamental *dis*agreements about justice—is quite problematic.

I wonder whether, on reflection, Rawls is happy with the width of this gap between the politics of a well-ordered society and the politics of a society like ours. There are two signs that he is not.

First, he himself seems quite willing to draw conclusions about American constitutional politics and law from his arguments about public reason etc. Though these inferences should be regarded as quite reckless given the divergence between the politics of a well-ordered society and the politics which the U.S. Supreme Court actually has to address,[15] Rawls seems unabashed about drawing them.

Secondly, Rawls is in general much less comfortable in his later work with the characterization of a well-ordered society which he gave in *A Theory of Justice*. He now denies what he then maintained—that in a well-ordered society people affirm the same conception of justice on the same moral and philosophical grounds. The point of *Political Liberalism* is to argue that in a well-ordered society people can (and probably must) affirm the same conception of justice on different moral and political grounds (pp. xvi–xvii). I wonder whether Rawls might be willing to yield a further concession. Maybe what is definitive of political philosophy— the philosophy of *politics*, after all—is that it asks how a society can be well-ordered in its procedures for debate and decision-making when its citizens disagree, not only about the good, but also about justice. The first concession, Rawls say, was motivated by the need to come to terms with the circumstances of "[a] modern democratic society" (p. xvi). But "pluralism of comprehensive religious, philosophical, and moral doctrines" (p. xvi) is not the only pluralism with which we have to deal in a modern democratic society. We also have to deal with justice-pluralism and justice-disagreement. Maybe political philosophy should be required to come to terms with that circumstance also.

VI.

Against all this and in defense of *Political Liberalism*, it may be argued that Rawls cannot simply confront disagreements about justice as a spectator—carefully noting the diversity of views, the extent of disagreement, etc. For he *is* a theorist of justice. He engages in these disagreements *as a participant*, and as an uncompromising opponent of conceptions other than his own. He surely cannot be required to make room, in his own normative conception of a well-ordered society, for other views about justice that are incompatible with his, views which from his point of view have simply got things wrong.

We may put this defense in terms that Ronald Dworkin once used to explain why the utilitarian calculus should exclude "external" preferences held by people as the upshot of political convictions incompatible with the grounds of utilitarianism itself. Dworkin said:

Utilitarianism must claim (as ... any political theory must claim) truth for itself, and therefore must claim the falsity of any theory that contradicts it. It must itself occupy, that is, all the logical space that its content requires. ... Suppose the community contains a Nazi, for example, whose set of preferences includes the preference that Aryans have more and

Jews less of their preferences fulfilled just because of who they are. A neutral utilitarian cannot say that there is no reason in political morality, for rejecting or dishonouring that preference, for not dismissing it as simply wrong, for not striving to fulfil it with all the dedication that officials devote to fulfiling any other sort of preference. For utilitarianism itself supplies such a reason: its most fundamental tenet is people's preferences should be weighed on an equal basis in the same scales, that the Nazi theory of justice is profoundly wrong, and that officials should oppose the Nazi theory and strive to defeat rather than fulfil it. A neutral utilitarian is in fact barred, for reasons of consistency, from taking the same politically neutral attitude to the Nazi's political preference that he takes to other sorts of preferences.[16]

We may not agree with this as an analysis of utilitarianism,[17] but the methodological point seems a fair one. If JAF is offered as a theory of justice, its principles must do *all the work there is to be done by principles of justice*. As a conception of justice, JAF is not required to be fair to, or to accommodate, its rivals. If a well-ordered society is a just society—and if Rawls is right about justice—then a well-ordered society will be one in which the principles he defends, and not any others, hold sway.

Moreover, this is not a trivial matter of a philosopher wanting to stake out his own convictions over as much of the field as possible. Justice is important: in a way, nothing is more important in the basic structuring of society. To form the belief that *justice* requires X rather than Y, is to form the belief that nothing less than X will do and that a compromise or accommodation with Y or anything else would be pernicious. Of course a given belief about what justice requires may be mistaken. But what one would be mistaken about, is what categorically and uncompromisingly ought to be done, so far as the basic structure of society is concerned.

That is what one might say in defense of Rawls's approach—an approach which characterizes a well-ordered society purely in terms of the principles of justice he thinks correct, without reference to the competition between them and what he regards as their fundamentally mistaken rivals. In Dworkin's terms, he is simply claiming truth for his own theory, and thus the falsity of any theory that contradicts it. He is—necessarily—occupying all the logical space that the content of his conception requires.[18]

I have no objection to this as a way of thinking about justice. But I have misgivings about it as a way of thinking about politics, certainly as a way of thinking about the politics of justice.[19]

What is normally understood by politics is that it is an arena in which the members of some group debate and find ways of reaching decisions on various issues in spite of the fact that they disagree about the values and principles that the merits of those issues engage. (The existence of disagreement and the felt need for decision notwithstanding disagreement are, if you like, the elementary "circumstance of politics"—as moderate scarcity, reasonable pluralism and limited altruism are among the "circumstances of justice.")[20] The empirical science of politics is the study of the ways in which this deliberation and decision-making actually take place. Normative reflection on politics—and ultimately political philosophy—amounts to reflection on the values and principles that are implicated in processes of deliberation and decision-making. To imagine that deliberative politics (or any form of peaceful politics) is possible is to imagine that people can agree on some of these procedural points even though they disagree on the merits of the issues that the procedures are, so to speak, housing. It is to imagine, in other words, that the procedural issues and the substantive issues are in some sense separable.

Now I can certainly think about politics as the partisan of a particular conception of justice competing uncompromisingly with its rivals in the political arena. But I cannot do so if my thinking about political and constitutional procedure is conducted entirely in the shadow of my substantive convictions. For me to think about politics, there must be limits on the "logical space" that my substantive views occupy. To think about politics, I must be willing at least part of the time to view even my own uncompromising convictions about justice as merely one set of convictions among others. I must be willing to address, in a relatively neutral way, the question of what is to be done about the fact that people like me disagree with others in society about justice.

That concession can be a demanding one. It is not just a matter of organizing neutral rules for a debating society. Political debate must issue in decision. To engage in politics is to subscribe to procedural principles (majority-rule is an example) that might yield outcomes at odds with my own substantive convictions, outcomes that my own substantive convictions condemn.

How could one contemplate this *on a matter of justice*? If justice is the *first* virtue of social institutions, how could there be any political virtue or principle that required one to support injustice simply on the ground that the other side won a vote in parliament, congress or court? If justice is the first virtue of social institutions, then surely nothing—including political procedures, including voting— is more important.

This response—which I have heard form others but which I am not attributing to Rawls—rests on an impoverished conception of the dimensions of political importance. To say that view Y, which we think unjust, should prevail because it has greater political support, is not to rank political or procedural considerations ahead of justice on some single dimension of moral importance. It is to come at the issue from a different direction. When we say that a view we think incorrect should prevail on political grounds, we approach it not in terms of intrinsic importance or priority, but in light of the basic circumstance of politics—the circumstance that even on the matters we think *most* important, a common decision may be necessary despite the existence of disagreement about what that decision should be.[21] The problem defined by that circumstance is the problem of selecting a substantive principle of justice to act on (together) when we disagree about which principles are true or reasonable and which not. To say then that justice is subordinated to procedural values in political decision-making would be to beg the question of which of the positions competing for political support is to be counted as just.

VII.

I began by looking at the relation between disagreements about justice and disagreements about the good. Two models were suggested: on the first, disagreements about justice are the upshot of disagreements about the good; on the second model, the two sorts of disagreements are independent of one another. We have seen that Rawls is probably not, after all, committed to the second model, at least not as a model of a well-ordered society. For on his account, a well-ordered society may exhibit disagreements about the good but it will not exhibit disagreements about the fundamentals of justice.

What about the kind of society with which we are familiar, in which *both* types of disagreement are present. Which of our two initial models is more accurate with regard to the less-than-well-ordered society like our own? Here, I do not think Rawls would want to rule out the first model, or at least some version of it. If a religious or philosophical tradition has nurtured a rich and resourceful conception of the good, it would be odd to expect its priests, ideologues, or philosophers not to have developed that conception also in a social or political direction. Social and political concerns after all are among the most pressing concerns we have: it would be odd if a tradition had views about what made life worth living but no views about the basis on which we ought to live our lives together. This seems indicated, too, by Rawls's use of the term "comprehensive" doctrine or conception to describe views about religion and value that compete in society. "Comprehensive" seems to indicate an ambition on the part of such conceptions to answer all the big questions, from which questions about justice and the basic organization of society can hardly be excluded. It is significant that one of Rawls's most prominent examples of a theory of the good is utilitarianism (p. 13): and utilitarianism certainly implies (some would say, it just *is*) a view about justice.

But if the first model explains even a part of people's disagreements about justice, then there is an interesting consequence for Rawls's account of the transition (so to speak) from a less-than-well-ordered society, in which people disagree about the fundamentals of justice, to a well-ordered society in which a particular conception of justice—say, JAF—is enshrined as a framework for public reason.

That consequence has to do with Rawls's distinction in *Political Liberalism* between an overlapping consensus and a *modus vivendi*. Both overlapping consensus and *modus vivendi* are models of the many-to-one relation between conceptions of the good and a single favored conception of justice.[22] Though Rawls is adamant that they are "quite different" from one another (p. 147), he conjectures that "an initial acquiescence in a liberal conception of justice as a mere *modus vivendi* could change over time ... into an overlapping consensus" (p. 168).

One way of understanding that change is as follows. So long as each conception of the good generates its own conception of justice—i.e. so long as each conception of the good is truly "comprehensive" in the way I described a paragraph or two ago—it is impossible for competing conceptions of the good to be related to a single conception of justice (such as JAF) in the strong moral relation that Rawls refers to as "overlapping consensus." Why? Because each conception of the good generates a direct competitor to the conception of justice which is putatively the recipient of allegiance in overlapping consensus.

Thus, among a range of rival conceptions of the good, G_1, G_2, ...G_n, we are likely to find that $G_1 \longrightarrow J_1$, $G_2 \longrightarrow J_2$, and so on (where J_1, J_2, ...J_n are rival conceptions of justice). Each of these pairs—G_1/J_1, G_2/J_2, etc—defines a *comprehensive* philosophical conception C_1, C_2, ...C_n.

Now suppose there is a liberal conception of justice, JAF, which could in principle represent a genuine overlapping consensus as between G_1, G_2, etc. From the point of view of J_1, J_2, etc, allegiance to JAF will be, at best, a mere *modus vivendi*. For J_1 and J_2 contradict JAF: they are rivals to JAF as they are to each other. They cannot offer JAF the sincere moral supporting that an overlapping consensus presupposes without compromising their own claims about justice. Moreover, inasmuch as J_1 is an integral part of C_1, J_2 an integral part of C_2, etc., the comprehensive conceptions C_1, C_2, ...C_n will not be able to support JAF in overlapping consensus either.

However, if JAF can secure itself for a period of time as a *modus vivendi* among C_1, C_2, ...C_n, it may cause each of the justice-components of those comprehensive conceptions to gradually lose ground, even within its general conception. J_1, for example, may gradually come to seem redundant even to the followers of C_1 as its work *qua* conception of justice is done—albeit as a *modus vivendi*—by the liberal conception of justice JAF. This opens up the possibility that over time, C_1 will decompose into its constituent parts—G_1 and J_1—with J_1 being quietly dropped, and the conception of the good, G_1, being left to forge a genuine moral allegiance to JAF. And similarly, for many of the other comprehensive conceptions.

If this process captures anything along the lines of what Rawls has in mind, it might also provide an additional basis for characterizing certain comprehensive conceptions of the good as unreasonable, from the point of view of JAF. "Unreasonable" has two meanings in *Political Liberalism*. On the one hand, as we have seen, it refers to a conception whose divergence from other conceptions is not intelligible in light of the burdens of judgment. On the other hand, it refers to a conception which makes claims for itself and its adherents without regard to a fair balance between its claims and those made in behalf of other conceptions (pp. 49ff). I have argued elsewhere that these definitions of "unreasonable" can come apart.[23] Here, though, I want to suggest that one way of defining "unreasonable," in the second sense, is that it characterizes any comprehensive conception, C_i, that has lived with other conceptions in *modus vivendi* for some time *without* being willing to abandon (or allow to wither away) its own tendentious theory of justice, J_i.

IX.

What I have just set out are some ideas on how we might think about the relation between disagreements about the good and disagreements about justice towards the end of the era or phase in which disagreement about justice remains a reasonable possibility.

However, these fascinating speculations about the withering away of reasonable disagreement about justice in a well-ordered society should not blind us to the fact that full-blooded disagreement about justice remains the most striking condition of our own politics. In these circumstances, we should be very careful about inferring anything for our politics—including our constitutional jurisprudence—from the purely theoretical possibility of a well-ordered society as John Rawls understands it. Because it may encourage or license such inferences, the argument in *Political Liberalism* needs to be hedged around with serious reservations and qualifications. Students of political philosophy need to be made aware of how much distance there is between the sort of theorizing about justice that goes on in works like *Political Liberalism* and the sort of theorizing that would be necessary if we were really to try making sense of the place that politics, process and constitution have in a society like our own.

Notes

[1] All page references in the text are to John Rawls, *Political Liberalism* (New York: Columbia University Press, 1993).

[2] See, e.g., *Political Liberalism*, op. cit., p. 134.

[3] As Rawls initially presents it, the idea of the burdens of judgment does have a political orientation. He says the burdens affect not only our estimation of the place that various ends and values have in our own way of life (p. 56), but also our assessment of the claims others might make against us. The latter is certainly an issue for the theory of justice.

[4] An arguable exception is a passage towards the end of Lecture IV ("The Idea of an Overlapping Consensus") in which Rawls hazards the suggestion that "different social and economic interests may be assumed to support different liberal conceptions" and to "give rise to ideals and principles markedly different from those of justice as fairness" (p. 167). He does not however dwell on this possibility.

[5] That is, Rawls seems to be committed to saying:
For all areas of dispute x, the existence of the burdens of judgment in x -> the lack of public reason in x.
From which it would follow:
For all areas of dispute x, the existence of public reason in x -> the absence of the burdens of judgment in x.

[6] That is not all we are trying to sort out, of course, For of course our most important question is: which is the better conception to govern the basic structure of society? However, I believe it is part of Rawls's general commitment to liberal principles (such as publicity or transparency) that the conception which governs the basic structure and the conception which sets the terms for public reason should be one and the same.

[7] See section VI. below.

[8] John Rawls, *A Theory of Justice* (Cambridge: Harvard University Press, 1971).

[9] Ibid., p. 198–99.

[10] Ibid., p. 196.

[11] Ibid., p. 197. (The ellipsis indicates the presence of an additional criterion of constitutional choice: the chosen constitution must not only be effective in yielding just choices, but it must also in itself do justice to those procedural rights—such as equal political participation—embodied in the first of the two substantive principles of JAF.)

[12] Ibid., p. 198.

[13] Idem.

[14] Cf. ibid., pp. 8–9.

[15] For an argument that American justifications of the judicial review of legislation commonly rest on a grave underestimation of the extent and character of political disagreement about rights and justice, see Jeremy Waldron, 'A Right-Based Critique of Constitutional Rights,' *Oxford Journal of Legal Studies*, 13 (1993), pp. 18–51.

[16] Ronald Dworkin, 'Rights as Trumps,' in Jeremy Waldron (ed.) *Theories of Rights* (Oxford: Oxford University Press, 1984), pp. 155–56.

[17] Rawls himself believed that it is an objection to utilitarianism that it is precisely *not* scrupulous in this way about which preferences it accommodates. See Rawls, *A Theory of Justice*, op. cit., pp. 30–31.

[18] Rawls insists throughout *Political Liberalism* that the appropriate thing to say in accepting JAF is not that it is "true" (and other views "false") but that it is "reasonable." (See *Political Liberalism*, pp. xx and 116.) The view attributed to him in the text is then the following: one cannot be expected to accommodate views that one regards as *unreasonable* within a framework defined by the only set of principles that can be regarded as reasonable.

[19] It might also be a grave mistake in thinking about *law*. If I understand him correctly in *Law's Empire*, Ronald Dworkin argues that one does not take law seriously unless one is willing to contemplate the possibility that some past political decisions have been based on views about justice other than one's own. To take law seriously is to be willing, in some circumstances, to keep faith with the tenor of past injustice. This is what law-as-integrity means and requires. When Dworkin says that "[W]e are all in politics together for better or worse, [and] that no one may be sacrificed, like wounded left on the battlefield, to the

crusade for justice overall," it is clear in context that "no one" means "no view about how society should be organized." See Ronald Dworkin, *Law's Empire* (Cambridge: Harvard University Press, 1986), p. 213. This is intriguing, in contrast to the view of Dworkin's excerpted above in the text. In that passage, however, Dworkin is talking about the internal workings of utilitarianism *as a theory of justice*. In the passage presently under discussion— in this footnote—Dworkin is talking about law and legality, which for him deal with aspects of a society's life that arise from the fact that people disagree about justice. See also Jeremy Waldron, "The Circumstances of Integrity," forthcoming in *Ronald Dworkin's Political Philosophy*, edited by Justine Burley (Basil Blackwell, 1995).

[20] See Rawls, *Political Liberalism*, p. 66. See also Rawls, *A Theory of Justice*, pp. 126–30. I have said a little more about this idea of "the circumstances of politics" in "Freeman's Defence of Judicial Review," *Law and Philosophy*, 13 (1994), 27, at pp. 34–35.

[21] In much the same way, Rawls is not required to say that justice matters *more* than the values implicated in one's favorite comprehensive conception; instead he should say that in thinking about justice we are proceeding along a different dimension of priority. (See Rawls, *Political Liberalism*, op. cit., pp. 156–58.)

[22] I should clarify this point. *Modus vivendi* and overlapping consensus are competing models of the many-to-one relation that might exist as between various conceptions of the good and a single conception of justice. The models set out at the start of this paper, by contrast, are models of the many-to-*many* relation between various conceptions of the good and various conceptions (plural) of justice.

[23] See Jeremy Waldron, "Justice Revisited" (A Review of Rawls, *Political Liberalism*), *The Times Literary Supplement*, 18 June 1993, pp. 5–6. Militant Islam provides an example of a comprehensive conception whose claims are (arguably) not unreasonable in light of the burdens of judgment but quite unreasonable in the sense of openness to accommodation with other conceptions.

The Appeal of Political Liberalism*

Samuel Scheffler

The appeal of liberalism derives to a considerable extent from its commitment to tolerating diverse ways of life and schemes of value. Yet this same commitment is also responsible for much of what is puzzling about liberalism. For what is the basis of liberal toleration? One answer rests the case for toleration on a pluralistic understanding of the nature of human value, on a conviction that the realm of value is irreducibly heterogeneous. Diverse ways of life should be tolerated, on this view, because they are routes to the realization of diverse human goods. A very different answer rests the case for tolerance on a general skepticism about value, on a conviction that there is no good sense to be made of the idea of objective value or the notion of a good life. On this view, diverse ways of life should be tolerated because there is nothing to the thought that some ways of life are better than others, and so there is no legitimate basis for *in*tolerance.

If the case for liberal toleration rests on some pluralistic thesis about the nature of human values, then both the depth of such toleration and the extent of its appeal seem called into question. For, inevitably, the pluralistic thesis will itself be controversial. Thus, on this interpretation, liberalism's professed toleration of differing conceptions of value turns out to depend on a more fundamental commitment to a particular conception of value, a conception which will be uncongenial or even abhorrent to some of the very evaluative outlooks that liberalism purports to tolerate, and which will not, therefore, serve to recommend liberal institutions to people who share those outlooks. Much the same will be true, it seems, if toleration is seen as the outgrowth of skepticism rather

* This essay is a slightly revised version of a paper presented at the Third Annual Philosophy Conference at the University of California, Riverside, on May 1, 1993. I am indebted to those present on that occasion for helpful discussion, and especially to David Gill, who raised the question that prompted most of the revisions in the present version. I am also indebted to John Rawls for illuminating discussion of his work over a period of many years.

Ethics 105 (October 1994): 4–22

than pluralism about value. For skepticism no less than pluralism represents a controversial understanding of the nature of values.

The most obvious way of defending liberal toleration, apart from the two just mentioned, is as a modus vivendi, a strategic compromise among contending social groups, none of whom is in a position to impose its preferred way of life on the others without intolerable cost, and each of whom therefore accepts a policy of mutual tolerance as the best that it can hope to achieve under the circumstances. That it will sometimes be possible to make a strong case for liberal toleration on pragmatic grounds of this sort seems hard to deny. Historically, the role played by such considerations has often been crucial. Yet a defense of toleration that rests entirely on pragmatic grounds seems unable to account for the moral appeal of the idea of tolerance, and, in any case, it retains its force only so long as the necessary balance of power in society is preserved. If one group gains enough strength that a policy of intolerance comes to seem tempting, the pragmatic argument provides no reason to resist the temptation.

The need to understand the basis of liberal toleration has taken on a renewed urgency at this historical moment. The liberal societies of the west are beset by a host of social problems whose source, according to many critics, lies ultimately in a culture of individualism and a breakdown of communal values for which liberal thought itself is responsible. While the tendency of this criticism is to suggest a need for greater social unity and cohesion, the very idea of a liberal society as a single national community with a common culture is also under attack, as such societies, with their increasingly diversified populations, struggle to come to terms with their own histories of exclusion and to accommodate the claims of "multiculturalism." In this context, it is more important than ever to arrive at a clear understanding of the basis of liberal toleration. More generally, liberalism needs to understand how it is to conceive of its relations to the diverse ways of life and forms of culture that characterize modern societies. The importance of this project of liberal self-understanding, as I shall refer to it, is only intensified by the need for liberal societies to orient themselves both in relation to those other societies, in Eastern Europe and elsewhere, that are struggling to establish liberal institutions for the first time, and in relation to societies like Iran, whose fundamentalist character presents a radical challenge to liberal thought.

John Rawls's book *Political Liberalism* constitutes a major contribution to this project of liberal self-understanding.[1] Rawls offers us a new way of thinking about the basis of liberal toleration. His "political

1. John Rawls, *Political Liberalism* (New York: Columbia University Press, 1993). Page references to this book will be given parenthetically in the text.

liberalism" addresses itself to the following question: "How is it possible for there to exist over time a just and stable society of free and equal citizens who still remain profoundly divided by reasonable religious, philosophical, and moral doctrines?" (p. 47). The core of political liberalism's answer to this question is that for such a society to be possible, its basic structure must be "effectively regulated by a political conception of justice that is the focus of an overlapping consensus of at least the reasonable comprehensive doctrines affirmed by its citizens" (p. 48). To understand this answer, obviously, we need to understand what is meant by notions like a "political conception of justice" and an "overlapping consensus."

To begin, we know from *A Theory of Justice* that a conception of justice is a "set of principles for assigning basic rights and duties and for determining . . . the proper distribution of the benefits and burdens of social cooperation."[2] A political conception of justice, Rawls now tells us, is one that has "three characteristic features" (p. 11). First, it is a moral conception, but "a moral conception worked out for a specific kind of subject" (p. 11), namely, for the "basic structure" of society, by which Rawls means a society's main social, political, and economic institutions. Second, a political conception of justice "is presented as a freestanding view" (p. 12). This means that "it is neither presented as, nor as derived from, [a comprehensive moral] doctrine applied to the basic structure of society, as if this structure were simply another subject to which that doctrine applied" (p. 12). Rather, a political conception "is a module, an essential constituent part, that fits into and can be supported by various reasonable comprehensive doctrines that endure in the society regulated by it" (p. 12). Third, the content of a political conception of justice "is expressed in terms of certain fundamental ideas seen as implicit in the public political culture of a democratic society" (p. 13). The suggestion here is that despite the diversity of people's comprehensive moral doctrines, there may be certain fundamental ideas implicit in a society's culture and institutions that command widespread agreement. A political conception of justice is one that is developed on the basis of this common ground.

If a political conception of justice can indeed be derived solely from ideas that are latent in the public political culture, then it may become the object of an "overlapping consensus." That is, it may be accepted by people who affirm very different comprehensive moral doctrines, because all of these people accept, albeit for different reasons, the fundamental ideas that function, in effect, as premises in the argument for the conception of justice. In an overlapping consensus,

2. John Rawls, *A Theory of Justice* (Cambridge, Mass.: Harvard University Press, 1971), p. 5.

Rawls writes, "the reasonable [comprehensive] doctrines endorse the political conception, each from its own point of view. Social unity is based on a consensus on the political conception; and stability is possible when the doctrines making up the consensus are affirmed by society's politically active citizens and the requirements of justice are not too much in conflict with citizens' essential interests as formed and encouraged by their social arrangements" (p. 134).

Not only will people's reasons for accepting the political conception vary, depending on which comprehensive moral doctrine they affirm, but in addition, different comprehensive moral doctrines may stand in different relations to the political conception. For example, some comprehensive doctrines may provide the political conception with a deductive basis, while others may provide reasons of other kinds for accepting it. Rawls says that "the point to stress here is that . . . citizens individually decide for themselves in what way the public political conception all affirm is related to their own more comprehensive views" (p. 38). What matters, he writes, is that "citizens themselves, within the exercise of their liberty of thought and conscience, and looking to their comprehensive doctrines, view the political conception as derived from, or congruent with, or at least not in conflict with, their other values" (p. 11).

These ideas enable Rawls to offer a model of liberal pluralism and toleration that represents an alternative to the three I canvassed at the outset. Like the model of liberalism as a modus vivendi, Rawls's model treats with utmost seriousness the deep differences in people's values and ways of life, and the potential for deadly conflict arising out of those differences. Yet, as he insists, the overlapping consensus that he envisions is not itself a mere modus vivendi. For, first, the object of the consensus is not just a set of institutional arrangements but is, rather, a moral conception, a conception of justice. And, second, all those who participate in the consensus accept that conception for moral reasons of one sort or another. As Rawls says, "All those who affirm the political conception start from within their own comprehensive view and draw on the religious, philosophical, and moral grounds it provides. The fact that people affirm the same political conception on those grounds does not make their affirming it any less religious, philosophical, or moral, as the case may be, since the grounds sincerely held determine the nature of their affirmation" (pp. 147–48). Because of these two differences between an overlapping consensus and a modus vivendi, there will also, Rawls says, be a third difference. An overlapping consensus will enjoy greater stability than a modus vivendi, because the commitment to the political conception of those who participate in the consensus is based on moral considerations rather than calculations of self or group interest and hence is not liable to be undermined by changes in the balance of power within the society. One's moral reasons for accepting the political conception are not weakened by an increase in one's power that would make it easier to press for a more advantageous set of institutional arrangements.

In a sense, then, Rawls's explanation of the basis of liberal toleration, if successful, may manage to combine the advantages of an appeal to a modus vivendi with those of an appeal to a pluralistic conception of value, while avoiding the pitfalls of either. Like the explanation in terms of a modus vivendi and unlike the one in terms of a pluralistic conception of value, Rawls combines respect for the facts of disagreement and diversity with a reluctance to rely on any controversial moral premises. However, like the explanation in terms of a pluralistic conception of value and unlike the one in terms of a modus vivendi, Rawls represents citizens as having moral reasons for their allegiance to the structures of toleration and the institutions of the liberal society. His aim, in other words, is to provide liberal institutions with a basis in moral reasons, without himself presupposing any controversial and contentious moral outlook. This aspiration is descended from Rawls's earlier aspiration, in *A Theory of Justice,* to derive a substantive conception of justice from the set of putatively "weak and widely shared" conditions and constraints that make up the original position. If Rawls can succeed in achieving his newer aim, then the earlier one is also vindicated, at least in part. For the notion of an overlapping consensus on fundamental ideas implicit in the public political culture supplies new content for the claim that the original position—construed now as a device for representing certain of those fundamental ideas—is made up of weak and widely shared assumptions.

Thus, from the standpoint of the project of liberal self-understanding, the potential advantages of "political liberalism" seem clear. Ultimately, however, the appeal of the view must depend, at least in part, on whether an overlapping consensus on something like Rawls's political conception of justice is a realistic possibility. In chapter 4 of *Political Liberalism,* Rawls offers what he calls "a model case" of such a consensus:

> It contains three views: one affirms the political conception because its religious doctrine and account of free faith lead to a principle of toleration and underwrite the fundamental liberties of a constitutional regime; while the second view affirms the political conception on the basis of a comprehensive liberal moral doctrine such as those of Kant or Mill. The third . . . is not systematically unified: besides the political values formulated by a freestanding political conception of justice, it includes a large family of nonpolitical values. It is a pluralist view, let us say, since each subpart of this family has its own account based on ideas drawn from within it, leaving all values to be balanced against one another, either in groups or singly, in particular kinds of cases. [P. 145]

By itself, this model case does little to encourage the thought that an overlapping consensus on Rawlsian principles could actually be achieved in a society like ours. For the three views it contains are not fully representative of the diverse schemes of value one finds in modern liberal societies; instead, all three appear to be drawn from the same relatively narrow portion of the broad spectrum of evaluative conviction. Although it seems plausible enough that these three views might converge on a liberal conception of justice, that tells us little about the prospects for a more inclusive consensus.

Later in chapter 4, Rawls presents a modified version of this model case which also includes classical utilitarianism. "This utilitarianism," he writes, "supports the political conception for such reasons as our limited knowledge of social institutions generally and on our knowledge about ongoing circumstances. It stresses further the bounds on complexity of legal and institutional rules as well as the simplicity necessary in guidelines for public reason. These and other reasons may lead the utilitarian to think a political conception of justice liberal in content a satisfactory, perhaps even the best, workable approximation to what the principle of utility, all things tallied up, would require" (p. 170).

Although the inclusion of classical utilitarianism serves to broaden the range of outlooks contained in the model consensus, and although its explicit purpose is just to illustrate the point that the different comprehensive doctrines represented in an overlapping consensus may stand in different relations to the political conception on which they converge, it is in some ways a puzzling addition. Rawls emphasizes that an overlapping consensus is a consensus not just on principles of justice but also on the fundamental ideas implicit in the public political culture from which those principles are derivable (p. 149). Indeed, what makes an overlapping consensus on a political conception of justice possible is precisely the fact that the political conception is developed from shared ideas. Accordingly, the original position is now to be construed as modeling certain of those shared ideas, and Rawls's arguments to the effect that his principles would be chosen in the original position are to be interpreted as beginning from those ideas. Yet many of these arguments are explicitly directed against utilitarianism. If utilitarianism is said to be included in the overlapping consensus on Rawls's two principles, then are we to imagine that utilitarians endorse Rawls's arguments for the rejection of utilitarianism even as they continue to affirm that view? This seems incoherent.

Moreover, even the fundamental ideas from which the arguments for the two principles proceed, and which the original position helps to model, are ideas which, according to Rawls himself, utilitarianism does not accept. For example, the "fundamental organizing idea" to which Rawls appeals is "that of society as a fair system of social cooperation between free and equal persons viewed as fully cooperating members of society over a complete life" (p. 9). Crucial to this idea of fair cooperation is said to be a notion of reciprocity, according to which "all who are engaged in cooperation and who do their part as the rules and procedures require, are to benefit in an appropriate way as assessed by a suitable benchmark of comparison" (p. 16). Yet in *A Theory of Justice* Rawls tells us that "the principle of utility is incompatible with the conception of social cooperation among equals for mutual advantage. It appears to be inconsistent with the idea of reciprocity implicit in the notion of a well-ordered society."[3] Elaborating on this point, he writes: "Implicit in the contrasts between classical utilitarianism and justice as fairness is a difference in the underlying conceptions of society. In the one we think of a well-ordered society as a scheme of cooperation for reciprocal advantage regulated by principles which persons would choose in an initial situation that is fair, in the other as the efficient administration of social resources to maximize the satisfaction of the system of desire constructed by the impartial spectator from the many individual systems of desires accepted as given."[4] If this is right, then it really is quite unclear how utilitarianism can be included in an overlapping consensus on Rawls's principles of justice, since it rejects the fundamental ideas that serve as premises in the arguments for those principles, as well as the arguments themselves.

Of course, as Rawls says, a utilitarian might conclude that, "given normal social conditions" (p. 171), Rawls's two principles represent "a satisfactory, perhaps even the best, workable approximation to what the principle of utility, all things tallied up, would require" (p. 170). The question is whether such a conclusion would be sufficient for utilitarianism to be included in an overlapping consensus, if it is also committed to rejecting the fundamental ideas from which Rawls's principles are derived as well as the arguments used to derive them. Moreover, the precise content and spirit of the imagined utilitarian conclusion are less clear than they may initially appear. We may recall that in *A Theory of Justice* Rawls considers two possible attitudes a utilitarian might take toward apparently nonutilitarian principles of justice. On the one hand, some utilitarians may say that "common sense precepts of justice and notions of natural right have but a subordinate validity as secondary rules; they arise from the fact that under the conditions of civilized society there is great social utility in following them for the most part and in permitting violations of them only under exceptional circumstances."[5] Rawls's project in *A Theory of Justice* is to a large extent

3. Ibid., p. 14.
4. Ibid., p. 33.
5. Ibid., p. 28.

motivated by the conviction that this attitude does not accord sufficient primacy to the principles of justice. On the other hand, a utilitarian might, Rawls suggests, argue that utility will actually be maximized if Rawls's two principles are "publicly affirmed and realized as the basis of the social structure."[6] However, Rawls maintains, such an argument would be tantamount to conceding the inadequacy of utilitarianism. For the publicity condition means that utilitarianism must be "defined" as "the view that the principle of utility is the correct principle for society's public conception of justice."[7] In other words, Rawls says, "what we want to know is which conception of justice characterizes our considered judgments in reflective equilibrium and best serves as the public moral basis of society. Unless one maintains that this conception is given by the principle of utility, one is not a utilitarian."[8] The upshot is that of the two possible attitudes that a utilitarian might take toward nonutilitarian principles of justice, the first represents too weak a form of endorsement, while the second is tantamount to the abandonment of utilitarianism. Thus neither attitude provides a model of how a committed utilitarian might genuinely affirm Rawls's principles as part of an overlapping consensus, and this only reinforces the doubts already mentioned about whether utilitarianism could indeed be included in such a consensus.

Even if it could, the question of how widespread a consensus on Rawls's principles of justice might realistically be achieved would remain. For a stable overlapping consensus in a society like ours would require the inclusion not only of fully articulated philosophical theories like utilitarianism but also of the many moral, religious, and broadly philosophical outlooks actually endorsed by citizens in our society. A stable overlapping consensus, one might say, must be a consensus of citizens, not of theories. Rawls recognizes this, and in chapter 4 of *Political Liberalism*, he tries to turn the point to his advantage. He argues, in effect, that in judging the prospects of an overlapping consensus on his conception of justice, it is a mistake to focus exclusively on committed partisans of fully articulated philosophical theories with clearly recognized implications for the justice of the basic structure of society. For most citizens do not hold any fully articulated and fully comprehensive moral doctrine. What they may well have instead is a loose network of values and convictions of varying degrees of generality, whose implications concerning Rawls's principles may or may not be clear to them. However, many of these people, having been raised in a liberal society, will have internalized the fundamental

---

6. Ibid., p. 181.
7. Ibid., p. 182.
8. Ibid.

idea of society as a fair system of cooperation on which Rawls's political conception rests and will have developed a strong allegiance to broadly liberal values and institutions. Indeed, rather than accepting liberal ideas as the consequence of their comprehensive moral doctrine, they may instead allow their commitment to a liberal order to shape the rest of their values. For example, they may find themselves shaping their understanding of their faith to render it consistent with such an order—perhaps emphasizing those strands in their tradition that lend support to tolerance and downplaying those that conflict with it. If this is correct, and if Rawls can in fact elaborate his conception of justice solely on the basis of ideas implicit in the public political culture of a liberal society, then such people may have strong reasons to affirm that conception. As Rawls puts it, "the comprehensive doctrines of most people are not fully comprehensive, and this allows scope for the development of an independent allegiance to the political conception that helps to bring about a consensus" (p. 168).

Although this argument has some force, there is an important ambiguity in Rawls's account of the sort of overlapping consensus he envisions, and this ambiguity affects the plausibility of his position. Recall that in an overlapping consensus, what people are said to affirm is a political conception of justice. And "a distinguishing feature of a political conception is that it is presented as freestanding" (p. 12), that is, as independent of any comprehensive moral doctrine. Now this suggests two puzzles. First, by whom must a conception be presented as freestanding in order to count as political? One possibility is that Rawls's presentation of his own conception is authoritative, so that that conception is political because *he* presents it as freestanding. But then, in order to know whether a given conception of justice is political we must be able to identify its authoritative presentation. What, for example, is the authoritative presentation of utilitarianism? Another possibility is that conceptions of justice are to be individuated partly by features of their presentation. Thus if you argue for Rawls's conception of justice by appealing to your comprehensive moral doctrine and I argue for it as a freestanding view, we are actually arguing for two different conceptions of justice, one political and the other not. But this seems needlessly confusing and potentially misleading, and in any case, it is a peculiar position to take if one is attempting to emphasize the possibility of consensus—to explain how people with divergent moral outlooks may nevertheless converge on a particular conception of justice. Still another interpretation is suggested when Rawls remarks at one point that what is characteristic of a political conception is only "that it *can* be presented without saying, or knowing, or hazarding a conjecture about, what . . . [comprehensive] doctrines it may belong to, or be supported by" (pp. 12–13; emphasis added). This leaves open the possibility that all conceptions of justice may be political, if all of them *can* be "presented as" freestanding. (How plausible would the presentations have to be?)

None of these three options seems to me especially attractive. It might be less confusing and more illuminating to use the adjective 'political' to describe arguments for conceptions of justice rather than the conceptions themselves. A political argument for a conception of justice would be one that appealed to ideas implicit in the public political culture, whereas a nonpolitical argument, say, would be one that appealed to a comprehensive moral doctrine. Thus one and the same conception of justice might in principle be supported by arguments of either type. Rawls might then be interpreted as asserting not that his conception of justice is a political conception but, rather, that his arguments for that conception are political arguments. And political liberalism might be construed as comprising two theses: first, that given the pluralistic character of modern societies, a just and stable order is possible only if the basic structure of society is effectively regulated by a conception of justice that is the focus of an overlapping consensus and, second, that the possibility of an overlapping consensus on a particular conception of justice is signaled by the availability of persuasive political arguments for that conception.

There is, however, a second and deeper puzzle underlying the one just mentioned, and it concerns the attitude that participants in an overlapping consensus are expected to have toward the "political conception of justice" on which they converge. In particular, the question is whether participation in such a consensus requires that one *regard* the conception of justice as a "political conception": that is, as a "freestanding" conception whose content "is expressed in terms of certain fundamental ideas seen as implicit in the public political culture of a democratic society." We know, in other words, that the participants in an overlapping consensus accept certain principles of justice as well as certain fundamental ideas implicit in the public political culture from which those principles are derivable. The question is whether they themselves also think of the principles as being expressed in terms of what they take to be ideas implicit in the public political culture, and as capable of being derived independently of any particular comprehensive moral doctrine. On the face of it, it would appear unwise to make this a requirement for participation in an overlapping consensus. For the more things that people must believe in order to be included in such a consensus, the more difficult it will be for a consensus actually to be achieved. In other words, if participation in the consensus requires affirmation not only of a particular set of principles of justice but also of certain metatheses about the status of those principles, then, other things equal, one would expect the consensus to include fewer people. Furthermore, Rawls's whole reason for drawing our attention to the possibility of an overlapping consensus is to suggest that people may affirm the same principles of justice even though they view these principles in very different ways, depending on which comprehensive moral doctrine they accept. Thus any requirement that the participants in an overlapping consensus must view the conception of justice as political would appear to be incongruous with the motivation for introducing the idea of such a consensus in the first place.

Suppose, for example, that someone—call her Jane—accepts Rawls's two principles of justice because she believes them to be implied by her comprehensive moral doctrine, which we may suppose to be some version of what Rawls calls "comprehensive liberalism." Jane does not, let us assume, think of the two principles as constituting a freestanding conception of justice, nor does she characterize them as such when she is explaining or defending them to others. Rather, she presents them to others as she herself conceives of them, namely, as derived from a certain comprehensive moral outlook. And although she recognizes that the two principles may be seen as giving expression to the idea of society as a fair system of cooperation, it does not occur to her to think of that idea as implicit in the public political culture; still less does she see the fact that it is implicit in the culture as crucial to its justificatory role. The importance to her of the idea of society as a fair system of cooperation derives instead from its relation to the ideal of "ethical autonomy" (pp. 77–78) that is at the core of her comprehensive doctrine. Yet Jane is, we may suppose, a sincere and indeed committed advocate of the two principles of justice and, as such, she is of course a staunch defender of the right of other people to affirm and defend comprehensive moral doctrines other than her own. If, by virtue of her failure to conceive of the two principles as amounting to a political conception of justice, a person like Jane does not qualify for inclusion in an overlapping consensus, then surely the prospects of achieving a widespread consensus are open to serious doubt. Moreover, to exclude Jane would seem inconsistent with the motivation for introducing the idea of an overlapping consensus to begin with.

Nevertheless, Rawls does at times appear to require that the participants in an overlapping consensus regard the conception of justice as political. He writes, for example, that "citizens are to conduct their fundamental discussions within the framework of what each regards as a political conception of justice based on values that the others can reasonably be expected to endorse and each is, in good faith, prepared to defend that conception so understood" (p. 226). Rawls makes this claim in the context of his discussion of "the idea of public reason." This idea arises because, Rawls believes, "it is essential that a liberal political conception include, besides its principles of justice, guidelines of inquiry that specify ways of reasoning and criteria for the kinds of information relevant for political questions" (p. 223). He therefore maintains that "the parties in the original position, in adopting principles of justice for the basic structure, must also adopt guidelines and criteria of public reason for applying those norms" (p. 225). These guidelines and criteria are to specify the modes of reasoning that may be used and the types of considerations that may be appealed to in discussing and resolving political questions in a society regulated by the principles of justice. They impose constraints on acceptable forms of political argument, constraints that Rawls refers to as "the limits of public reason." These limits hold not only for public officials but also for "citizens when they engage in political advocacy in the public forum, and thus for members of political parties and for candidates in their campaigns and for other groups who support them" (p. 215). Indeed, the limits govern "how citizens are to vote" (p. 215), at least when "the most fundamental political questions" are at stake (p. 216). Among the most important of the constraints imposed by the limits of public reason is that "in discussing constitutional essentials and matters of basic justice we are not to appeal to comprehensive religious and philosophical doctrines—to what we as individuals or members of associations see as the whole truth" (pp. 224–25). In other words, the limits of public reason tell us that we are "to conduct our fundamental discussions in terms of what we regard as a political conception. We should sincerely think that our view of the matter is based on political values everyone can reasonably be expected to endorse" (p. 241).

Rawls's discussion of public reason raises a variety of questions. For one thing, it seems puzzling to suggest that the parties in the original position adopt guidelines that specify, among other things, that we are "to conduct our fundamental discussions in terms of what we regard as a political conception" of justice. For the idea of a political conception of justice is not one that is obviously available to the parties in the original position. What makes Rawls's conception political is the fact that it is elaborated on the basis of fundamental ideas that are implicit in the public political culture. The function of the parties in the original position is to help model certain of those fundamental ideas, not to endorse them or to argue from them to something the parties regard as a political conception. In other words, the parties' sole concern is to choose a conception of justice that will maximize their share of primary social goods. They do not themselves decide that they want a political conception of justice based on ideas implicit in the public political culture; rather, the fact that they model such ideas means that *we* have reason to regard the principles they select as having the status of a political conception.

More generally, the idea that the parties in the original position adopt "guidelines of inquiry" which include "principles of reasoning and rules of evidence" (p. 224) requires further explanation. Rawls says that the "argument for those guidelines . . . is much the same as, and as strong as, the argument for the principles of justice themselves" (p. 225). Perhaps so; but in the case of the guidelines, the array of options from which the parties choose and the basis of their choice require further elaboration. Moreover, there is the following difference between the choice of such guidelines and the choice of principles of justice. In order to make their choice among rival conceptions of justice, the parties do not themselves need to employ any particular conception of justice. If they did, the justificatory force of their choice would be open to serious doubt. In choosing among candidate principles of reasoning and methods of inquiry, however, the parties must already be employing certain methods of reasoning and modes of inquiry, which are given by stipulation as part of the original position construction. Thus, in the absence of some further explanation of the relation between the methods of inquiry the parties employ and the methods of inquiry they adopt, there is a danger that any choice they make will appear question begging.

For present purposes, however, what is most striking about Rawls's discussion of public reason is how emphatically it serves to reinforce the concern that by requiring the participants in an overlapping consensus to conceive of the conception of justice they endorse as political, Rawls risks undermining the plausibility of the idea that an overlapping consensus might actually be achieved. The principle that ordinary citizens, when engaged in political advocacy and even when voting, must appeal only to what they regard as a political conception of justice and never to their own comprehensive moral doctrines is an extraordinarily strong one. Accordingly, it seems much harder to envision a wide variety of comprehensive doctrines converging on this principle of public reason in addition to the two principles of justice than it does to envision them converging on the principles of justice alone. Indeed, the plausibility of this putative principle of public reason is open to serious challenge. For it does not seem difficult to think of instances in our own society in which people have appealed to comprehensive moral doctrines in ways that many would regard as appropriate, or at least not inappropriate. Toward the end of his discussion of public reason, Rawls himself considers the examples of the abolitionists and of Martin Luther King, Jr., and in the face of these examples he modifies his principle to allow that citizens may in certain circumstances appeal to their comprehensive doctrines if this is necessary to strengthen the ideal of public reason itself. But there are many other examples that could be cited in addition to the two that Rawls mentions: such as the religiously inspired opposition of Quakers and others to the war in Vietnam; the religiously motivated opposition of many people to capital punishment; the central role traditionally played by black churches in the political life of the African-American community; the opposition by certain religious denominations to United States policies in Central America during the 1980s and the associated movement to provide sanctuary in churches for Central American refugees; and the religiously based advocacy of policies to eliminate homelessness and poverty. Note, moreover, that all of the examples I have cited are instances in which comprehensive religious doctrines have been drawn on in the context of public political advocacy, in ways generally congenial to the political left. If we broaden our horizons to include nonreligious appeals to moral principles, to include citizens' reasons for voting as well as the content of their public advocacy, and to include positions taken across a wider range of the political spectrum, then the number of examples will only multiply. The idea that in all such examples the reliance on a comprehensive moral or religious doctrine must either be necessary to strengthen the ideal of public reason or else unjustified seems highly questionable. And in any event, the availability of so many examples does nothing to enhance the plausibility of the idea that an overlapping consensus might actually converge not only on Rawls's two principles of justice but also on the guidelines of public reason as he describes them.

Given the contentiousness of some of Rawls's claims about the limits of public reason, and given that their effect is also to make the achievement of an overlapping consensus seem less likely, it is natural to wonder how important it is for Rawls's purposes to insist on those claims. In an attempt to ascertain this, let us imagine a society in which an overlapping consensus on Rawls's two principles of justice has actually been achieved and in which a constitution consistent with those two principles has been adopted. Let us further suppose, however, that citizens in this society view the status of the two principles in different ways, depending on their comprehensive moral doctrines. Thus there is no consensus on the proposition that the two principles of justice constitute a political conception, still less on the proposition that citizens are to conduct their discussion of constitutional essentials and basic justice in terms of what they regard as a political conception. Despite the absence of consensus on these two points, the constitution of the society guarantees the basic rights and liberties of all citizens, in accordance with the principles of justice, and this excludes any attempt to use the coercive power of the state to enforce a particular comprehensive doctrine. Similarly, any attempt to deny basic justice to some people in the name of a particular comprehensive doctrine is ruled out. Moreover, since all citizens, by hypothesis, affirm that the two principles are to regulate the basic structure of their society, they all regard those principles as the "final court of appeal for ordering the conflicting claims of moral persons."[9] Thus it is to the two

9. Ibid., p. 135.

principles, rather than their own comprehensive moral doctrines, that citizens naturally appeal when discussing constitutional essentials and matters of basic justice. In addition, citizens are aware of the existence both of widespread agreement on the principles of justice and of widespread disagreement in people's comprehensive moral doctrines. This awareness, when coupled with the commitment to mutual respect that is implied by citizens' common affirmation of the two principles, gives rise to an ethos of restraint, a reluctance on the part of many citizens to appeal in the public arena to their own comprehensive moral doctrines. After all, the fact that they are in agreement about the principles to regulate the basic structure of their society is what matters for fundamental political purposes, and, we may suppose, they have no need and little desire to alienate those they respect by insisting on divisive moral or religious claims.

The upshot of this discussion is that some limits of public reason may be a consequence of, and still others may be encouraged by, the existence of an overlapping consensus on the two principles alone, without any need for citizens to conceive of those principles as a political conception of justice or to agree that they must conduct their discussion of fundamental political questions in terms of what they regard as a political conception. If this is correct, and if the requirement that citizens view the conception of justice as political has the disadvantages I have said it does, then Rawls may have little reason to insist on that requirement.

The point I have been trying to make may be put another way. One of Rawls's aims in *Political Liberalism,* if I understand him correctly, is to respond to those critics of his earlier work who charged that while purporting to offer a neutral and universal justification for his principles of justice, it rested tacitly but unmistakably on a liberal conception of value. In response, Rawls denies that his theory aspires to universal validity but also that it rests on any comprehensive conception of value. Instead, he argues, his theory is addressed to societies of a certain type at a particular historical moment. These societies have a tradition of democratic thought and constitutional interpretation but there exist within them deep disagreements about fundamental political questions and also a wide diversity of comprehensive moral and religious doctrines. Given these historical facts, there is a real question about how a shared and workable conception of justice for these societies can be arrived at. It is to this question that Rawls's theory is addressed, and his answer involves not the endorsement of a particular comprehensive doctrine but, rather, an attempt to bypass the disagreements among such doctrines. What he tries to do, as we know, is to identify certain bases of agreement that are implicit in the public political culture and which therefore represent common ground among the citizens of democratic societies. He then attempts to use these "fixed points" as premises in an argument for a conception of justice to which all or nearly all may be able to agree. This is what Rawls is trying to do: to argue from views that are widely shared in our culture to a definite conclusion about justice, thereby offering a conception of justice that may command widespread agreement despite the pluralism and disagreement that characterize our society. If his argument is successful, then the conception he identifies may serve as the object of an overlapping consensus among people who have different comprehensive moral doctrines and whose affirmation of the theory is therefore based ultimately on different reasons. In order to be successful, it is important that Rawls's argument be a "political" one: that is, that it rely as much as possible on shared ideas and avoid reliance on any comprehensive moral doctrine. However, if what I have been urging is correct, it is not important that the citizens who are included in the overlapping consensus should themselves think of Rawls's conception as political. Any requirement that they do so would make an overlapping consensus more difficult to achieve, would add little that is plausible to an adequate account of public reason, and would mandate a degree of metaethical uniformity that is incongruous with the motivation for introducing the idea of an overlapping consensus in the first place. For all of these reasons, such a requirement would weaken rather than strengthen Rawls's reply to his critics. Or so it seems to me.

This conclusion is not altered, incidentally, if we take into account the added complication that Rawls characterizes his conception of justice not only as political but also as constructivist. It is constructivist because its principles "may be represented as the outcome of a certain procedure of construction" (pp. 89–90). That is, the principles are constructed from ideas of society and the person via the device of the original position. A constructivist conception, Rawls says, neither asserts nor denies that its principles are true; it "does without the concept of truth" altogether (p. 94). Political constructivism, which is "part of" political liberalism, asserts instead that the constructivist conception is "reasonable for a constitutional regime" (p. 126). Although many citizens "may want to give the political conception a metaphysical foundation as part of their own comprehensive doctrine" (p. 126), political constructivism refrains from doing this and restricts itself to the claim that the conception is reasonable. "The advantage of staying within the reasonable," Rawls writes, "is that there can be but one true comprehensive doctrine, though . . . many reasonable ones. Once we accept the fact that reasonable pluralism is a permanent condition of public culture under free institutions, the idea of the reasonable is more suitable as part of the basis of public justification for a constitutional regime than the idea of moral truth. Holding a political conception as true, and for that reason alone the one suitable basis of public reason, is exclusive, even sectarian, and so likely to foster political division" (p. 129). The question, however, is who exactly is supposed to believe that "the idea of the reasonable is more suitable as part of the basis of public justification for a constitutional regime than the idea of moral truth." It is easy to see that there may be an advantage to Rawls in offering a purely constructivist argument for his principles—in asserting, that is, not that the principles are true but merely that their source in ideas implicit in the public political culture enables them to provide a reasonable basis of public justification. For if he can give people a reason to affirm his principles whether or not they accept the idea of moral truth, he maximizes the appeal of those principles and enhances the prospects of an overlapping consensus. He makes it possible, in other words, for people to agree on the principles even if they disagree about the metaphysical status of those principles. But if citizens are also required to agree that "the idea of the reasonable is more suitable as part of the basis of public justification . . . than the idea of moral truth," then Rawls risks squandering these very gains, for he is then insisting on a partial but nevertheless significant degree of uniformity in the way people regard his principles.

Up to this point, I have been exploring the appeal of political liberalism by examining the prospects for an overlapping consensus on a political conception of justice in a modern democratic society like our own. Before concluding, I want to take up one other issue that bears on the appeal of political liberalism, and this concerns the relevance of this form of liberalism for those societies whose traditions are not liberal or democratic. Thus I want to turn from political liberalism's domestic policy, as it were, to its foreign policy. As we have seen, Rawls's work as he now presents it is addressed to modern democratic societies at a certain historical moment. His political liberalism seeks to establish a liberal conception of justice on the basis of ideas that are implicit in the public political culture of such societies. If, however, political liberalism appeals in this way to the public political culture of democratic societies, then the justification of liberal principles and institutions that it offers appears to presuppose a society in which liberal values are already well entrenched. It is not clear that political liberalism provides any reason for establishing liberal institutions in societies that do not already have liberal traditions. Thus, to put it another way, it is not clear that political liberalism could ever provide the original justification for a society's liberal institutions. Liberal traditions and institutions must, it seems, precede political liberalism: that is, they must already exist in order to create the conditions that make possible the sort of justification offered by political liberalism. This is not merely a historical problem; it raises doubts about whether political liberalism has anything to offer to those aspiring democracies in Eastern Europe and elsewhere that have no liberal traditions and whose public political cultures therefore lack the implicit ideas to which Rawls appeals. If in fact political liberalism has nothing to offer such societies, then its defense of liberal principles and institutions may seem intolerably weak. In renouncing any universalistic ambitions, Rawls may now seem to have gone too far in the other direction and to have produced a version of liberalism that is so historically specific and so dependent on a prior history of liberal institutions as to be of little relevance in those situations where the justification of liberalism matters most: that is, where liberalism is confronted by, and must engage with, societies whose traditions and practices are not liberal.

In a recent essay titled "The Law of Peoples," Rawls makes clear that his defense of liberalism does not in fact aspire to the kind of universality that some liberals would prefer.[10] In that lecture, he attempts to develop what he calls a "liberal law of peoples," which applies even to societies that are not themselves liberal. Yet he also makes it clear that this law does not require nonliberal societies to become liberal. On the contrary, Rawls argues that "not all regimes can be reasonably required to be liberal," and that a society that is not liberal may nevertheless be "well ordered and just."[11] Rawls's development of the law of peoples raises many questions that I cannot pursue here. For present purposes, however, what is noteworthy is that it appears to confirm the suspicion that Rawls's justification of liberal institutions is limited in certain striking ways. Political liberalism makes no general claim about the superiority of liberal over nonliberal societies, nor does it provide arguments as to why heretofore nonliberal societies should become liberal. Rawls seems to regard this reticence as a virtue, in part because he is sensitive to the charge that more ambitious claims on behalf of liberalism represent a form of western ethnocentrism, and because he believes that it is not necessary to make such claims in order to develop a law of peoples that applies to all nations and which specifies certain minimum standards of acceptable conduct.

Yet, it may be objected, political liberalism does not merely refrain from asserting that all societies should become liberal; what is more disturbing is that it cannot give any nonliberal society a reason why it should become liberal. It simply has nothing to offer to those societies that may be attempting, in the face of considerable opposition and without the benefit of any significant democratic tradition, to develop liberal institutions for the first time and which look naturally to the liberal philosophers of the democratic west for what is literally "moral support."

10. John Rawls, "The Law of Peoples," *Critical Inquiry* 20 (1993): 36–68.
11. Ibid., pp. 37, 44.

This seems to me a legitimate concern, although Rawls might respond that there is in fact a difference between the reasons why liberal institutions take root in a society for the first time and the justifications for such institutions that become available at later stages. Thus it might be said that liberal institutions take hold, when they do, for a variety of reasons—which may include the need for a modus vivendi, the collapse of alternative institutional schemes, or the desire to emulate the perceived economic success of existing liberal democracies—but which almost certainly do not include a society's happening to converge from the outset on a particular liberal comprehensive moral doctrine. Moreover, and this may be one of the sobering messages of *Political Liberalism,* liberal institutions founded on the sorts of reasons just mentioned are bound to be precarious until a society has lived under them long enough to develop a tradition of tolerance, a commitment to the virtues of liberal citizenship, and an ethos of reasonableness and fair reciprocity. These things are resources that can help to stabilize liberal institutions by making an overlapping consensus on liberal values and principles possible. But their development takes time and reasonably favorable conditions. It cannot happen overnight at the drop of an argument, even a good one. Once it does happen, however, and this may be the more encouraging message of *Political Liberalism,* then a liberal society may be able to flourish despite the deep disagreements that are bound to persist.

If this response seems insufficiently robust, there is one further thing that might be said consistently with the spirit of Rawls's book, namely, that if an overlapping consensus on liberal principles can indeed be achieved in modern democracies, then accepting any one of the doctrines included in such a consensus may give one reason to support a liberal scheme. In other words, the distinctive contribution of political liberalism may be to suggest that there are many ways to arrive at liberal principles and that that very fact is a source of liberalism's strength. For if the reasonable comprehensive doctrines that thrive under conditions of freedom all converge on liberal principles, then what may be said to those in societies seeking to establish liberal institutions is that such institutions represent common ground among the various outlooks likely to endure under conditions that encourage the free exercise of human reason. Of course, however, this can be said only if an overlapping consensus is a realistic possibility in modern, pluralistic democracies. This brings us back to the questions raised earlier. Until those sorts of questions are convincingly answered, the suspicion is bound to persist, especially among those who would defend liberalism on the basis of a comprehensive moral doctrine, that Rawls's position depletes the moral resources of liberalism without managing in exchange to broaden its justificatory appeal.

Justice and the Aims of Political Philosophy*

Kurt Baier

I

In his two most recent publications, Rawls lays great stress on the relatively parochial nature of the proper aims of political philosophy and the suitable method for attaining them.[1] In general, "the aims of political philosophy depend on the society it addresses" (p. 1); in constitutional democracies one of the important long-term ends is attaining (or maintaining) stable social unity (p. 24). Perhaps the greatest obstacle to achieving this aim is our disagreement about how certain familiar values, such as freedom, equality, and efficiency, are to be understood, mutually accommodated, and realized in such a constitutional democracy; or more specifically, in the United States at this time.[2] Rawls's own "justice as fairness" may be a solution to this problem provided it also satisfies a certain "practical" condition which he now considers essential for Western political philosophers to meet because "political philosophy must be concerned, as moral philosophy need not be, with practical political possibilities" (p. 24). Rawls now argues that the best way for political philosophers to attain stable social unity is to aim for a certain sort of agreement among citizens, which he calls "an overlapping consensus" and which is the minimum sufficient for stable social unity. Under such a consensus, a given conception of justice is "affirmed by the opposing religious, philosophical, and moral doctrines likely to thrive over generations in a more or less just constitutional

* Some points in Sec. II of this article are adapted from my comments on Rawls's presentation of his "The Idea of an Overlapping Consensus" at the Chapel Hill, North Carolina, colloquium in October 1986. In Sec. VII, I borrow some ideas from the first of my three Perspectives Lectures given at Notre Dame in 1977 under the title "The Varieties of Justice." I am indebted to John Rawls and to some participants on these two occasions for some critical and clarifying remarks.

1. John Rawls, "Justice as Fairness: Political not Metaphysical," *Philosophy and Public Affairs* 14 (1985): 223–51, and "The Idea of an Overlapping Consensus," *Oxford Journal of Legal Studies* 7 (1987): 1–25, with which I shall mainly be concerned; unless otherwise specified, parenthetical references in the text refer to this latter article.

2. John Rawls, "Kantian Constructivism in Moral Theory: The Dewey Lectures 1980" (which Rawls would now retitle "Kantian Constructivism in Political Theory"), *Journal of Philosophy* 77 (1980): 515–72, 517–18.

Ethics 99 (July 1989): 771–790

democracy, where the criterion of justice is that conception itself." Rawls now believes that a nonutopian (p. 22) conception of justice, one that has some hope of gaining the support of such a consensus (p. 1), must satisfy four conditions: (*a*) it must be capable of bypassing philosophy's long-standing controversies (pp. 12–13); (*b*) to be thus capable, it must be "political"; (*c*) it also must be liberal; (*d*) and it must steer a course between two extreme strands of liberalism.

a) To be capable of by-passing philosophy's long-standing controversies, this conception of justice must be capable of being supported by "the method of avoidance," by which we neither "assert nor . . . deny any religious, philosophical or moral views, or their associated philosophical accounts of truth and the status of values. Since we assume each citizen to affirm some such view or other, we hope to make it possible for all to accept the political conception as true, or as reasonable, from the standpoint of their own comprehensive view, whatever it may be" (pp. 12–13).

b) To be "political," in Rawls's sense, it must—as I shall say—be narrow in scope and have a local political base.

It is narrow in scope if it is particular rather than "general (or universal)" and limited rather than "comprehensive" (p. 3, n. 4; p. 14, n. 23). It is particular if it is intended, at least in the first instance, for the appraisal solely of the basic structure of society rather than for the appraisal of many (or all) subjects to which justice applies (p. 3, nn. 3, 4). Thus a conception of justice that is particular could not be used, at least in the first instance, in the appraisal of international relations or of terrorism. A conception of justice is limited if for its appraisals it relies not on ideals, principles, and standards intended for much or all of our conduct (as is, I suppose, benevolence, courage, charity, or prudence), but on ideals, etc., intended for only a limited area of our life (such as, I suppose, individual political conduct; p. 3, n. 2).

A conception of justice has a local political base if it is worked up "from the fundamental intuitive ideas latent in the public political culture of a democratic society" (pp. 6–7) rather than from within a comprehensive religious, philosophical, or moral conception, such as utilitarianism or the theory of natural law or even philosophical (as opposed to political) liberalism, such as that of Kant or Mill, which "applies to the political order as if this order was but another subject, another kind of case, falling under that conception" (p. 3).

Rawls believes that only a political conception (in this sense of "political") has any hope of achieving an overlapping consensus because only such a conception can appeal to ideals already held and can bypass the disagreements arising from the inescapable diversity and mutual incompatibility of general and comprehensive religious and philosophical, including moral, doctrines likely to flourish there. A conception that is wide in scope would require a corresponding "enveloping" consensus, as we might call it, a consensus on the various competing comprehensive doctrines. But such a consensus cannot be hoped for and would not even be desirable in a constitutional democracy which is inevitably pluralistic (p. 4, n. 7). For a "public and workable agreement on a single general and comprehensive conception could be maintained only by the oppressive use of state power" (p. 4).

c) Rawls does not appear to think that only justice as fairness has hope of an overlapping consensus in our society, for he thinks that it is "also likely that more than one political conception may be worked up from the fund of shared political ideas; indeed this is desirable, as these rival conceptions will then compete for citizens' allegiance and be gradually modified and deepened by the contest between them" (p. 7).

However, he does think that "a workable conception of political justice for a democratic regime must be in an appropriate sense a liberal one" (p. 5). A liberal conception, as Rawls defines it, has three elements: (i) it specifies certain basic rights, liberties, and opportunities; (ii) it assigns a special priority to these rights etc.; (iii) it assures "to all citizens adequate all-purpose means to make effective use of their basic liberties and opportunities" (p. 18).[3]

d) A conception of justice steers the required middle course only if it can gain a stronger support than is provided by a Hobbesian "*modus vivendi* secured by a convergence of self- and group interests even when coordinated and balanced by a well-designed constitutional arrangement" (p. 23). Such a modus vivendi admittedly can secure agreement but not one that is "stable with respect to the distribution of power" (p. 12). At the same time, a conception of justice should not have to count on the support of "a comprehensive moral doctrine such as that of Kant or Mill . . . which cannot gain sufficient agreement" (p. 18). Thus, the Hobbesian balance of conflicting interests secures, at best, unstable agreement, and philosophical (as opposed to political) liberalism (p. 23) expects more agreement than is attainable or even desirable in a constitutional democracy.

This concludes my—necessarily impoverished—summary of Rawls's claims in his most recent papers, especially "The Idea of an Overlapping Consensus." In Sections II–VI of this article I examine these claims and some of their implications. In Section VII I offer some speculative remarks about various conceptions of justice and of the concept of justice and examine their bearing on Rawls's claims about the relation between moral and political philosophy.

II

Rawls clearly thinks that we do not now have a consensus on a conception of justice. He sketches a scenario of the progress of a society from a

---

3. Rawls also offers a "fuller idea of a liberal conception of justice" in n. 27 on the same page. We need not compare the two but should note that both contain requirement iii which would seem to be in conflict with libertarian conceptions of justice. Compare Rawls's discussion of Nozick in his "The Basic Structure as Subject," in *Values and Morals,* ed. A. I. Goldman and J. Kim (Dordrecht: Reidel, 1978), sec. 3.

Hobbesian modus vivendi (pp. 9–12) to an overlapping consensus on such a conception (pp. 18–21). Under the former, toleration of different religious, metaphysical, and moral doctrines is grudgingly accepted as a faute de mieux. Under it, all or most citizens consider it the government's duty to uphold the true doctrine and repress false ones. The government is expected to return to intolerance as soon as there is a favorable change in the distribution of power. The people acquiesce in the practice of tolerance only because they lack the power to suppress opposing views and prefer toleration as a lesser evil to prolonged inconclusive war. Such an acquiescence depends on a fortuitous conjunction of contingencies (p. 1) and is therefore doomed to instability when the distribution of power changes.

In a genuine consensus on a political conception of justice in an essentially pluralistic society, tolerance, readiness to meet others halfway, reasonableness, and the sense of fairness are regarded as very great virtues, and when they are widespread and sustain the public conception of justice, they are regarded as constituting "a very great public good, part of a society's political capital" (p. 17). Rawls concludes that when there is such a consensus, then the values that conflict with it "may be normally outweighed" (p. 17). Hence such a situation will be stable even if the distribution of power changes and conflicting values become more widespread. Of course, this is so only to the extent that the values enshrined in the conception of justice for the basic structure of a constitutional democracy are placed by the bulk of at least the politically active members above the values enshrined in the conflicting religious, metaphysical, or moral doctrines.

Where are we now in this scenario sketched by Rawls? Obviously, Rawls must believe, we are no longer at the stage of a Hobbesian modus vivendi, for we have agreement on the workings of the legal process which we allow to adjudicate those of our disagreements on which we cannot simply agree to differ. This is not a mere Hobbesian modus vivendi, for the currently dominant group does not attempt or even want to use its power to impose its conception of justice on the whole community by an oppressive use of the state power, say, by suitable indoctrination of the young through compulsory public education or by censorship of and punishment for the expression of opposing views. Of course, the current majority probably hopes that its conception will remain the dominant one, and it uses whatever means it has within the limits permitted by the political process to ensure that its conception is given effect, but it recognizes the possibility or even probability that there will be a shift in the distribution of power and with it the dominance of another conception of justice. But they believe, and believe that most others believe, that the methods defined by the legitimate political process will continue to be generally accepted, whatever the adjudications resulting from the use of these methods in particular cases. They do not treat the limitations imposed by the legitimate political process as a necessary evil, but recognize and appreciate the great value to all of stable general adherence to that process.

Have we then reached a consensus on the principles of justice? I think the answer must be no, for there still are many different and conflicting conceptions of justice, for instance, the perfectionist, the utilitarian, the libertarian, the socialist, and now Rawls's justice as fairness, not all of them even liberal. But although there seems to be no consensus on a conception of justice, there is a consensus on something else, namely, on the procedures for making and interpreting law and, where that agreement is insufficiently deep to end disagreement, on the selection of persons whose adjudication is accepted as authoritative.[4] It is not the case that this agreement "is contingent on circumstances remaining such as not to upset the fortunate convergence of interests" (p. 11). On the contrary, such an agreement on the process of adjudication when interests conflict—call it a "constitutional consensus"—is valued for its own sake and for much the same reasons as a consensus on a principle of justice would be valued: it maintains stability over a wide range of distributions of power, and it fosters the virtues of tolerance, respect, and reciprocity (p. 12).

It would seem, then, that the practical aim of political philosophy— stable political unity—can be achieved in the absence of a consensus, whether overlapping or enveloping, on a narrowly political conception of justice.

An objector may perhaps concede that a constitutional consensus can achieve stability but insist that it cannot achieve adequate social unity. For, he may say, under such a consensus people would disagree not only on the good but also on the just and the right. Their agreement would be confined to a procedure, not for settling disagreements, but merely for what is to be done in the face of unsettleable disagreements about what is the just or right thing to do. And this would be too "thin" a consensus to constitute social unity. If we cannot have genuine political community under political liberalism because we cannot have agreement on the good, at least we must have agreement on the principles of justice, if we are to have anything deserving the name of social unity.

But would a consensus on justice as fairness, which ultimately is only pure procedural justice,[5] be significantly "thicker" in terms of social unity than a constitutional consensus? Suppose you and I disagree on the validity of the claims we both advance to the ownership of a particular horse and that we finally agree to toss a coin to settle the issue one way or the other rather than let the dispute drag on forever. This would not

4. For a helpful account of authority, see Joseph Raz, *The Authority of Law* (Oxford: Clarendon, 1979), esp. chap. 1, and "Authority, Law and Morality," *Monist* 68 (1985): 295–324, esp. 296–305; also my "The Justification of Governmental Authority," *Journal of Philosophy* 69 (1972): 700–716.

5. John Rawls, *A Theory of Justice* (Cambridge, Mass.: Harvard University Press, 1971), pp. 120, 136; henceforth *TJ*.

be regarded by us as pure procedural justice since we both believe that there is a substantive issue on which we cannot agree. We therefore abandon the quest for a just solution and let our conflict be settled by a mutually acceptable procedure.

Our current constitutional consensus is somewhat like this: a consensus that is neither on substantive nor on procedural justice. The former is not available, and the latter is inappropriate. We prefer to abide by the established legal procedures, which embody at least some (though perhaps confused or inconsistent) principles of substantive justice because we consider this solution superior to settling the issue by force, or to leaving it unsettled until we can come to agree on justice, or to settling it by pure procedural justice, such as tossing a fair coin, which last would settle it as if neither of us had any claim of substantive justice.

A constitutional consensus is a special case of imperfect (impure) procedural justice. We believe that our method does not always yield a solution in conformity with the requirements of justice. We believe this not because experience has taught us over the long run that the use of this method usually though not always yields substantively just solutions but, rather, because we have no way, convincing to all of us even in the long run, of telling whether the contentious solutions produced by our method were just or unjust.

It seems to me, then, that if social unity cannot be achieved in a democratic society, as Rawls argues it cannot be, by the establishment of a consensus on "the meaning, value and purpose of human life" (pp. 2–3), then the best we can hope for is indeed an agreement on justice to adjudicate between different and conflicting conceptions of the good. But even that is, on Rawls's own showing, at bottom, only an agreement on pure procedural justice, and it is not clear that the kind or degree of social unity achieved by an overlapping consensus on principles of pure procedural justice is significantly greater than that achieved by a constitutional consensus.

III

Let us, however, assume that a constitutional consensus, because it apparently lacks agreement on a conception of justice, is insufficient for stable social unity and that, therefore, contemporary Western political philosophers must present a conception of justice "such that there is some hope of gaining the support of [at least] an overlapping consensus" (p. 1) on it. A crucial question must therefore be exactly what conditions must be satisfied for such a consensus to exist. There would seem to be three dimensions in each of which a certain point would have to be reached if there is to be an "adequate" consensus: (i) the "level" of the consensus, depending on the degree of specificity with which that conception is formulated; (ii) the "extent" of the consensus, depending on the extent of support among the population; (iii) the "intensity"—as I

118

shall call it—of the consensus, depending on the intensity of the agreement by those who agree. The three would seem to be interrelated. The greater the degree of specificity, the smaller the extent and the intensity required for adequacy, and so on, that are likely to be achieved. It may well be that for some low degree of specificity we already have a consensus of adequate extent and intensity. I shall discuss dimension i in this section and return to the other two dimensions in Section VI.

Although there seems to be an important connection between the concept of justice and various conceptions of it, as Rawls distinguishes the two,[6] I shall here assume that we do in fact agree on the concept of justice, that we have the same conception of the concept. (I shall say more about this in Sec. VII.) For the moment I shall consider only the level of the consensus depending on the degree of specificity with which the principle of justice is formulated: the higher that degree, the higher the level of consensus achieved, given the same magnitude of the other two dimensions, extent and intensity.

A fairly low level of consensus would be achieved if there were consensus on the following: "Institutions are just when no *arbitrary distinctions* are made between persons in the assigning of basic rights and duties and when the rules determine a *proper balance* between competing claims to the advantages of social life."[7] A much higher level would be

6. Ibid., pp. 4 ff. Thus, even if you and I agree on the principle of giving everyone his due, this need not be an agreement on the principle of justice if we disagreed on the concept of justice: not, for instance, if you thought the function of this principle was to distribute to people what the actually accepted rules of the institutions spelling out what is due from whom to whom award to them, whereas I think that their function is to distribute to them what is really due to them, i.e., what is awarded them by such institutions as long as they conform to some further principle, say, Rawls's justice as fairness. For further clarification, see nn. 7 and 19 below.

7. Rawls, *TJ*, p. 5; my emphasis. Rawls offers this formulation as an account of having the concept of justice because we "can agree to this description of just institutions since the notions of an arbitrary distinction and of a proper balance, which are included in the concept of justice, are left open for each to interpret according to the principles [i.e., the conception] of justice that he accepts" (*TJ*, p. 5). But note: (i) On the same page, Rawls says, "it seems natural to think of the concept of justice as distinct from the various conceptions of justice and as being specified by the role which these different sets of principles, these different conceptions have in common." On this account, having the concept of justice need not carry any implications of what are the empirical criteria by which we must appraise actual institutions as just or unjust. As Rawls suggests, this is one reason why it is more likely that we can agree on the concept of justice than on conceptions of justice. (ii) By contrast, Rawls's formulation in the first sentence of this note does carry such normative implications. Thus, the reason why we can agree on this conception of the concept is not that it is normatively noncommittal, but that it is so highly nonspecific that its normative implications will hardly ever come down on one side or the other of a disagreement about the justice or injustice of an institution. (iii) It is not the case that plainly we agree on the concept of justice. The history of ethics shows that there are many different conceptions of the concept. In Sec. VII I shall examine what I take to be five different conceptions of the concept of justice.

reached by agreement on Rawls's first formulation of the principles,[8] and a higher level still through his final formulation.[9]

It would seem, then, that we cannot say without prior clarification of the required specificity whether we already have an adequate consensus on a conception of justice, or only a constitutional consensus. For whether we have one or the other is likely to depend on how specific is our formulation of the principle(s) of justice. Suppose the level of specificity required is no higher than this: principles of justice (in the sense of principles with the appropriate function of "assigning basic rights and duties and [of] determining what people should take to be the appropriate distribution of benefits and burdens of social cooperation")[10] are principles of justice (in the sense of principles providing empirical criteria for correctly distinguishing the just from the unjust) "when no arbitrary distinctions are made between persons in the assigning of rights and duties and when the rules determine a proper balance between competing claims to the advantages of social life."[11] If we think of principles of justice on this high level of abstraction then, probably, we already have a consensus on the principles of justice. But if they must be formulated at the very high level of specificity of Rawls's final formulation in *A Theory of Justice*,[12] then we almost certainly do not have an adequate consensus.

IV

The question, therefore, arises what level of consensus is adequate. In *A Theory of Justice*, Rawls claims that, despite the diversity and incompatibility of our different conceptions of justice, we each have one or other such conception and therefore understand the need for, and are prepared to affirm, "a characteristic set of principles for assigning basic rights and duties for determining what [we] take to be the appropriate distribution of the benefits and burdens of social cooperation."[13] This suggests to me the view that, since we understand the need for agreement on principles of justice at the level of specificity at which we now have disagreement, the political philosopher should present principles of justice with a high degree of specificity, perhaps as high as Rawls's final formulation.[14]

However, Rawls also says things that suggest something rather different. "We suppose that these [implicitly shared fundamental] ideas and principles can be elaborated into a political conception of justice, which we hope can gain the support of an overlapping consensus. Of course, whether this can be done can be verified only by actually elaborating a

8. Ibid., p. 60.
9. Ibid., pp. 302–3.
10. Ibid., p. 4.
11. Ibid., p. 5.
12. Ibid., pp. 302–3.
13. Ibid., p. 4.
14. Ibid., pp. 302 ff.

political conception of justice and exhibiting the way in which it could be thus supported. It is also likely that, as we have seen, more than one political conception may be worked up from the fund of shared political ideas; *indeed this is desirable,* as these rival conceptions will then compete for citizens' allegiance and will be gradually modified and deepened by the contrast between them" (pp. 6–7; my emphasis). And in a long and important footnote he adds, "a comprehensive doctrine, whenever widely, if not universally shared in society, tends to become oppressive and stifling" (p. 4, n. 7, sec. 5).

It is not clear to me why a widely and freely adopted comprehensive doctrine, such as "the philosophical liberalism" of Mill or Kant, should be stifling whereas a widely shared narrowly political doctrine, such as "political liberalism," is not. It is, therefore, unclear to me whether development in the direction of an overlapping consensus on a political conception of justice with the degree of specificity of the final version (or some other higher or lower degree) is really desirable. If a constitutional consensus, such as we appear to have now, provides stable social union and if the competition of rival conceptions "worked up from the fund of shared political ideas" is desirable and if there is a danger that wide agreement on a very specific principle of justice, even if political, would tend to become "oppressive and stifling," should political philosophers hope or press for a higher-level consensus than we already have? Can we even define that level of specificity so that we know exactly what to aim at, or what to maintain when we have reached it? Is there any reason for going beyond the level of consensus we have now, supposing that what we now have gives us stable social unity?

V

Let us, however, set aside these difficult questions and grant, at least for argument's sake, that contemporary Western political philosophers should regard it as their aim to formulate a conception of justice, whatever may be the appropriate degree of specificity, that has "some hope" of commanding an adequate consensus rather than be satisfied with the present constitutional consensus. There remains the question why, as political philosophers, they must advance only (liberal) conceptions that are (narrowly) political (rather than philosophical) and why they must not widen these conceptions except where and to the extent that this is necessary to refute a comprehensive religious, metaphysical, or moral conception that conflicts with the political conception advanced by the philosopher.

Here, the three main points in question are (i) whether in order to produce or maintain stable social unity it is necessary or helpful to achieve a high-level consensus on a conception of justice for the basic structure; (ii) whether the characteristics of a constitutional democracy, such as pluralism in religion, metaphysics, and morality make it impossible or highly unlikely or even undesirable to achieve anything wider than an overlapping consensus; and (iii) whether the presentation of a political conception of justice is always the only or the best way to bring about or maintain such a consensus.

We have already seen what distinctions and qualifications are necessary when considering i. As far as ii is concerned, Rawls himself concedes that, when people regard certain questions as so important that they advocate the use of force to ensure a correct settlement, we may have no alternative but to deny this and to assert something concerning which we had hoped as it turns out, vainly, to use the method of avoidance (p. 14). Rawls himself, even in a recent paper, defends the thesis of the priority of the right over the good, which would seem to be one of those long-standing philosophical controversies on which one might have wished to employ the method of avoidance.[15]

Thus clearly Rawls thinks that in certain circumstances it is both possible and desirable to achieve a wider than an overlapping consensus, or at any rate, that in these circumstances political philosophers must risk the attempt. However, he regards any widening of the conception of justice beyond the political as something they should engage in only when it is forced on them by the existence of comprehensive doctrines in conflict with the presented political conception of justice.

This brings us to iii. Should political philosophers venture beyond a political conception only when there already exist "dangerous" comprehensive doctrines in conflict with the liberal conception of justice they favor? It seems to me that political philosophers need not wait until such "dangerous" doctrines have begun to spread. If our presentation of a wider conception can have any effect once these passions of intolerance have arisen and their propagation is organized by believers (and perhaps others who expect to reap personal gains from the spread of hatred and mistrust), might it not also help to prevent these views from gaining adherents in the first place? Insofar as such hostile movements are based on comprehensive conceptions in conflict with liberal conceptions of justice, political philosophers concerned to reach or maintain an adequate consensus on such a conception or even on a constitutional consensus might do well to refute such comprehensive conceptions before they become popular.[16]

15. John Rawls, "The Priority of Right and Ideas of the Good," *Philosophy and Public Affairs* 17 (1988): 251–76.

16. In his illustration, Rawls says, "we do not state more of our comprehensive view than we think would advance the quest for consensus. The reason for this restraint is to respect, as far as we can, the limits of free public reason" (p. 14). The second of these two sentences is somewhat puzzling for it suggests that any widening of the conception advanced amounts to a failure to respect the limits of free public reason. But why should that be so? Under a constitutional consensus, we could offer, for instance, a doctrine of philosophical (rather than political) liberalism, such as that of Kant or Mill (pp. 5–6, 23–24) without, surely, infringing these limits. We would infringe them only if we pushed these doctrines in illegitimate ways, say, by indoctrination and suppression of contrary views. Thus, the only valid reason for political philosophers not to advance a doctrine more comprehensive than a narrowly political one would seem to be that it would not have a chance of achieving

Of course, this does not mean they should present fully comprehensive doctrines. For major parts of these would be simply irrelevant. It would be a waste of time for political philosophers to argue about transubstantiation or the role of memory in personal identity or the merits of virtue ethics versus duty ethics, or even "the status of values as expressed by realism and subjectivism" (p. 13). But it would not be irrelevant to include all those aspects of a moral doctrine that have been developed for a broader subject than the basic structure. For if they are convincing, that might help in converting those who are attracted by comprehensive religious or metaphysical doctrines that are in real conflict with a (narrowly) political conception of justice.

Our main problem does not seem to be that as political philosophers we take on unnecessary quarrels with rival comprehensive conceptions that are compatible with our narrowly political (liberal) conception of justice. It is, rather, that there are, and that we must attempt to refute, rival comprehensive conceptions that are in conflict not only with our liberal political conception of justice but even with the existing constitutional consensus. I share Rawls's aim to make political philosophy independent of the interminable controversies in religion and metaphysics, but I do not see political philosophy as similarly isolable from ethics. It seems to me that social justice is a branch of justice and justice a branch of morality. I think a consensus on a conception of justice might be easier to reach or maintain if political philosophers did not detach themselves from the relevant parts of moral philosophy. I return to this topic in Section VII.

VI

Let us now ask in precisely what sense the aims of political philosophy, unlike those of moral philosophy, are or should be practical. According to Rawls, the relevant difference between the politician and the political philosopher would seem to be a matter of the scope of the practical political concern: "The politician, we say, looks to the next election, the statesman to the next generation, and philosophy to the indefinite future" (p. 24). For this reason, Rawls thinks, political philosophy is compelled "to consider fundamental institutional questions and the assumptions of a reasonable moral psychology" (p. 24). For this reason also "the political conception [of justice presented by the political philosopher] needs to be such that there is some hope of its gaining the support of an overlapping consensus" (p. 1). Thus the relevant difference between the three would seem to be only the time frame of their practical aim. And this in turn suggests that the political philosopher must eliminate or at least rank lower those "utopian" (p. 22) conceptions with regard to which there is little or no hope that they will "gradually over generations become the

---

consensus. But if that is so, it will also be hopeless to "deny" such conflicting comprehensive views once they have become widespread. And respecting the limits of free public reason seems irrelevant. For further remarks on this topic see Sec. VI below.

focus of an overlapping consensus" (p. 24), just as the politician must eliminate or rank lower those political platforms that would jeopardize his election.

To clarify the question, we can distinguish two dimensions of practicality and its opposite. One ranges from the "stronger" realizability to the "weaker" foreseeability and their opposites, the other from the stronger empirical confirmability to the weaker imaginative envisageability and their opposites. This creates four senses. In order of strength, they are: the empirically realizable, the empirically foreseeable, the imaginatively realizable, and the imaginatively foreseeable. I begin by examining the stronger interpretation in each dimension.

On the first dimension, Rawls appears to favor the stronger interpretation. The political philosopher (unlike, presumably, the political scientist) is not merely trying to foresee which, if any, conception will gain consensus but tries, by a suitable presentation of one of the conceptions that have a hope of achieving a consensus, to make a difference to which conception will be accepted.

Three comments. First, this will pose a difficult (but perhaps unavoidable) choice for the political philosopher. He may have to play two potentially conflicting criteria against each other. Suppose among the conceptions that appear to have some hope of gaining consensus are justice as fairness, the libertarian, the socialist, and the utilitarian conceptions. And suppose also that, in his view, justice as fairness is the one that is best supported by those political values embedded in our culture that the philosopher most favors but that the utilitarian and the libertarian conceptions are more likely to gain consensus. Which conception should he present? If he presents justice as fairness, is he unacceptably utopian; is he failing to work for his proper end as a political philosopher?

Second, as far as practicality is concerned, I cannot see a significant difference between the aim of the political and the moral philosopher. Both present (among other things) conceptions of justice. Both will want to achieve adequate consensus on them. Both will attempt to work these up from values embedded in the culture. Both will be faced by the same choice between two potentially conflicting criteria: likelihood of gaining consensus and their own ranking of merit.

Third, there is a possible (though perhaps only partial) explanation of why someone might think that political philosophers have a practical aim while moral philosophers do not. The explanation is a failure to note an important difference between a politician and a statesman, on the one hand, and a political philosopher, on the other. The former, by their specifically political role, have various forms of power by whose exercise they shape the legally enforceable rules that determine the distribution of the benefits and burdens of cooperation. In their selection of principles to be presented they are often strongly motivated by the aim of retaining or extending this power. For them the choice of a principle to present will often be a means to achieving consensus, not on a principle they judge the morally best but, through its sufficiently wide acceptance *as* the best (even if they themselves do not share this appraisal), on a means to gaining or retaining the desired political power. In this respect, then, they are more "practical" than the moral, but also than the political, philosopher but in a different sense of "practical": their primary aim is power, not stable social unity or consensus.

Concerning the second dimension, empiricalness, the main problem is this. If a political philosopher is serious about rebutting the charge of utopianism and ignoring practical aims, he is likely to want to clarify how the existence of a consensus on a conception of justice can be empirically ascertained, what would constitute a consensus sufficient for stable social unity, and what features of a conception of justice increase or decrease the likelihood of such an adequate consensus. He would want to determine empirically under what conditions the presentation of a political conception is the best way to gain a consensus sufficient for stable unity.

It is unclear to me whether Rawls expects the political philosopher to be thus empirical. If not, if he is satisfied with a merely imaginatively realizable or foreseeable consensus on a principle of justice, is he not open to the charge of utopianism or failing to be practical in the sense explained? Are scenarios, such as those sketched by Rawls, of the transition from a Hobbesian modus vivendi to an overlapping consensus, more than armchair sociology or political science?

However, Rawls does not seem to want anything stronger than this. In the concluding sentences of "The Idea of an Overlapping Consensus," he says, "Political philosophy assumes the role Kant gave to philosophy generally: the defense of reasonable faith. In our case this becomes the defense of reasonable faith in the real possibility of a just constitutional regime" (p. 25).

If that is the extent of the practical aim of political philosophy, is moral philosophy even less practical than this? Does the moral philosopher not have to take consensus into account at all? Is morality a purely individual matter? Can we simply agree to differ? Do we not, in cases of moral disagreement, say, on abortion, need something like our constitutional consensus, quite as much as when we disagree on justice?

We have already noted the possible correlation between consensus and degree of specificity of the presented formulation of a conception of justice. Now we must attend to the two other dimensions, the extent and the intensity of the consensus.

What I call "extent" covers the number of the relevant people consenting. Rawls speaks of "the bulk of the politically active citizens." To settle the questions empirically, we would have to settle who exactly the politically active citizens are (the voters, the party members, the organizers, the readers/writers of political tracts, the marchers?) and what proportion of them is sufficient to amount to "the bulk."

What I call "intensity" spans the range of attitudes from reluctant to indifferent acquiescence, active support, explicit (self-conscious, reasoned) intellectual agreement, implicit agreement, that is, agreement that would become explicit under the appropriate conditions.

But perhaps all this is misguided, like asking how many hairs a person must have on his head if he is not to be regarded as bald. Perhaps we need a further theory which would allow us to determine "adequate" consensus by some "indicator"; thus, recidivism is often thought to be such an indicator of the deterring or rehabilitating efficacy of a type of punishment. But what would be a plausible indicator of consensus and its extent or intensity?[17]

It is unclear, then, what exactly Rawls wishes to emphasize about the aims of the political philosopher and how they must modify his writings to serve these aims when he stresses the practical aspect of his task, and why he thinks this is different from that of the moral philosopher.

VII

I now want briefly to formulate, explore, and contrast several of the conceptions of the concept of justice[18] which have been most widely advanced in the philosophical literature, and to draw attention to another which, though not to my knowledge previously advocated, is yet, at any rate by my lights, one that more accurately represents our intuitive understanding of justice than do the others. If I am right in this, then, since

---

17. In any case, Rawls does not seem to favor this approach, for he says (p. 5, n. 8), "Free and willing agreement is agreement endorsed by our considered convictions on due reflection, or in what I have called 'reflective equilibrium'" (see *TJ*, pp. 19 ff., 48 ff.).

18. I distinguish between (i) a conception of the concept of justice and (ii) (following Rawls) a conception (or principle or criterion) of justice. (i) A conception of the concept A I take to be a view of what it is for a linguistic community to have the concept A. Often there is no question but that a certain linguistic community has a certain concept, e.g., that the contemporary Anglo-American linguistic community has the concept of happiness, whereas it is not clear that the ancient Greeks had exactly the same concept. Where there is no such doubt, adherents of different conceptions of the concept normally disagree about what is the correct conception of the concept. Ryle took it that Descartes's linguistic community had the same concept of mind as Ryle's, but he thought that Descartes's conception of the concept was a misconception; he did not think it was a correct conception of a different superior or inferior concept. In other cases, as with Rawls's primary goods or reflective equilibrium, the conception advanced is a proposal for the introduction of a new concept. In the former case, the existence of the concept (the practice) precedes the conception, in the latter the conception precedes the existence of the concept (the practice). I assume that our linguistic community has a single (reasonably coherent) concept of justice, that different thinkers, especially philosophers, form different conceptions of that concept, and that some of these are misconceptions. One could but I do not here raise the difficult question of whether there are or were other concepts comparable to our concept of justice that are superior to ours, say, the Greek concept of *dikaiosyne*. (ii) The concept of justice is a normative moral concept. It determines how to distinguish the just from the unjust, and it morally requires those who can be either just or unjust to be just rather than unjust. In contradistinction to a conception of the concept of justice, a conception of justice is a view of how to tell what would satisfy this moral requirement. A correct conception of the concept of justice must enable us to tell what is a correct, what an incorrect, conception of justice.

this conception of the concept also involves a particular principle, or conception, of justice, albeit a highly nonspecific one, we already have a consensus on a conception of justice, though we may not be aware of this, since we may not yet realize that this is a correct conception of our concept of justice.

First, then, a brief delineation of five conceptions of the concept of justice. The first of these is probably the oldest and most widely held. Plato attributes it to Simonides, it was embraced by Cicero and Justinian, and philosophers have defended it more or less continuously since then.[19] On this view, justice consists in giving everyone his due, where something is due to someone if he has a right to it or if he deserves it. It is due to him from another if she has a duty or if, though she has no duty, she morally ought to secure it for him.

I think this is not a conception that captures all our important commonsense intuitions about the concept. If I have undertaken to get you to the church on time, then that is what is due to you from me and if I get you there on time, I have given you that due. But I have not exhibited the virtue of justice, I have not been just to you or done you justice. I have done my duty by you, I have lived up to my commitments, I have done what was morally required of me. Nor of course have I been unjust to you. Indeed, I would not have been unjust to you if I had not got you there on time either, though I would have failed in my duty, and so on. This is simply not a case in which either justice or injustice is applicable, as we commonly conceive of it.

The second conception is a slight modification of the first. It takes justice to be that part of morality which has to do with what is morally required of one, what others have a right to against one, and what can justifiably be exacted. This conception (developed by J. S. Mill as an account of duty) finds (misguided) support in Kant's division of morality into the domain of the *Rechts-* and *Tugendpflichten,* by the frequent (but misleading) translation of the former as *juridical duties* or *duties of justice.* Unlike the first conception, it includes duties, such as driving on the right, which are not due to anyone in particular, and it excludes what another deserves but has no right to. This does indeed delineate an important part of morality, namely, that which contrasts with what goes beyond the call of duty; but, like the first conception and for much the same reason, it does not seem to me to pick out our concept of justice.

These first two conceptions of the concept construe justice as an excellence of any individual moral agent who behaves in ways that conform to certain high-level principles. They identify the principles of justice with the principles enjoining the doing of one's duty, and the respecting of other people's rights and deserts.

---

19. See, e.g., the important and illuminating paper by Joel Feinberg, "Noncomparative Justice," *Philosophical Review* 83 (1974): 298.

The third is what Rawls calls "formal justice."[20] It is the impartial and conscientious administration of the institutions composing the basic structure of a society, that is, those institutions that determine people's rights and duties in a particular society. On this interpretation, justice is the conscientiousness of a judge or of those playing analogous adjudicative roles—for example, parent, teacher, administrator—rather than that of any moral agent irrespective of what institutional role he plays or whether he plays any such role. This seems to me to capture one important element of the concept. Those who think of justice as treating equals equally and unequals unequally[21] may have in mind such conscientious and impartial administration of institutions with adjudicating roles. However, as Rawls says, following Sidgwick, "law and institutions may be equally executed and yet be unjust."[22]

The fourth conception identifies justice with a certain excellence of institutions, namely, conformance with a certain principle, which we could call the principle of equitability. On this fourth conception, justice (or justness) is the characteristic excellence of the conventional devices determining what is due from whom to whom. These devices include those institutions which make this determination possible by assigning certain rights, duties, and normative powers[23] (such as authority) to certain roles, for instance, those of legislator and citizen, parent and child, employer and employee. But they also include noninstitutional devices such as publicly recognized precepts, rules, and principles that hold for classes of people not defined as institutional role players, for example, females, children, and persons in a good position to rescue someone in distress. We can call equitable or inequitable also those states of affairs that conform to these judgments and principles. Hence on this fourth conception they too could be called just or unjust. Thus, if the legal principles that led to *Plessy v. Ferguson* (U.S. Supreme Court 163, US 537 [1896], upholding racial segregation in public transport and education) violate the principle of equitability, then the state of affairs created by the correct enforcement of that ruling is also inequitable and therefore on this conception unjust.[24]

20. Rawls, *TJ*, pp. 58–59.

21. For example, William K. Frankena, *Some Beliefs about Justice*, Lindley Lecture (Lawrence: University of Kansas Press, 1966).

22. Rawls, *TJ*, p. 59.

23. In the sense explicated by Joseph Raz, "Voluntary Obligations and Normative Powers," *Proceedings of the Aristotelian Society* 46, suppl. (1972): 79–102. An example is the power of assuming obligations by promising or of imposing duties on others by legislating.

24. Thus, the provisions of a certain peace can be equitable and so just on this conception, if the peace treaty requires each party to provide to the other what has become due to or deserved by the other from it as a result of what happened in the preceding war. Similarly, a declaration of war can be equitable and so just, on this conception, if a country is due or deserves certain things from another which it can attain only by making war on the other. It is less plausible, on this conception, to speak of a just war since if the declaration of war by one party is just, engaging in war by the other party will not be just—unless the other party engages in war for unrelated reasons.

Thus, the principle of equitability applies to a good deal more than Rawls's basic structure and therefore might well have to be formulated in a less specific way than Rawls's two principles if it is to fit the many different contexts to which it must be applicable.

What is the content of this important moral principle? Perhaps the least controversial approach to this difficult question would seem to be this. Since this principle imposes a significant constraint on the content of a very wide range of social devices that determine the distribution of the benefits and burdens of social interaction regulated by them, its content must be such that all those whose interaction is regulated by it have at least adequate if not compelling reason to accept it (or at least welcome its social adoption). For then they will comply voluntarily insofar as they are reason-guided, with the requirements of social devices that conform to this principle.[25] Being "to everyone's advantage" or "for the good of everyone alike" would seem to be intended as more or less equivalent formulations of this principle.

The fifth conception combines the first, third, and fourth.[26] It ties justice to certain special institutions but subjects these to the principle of equitability. At the same time, it makes justice applicable not only to actions, persons, and institutions but also to judgments, states of affairs, and the world.[27] On this view of the concept, what can be just or unjust are only those persons (as well as their acts and the consequences of these acts) who play roles analogous to those of judges—those that dispense or mete out (what they purport to be) justice, those whose judgments of what is due from whom to whom constitute "declaratory justice," whether first-order (when people were not required to know what was due) or corrective (when they knew, or ought to have known but failed to act accordingly).

Thus on this conception anyone can receive justice and suffer injustice, but the only persons who can be just or unjust are those "dispensing justice." They are just if they follow the rules of equitable devices determining what is due from whom to whom. They are unjust if they fail to follow the rules of such an equitable device.[28]

25. Rawls's difference principle can be seen as the application, whether defensible or not, of the principle of equitability to the design of a market economy under certain conditions, i.e., "chain connection" (*TJ*, pp. 81 ff.). What Rawls calls the "General Conception" of justice (*TJ*, p. 302) can be seen as its application under somewhat different conditions to the distribution of all types of primary goods. What generates the different formulations of the principle seems largely or entirely due to the different contexts and circumstances of application.

26. Rawls's conception of the concept of justice can perhaps be construed as a combination of the second and fourth.

27. In "Noncomparative Justice," Feinberg examines the notion of cosmic justice/injustice but lists only two senses, the justice/injustice done by or to the cosmos. But this makes sense only if one thinks of the cosmos as something analogous to a person. More commonly, cosmic justice/injustice is the justice/injustice done or received in the cosmos.

28. This account leaves unclear whether such dispensers of justice are just or unjust if they follow the rules of an inequitable device, and whether the persons subject to such an inequitable device suffer an injustice. If such dispensers are unjust, then they can be

On this conception, justice is that part of morality which deals with the authoritative interpretation of the principle of equitability and its application to the rules of institutions authoritatively laying down what is due from whom to whom and the application of these rules by authoritative judges to particular cases brought before them. On this conception, a world in which each person is concerned to, and does, give to all what is due to them from her, but which lacks an agency with the task of determining authoritatively what is thus due, and of suitably nudging those who are or might be reluctant to provide what is due, would be a morally admirable one, but not one that is just; not of course because it would be an unjust one, but because such a world has no need and no work for justice so conceived. The moral excellence of the people in this wonderful world can be characterized without reference to justice: they never wrong anybody; they always discharge their duties and obligations to others; and they honor one another's rights and deserts. But no one in this world is just or has justice dispensed to him or receives injustice. Concern for justice and about injustice arises only when as is, alas, usually and perhaps necessarily the case in our sort of world (as Hobbes and Locke noted), people do not always agree on what is due from whom to whom and do not always give to others what they know or believe is due from them to others. In this wonderful world (where a stricter version of Rawls's ideal, or strict, compliance holds),[29] institutions of justice would wither away.[30]

On this version, certain role players can be not only just or unjust, but just or unjust to others. Since what is due from one person to another will normally be either a benefit or a burden, a judge's adjudication will be just if he either allocates no smaller a benefit or no greater a burden than is due to the person. If a judge is just, he will also be just to the persons between whom he adjudicates. If he grants one of them a greater benefit or imposes a lesser burden than is his due, he is unjust, but not to him: he is unjust to the other person from or to whom he judged that benefit to be due.

---

so unintentionally and unknowingly. In this case, if their victims suffer an injustice, then they do so without the dispensers' being iniquitous. It seems plausible to say that, as long as they do not believe that the rules they apply are inequitable, such dispensers are meting out justice, but that they are not just, even though they believe they are. There may then be cases in which they mete out justice without being either just or unjust.

29. Rawls, *TJ*, p. 8. Stricter because compliance occurs (as in an ideal state of nature) without the need for institutions of declarative justice.

30. As is well known, Marx thought that in a classless society, in the so-called realm of freedom, where everybody gets what he needs, there is no call for such an authoritative determination of what is due from whom to whom, let alone for institutions' enforcing such determinations. In this even more wonderful world, each will willingly give according to his ability, and this will produce and will be known to produce enough, perhaps more than enough, for each to be given according to his need (or is it his desire?). In this world of abundance, Marx thought, it will be unnecessary or pointless to determine how much or how little is due from whom to whom.

130

An interesting special case is that of judging character, a practice we all can and tend to engage in. The function of judgments of character is to acquaint members of the moral community with how well given individuals have, in the opinion of their peers, performed as moral agents. Such information is important for the formation of trust and distrust, without which morality could not work. Since every member of the moral community to a considerable extent depends, for the good life, on the reputation he has with others, the expression of such judgments constitutes powerful pressure in the direction of moral conformity. A good reputation is obviously an important asset, a bad reputation a liability. At the same time, a deservedly bad reputation serves to protect others against unwarranted trust. Thus, everyone has a legitimate claim to other people's making judgments no less favorable than is warranted by the facts. And his neighbors have a right to judgments no more favorable than is warranted by the facts.

This imposes a role-duty of conscientiousness and veracity on character judges. Since a bad reputation is a burden and a good reputation a good, it is clear that a person who judges another less favorably or more unfavorably than is warranted by the facts is wronging him, by being unjust to him. In the first case the injustice takes the form of failing to do him justice, in the second case of doing him an injustice. By contrast, if he judges him more favorably or less unfavorably than is warranted by the facts, he is not unjust to him, nor is he doing him or others an injustice nor failing to do him or them justice. The reason for this is, of course, that in this case the judgment of declaratory justice does not merely say or imply what is due to a person from another or from her to him. The judgment itself is the deliberate giving or not giving to the person judged of something which the judge knows or ought to know is due to that person or to others from the judge. What is due to her is that she not be judged less favorably or more unfavorably, what is due to others, that she not be judged more favorably or less unfavorably than is warranted by the facts. Hence judging her more favorably or less unfavorably than is warranted by the facts is an injustice not to her but to others, yet it is not the sort of injustice to them which is a failing to do them justice or doing to them an injustice.

On this fifth conception of the concept of justice, judgment of character is the main case in which the just or unjust behavior is both a judgment (though merely implicit) of what is due to someone from the judge himself and the giving or not giving her of what is her due. Perhaps it is attention to this special case that has misled some into thinking that the first conception offers the best account of our concept of justice.

On this fifth conception of the concept of justice and its implied conception of justice (the highly abstract principle of equitability) we may well already have an adequate consensus on this conception of justice. It is, of course, not clear that Rawls's two principles can be derived from this more abstract principle, and it is fairly clear that, even if there already is a consensus on it, there is no consensus on Rawls's two principles.

VIII

If I am right about the main points I made, then the following would seem to be reasonable conclusions.

1. Our existing constitutional consensus would seem to be sufficient for stable social unity, even though it does not amount to a consensus on a highly specific principle (or set of principles) of justice for the whole basic structure.

2. It is not clear that an overlapping consensus on a conception of justice would produce greater stability and social unity than our existing constitutional consensus or that, if it did, this would be desirable.

3. On one interpretation of the concept of justice, we may already have an adequate consensus on a principle of justice for the whole basic structure, namely, the principle of equitability.

4. Political philosophers need not necessarily present a (narrowly) political conception of (social) justice, but may, while avoiding unnecessary because irrelevant entanglements with the long-standing controversies in religion and metaphysics, present a political conception that can be seen as the application of the general moral principle of equitability to the special context of the basic structure. For this would add the backing of morality to the political conception presented.

5. There is no significant difference between the aims of political and moral philosophy, as far as practicality is concerned. Both must draw on the values embedded in our culture. Both must present conceptions that have a hope of commanding an adequate consensus. Neither is practical in the sense that its practitioners' theories and judgments are exercises of normative powers or of political power, nor attempts to gain or retain or increase such power. In this respect, political philosophers differ significantly from politicians and statesmen, but not from moral philosophers.

JOSEPH RAZ   Facing Diversity: The Case
                             of Epistemic Abstinence

Both friends and foes often emphasize the way liberal thought is concerned primarily with individuals. The pursuit of freedom is often pictured as the protection of the individual from the tyranny of the majority.
All too often this concern with individuals is taken to show liberalism's
neglect of the importance of communities. Whatever truth this accusa-
tion may have when leveled at the way some writers have understood
the liberal ideal, it is misguided when aimed at the ideal of individual
freedom itself. People's individuality expresses itself in ways fashioned
by social practices, and through their ability and inclination to engage in
socially formed relations and pursuits. Concern for individual freedom
requires recognition that an important aspect of that ideal is the freedom
of people to belong to distinctive groups, with their own beliefs and practices, and the ability of such groups to prosper.

In recent years several liberal writers have made the response to pluralism—the response to the fact that our societies consist of groups and
communities with diverse practices and beliefs, including groups whose
beliefs are inconsistent with each other—central to their concern. In
their work the connection between individual freedom and group pros-
perity becomes particularly evident.

This article examines the contemporary philosophical responses of
John Rawls and Thomas Nagel to the diversity of opinions, customs, and
ideologies prevalent in our societies. While these responses differ in
many important respects, they share a common core; they manifest, and
try to defend, a common attitude marked by three features. First, the

    I am grateful to G. A. Cohen, Simon Coval, Gerald Dworkin, S. White, and the Editors
of *Philosophy & Public Affairs* for helpful comments.

response of both thinkers to diversity is basically tolerant. They allow, to use Rawls's words, "for a plurality of conflicting, and indeed incommensurable, conceptions of the meaning, value and purpose of human life."[1] Second, the justification of tolerance is based not on the positive value of diversity, nor on the dangers of entrusting governments with the power to suppress it, but on considerations of fairness.[2] Third, these considerations lead them to draw boundaries, based on epistemic distinctions, to the reasons on which governments may act. They advocate an epistemic withdrawal from the fray. Governments, like everyone else, should of course act for good reasons. This would seem to require governments to ascertain which reasons for action are valid and which are not. But, says Rawls, governments should not be concerned with the truth or falsity of the doctrine of justice which guides them. Nagel, following a slightly different line of reasoning, suggests that the reasons for certain views are so personal that a (true) doctrine of justice must disqualify such views, even if true, from serving as reasons for governmental action.

At least since Mill propounded the harm principle, liberal political thought has been familiar with arguments that certain true beliefs that individuals are justified in relying upon in the conduct of their private affairs may not be relied upon by governments. The arguments put forward by Rawls and Nagel are, however, novel. For never before has it been suggested that governments should be unconcerned with the truth of the very views (the doctrine of justice) which inform their policies and actions, and never before has it been argued that certain truths should not be taken into account because, though true, they are of an epistemic class unsuited for public life.[3] The purpose of this article is limited and is purely critical: it is to challenge the cogency of the reasons offered by both writers for epistemic abstinence.

I. EPISTEMIC ABSTINENCE

Some of Rawls's recent writings are concerned to explain and defend the foundations of his enterprise. When *A Theory of Justice* first appeared it

1. John Rawls, "Justice as Fairness: Political not Metaphysical," *Philosophy & Public Affairs* 14, no. 3 (Summer 1985): 225 (hereafter referred to as "Political not Metaphysical").
2. I take it that Nagel's concern with impartiality is a concern with one aspect of fairness.
3. Notice that the novelty in Nagel's position is in disqualifying certain true beliefs from providing justification for governmental action without showing that the beliefs are suspect and unreliable.

impressed people not only by the scope of its conclusions, by the body of theory which seemed derivable from its principles of justice, but also by the depth of its foundations. In an age where there seemed little to choose between the intellectually barren battle of dogmatic ideologies (capitalist and Marxist in particular), on the one hand, and the narrow, uninspiring, pragmatic squabbling over details within each camp, on the other hand, *A Theory of Justice* demonstrated that there is room for rational theory-building on a grand scale.

The scale was impressive partly because it rejected the hand-to-mouth, piecemeal intuitionism of the many articles on "relevant" topics such as racism, conscientious objection, and abortion, and showed how such diverse problems can be treated systematically as part of a unified theory based on a few leading ideas. Moreover, it was a theory which addressed the central aspects of our society, the fundamental issues of the distribution of power, status, and resources, and not merely peripheral areas of discontent such as conscientious objection and civil disobedience, or particularly topical and urgent problems, such as racism.

But the scale was equally impressive because in its advocacy and use of the method of reflective equilibrium and of contractarian arguments the theory revived Aristotelian and Kantian themes, and promised a method of resolving by rational argument the ancient disputes of political morality, and, as the more daring souls hoped, of morality generally. This revival of theoretical interest in the foundations of morality is the target of much of Rawls's recent writing, which is designed to disavow any such claims or aspirations. Instead, Rawls claims that the road to a theory of justice of an unmistakably liberal cast is through a good deal of epistemic abstinence.

Justice for Our Times

Epistemic abstinence is only one aspect of Rawls's modest conception of political theory. Four themes have to be distinguished, all of which are captured by the slogan "Justice as Fairness: Political not Metaphysical." First, it is a theory of *limited applicability*; second, it has *shallow foundations*; third, it is *autonomous*; and finally, it is based on *epistemic abstinence*. I will explain these features one at a time, starting with the first.

Rawls's theory has limited applicability. We know that it is not a comprehensive theory of justice; it is a theory of the justice of the basic structure of society only.[4] What I have in mind here is the theoretically more startling fact that the theory does not apply to the basic structure of all societies: "Justice as fairness is framed to apply to what I have called 'the basic structure' of a modern constitutional democracy."[5] This must have surprised the many early readers of Rawls who remember him limiting the application of his theory in a different way, that is, to the description of perfectly just societies only, leaving out all the principles which apply only in societies which fall short of this ideal. Many readers saw this as making the theory irrelevant to our countries.[6] The new limitation on the applicability of the theory is designed not only to make it political and not metaphysical, but also to render it realistically relevant to contemporary circumstances, and to remove any trace of utopianism.

Rawls has never attempted a precise or exhaustive analysis of the features of modern constitutional democracies which make his theory suited to them. To my mind this is one of the very attractive features of his position. It is not merely the result of a desire to avoid pedantry; it should be seen as fundamental to the nature of Rawls's whole enterprise. The firm starting point is the society of the here and now, and every society sufficiently like it. Generalizations regarding the basic features of the society of the here and now are not definitive of the boundaries of the enterprise. They are but (empirical) assumptions or conclusions which can be reexamined and revised. The only definitive foundation is the rootedness in the here and now.[7] This feature goes very deep. It af-

---

4. See John Rawls, *A Theory of Justice* (Cambridge: Harvard University Press, 1971), sec. 2, and "The Basic Structure as Subject," in *Values and Morals*, ed. A. Goldman and J. Kim (Dordrecht: Reidel, 1978), p. 47.

5. Rawls, "Political not Metaphysical," p. 224.

6. It would seem that Rawls, as many suspected, thinks that the United States and other modern Western democracies are basically just societies. This, as we will see, is a necessary, indeed a crucial, assumption if his theory is to be applicable to the contemporary societies it is meant for. On the limited applicability of the original theory see *A Theory of Justice*, pp. 245–46.

7. To ask what is the scope of the indexical is to misunderstand its function. It is ineliminable. The writer's theory must, to be successful, apply to his society at the time of writing, but there is no general answer as to which other societies and what other times it applies to. The applicability of the theory to different societies must be examined on a case-by-case basis. General guidelines can be useful, but they should never be understood as exhausting the range of relevant considerations.

The reflections here and in the text above go beyond anything Rawls can be regarded as committed to. They explain some of the background which makes me assent to his claim of limited applicability.

fects not only the conditions of applicability of Rawls's theory but also the very aim of political philosophy. "The aims of political philosophy depend on the society it addresses."[8] Only because we live in societies of this kind is the construction of a theory of justice along Rawls's lines, a theory which has the aims he set it, a proper task for political philosophy. In parallel, these conditions of contemporary democracies determine not only the content but the very function and role of a doctrine of justice.

While Rawls gives no precise and exclusive enumeration of the contemporary conditions which make us subject to his theory of justice, two factors or clusters of factors figure prominently in his argument. First and foremost is *the fact of pluralism.* There is "a diversity of general and comprehensive doctrines" and a "plurality of conflicting and indeed incommensurable conceptions of the meaning, value and purpose of human life" which are "affirmed by the citizens of democratic societies." "This diversity of doctrines—the fact of pluralism—is not a mere empirical condition that will soon pass away; it is . . . a permanent feature of the public culture of modern democracies."[9] Second, our societies share a rich enough *common culture* consisting in principles accepted by all as valid. We have a public culture and a public reason which can be appealed to as standards whose validity is, in spite of the fact of pluralism, beyond dispute.

This delicate balance between diversity and agreement sets the task of political philosophy in constructing a theory of justice and identifies the presupposition of both its success and its applicability. "Conditions for justifying a conception of justice hold only when a basis is established for political reasoning and understanding within a public culture. The

8. John Rawls, "The Idea of an Overlapping Consensus," *Oxford Journal of Legal Studies* 7 (1987): 1 (hereafter referred to as "Overlapping Consensus"). This is the opening sentence of the article.

9. Ibid., p. 4. Altogether Rawls lists seven features: "(1) the fact of pluralism; (2) the fact of the permanence of pluralism, given democratic institutions; (3) the fact that agreement on a single comprehensive doctrine presupposes the oppressive use of state power . . . (4) the fact that an enduring and stable democratic regime, one not divided into contending factions and hostile classes, must be willingly and freely supported by a substantial majority of at least its politically active citizens; (5) the fact that a comprehensive doctrine, whenever widely, if not universally, shared in society, tends to become oppressive and stifling; (6) the fact that reasonably favourable conditions . . . which make democracy possible exist; and finally, (7) the fact that the political culture of a society with a democratic tradition implicitly contains certain fundamental intuitive ideas from which it is possible to work up a political conception of justice suitable for a constitutional regime."

social role of a conception of justice is to enable all members of society to make mutually acceptable to one another their shared institutions and basic arrangements, by citing what are publicly recognized as sufficient reasons, as identified by that conception."[10]

This task of a political philosophy for our time—to construct a conception of justice out of the beliefs and principles which are part of our common culture, the beliefs which transcend the diversity endemic to our culture—brings us to the second sense in which the theory is political and not metaphysical. A theory of justice for our time has *shallow foundations*. Its justification starts with the fact that certain beliefs form the common currency of our public culture. It does not seek deep foundations for these beliefs; it concerns itself neither with their justification nor with its absence. A theory of justice "tries to draw solely upon basic intuitive ideas that are embedded in the political institutions of a constitutional democratic regime and the public traditions of their interpretation. . . . it starts from within a certain political tradition."[11]

The shallowness of the foundations is not forced on Rawls by the limited applicability of his theory. It is, in his mind, a result of its other two features, its autonomy and its epistemic abstinence. The *autonomy* of the theory of justice is its autonomy from general moral theory. As Rawls explains, his theory "is not to be understood as a general and comprehensive moral conception that applies to the political order,"[12] or to our concrete historical circumstances. Naturally, a theory can have limited applicability simply through including the conclusion that a universal theory bears on a particular subject or in particular circumstances. But Rawls's theory is no application of any more general moral doctrine. It is a self-standing political theory, which is not to be justified by its relations to a wider moral doctrine. This is one explanation of its shallow foundations: it starts not with general moral truths but with the givens of our common culture, which it takes as facts, irrespective of their validity or truth. And that is as far as it goes.

Embracing autonomy and shallow foundations is Rawls's response to the fact of pluralism. We should reconcile ourselves to pluralism. It

10. John Rawls, "Kantian Constructivism in Moral Theory," *Journal of Philosophy* 77 (1980): 517 (hereafter referred to as "Kantian Constructivism").

11. Rawls, "Political not Metaphysical," p. 225. See also p. 228, and "Overlapping Consensus," p. 6.

12. Rawls, "Overlapping Consensus," p. 3.

should be accepted not merely as a permanent fact, but as one which shapes the doctrine of justice. That doctrine must derive from the elements in our culture which transcend pluralism, which form its common public culture. The beliefs, attitudes, and institutions which constitute that public culture may well have a sound foundation in some comprehensive, possibly universal, moral theory. Alternatively, they may lack sound foundations. Neither matters. The common culture matters to Rawls as a fact, regardless of truth. That is the meaning of the shallow foundations. They, and the autonomy of the doctrine of justice, allow the generation of a theory of justice which can form the basis of a consensus in the face of pluralism.

While Rawls regards the limited applicability and shallow foundations of his theory as independent though complementary aspects, he thinks that together, and combined with his doctrine of the social role of justice which informs them, they force on him the fourth measure of modesty we referred to above. The doctrine of justice must adopt a posture of epistemic abstinence. Rawls's *epistemic abstinence* lies in the fact that he refrains from claiming that his doctrine of justice is true. The reason is that its truth, if it is true, must derive from deep, and possibly nonautonomous, foundations, from some sound comprehensive moral doctrine. Asserting the truth of the doctrine of justice, or rather claiming that its truth is the reason for accepting it, would negate the very spirit of Rawls's enterprise.[13] It would present the doctrine of justice as one of many competing comprehensive moralities current in our society, and this would disqualify it from fulfilling its role of transcending the disagreement among these many incompatible moralities.

To fulfill its social role of forming a basis for a consensus on the fundamental structure of society—thus enabling the citizens of a pluralistic society to discuss the constitutional principles of their society, and the implications of these principles, by reference to reasons which are acceptable to all regardless of their political, moral, and religious views—a doctrine of justice must be advocated on the ground that it commands or is capable of gaining a consensus of opinion, and not on the ground

---

13. As G. A. Cohen observed to me, this conclusion does not follow if all members of the community regard the doctrine of justice as self-evident. Then they could all agree to its truth without getting involved in any disagreements arising out of their comprehensive ethical and political views. Rawls has, of course, sufficient empirical evidence to know that his theory of justice is not accepted as self-evident by all in our society.

that it is true. "Questions of political justice can be discussed on the same basis by all citizens, whatever their social position, or more particular aims and interests, or their religious, philosophical or moral views. Justification in matters of political justice is addressed to others who disagree with us, and therefore it proceeds from some consensus."[14] "By avoiding comprehensive doctrines we try to bypass religion and philosophy's profoundest controversies so as to have some hope of uncovering a basis of a stable overlapping consensus."[15] "Some might say," adds Rawls, "that reaching this reflective agreement is itself sufficient grounds for regarding that conception as true, or at any rate highly probable. But we refrain from this further step: it is unnecessary and may interfere with the practical aim of finding an agreed public basis of justification."[16] The social role of justice can be purchased only at the price of epistemic distance.

Justice in Our Time, or Has Rawls Become a Politician?

Having concluded this preliminary examination of Rawls's conception of his enterprise, let us turn to some interpretative and critical questions. The last quotation, which is of crucial importance, provides a point of departure. It emphasizes the practical aim of the doctrine of justice. This seems to be the natural concomitant of epistemic abstinence. The aim is not to direct us towards true, valuable ideals, but to achieve certain practical political goals—to "help ensure stability from one generation to the next,"[17] to secure stability and social unity,[18] and to achieve this through bringing about a consensus on certain constitutional principles. "The aim of justice as fairness as a political conception is practical. . . . it presents itself not as a conception of justice that is true, but one that can serve as a basis of informed and willing political agreement."[19] A society that has achieved consensual unity and stability by endorsing a common doctrine of justice is called by Rawls "a well-ordered society":

> To say a society is well ordered by a conception of justice means three
> things: (1) that it is a society in which all citizens accept, and acknowl-
> edge before one another that they accept, the same principles of jus-
> tice; (2) that its basic structure—its main political and social institu-

14. Rawls, "Overlapping Consensus," p. 6.
15. Ibid., p. 14.   16. Ibid., p. 15.   17. Ibid., p. 1.
18. Rawls, "Political not Metaphysical," p. 251; see also pp. 249–50.
19. Ibid., p. 230.

tions and the way they hang together as one system of cooperation—is publicly known, or with good reason believed, to satisfy those principles, and (3) that citizens have a normally effective sense of justice, that is, one that enables them to understand and to apply the principles of justice, and for the most part to act from them as their circumstances require. *I believe that social unity so understood is the most desirable conception of unity available to us; it is the limit of the practical best.*[20]

This is of course the stuff of all democratic politics. It is concerned with give and take, with exploring a common ground for agreement on common policies and principles. When politics is concerned with fashioning a constitution, it requires near unanimity, and, of course, it deals with principles which will provide the framework within which all other political issues will be resolved. It sounds as if Rawls's practical aim is to engage in practical constitutional politics, with one difference: whereas politicians, at least sometimes, try to secure agreement by convincing people that the principles underlying their proposals are true, Rawls abjures this argument, and seeks to secure agreement simply by pointing out that certain principles are already implicitly agreed to, or nearly so.[21]

There is nothing wrong with engaging in politics, though some may doubt whether this is really what political philosophy is about. The suggestion that political philosophy should be no more than the sort of politics where the only thing that counts is success in commanding general agreement, the kind of politics where any principle, whatever its content, will be accepted provided it commands general assent, and where every principle will be compromised or rejected if it fails to gain universal approval, is objectionable. But is this really what Rawls has in mind?

Rawls assures us that "political philosophy is not mere politics." But

20. John Rawls, "The Priority of Right and Ideas of the Good," *Philosophy & Public Affairs* 17, no. 4 (Fall 1988): 269, italics added (hereafter referred to as "The Priority of Right"). The language and emphasis of this article, seen here in the use of the expression "the practical best," while not explicitly withdrawing from epistemic abstinence, is inconsistent with it. I will return to this point below.

21. Rawls is aware that there may not be enough common ground in a society actually to reach an overlapping consensus on a doctrine of justice. Narrowing down apparent differences is all that can be aspired to. Alternatively, the desire to reach agreement may lead people to modify those of their views which stand in the way of a consensus, thus making it possible after all. See "Political not Metaphysical," p. 228, and "Overlapping Consensus," pp. 7, 16, 19.

he simply points out that it takes a longer view.[22] It is essentially constitutional politics. It would be wrong, however (though, given much of what he says, entirely understandable), to regard the politics Rawls advocates as an unprincipled search for consensus at all costs. Two crucial elements in his thought rebut this misinterpretation. First, his aim is to reach "a consensus that includes all the opposing philosophical and religious doctrines likely to persist and to gain adherents in a more or less just constitutional democratic society."[23] In other words, only because our societies are nearly just societies can it be right for political philosophy to regard the pursuit of consensus as its overriding goal, and the consensus need not encompass every passing fashion, but only those comprehensive outlooks which are likely to persist in nearly just societies.

There is a problem here. The doctrine of justice itself reflects the consensus of our societies. Is it not inevitable that they will live up to their own standards? Rawls unflinchingly recognizes the self-referential nature of the condition. The consensus to be sought, he says, is one between the opposing doctrines likely to thrive "over generations in a more or less just constitutional democracy *where the criterion of justice is that political conception itself.*"[24] Of course, a society may avow principles which it does not live up to. There is no reason to refuse to pursue consensus in such a society. The consensus sought is among the competing moral, religious, or philosophical theories. The fact that the practice of that society does not conform to them is not reflected in the consensus view of justice which emerges, and does nothing to discredit it. So perhaps the condition of near justice imposed by Rawls is vacuous, and does little to qualify the unqualified pursuit of consensus at any price.[25] Though I do not know what non-self-fulfilling condition Rawls may have in mind, it is clear that he means this condition, or something like it, to

22. Rawls, "Overlapping Consensus," p. 24.
23. Rawls, "Political not Metaphysical," pp. 225–26; see also pp. 246–47, 249, and "Overlapping Consensus," pp. 1, 9.
24. Rawls, "Overlapping Consensus," p. 1.
25. A similar problem applies to a second, related condition imposed by Rawls. The consensus is between conceptions of the good which are "each compatible with the full rationality of human persons" ("Political not Metaphysical," p. 248). But Rawls suggests that the concept of the person he is employing is itself simply the one current in our culture. I will return to this text, and discuss the related statement on p. 9 of "Overlapping Consensus," below.

have substantial bite and to place the pursuit of consensus in a context which makes it an appropriate aim.

That consensus is the goal only in nearly just societies is an external condition on Rawls's methodological conception. It limits its applicability. The second corrective to the "consensus at any price" understanding of Rawls is the internal condition built into the special meaning he gives the expression "an overlapping consensus." He discusses this as part of his explanation of why an overlapping consensus is to be distinguished from a mere *modus vivendi*. Of the various marks of that distinction two are relevant here.[26]

First, and this factor explains all the others, a *modus vivendi* is a compromise based on self- or group interests; it reflects no principles other than the fact that it is an acceptable compromise.[27] A theory like Rawls's is genuinely a theory of justice. Not every consensus can be presented as a theory of justice. To be that, it must be a moral conception (though of course neither a comprehensive nor a deep one). It must possess internal coherence in expressing "conceptions of person and society, and concepts of right and fairness, as well as principles of justice with their complement of the virtues."[28] Second, the theory of justice is one which each of the many incompatible comprehensive moral, religious, and philosophical views can accept from its own standpoint. It is not, or not merely, based on a consensus among members of a society; it is primarily a consensus among the different conceptions of the good in that society: "We hope to make it possible for all to accept the political conception as true, or as reasonable, from the standpoint of their own comprehensive view, whatever it may be."[29]

These internal conditions on a doctrine of justice make it much harder to achieve. A prudential give and take among relatively rational individuals may well lead to a compromise, but it is likely to lack the complexity and the structure of internal justification required by Rawls. Rawls's aim is a genuinely philosophical conception of justice, not merely a political expediency. It is not surprising that he is not particularly optimistic

26. It is worth remembering that the distinction is introduced for a different purpose— that is, to show that the doctrine of justice is not advocated on purely prudential grounds. See Rawls, "Political not Metaphysical," p. 247.

27. See, for example, Rawls, "Overlapping Consensus," pp. 1, 2, 10, 11.

28. Rawls, "Political not Metaphysical," p. 247.

29. Rawls, "Overlapping Consensus," p. 13.

about the chances of actually achieving consensus on a theory which meets these conditions. "All this is highly speculative and raises questions which are little understood." All we can do is hope that a basis for such a consensus may be found, and that a consensus may emerge on that basis.[30]

Can There Be Justice without Truth?

These comments help to explain in what sense Rawls's theory is both philosophical and practical. It is philosophical in that it calls for a complex moral doctrine of justice. Yet it is practical, for the one and only reason Rawls mentions for the desirability of setting political philosophy this task is that it is necessary to ensure consensus-based social stability and unity. These practical goals explain the desirability of a doctrine of justice based on overlapping consensus, and one which is internally coherent and complex, that is, which constitutes a moral doctrine.[31] The fact that political philosophy can only assure us of the possibility of consensus and that its actuality is merely speculative does not make the philosophical enterprise any less practical.[32] The only reason for philosophy to establish the possibility of stability is, presumably, that that is the only way philosophy can contribute towards achieving noncoerced social unity and stability.

But why should philosophy contribute to these goals rather than to others? Presumably because they are worthwhile goals. So it would appear that while the goal of political philosophy is purely practical—while it is not concerned to establish any evaluative truths—it accepts some such truths as the presuppositions which make its enterprise intelligible. It recognizes that social unity and stability based on a consensus—that is, achieved without excessive resort to force—are valuable goals of sufficient importance to make them and them alone the foundations of a theory of justice for our societies. Without this assumption it would be unwarranted to regard the theory as a theory of *justice*, rather than a theory of social stability. In an uplifting conclusion Rawls declares that

30. Rawls, "Political not Metaphysical," p. 250; "Overlapping Consensus," p. 25.
31. Rawls, "Political not Metaphysical," pp. 250–51; "Overlapping Consensus," pp. 1, 11–12.
32. Naturally, the theory, if successful, establishes the truth of instrumental judgments to the effect that certain policies make stability and unity possible, or likely. Every practical inquiry does that. I take Rawls's point to be merely that the theory need not go into moral issues.

political philosophy aims at "the defence of reasonable faith in the real possibility of a just constitutional regime"[33]—by which he surely means that the real possibility, which he has argued for, of achieving consensus and securing stability is reason for faith in the possibility of a truly just regime, not merely the possibility of a regime which is called just by its members.

My argument is simple. A theory of justice can deserve that name simply because it deals with these matters, that is, matters that a true theory of justice deals with. In this sense there are many theories of justice, and they are all acceptable to the same degree as theories of justice. To recommend one as a theory of justice for our societies is to recommend it as a just theory of justice, that is, as a true, or reasonable, or valid theory of justice. If it is argued that what makes it *the* theory of justice for us is that it is built on an overlapping consensus and therefore secures stability and unity, then consensus-based stability and unity are the values that a theory of justice, for our society, is assumed to depend on. Their achievement—that is, the fact that endorsing the theory leads to their achievement—makes the theory true, sound, valid, and so forth. This at least is what such a theory is committed to. There can be no justice without truth.[34]

33. Rawls, "Overlapping Consensus," p. 25.

34. I have been equating 'true', 'sound', 'valid', and so on. Could it be that Rawls merely refuses to endorse truth, while being willing to apply one of the other adjectives? I think that the text suggests otherwise. The important point, however, is that he is committed to applying to the theory of justice whichever adjective is appropriately applied to moral propositions. There is no room for epistemic distance.

Noncognitivists and some others will find the reference to the possible truth of a theory of justice unintelligible. Theories of justice, in their view, are not the sort of things which can be either true or false. I am not taking sides in this debate here. My argument is purely an *ad hominem* one. Rawls is happy to contemplate the possibility that theories of justice are bearers of truth values, and that at least one is true. His argument is that the truth or falsity of a theory of justice does not matter to its acceptability. His is the theory of justice for us even if it is false. Therefore, his epistemic abstinence gives no support to noncognitivists or others who find the application of "truth" to theories of justice objectionable. He cannot and does not wish to rely on arguments from that source. Neither does he claim that it is unknowable whether a theory of justice is true or false. He is willing to contemplate the possibility that there are some who know what the true theory of justice is, and that it is incompatible with his. He is, in effect, arguing that such persons should nevertheless support his theory rather than the incompatible true theory, for his theory is the theory for us.

My argument above is not so much that such a claim is not morally justified as that it is incoherent, for in claiming that this is the theory of justice for us for such-and-such reasons, one is claiming that those reasons show (or make) this the true theory of justice (if truth applies to theories of justice).

2. POLITICAL INDEPENDENCE

Justice as Fairness: Practical or Theoretical?

The previous section concludes my main argument, which is directed against the epistemic abstinence that is one of the four features central to Rawls's recent writings on the justification and standing of his theory. In the present section I will discuss the remaining features—the autonomy of the theory of justice and its shallow foundations. I will conclude that Rawls's theory is strengthened if the thesis of the shallow foundations is jettisoned, and the idea of an overlapping consensus, to which it led, radically reinterpreted. Furthermore, a weak thesis of the autonomy of the theory of justice, which is completely independent of the discarded theses of epistemic abstinence and shallow foundations, should replace Rawls's strong autonomy. First, however, let us note the consequences of reuniting the practical and theoretical aspects of the theory of justice.

In his attempt to sustain his epistemic abstinence Rawls claims, as we saw above, that the theory of justice should be judged by its success in performing a practical task. It should not be regarded as a theory claiming truth for itself. Even if it is false it is still successful, it is still the theory we should accept, if it fulfills its practical role. My reply above was that if fulfilling the practical role assigned it by Rawls vindicates the theory of justice, then it shows it to be true (assuming *ad arguendum*, as Rawls does, that it can be true or false). Once epistemic abstinence is avoided we recognize that the practical role of the principles of justice in achieving consensus-based unity and stability is a theoretical consideration bearing on the truth (or validity) of the principles. We reject the dichotomy between the practical and the theoretical, and we are able to see how they are interrelated.

As a result we no longer need to see, nor can we see, in the achievement of consensual unity and stability the be-all and end-all of the theory of justice. It becomes one among many considerations bearing on the truth of the theory. In "The Priority of Right and Ideas of the Good," for example, Rawls follows his positing of the well-ordered society as the practical goal of a theory of justice with a passage pointing to the two ways in which a well-ordered society is good for people individually.[35] In

---

35. Rawls, "The Priority of Right," p. 270. As Rawls points out, the goal is also a social goal achieved only through social cooperation. This is one aspect of his theory which may disprove the criticism that it is individualistic. Much depends on whether Rawls's theory

"Justice as Fairness: Political not Metaphysical" he says that "the over-arching fundamental intuitive idea, within which other basic intuitive ideas are systematically connected, is that of society as a fair system of cooperation between free and equal persons. Justice as fairness starts from this idea as one of the basic intuitive ideas which we take to be implicit in the public culture of a democratic society."[36] Later he observes that "since the question of which conception of political justice is most appropriate for realizing in basic institutions the values of liberty and equality has long been deeply controversial within the very democratic tradition in which citizens are regarded as free and equal persons, the aim of justice as fairness is to try to resolve this question by starting from the basic intuitive idea of society as a fair system of social cooperation in which the fair terms of cooperation are agreed upon by citizens themselves so conceived."[37] These passages can be read as providing arguments to show that Rawls's doctrine of justice is true. They are all points which speak in its favor.[38] It is true, we can understand these passages as saying, because it represents a correct balance between freedom and equality, the balance which is required by a doctrine which is to be, as any doctrine of justice must be, a fair system of cooperation between free and equal people. Rawls's epistemic abstinence stops us from reading them in this way. His epistemic abstinence means that his doctrine of justice should be accepted even if false. To be consistent with epistemic abstinence these passages must be understood as pointing simply to beliefs which command general consent in our culture. Even that fact is not used to show that the principles are true. It merely shows that they can form part of a doctrine of justice which fulfills the practical role assigned to it by Rawls—that is, securing consensual unity and stability.

Once we are rid of the epistemic abstinence, however, we can reverse the connection between the goal of consensual stability and unity and that of achieving a fair system of cooperation between free and equal

---

yields the conclusion that a well-ordered society is intrinsically good, or whether it is good only instrumentally in enabling individuals to achieve their individual aims. If it is intrinsically good, then Rawls's theory is not individualistic, as it recognizes an essentially social goal as intrinsically good.

36. Rawls, "Political not Metaphysical," p. 231.

37. Ibid., p. 244. See also "The Priority of Right," p. 253.

38. As do other passages, especially the long discussion in "The Priority of Right" of the goodness of justice as fairness.

people. Being epistemically unshackled, we can conclude that the achievement of consensual unity and stability is worthwhile because (at least in part) without them there can be no fair cooperation between *free and equal people.*[39]

Digging Deeper

If the fact that the principles of justice enable us to establish a fair system of cooperation between free and equal people counts in their favor, what is the relevance of the popularity of the ideal of a fair system of cooperation in modern constitutional democracies? Would it not have been an argument for Rawls's doctrine of justice that it secures such cooperation had we lived in a society in which its value is not generally appreciated? Rawls thinks it important to start from the common beliefs of our culture. We called this feature of his theory its shallow foundations. But what purpose does it serve? Possibly he feels committed to it by his epistemic abstinence. If we shun the question whether the theory is true, we must instead make sure that it is acceptable to people, given their current beliefs. Can the shallow foundations survive the rejection of epistemic abstinence?[40]

Several possible reasons for assigning weight to the general belief in the desirability of a fair system of cooperation between free and equal people ought to be mentioned only to be rejected. First, it may be said that if a doctrine of justice is to fulfill its social role, it must rest on wide social support, which will enable it to form the common background of political debate.[41] To understand the ideal of a fair system of cooperation in this way is to revert to the view which denies it primary justificatory force. If Rawls's understanding of our common culture is correct, this point shows that his doctrine of justice may come to be accepted by people in our countries. But while acceptability may indeed be an important condition for any satisfactory theory of justice, it cannot be its main virtue. That has to involve considerations which bear directly on the justice of its recommendations. Not every feasible doctrine is a valid one. Feasibility or workability can only be a small part of such an argument. Second, some readers have understood Rawls's shallow foundations as hav-

39. Many of Rawls's readers have understood him in this way all along. They fail to realize that this reading is inconsistent both with his epistemic abstinence and with his shallow foundations, on which more below.

40. My argument in the previous section amounts to showing that shallow foundations are in any case inconsistent with epistemic abstinence.

41. See, for example, Rawls, *A Theory of Justice*, pp. 454–55.

ing evolved from, and having inherited the status of, his doctrine of reflective equilibrium. According to this reading of his recent work, the social acceptability of certain beliefs shows them to be true, for it shows them to be held in reflective equilibrium. Reflective equilibrium is interpreted by such readers as requiring social convergence, rather than merely a certain mode of individual endorsement. I see no reason to accept this understanding of the point. It is true that it has the merit of reconciling relying on the desirability of a fair system of cooperation with relying on its popularity in our culture. Its popularity, on this interpretation, establishes its desirability. But this interpretation does violence to the essential features of Rawls's position. For him reflective equilibrium is the fundamental method of justification; it is an epistemic doctrine of universal application. His advocacy of shallow foundations, on the other hand, is limited to a theory of justice for our society. In fact the correctness of shallow foundations is itself to be judged in reflective equilibrium. The two cannot be identified.

Is it possible, however, that shallow foundations are truth-making in our culture? Is it possible that Rawls believes that a fair system of cooperation among free and equal people is a valid ideal for us because it is generally acceptable in our culture? It is difficult to see how the popularity of a (putative) ideal bears on its validity except insofar as it reflects on the feasibility of its implementation. One possibility is that Rawls starts from the presupposition that our countries are just. We do not know what makes them just, as there are many incompatible opinions and arguments regarding their justification. So we jettison any deep theory, which would have to adjudicate between the competing views, and embrace shallow foundations. For we know that since our countries are just, the views which are common ground must be sound. This presupposition makes the theory essentially complacent. Any moral and political theory must be open to the possibility that the societies to which it applies are fundamentally defective. Radical criticism of common institutions and common beliefs is, at least in principle, part of the function of such theories.[42]

Another suggestion might be that commonly endorsed beliefs enjoy

42. Nor does Rawls claim otherwise, for he is willing to consider, in conformity with his epistemic abstinence, the possibility that such ideals are invalid but should be accepted nonetheless. Notice that my point in the text above is consistent with the view that every criticism must, in some sense, be rooted in the culture and the tradition it addresses. Those who believe that this is so can admit the possibility of radical criticism, rooted, for example, in a sociologically deviant strand of the culture.

the consent of (just about) everyone, and that consent is the foundation
of moral or political validity, or at least an overriding consideration, vali-
dating principles however objectionable they are on other grounds. But
there is nothing in Rawls's account to show that the common acceptance
of such principles is achieved under conditions which amount to a free
and informed consent to them;[43] and it is doubtful whether consent
which is not free and informed is binding in the required way. It would
seem therefore that if the desirability of a fair system of cooperation
should count in favor of Rawls's principles of justice, then it is the validity of this ideal, and not its popularity, which is required to support the
argument. Shallow foundations have to be abandoned along with epistemic abstinence.

What Sort of Autonomy?

I suggested earlier that Rawls sees epistemic abstinence, the shallow
foundations of his doctrine of justice, and its autonomy as closely connected and mutually supportive. Must his view of the autonomy of the
doctrine of justice suffer the fate of the other two facets of his recent
writings? Not necessarily. An autonomous political theory is a theory
which argues for the truth of propositions about specifically political values, virtues, and so on. Being autonomous, it is not concerned with nonpolitical moral truths.[44] But its whole purpose and function is to argue
for political moral truths. Rawls's argument leads from the political values of consensus-based social stability and unity, or of a fair system of
cooperation, to the political doctrine of justice. All these are autonomous
political values, for (a) "social unity and stability" and "a fair system of
cooperation" are social predicates which only indirectly bear on individual behavior, and (b) the justification of the value of stability and unity
is independent of other moral values. Politics is not morality applied to a
special subject.

Can Rawls's conception of the autonomy of political morality, of its
independence from all comprehensive moral doctrines, be sustained?
The key to the problem is the role of overlapping consensus. So far we
have seen one way, and I take it to be the main way, in which that idea
figures in the argument. It plays a crucial instrumental role. Principles

---

43. Needless to say, Rawls does not rely on this argument, at least not explicitly.
44. I distinguish below two senses in which a political theory may be called "autonomous."

which command an overlapping consensus fulfill the social role of justice, that is, they help secure consensual social stability and unity. They
do so in a special way which suggests that overlapping consensus may
play a second, justificatory role. Consensual stability and unity are, as we
saw, achieved through the fact that everyone (or almost everyone) agrees
with the theory of justice for his own reasons. Starting from different
standpoints, all end up endorsing the same principles.[45]

This seems to suggest that the people who are governed by the principles of justice accept them each from the point of view of his or her
own comprehensive conception of the good. For them political philosophy does not appear to have shallow foundations. They regard it as an
application of their comprehensive morality to the special problems of
politics. In what sense is it then autonomous? For whom is it autonomous? Recall the passage we examined before: "Some might say that
reaching this reflective agreement is itself sufficient grounds for regarding that conception as true, or at any rate highly probable. But we refrain
from this further step: it is unnecessary and may interfere with the practical aim of finding an agreed public basis of justification."[46] Why might
the fact of a reflective agreement indicate that the conception of justice
agreed on is (probably) true? One reason might be that it is unlikely that
all reasonable conceptions of the good are false. Therefore whatever they
all agree on is probably true. A second reason, which seems closer to the
spirit of Rawls's argument, is that achieving reflective agreement secures the social role of justice (helping to ensure consensus-based stability and unity), and this shows that the conception of justice agreed on
is true.

It seems that Rawls concurs but fears that saying so would interfere
with securing an agreed public basis for justification. Naturally it is not
the fact of the agreement which interferes with finding agreement.
Rather what is suspect is the claim that its fulfilling the social role of
justice, securing a consensus-based stability and continuity, shows that
a theory of justice is true. This claim may not command agreement, and
if put forward as part of the theory of justice will make it controversial
and jeopardize its ability to fulfill its role. It would appear that the theory
is supported by arguments whose advocacy would be self-defeating.

45. See, for example, Rawls, "Overlapping Consensus," pp. 9, 13.
46. Ibid., p. 15.

What Rawls needs is not epistemic abstinence so much as an esoteric doctrine.

What about us, Rawls's readers? How are we to treat his arguments? Are we to accept his theory of justice as an autonomous political doctrine for the reasons he explains, or should each of us accept it as part of his or her comprehensive conception of the good? How does Rawls himself view his theory? Is it, in his eyes, part of an autonomous political theory with shallow foundations? Or is it part of his comprehensive conception of the good? One cannot have it both ways.

A distinction between two ways in which a political theory can be autonomous will help here. It is weakly autonomous if it is part of a pluralistic comprehensive conception of the good. A pluralistic conception of the good recognizes the existence of irreducibly many intrinsic goods, virtues, and values. Some independent goods are essentially political. Distributive justice may be such a value. It manifests itself politically, in the constitutional structure of society, and in its observance. The personal virtues which are associated with distributive justice are political virtues. They mark the quality of people as citizens. They are forms of individual excellence which are manifested in public attitudes and actions. Political theory understood as dealing (at least in part) with irreducibly political values can nevertheless be part of a comprehensive moral view. It is justified by establishing how its values fit and make sense together with the other values embraced in the comprehensive conception. By contrast, a strongly autonomous political theory is a theory whose validity or truth does not depend on nonpolitical considerations.

Which is Rawls's own view? His is a theory which makes no claim to truth or validity, and is thus independent of any moral foundations. It is strongly autonomous. Which view should be attributed to Rawls once his theory is freed from its stance of epistemic self-denial? It seems clear that even then Rawls should be understood to endorse strong autonomy. Weak autonomy would make the theory part of particular comprehensive conceptions of the good, and it is the thrust of Rawls's whole argument to deny this, to suggest that a theory of justice for our times should not be part of a comprehensive conception of the good.[47]

47. This is confirmed by "The Priority of Right," pp. 252–53, where Rawls draws a similar distinction between two conditions of autonomy (the first corresponding to my weak autonomy), and asserts that both obtain. The discussion on pp. 261–62 of the same article may, however, suggest that all that is required is weak autonomy within an overlapping consensus of comprehensive, and otherwise divergent, moral theories.

There are at least two decisive objections to viewing political philosophy as strongly autonomous.[48] First, justification of moral and political
values depends in part on the way they can be integrated into a comprehensive view of human well-being.[49] Moral and political justification is
in part holistic. Second, the practical implications of any value depend
on whether it conflicts with other values, and if so, which of the conflicting values prevails in particular circumstances of various kinds. Since a
strongly autonomous political theory prevents us from considering its political values in the comprehensive context of a complete moral theory, it
cannot yield practical conclusions. It can neither assure us that conflicts
do not arise nor adjudicate when they do arise.

The question of possible conflicts between his doctrine of justice and
other values is specifically addressed by Rawls: "How can a political conception of justice express values that, under the reasonably favourable
conditions that make democracy possible, normally outweigh whatever
other values conflict with them?" His answer, in brief, is that "the values
which conflict with the political conception of justice and its sustaining
virtues may be normally outweighed because they come into conflict
with the very conditions that make fair social cooperation possible on a
footing of mutual respect."[50] One might quarrel with this answer in various ways. One is to face Rawls with a dilemma. If what he means is that
general compliance with the principles of justice is necessary to achieve
the goal stated, it does not follow that absolute compliance in each case

48. My characterization of strong autonomy is too vague to allow conclusive discussion.
For example, if autonomy is infringed by justifying political values by reference to individual well-being, then on the humanistic assumption that what matters in the end is the
well-being of people, valid political theory cannot be strongly autonomous. I will, however,
understand strong autonomy as allowing appeal to individual well-being in justification of
political values and institutions. What is not allowed is appeal to other concrete virtues and
values which are not themselves political.

49. Goods and values are often said to be interdependent in another sense as well: they
are said to depend on each other in their operation, in that they are merely conditionally
good. They are good in a normal context. Trust is good in most circumstances, but there
will always be circumstances in which any good turns bad and any virtue loses its value.
This argument convinced Kant that only the good will is unconditionally good (*Ground-
work of the Metaphysics of Morals*, chap. 1). I do not wish to endorse this thesis of interdependence.

50. Rawls, "Overlapping Consensus," p. 17. Rawls makes other comments in this context. But they seem to be addressed to a conflict between his doctrine of justice and comprehensive moralities which are fundamentally hostile to it. My argument assumes that
one accepts Rawls's doctrine of justice in its own right and is merely worried about conflicts between it and other moral values.

is necessary. So particular conflicts require examination of their particular circumstances. If, on the other hand, what Rawls means is that one person or institution can be just to another in the individual case only if he deals with him in conformity with the principles of justice, this leaves open the question whether being absolutely just to another is always more important than all other possible moral considerations.

Whatever one's response to this objection, the important point is that Rawls agrees that a doctrine of justice yields practical conclusions only if its requirements are compared with and assessed in relation to other values. This amounts to the (inevitable) abandonment of strong autonomy, and to an acceptance of weak autonomy instead.

Political Theory as Morality's Foreign Office

In a way, only now, having rejected Rawls's epistemic abstinence, his shallow foundations, and his thesis of the strong autonomy of his theory, are we able to do full justice to the idea of an overlapping consensus. Our recent reflections started with a quandary: Does the theory of justice rest on the need to secure a consensus-based social unity and stability, or is it nested in a sound comprehensive conception of the good? The specific purpose of Rawls's recent writing is to deny that his theory of justice is to be accepted because it is part of a true comprehensive moral theory. At the same time he maintains (or rather would maintain if he were to abandon his epistemic self-denial) that it is true or valid (in part) because everyone who accepts it accepts it as part of his comprehensive moral theory. Does this mean that all who so accept it are mistaken in doing so,[51] but the fact that we are all mistaken makes the theory true?

This is the only possible interpretation on the assumption that Rawls's theory is strongly autonomous.[52] But having rejected the strong autonomy thesis, we can explore the possibility that the theory of justice is defended by Rawls—or rather by some of his arguments—as part of a comprehensive moral theory. That defense is best reconstructed as resting on four limbs:

(1) *The embeddedness of the justification*: The doctrine of justice is part of a true comprehensive moral theory.

51. That is, everyone has the wrong reasons for accepting it.

52. It is true that Rawls refuses to judge whether the various comprehensive moral theories are true or false. But he is committed to condemning them all as falsely endorsing a nonautonomous theory of justice, or else he must abandon his claim that the theory is autonomous.

(2) *The ad hominem element*: Those who do not accept the true comprehensive moral theory are nevertheless committed to its doctrine of justice, for it is consonant with their comprehensive views
as well.

(3) *The interdependence of arguments*: The *ad hominem* element is
essential to the justification of the doctrine as part of the sound
and comprehensive moral theory.

(4) *The similarity of the arguments*: The reason the doctrine of justice can be argued for *ad hominem* is the extensive similarities
among the diverse moral theories in our societies.

The special character of the defense lies not in its being independent
of the true, comprehensive moral theory, but in the fact that (a) the doctrine of justice is embedded in both true and false moral theories in a
similar way, and (b) that way includes cross-reference in each theory to
the fact that it is so embedded in the others. An outline of Rawls's reconstructed argument will show how these features figure in it.

First, every (comprehensive) moral theory must address the question:
How are those who disbelieve it to be judged and treated? It may declare
that their disbelief is irrelevant. Moral principles apply to all regardless
of their beliefs, and everyone is judged by them in the same way. Many
theories do not take this line. They may, for example, regard responsibility as dependent, at least to a degree, on people's frame of mind when
they engaged in the activities on which they are being judged. Some
religions distinguish between universal principles that bind all, and principles that bind only believers in the right faith. Such theories have a
special doctrine regarding the way one should behave towards nonbeliev-
ers. One's duties and responsibilities towards them and their duties and
responsibilities may differ from those which bind the religiously or morally faithful.

Second, the true moral theory for our societies recognizes that there is
special value in people's freely developing their own understanding of
the meaning of life and the ways one can flourish, and also in people's
living in accord with their own freely developed conception of the good.
This means that those whose lives are not guided by such freely chosen
conceptions of the good are diminished and that those who are so guided
are better off for being so guided, even if their particular conceptions of
the good are mistaken.

This is a very crude version of the sort of belief in the value of autonomy that Rawls attributes to Kant and Mill—that is, a belief in the value
of autonomy as part of a comprehensive theory of the good and of the
meaning of life. Rawls, of course, abstains from expressing judgment on
it,[53] though it seems to me that his claim that we have a higher-order
interest, which dominates all other interests,[54] in "realiz[ing] and exer-
cis[ing]" our "capacity to form, to revise, and rationally to pursue a conception of the good"[55] commits him to nothing less. In any case, the preceding argument suggests that the idea of an overlapping consensus
must make each of us situate the doctrine of justice within *some* comprehensive conception of the good. It is reasonable to attribute this kind
of liberalism to Rawls. But this conception can be seen as an example
only. If not this, then his liberalism must rest on some other conception
of the good, which needs spelling out.

Third, it follows that while one may try to convince others of the error
of their ways, one should not force or manipulate them to live in ways
other than those they accept. They should be given opportunities freely
to develop their own conceptions of the good. It is vital to the validity of
the argument that this point is self-referential. Only if people agree that
giving them opportunities to develop their own conceptions of the good
is valuable do they develop their ideas and conceptions of the good in the
spirit required according to the above claim about people's higher interests. Their higher interests, that is, are understood to include self-rec-
ognition, recognition that these are people's higher interests. This fact
applies to my concern for my own life too. While I am concerned to lead
the life that I now believe to be the right one, I am even more concerned
to be able to lead the life that conforms to my freely developed conception
of the good as it may be from time to time. Hence the way to relate to
others who do not share our conception of the good is to establish a
scheme of cooperation, to which all could agree, and which would enable
all to pursue their own conceptions of the good within fair terms of cooperation.

Fourth, as a matter of fact the conclusions reached in the previous
point (everyone should be allowed to pursue his own conception of the

53. See Rawls, "Political not Metaphysical," pp. 245–46; "Overlapping Consensus," pp.
5, 9.
54. Except the other higher-order interest in living in a just society.
55. Rawls, "Kantian Constructivism," p. 525.

good, within a framework which commands general consent), though not the grounds for them, are part of the common culture of modern constitutional democracies. We therefore know that other people freely accept them as true, though not necessarily for the reasons that we do. This means that there is reason to hope that an agreement on principles of justice based on these two requirements is forthcoming.

Fifth, the last point shows how our own endorsement of a doctrine of justice from the point of view of our own conception of the good (as explained in the second point above) depends on that doctrine's acceptability to other people in our society, who do not share our conception of the good. Hence there is here a possibility of give and take. We are willing, upon reflection, to modify our own interpretation of the common culture, and those aspects of our conception of the good on which it depends, in order to reach the kind of agreement that our conception of the good recommends, that is, in order to overcome some differences of opinion between us and others. The fact that an agreement is demanded of us by our own conception of the good renders that conception open to revision in order to secure that agreement.

As is clear, this is not Rawls's own argument. It is a reconstruction to which we have been driven in view of the difficulties we found in sustaining Rawls's espousal of epistemic self-denial and shallow foundations, and the strong autonomy of his theory of justice. The reconstructed argument preserves the limited applicability of the theory, the doctrine of a higher-order interest in autonomy, and the central role of the idea of an overlapping consensus. It does not make much of Rawls's insistence on the importance of social unity and stability. These can lead to an alternative reconstruction, which relegates Rawls's statements about higher-order interests to the body of the doctrine of justice rather than to its deep justification. This second reconstruction simply says that the true moral theory for our society regards consensus-based social unity and stability as of paramount importance. Therefore, since only principles which command general consensus among all viable comprehensive moralities current in our society can secure stability and unity, the doctrine of justice should rest on an overlapping consensus. And Rawls's theory of justice happens to command, or nearly to command, such a consensus. This reconstruction is closer to the view that the theory of justice is weakly autonomous.

Consensus and Stability

Rawls's response to pluralism has two aspects; he attempts to avoid taking sides in the argument among conflicting conceptions of the good in
two ways. First, by opting for shallow foundations and epistemic abstinence, he seeks to avoid basing his doctrine of justice on controversial
grounds. Second, the practical implications of his doctrine of justice are
meant to avoid favoring one conception of the good over any other.
Within the framework set by the principle of justice each is allowed to
pursue his conception of the good, in his own way. As regards the first
aspect of Rawls's response to pluralism, we have seen that his own arguments can sustain neither epistemic abstinence nor shallow foundations. Our reconstructed argument based on the idea of an overlapping
consensus makes the doctrine of justice morality's department of foreign
affairs. It is a special part of a comprehensive conception of the good, but
it is a part of it all the same. The reconstruction was designed to guarantee the noncontroversiality of the doctrine of justice which emerges
(where noncontroversiality means a *potential* overlapping consensus,
one which can be reached by people motived to seek consensus who rationally explore the implications and the flexibility of their comprehensive conceptions of the good). Whether such a noncontroversial doctrine
of justice can in fact be justified depends on the success one may have
in filling in the bare outlines of the reconstructed argument offered here.
The difficulty is that we have moved a long way from Rawls's original
intentions. The evaluation of the principles of justice depends, according
to the reconstructed argument, on the soundness of a comprehensive
moral theory which yields them. For it was that comprehensive moral
theory which through its own internal logic came to regard overlapping
consensus as necessary to secure justice. If the sound conception of the
good does not contain the reconstructed argument, then the doctrine of
justice falls with it. So we have to await a statement of Rawls's general
moral theory to answer the question. It would not do to take too seriously
the reconstructed argument above. It is too sketchy, and it is not Rawls's.

This is not the place to discuss the other aspect of Rawls's response to
the fact of pluralism. I would like, however, to remark here that the success of his principles of justice in being at least roughly neutral between
different conceptions of the good (meaning here "that the state is to ensure for all citizens equal opportunity," that is, equal chances of success,

"to advance any conception of the good they freely affirm")[56] seems to me essential to their persuasiveness. It is true that the neutrality of the principles of justice is subject to several exceptions, the most important being that conceptions of the good inconsistent with the principles of justice are likely to be at a disadvantage. In reiterating this second point in "The Priority of Right," Rawls has expressed himself in a way which may suggest to the incautious reader that his theory does not aspire to (rough) neutrality (in this sense of the term).[57] His words there, however, should not be so understood. If one reason supporting his doctrine of justice is that it is roughly neutral, then this exception can be easily accommodated. It does no more than admit that given the denial by some conceptions of the good of an equal opportunity to those who pursue other conceptions, neutrality can be achieved only by disadvantaging the intolerant conceptions. It follows, of course, that the feasible neutrality is not complete. But this is consistent with arguing that Rawls's theory is as neutral as any can be.

Why does the case for Rawls's doctrine of justice rest on the (rough) neutrality of his principles? Rawls's general argument rests on the assumption that in the original position people would opt for the principles of justice because they insure themselves against the worst eventualities. For this reason they would opt for a distribution of primary goods as equal as is consistent with making the lot of the worst off as good as possible. This conclusion follows only if the distribution of primary goods correlates fairly accurately with what people care most about. Only if it does will insuring themselves against the worst allocation of primary goods amount to insuring themselves against the worst eventualities. According to Rawls, people care most about their ability to realize their own conceptions of the good.[58] So the success of his argument for the principles of justice depends on the claim that primary goods provide an equal chance of advancing any conception of the good a person may have (excluding those inconsistent with the principles of justice). If they do,

56. Rawls, "The Priority of Right," p. 262.
57. See ibid.: "The priority of right excludes the first meaning of neutrality of aim, for it allows only permissible conceptions (those that respect the principles of justice) to be pursued."
58. I am inclined to say that they care most about realizing the sound conception of the good.

then the principles of justice are as neutral as possible in ensuring to all people the same chance of realizing their conceptions of the good regardless of what those conceptions are.[59] Elsewhere I, like many other writers, have criticized Rawls's principles of justice for failing to be neutral in this sense; I will not return to this issue here.[60]

There is, however, one more aspect of Rawls's argument which should be considered here. This is the argument for overlapping consensus from the need for social stability and unity. That need can be taken for granted.[61] Does it vindicate the idea of an overlapping consensus? This requires three restrictive elements: first, social unity and stability are to be secured through agreement on principles; second, the whole community, or at least all those who adhere to conceptions of the good which are likely to survive within it, will agree on the same set of principles of constitutional government; third, the principles agreed upon form a coherent and complex body of theory with its own internal structure of justification—that is, they are mutually supportive.

The third element is, as was mentioned above,[62] the only one explicitly justified by Rawls. He regards it as necessary to guarantee stability. Without such deep agreement, shifting power relations, or temporary changes in alliances within the community, may undermine the consensus, and with it social stability. If this argument holds, then it will also justify the other restrictive requirements. I doubt, however, whether any of them plays the central role in securing social unity and stability assigned to them by Rawls. Rather, affective and symbolic elements may well be the crucial cement of society, and to these one has only to add the little power individuals have to affect societal affairs.

Stable societies are marked by a high degree of identification of individuals with their society. People are proud members of their nation. The identification is marked by attachment to national symbols, cultural and conventional as well as legal (language, literature, foods, flag, and anthem). These evoke emotion, and create common bonds among those who share these attitudes. They are important elements in shaping one's

59. In "The Priority of Right," pp. 275–76, Rawls seems to display an indifference to the considerations adumbrated above which appears to me to undermine his own theory.

60. See Joseph Raz, *The Morality of Freedom* (Oxford: Oxford University Press, 1986), chap. 5.

61. Though only in the sense of assigning it some importance. There is no reason I know of for assigning it absolute importance.

62. See Section 1.

imagination, and in defining one's historical horizon. People share a common pride in a shared historical experience. Such identification normally includes attachment to certain values. But these are normally expressed at a high level of abstraction (liberty, equality, fraternity) which is compatible with complete disagreement about constitutional principles (for example, between royalists and republicans, or between fascists, democrats, and revolutionary communists).

Obviously there may also be agreement on some constitutional principles. But there need not be complete agreement. There may, for example, be an overlapping agreement in a sense different from Rawls's—that is, agreement between any two people about some of the prevailing constitutional principles, so that each principle enjoys a measure of support, although no one agrees to them all. Or there may be other forms of overlap.

Symbolic and affective identification and a partial cognitive overlap may be a very firm foundation for social unity and stability, especially when we remember that individuals find it both prudentially and morally undesirable to undermine the status quo, or even to try to evade its consequences, given the small chances of success. Of course, many factors contribute to the stability of a country's political system: the nature of its culture, its history of past conflicts, the depth of feeling concerning current rivalries, and so on. The point is that they are only partially sensitive to the existence of anything remotely like Rawls's overlapping consensus. The latter is neither necessary nor sufficient, and even were it to exist it would play only a partial, perhaps even a merely subsidiary, role in securing unity and stability. None of this denies that common agreement to a theory of justice will contribute to such goals. But given the way the world actually works, the modesty of that contribution raises doubts as to whether Rawls has identified the concerns which should dominate political philosophy today. No reason seems to have been given for political philosophy to abandon its traditional goals of understanding the moral presuppositions of existing institutions and criticizing them and advocating better ones—in the full light of reason and truth.

3. Impartiality against Truth

Thomas Nagel has recently offered an ingenious argument which he presents as an attempt to capture the sound intuitions behind the position advocated by Rawls, among others. Like Rawls's own arguments, it rests on the advocacy of epistemic abstinence. Does it fare any better? Its examination occupies the rest of this article.

The Role and Limits of Justification

Traditionally, normative political theory sought to determine and to explain the truth of value judgments concerning political authority and its actions. One wonders whether this goal is shared by Nagel. "Political stability," he remarks, "is helped by wide agreement to the principles underlying a political order. But that is not all: for some, the possibility of justifying the system to as many participants as possible is of independent moral importance."[63] Justification, he explains, is a normative concept, which may facilitate agreement, but is neither necessary nor sufficient to that end. Justification, as I understand it, is the explanation of the truth of a value judgment—in this case concerning the scope and limits of legitimate authority. It seems, therefore, that Nagel's object is to argue for the truth or validity of certain principles of governmental action. But things are not so simple.

The goal of justification, says Nagel, is "to persuade the reasonable." The attempt to justify has a practical point. Its point is not, or not only, to discover under what conditions governments have a right to rule. It is not, or not only, to learn the truth. Rather it is to secure the independent practical value of convincing the reasonable. That is why Nagel can conclude that "given the actual range of values, interests, and motives in a society, and depending on one's standards of justification, there may not be a legitimate solution [that is, a valid justification], and then one will have to choose between illegitimate government and no government."[64] But if government lacks justification, is it rational to choose it nonetheless? If it is rational, that must be because having a government is desir-

63. Thomas Nagel, "Moral Conflict and Political Legitimacy," *Philosophy & Public Affairs* 16, no. 3 (Summer 1987): 218 (hereafter referred to as "Conflict and Legitimacy"). Much of the time Nagel appears not to express his own views but rather those of "some," as here, or of "liberals" or "liberal theory." I will assume that normally Nagel agrees, at least tentatively, with these views. Nagel does not share the sensitivity displayed by Rawls to the range and variety of liberal views. The idea that liberalism can be identified with some political theory put forward by one or more writers over the last few years shows little respect for the history of the subject, as well as for the vitality and richness of the liberal tradition.

64. Ibid.

able in that it serves some value. But then that fact would provide the
sought-for justification.[65] If justification is simply the explanation of the
truth of a value judgment, then the choice that Nagel refers to can never
be a rational one. Justification for Nagel, it would therefore seem, must
be something different. Rather than being the road to normative truth in
general, it seems to be but one practical value among many. If no justification is available it may still be worth having an unjustified—that is,
illegitimate—government for the sake of other values that this may
serve. As we shall see, the gap between truth and justification is both
the source of the appeal of Nagel's proposal and the root of its weakness.

Convincing the reasonable is valuable in itself. It is, one might say,
always nice to have everyone agree that one's actions are sensible and
just. But there can be no doubt that this is at best a luxury.[66] The matter
acquires urgency, according to Nagel, when the action concerned is that
of a political authority. The reason is that political authorities exercise
coercion over their subjects. That is why their actions should enjoy the
consent of their subjects: "This question is part of the wider issue of
political legitimacy . . . of justifying coercively imposed political and social institutions to the people who have to live under them."[67]

Several of the points I have attributed to Nagel now have to be un-
packed. First, convincing those subject to governmental power, securing
their actual agreement, is ultimately what is desired. One's duty to
others, however, is confined to acting on grounds which are known and
which will convince if reasonably attended to. If they fail to convince,
that is not one's fault. Hence the objective of one's action is convincing
the reasonable. The basic motivation is to secure consent, but it is
hedged by a certain understanding of the limits of one's responsibilities
towards others. Responsibility lapses if its failure to achieve its object is
due to other people's unreasonableness.

Second, the special need to base political action on consent arises from
its coercive character. "This element of coercion imposes an especially

65. Remember that the issue is not whether one is justified in obeying the government.
One may be justified in obeying an illegitimate government. The question is whether the
government is legitimate or justified.

66. The luxury is in the desire to secure actual agreement. Possibly, whenever we act,
the reasons for our actions, the maxim of our action, should be objectively valid. This may
be enough to secure the agreement of the reasonable under ideal conditions.

67. Nagel, "Conflict and Legitimacy," p. 218.

stringent requirement of objectivity in justification."[68] The result is that only the consent of those who are coerced by a political act (or against whom it would be coercively enforced) need be secured. This may narrow the scope of the constraints of impartiality that Nagel is seeking to justify more than he intends. Those constraints will not apply to noncoercive action like declaring a certain religion the state religion, or to the granting of other (inexpensive) public honors and privileges to that religion or to its practitioners. But these are marginal matters. Once the core of Nagel's contention is established, there may well be ways of extending it to certain peripheral regions.

Rational Consent

Justified coercion is based on consent. This is Nagel's first principle. I will call it the principle of consent. The consent he requires is individual consent to every single measure. His object is to set a limit to the measures governments may adopt. Any measure of which a citizen would reasonably say "I withhold my consent to that" is ruled out. This requirement goes well beyond such consent as is secured by the existence of a democratic government.[69] Nagel's interpretation of the principle, however, involves strands of thought which some who are attracted by its basic idea may not wish to follow. His is a rationalist notion of consent: the reasonable consent when reason indicates that consent is due. Reason always indicates that consent is, other things being equal, due when the proposed action confers a clear advantage, or is part of a scheme which is imposed on a group, compliance with which secures advantages for all.[70] Refusal to consent to such measures as the compulsory wearing of car seat belts, compulsory vaccination whose benefits are clear, and so on is not protected by Nagel's principle as he understands it. Others have distinguished between theories based on benefit to the governed and those based on their consent. Nagel elides the two.

It may be suggested that Nagel feels forced into this position by a misunderstanding of the limits he sets to justification. The principle that we need justify our actions only to the reasonable seems to leave no room for a gap between reason and consent. If an action is to my benefit, then by reason I ought to consent to it. No one has to justify it to me if I

---

68. Ibid., p. 223; cf. also p. 238.
69. I discuss below the way in which Nagel attempts to incorporate democratic principles into his theory.
70. Nagel, "Conflict and Legitimacy," p. 224.

unreasonably fail to consent. So far this seems plausible enough. Other people's actions should not be restricted by my unreasonableness. But Nagel is using the principle to set the limit to the justification of coercion, and this puts a completely different complexion on the problem. I am the one to be coerced. It is not so much a matter of whether others are limited by my unreasonableness, though it is that as well. It is primarily a question of whether whenever I act unreasonably I am liable to be coerced, whether my reasonableness sets the limits of my freedom. Is there no right to err freely, to act unreasonably against one's own interests?

One way to argue for such a right is to show that it is sometimes more important for a person to choose freely than to choose correctly, that acting freely is itself an important ingredient of individual well-being. Nagel, like Rawls, shuns such arguments as being sectarian—as dependent on accepting a particular conception of the meaning and value of life rather than remaining neutral. Others have strongly argued that respecting persons is an imperative binding on us independently of any conception of the good, an imperative that enjoins us to respect the will of others, rather than their intellect.[71] Nagel is not prevented from accepting such views by his principle of the limits of justification. Even those who act unreasonably need to be reasonably convinced that curtailing their freedom when they act unreasonably is justified. That one person's conduct in acting against his own best interests is unreasonable does not mean that the act of another in coercing him can be justified to the reasonable. Nagel's rationalistic version of the contractarian argument is independent of his view on the limits of justification.

It would be a mistake to conclude that Nagel's principle applies only to and to all measures restricting one person for the benefit of others. This is the line adopted by what I shall call "moral contractarians," that is, those who wish to derive all of morality from the agreement of individuals with nonmoral motivations and principles only. This is not Nagel's road. His contractarianism is political only.[72] People have, right or wrong, moral beliefs. These are to be justified by other means. People's political

71. In *The Morality of Freedom*, p. 57, I have followed the first route mentioned here. The justification of authority must take into account that often it is better for people that they control their own lives than that their actions be to their own advantage. Robert Nozick's *Anarchy, State, and Utopia* (New York: Basic Books, 1974) is a most powerful argument for the second line of argument.

72. This is what Nagel calls the "mixed" theory, which he thinks is characteristic of contemporary liberalism. See "Conflict and Legitimacy," p. 219.

morality is special. Given that it sanctions coercion, it must rest on agreement. That agreement is forthcoming not only to very basic paternalistic measures but also to the prevention of harm to others, since such measures are based on values that are generally shared and therefore agreed to.

The problem of legitimacy is that of justifying governmental action which rests on values not generally shared. But why should their being commonly shared or not matter? All that Nagel's principle of consent requires is appeal to principles which are true and which can be shown to be true to the reasonable. Given Nagel's rationalistic political contractarianism, he can object neither to the exclusive reliance on reason (rather than the will) nor to the reliance on moral principles. They can be established independently of consent, and he specifically eschews reliance on skepticism concerning moral values.[73] In other words, given the acceptance of the rationality of moral beliefs, and a rationalistic interpretation of consent, Nagel's first principle lacks any bite. It adds nothing to the demand that coercive political action should be based on well-reasoned principles. If it is so based it can also meet the test of convincing the reasonable.[74]

Impartiality and Belief

Nagel is of course aware of this. His principle of consent acquires its practical significance from its combination with a second principle: the principle of impartiality. The theory which Nagel explores, which he once refers to as "true liberalism," requires that consent shall be secured not through any rational reasons, not through any successful appeal to the truth or rationality of the relevant moral principles, but through appeal to impartial grounds only. "The defense of liberalism requires that a limit somehow be drawn to appeals to *the truth* in political argument."[75]

73. Ibid., pp. 228–29.

74. But does Nagel, in the passages discussed above, do more than predict the likelihood of consent in cases of clear self-interest (and clear potential harm to others)? I think he does. Nagel has distanced himself from the need to rely on actual consent by relying on the consent of the reasonable. This requires a test of reasonableness which goes beyond saying that the reasonable consent when there is good reason to consent. Nagel provides no such test, and the discussion referred to above suggests that he regards consent of the reasonable to follow good reason. In the absence of such a test the principle that the reasonable consent when there is good reason to consent is a logical truth, not a prediction or a moral principle. This shows that consent has lost its moral force; it necessarily trails clear good reason.

75. Nagel, "Conflict and Legitimacy," p. 229.

That limit is in the idea of impartiality, understood not only in the sense of giving equal weight to the interests of all: "Liberal impartiality goes beyond this, by trying to make the epistemological standpoint of morality impersonal as well."[76] This means, as we will see in a moment, that the reasons, or the method of reasoning, used to justify the different principles must be acceptable to all. But Nagel approaches this idea obliquely.

[I] The idea is that when we look at certain of our convictions from outside, however justified they may be from within, the appeal to their truth must be seen merely as an appeal to our beliefs, and should be treated as such unless those beliefs can be shown to be justifiable from a more impersonal standpoint. . . . This does not mean we have to stop believing them—that is, believing them to be *true*. Considered as individual beliefs they may be adequately grounded . . . the standards of individual rationality are different from the standards of epistemological ethics.[77]

One aspect of this passage seems to me puzzling, yet Nagel regards it as crucial to his argument. If we rely on beliefs which are, for us, "from within" well grounded, how can we be deemed to be appealing merely to the fact that we have certain beliefs rather than acknowledged for what we are actually doing—that is, appealing to their truth? "The reason is," says Nagel,

[II] that unless there is some way of applying from an impersonal standpoint the distinction between my believing something and its being true, an appeal to its truth is equivalent to an appeal to my belief in its truth. . . . I have to be able to admit that I might turn out to be wrong, by some standards that those who disagree with me but are also committed to the impersonal standpoint can also acknowledge. The appeal to truth as opposed to belief . . . must imply the possibility

76. Ibid., p. 230. Nagel embeds this discussion in his familiar view about points of view that vary in "objectivity": "On the view I would defend, there is a highest-order framework of moral reasoning . . . which takes us outside ourselves to a standpoint that is independent of who we are. It cannot derive its basic premises from aspects of our particular and contingent starting points within the world, though it may authorize reliance on such specialized points of view if this is justified from the more universal perspective" (ibid., p. 229). I shall not consider the significance of this way of considering the issue. To my mind it is inessential and distracting. As we saw, the substantive issue, according to Nagel, is whether there is ever justification for "a kind of epistemological restraint" (ibid.), namely, not acting for valid reasons. This issue does not depend on the metaphor of "points of view."

77. Ibid., p. 230.

of some standard to which an impersonal appeal can be made, even if it cannot settle our disagreement at the moment.[78]

This, especially the last sentence, which seems to make the point most succinctly, must be right. But is it compatible with the drift of the previous quotation? As Nagel reminds us, to believe in a proposition is to believe it to be true. That belief is not, and cannot be (very special cases, which I will disregard, excepted), the believer's reason for thinking that the proposition is true. My belief in a proposition is, *a fortiori*, no reason for others to accept it.[79] When a person relies on a proposition, his belief in the proposition merely shows that he has confidence in its truth. It does nothing to justify that confidence or to point to its sources. I believe that it is dark outside not because I believe that it is dark outside, but because there is no light showing through my window. If I act relying on my belief, my reason for the action is not the fact that I hold the belief but, as Nagel puts it, its truth.

Notice that in all this the position of the believer is the same as that of the observer. Neither would accept the fact that the believer believes in a proposition as a ground for action. Both will accept the truth of the proposition as a ground for action. Moreover, and this is the crucial point, both know that only if the believer is capable of distinguishing between believing a proposition and its truth as grounds for accepting it, for acting on it, and so on can he have beliefs at all. For the points just made are at the core of the notion of believing, and while persons need not be able to articulate them to have beliefs, they must recognize them, and apply them correctly, to be capable of having beliefs. The logical prerequisites of the capacity to believe include recognition of the possibility of error and of an impartial or objective recognition of such an error. Nothing less is required by the fact that to believe a proposition is to believe it to be true, and by the distinction between the fact of believing a proposition and its being true.

But if all this is so—and this I take to be the burden of passage II above—Nagel's earlier statement (in passage I) must be false. There is, as we saw, complete symmetry in the matter between the believer and the spectator. It therefore cannot be "that when we look at certain of our

78. Ibid., p. 231.
79. Though, of course, if I witnessed the events I believe in, or have special competence to judge such matters, or have access to adequate evidence, then my belief, together with such facts, is reason supporting a similar belief.

convictions from outside, however justified they may be from within, the appeal to their truth must be seen merely as an appeal to our beliefs." If it is an appeal to their truth, rather than merely to their existence, from the inside, it must be recognized as such from the outside as well. The conditions separating appeal to truth and appeal to mere belief are one and the same from all perspectives. In particular, from within as well one can sustain the view that one is relying on the truth of a belief only if one recognizes that one may be wrong by objective and impartial standards.[80]

Impartiality and Acceptable Reasons

Perhaps, however, none of this touches the heart of Nagel's point. Clearly nothing in the above denies one contention in passage I, namely, that one should not rely in justifying coercive political actions on principles the reasons for which are not acceptable to all those subject to the authority. I referred rather vaguely to the acceptability of reasons, meaning something like: If p is an acceptable reason for a certain action, or for the adoption of a certain principle or the institution of certain political arrangements, then while there may be disagreement over whether p is the case, whether it is not overridden or defeated by other reasons, and so on, it is nevertheless agreed that p, if true, is a reason for the claimed conclusion. When the reasons proposed for coercive political actions meet this test they are acceptable reasons, they are what Nagel calls "a common ground of justification," though evidently their acceptability is far from guaranteeing actual agreement.

Nagel's own explanation of his requirement of the common ground of justification is different. For him it requires

> first, preparedness to submit one's reasons to the criticism of others, and to find that the exercise of a common critical rationality and consideration of evidence that can be shared will reveal that one is mistaken. This means that it must be possible to present to others the basis of your own beliefs, so that once you have done so, *they have what you have.* . . . Public justification requires, second, an expectation that if others who do not share your belief are wrong, there is

80. Indeed, as we saw, the very possibility of belief depends on that recognition. Those who lack it cannot be said to be relying on their beliefs either. Nagel's suggestion of a contrast between those who rely on their believing and those who rely on the truth of their beliefs is chimerical; it is logically impossible to do the first.

probably an explanation of their error which is not circular. That is, the explanation should not come down to the mere assertion that they do not believe the truth.[81]

While I agree with the second requirement, the core of the first is so stringent that it rules out reliance on common everyday observations of fact, as well as much scientific knowledge. We often rely on sense perception and on memory as important reasons for our beliefs. Similarly we rely on our situation (right next to the accident, in the bright light of day, and so on) as reasons to trust our sense perceptions or our memories. All these are acceptable reasons in the sense I explained. Others may doubt whether the Centurion saw Jesus rise from his grave. But they agree that if he did, it is evidence, even though perhaps not conclusive evidence, of the Resurrection.

This point is of crucial importance to Nagel's argument. If he relaxes the test to allow for the acceptability of ordinary reasons (for example, by admitting counterfactuals such as "had they been in your situation they would have shared what you have"), then many religious doctrines he is particularly eager to exclude[82] are admitted with them. In fact many Roman Catholic, Anglican, and other Christian and Jewish theologians rely on nothing but acceptable reasons, such as eyewitness evidence to historical events, often of a public nature, and ordinary methods of reasoning, such as are invoked in the ontological or other arguments for the existence of God.

But have I not missed the point? Is it not obvious that Nagel's aim is to exclude revelation and the judgment that certain beliefs are self-evident from public reliance? Perhaps, but does he provide any reason for doing so? He could have argued that revelation is unreliable and self-evidence an incoherent (or perhaps merely an unreliable) ground for belief. But he does not. To do so would undermine the justification for accepting the beliefs based on revelation or self-evidence by the people who hold them. Nagel's strategy depends on accepting that the people who hold certain beliefs are justified in doing so, and yet asserting that for epistemic reasons those beliefs may not be relied upon in supporting public policies.

Perhaps one should distinguish between private and public revelation.

81. Nagel, "Conflict and Legitimacy," p. 232.
82. Cf. ibid., pp. 229, 232.

But why should the number of people actually present matter? A more promising distinction is between revelation which relies on sense perception and is admissible, and that which does not rely on a familiar and trusted mode of acquiring knowledge and so is suspect. Again this argument fails to draw the line between what is rational for the private believer and what is rational for the polity. Notice that the second kind of revelation may be public. Thousands may testify that they felt in some mysterious way the presence of a mysterious and wonderful being, and heard, in their mind's ear, his message, even though the place was completely quiet. The identity of the reports of many people of what they felt at the same time and place makes this revelation public. One may think that the fact that many had the same experience at the same time lends credence to the report of each one of them. But it does not differ in principle from the report of a single person of the same experience, even when it was not witnessed by others. Either such reports are acceptable by all, or they are not to be trusted even by the person who had the experience.

We do in fact hold ourselves open to accept reports of extrasensory perceptions, as in the case of diviners. Our grounds for either confidence in or mistrust of their ability to identity the presence of water underground are inductive: their past successes or failures. But so is their own reason for confidence in their own ability. If I suddenly feel that there is water under the ground I am standing on at the moment, I will not, nor should I, have any confidence that water is to be found there.[83] Once my ability is empirically proven I will acquire confidence in it, and so should other people. It is true that the level of evidence which makes it rational for a person to come to hold a certain belief is not the same as that which makes it rational for a public authority to come to adopt a policy based on such a belief. It may be rational for people to come to believe that certain drugs are safe, or that they are dangerous, by evidence which falls short of the level required to justify the Food and Drug Administration in licensing or banning them. But that is a common phenomenon which seems to have no bearing on the issues discussed by Nagel.

Nagel gives us little indication of what sort of grounds are cogent

83. Does the fact that having the feeling means having the thought that there is water there give me confidence? I do not think so. I would feel assaulted by the thought. It is there for reasons beyond my comprehension. Even though I have it, I know that I cannot trust it.

enough to justify one in accepting certain beliefs as true, and yet not acceptable as grounds for coercive political action. Oddly enough he mentions just about any kind of public issue as falling, at least prima facie, within that category "in the present state of moral debate." The enforcement of religious views, abortion, sexual conduct, and the killing of animals for food are examples of matters all current beliefs on which fail the impartiality test. So do issues concerning the morality of nuclear deterrence, the death penalty, and the fundamental problems of economic and social policy governed by different conceptions of social justice.[84] That he does not wish to exclude the last three from coercive political action is due not to the impartiality test but to other considerations.[85]

These reflections demonstrate that Nagel's principle of impartiality in itself does little to justify the "true liberal" policies which he invokes it to justify. But the doubts that Nagel's list of cases raises go to the very heart of his understanding of his principle. He seems to regard any widespread disagreement over policies as indicating a failure to meet the condition of epistemic impartiality, and provides no independent analysis of the grounds resorted to in such debates. But as Nagel himself says, the existence of a common ground of justification is far from guaranteeing agreement, "nor does it mean that only one belief is reasonable on the evidence. I may hold a belief on grounds that I am willing to offer in objective justification, suitable for the public domain, while acknowledging that others who consider that justification and yet reject the belief are not being irrational or unreasonable, though I think they are wrong."[86] "Reasonable belief is partly a matter of judgment, and is not uniquely determined by the publicly available arguments."[87]

If the existence of a common ground does not guarantee actual agree-

84. See ibid., pp. 233–34.

85. Nagel regards these matters as essentially public in nature, so that the government must adopt some position on them, or at least as matters which are accepted by all as matters of public concern (see ibid.). These are especially weak arguments. Issues of social justice are accepted as matters of public concern in precisely the way that abortion is. And while the morality of *state*-wielded nuclear deterrence or capital punishment is inevitably a matter on which the state must take a view, the state's relation to nuclear weapons owned by private individuals or to capital punishment meted out by them is on a par with its relation to private abortions. Is it reasonable to hold that considerations which determine the morality of nuclear threats and of the death penalty should determine public policy regarding their use by the state, but should be excluded from affecting public policy regarding their use by individuals?

86. Ibid., p. 234.   87. Ibid., p. 235.

ment even when the evidence is shared—let alone when it is not, as of course in reality it rarely is—how can disagreement be a reliable indicator of the absence of a common ground of justification? We require a direct analysis of the way such arguments are conducted, of the reasons actually advanced for different policies. None is offered. Nagel, when addressing the difficulty of applying his impartiality test, refers back to his distinction between appeal to the fact that one holds a belief and appeal to the truth of that belief as providing the touchstone;[88] but since that distinction is incoherent it does not advance matters.

We are left in a frustrating position. We know that the test of "sharing all the evidence" must be relaxed. But nothing in the rest of Nagel's discussion suggests how to relax it. I suspect that the principle of impartiality, when relaxed to admit all acceptable reasons, fails in the task that Nagel assigns it. Like Nagel's principle of consent, it too is a toothless tiger. It can rule out only blatantly irrational beliefs. It does not rule out as grounds for coercive political action any beliefs that individuals are justified in holding to be true. No one is justified in holding beliefs that are not based on acceptable reasons. But the heart and soul of Nagel's argument is for epistemic restraint in appealing to truth, for the contention that some truths which individuals are justified in believing, they are not justified in relying on politically. This seems an impossible task, given that to be personally justified in believing a proposition one must accept that one's belief is in principle subject to impersonal, impartial standards of correctness. Those who comply with this condition do subject their beliefs to valid impersonal tests. It may be that others do not see it that way, and deny the validity of those tests. But given that the tests are both valid and publicly, objectively, and impartially available, it seems impossible that others can *reasonably* deny the validity of those tests, unless they lack information. And that lack can be remedied, and so cannot serve as the basis of Nagel's theory. Ultimately Nagel's principle is bound to fail because it depends on driving a wedge between appeal to truth and acceptance of objective standards of justification; and that wedge comes unstuck.

Impartiality and Respect

Nothing in the above undermines a cluster of related valid points. First, within certain limits, people may seek to promote their personal prefer-

---

88. See especially ibid., p. 236.

ences for a certain worthwhile environment and style of life by political action. But in doing so each person's preferences are to count equally. Such cases are part of the case for a democratic constitution.[89] They do not involve any epistemic restraint, for there is no suggestion that there is any truth withheld. I simply believe that plenty of music opportunities are valuable. You believe that open spaces are important. We are both right. But scarcity of resources imposes a need to choose. That is why numbers count.

Nagel notices correctly that a "large range of legislative and communal issues . . . are put under the control of the preferences of the majority, or of coalitions among minorities."[90] He does not justify this practice by reference to his condition of impartiality, and it seems doubtful whether it can so be justified. This practice is an expression of a democratic outlook which, in matters of the consent of the governed, is much less demanding than Nagel's contractarian view. The problem is not that democratic governments decide many issues on the basis of nothing better than the subjective preference of their subjects. Rather it is that the principle decreeing that matters should be so resolved does not seem to meet the condition of impartiality. There is little consensus, and not much argument in the public arena, on when people should vote simply to express their personal preferences, and when they should vote in support of valid general principles. I can think of no reason why this issue should be more immune to Nagel's impartiality test than issues of economic and social justice, and so on. It is possible that this part of Nagel's argument is out of line with its main thrust.

Second, there are reasons, not based on preferences, which apply to one individual but not to others. These arise out of commitments and undertakings, status and office, as well as through the fundamental fact that every person is a different person. Needless to say, such reasons should not be imposed on people to whom they do not apply. But neither they nor individual preferences involve any epistemic restraint. Both the agent and others agree that those preferences and reasons exist, and that they apply only to the agent.

Third, there are principles and ideals which apply to all, but which call for no political enforcement or support. They may be inimical in nature

---

89. See my "Skepticism, Liberalism and Democracy," *Iowa Law Review*, in press.
90. Nagel, "Conflict and Legitimacy," p. 239.

to any political intervention, being based on strong voluntaristic principles. Or they may be concerned with dimensions of human life to which politics can make no difference. Obviously such ideals should not be, cannot be, pursued politically. Equally obviously no measure of epistemic restraint is exercised in reaching this conclusion.

Finally, principles calling for coercive action may indeed require justification of a special kind, with the result that measures which are admirable if undertaken voluntarily may not be coercively imposed. Again, this view requires no epistemic restraint. It calls for no holding back on the truth, but rather for a recognition that different measures require different justifications, that different propositions are true only if justified by different arguments.

My criticism of Nagel turns on the cogency of his analysis, rather than on the attractiveness of his vision. There is a deep appeal in the idea that coercive measures are justified only if based on the consent of those subject to them. It seems to solve at a stroke the problem of justifying coercion. According to Nagel, it expresses Kant's categorical imperative that one should treat humanity never merely as a means but always also as an end.[91] Ultimately we have to account for the importance of both coercion and consent in our political outlook. For the present, suffice it to point to the dilemma facing contractarian theories of politics (that is, those which allow that moral principles other than political ones are to be justified on other grounds, and form the basis on which consent to political principles is sought). They may, with Rawls, attempt to base political principles on an overlapping consensus. That is, they may seek principles to which all viable ideologies in the relevant political morality implicitly agree, or are committed to agreeing, or nearly so. Or they may, with Nagel, look for principles based on reasons which are generally acceptable in the relevant society.

Rawls's route seems barren in pluralistic societies, like ours. The degree of existing diversity is just too great. Furthermore, as argued above, there seems little reason to reject valid or true principles, the implementation of which may actually be of benefit to all, just because a small sector of the population cannot be convinced of this fact. Nagel's alternative relies on the dubious epistemological claim that there can be reasons for belief and for action which are *quite reasonably* not recognized

91. Ibid., pp. 223, 238.

as such by people generally but which are valid nevertheless. If one rejects this possibility, then it is tempting to say that our duty to act only on political principles to which the reasonable consent is simply the duty to act on well-founded, valid principles. For that is what the reasonable consent to. This eliminates the independent role of consent.

The problem is not why one should assign consent any role. It is more fundamental. The puzzle is how one can give consent a viable role, without saying that only principles already agreed to by all can be relied upon. One must find a reasonable interpretation of the intuitively appealing idea that political principles must be accessible to people as they are. It is not enough, according to this intuition, that those who are totally rational and open to rational conversion will be persuaded, and be radically changed. Politics must take people as they come and be accessible to them, capable of commanding their consent without expecting them to change in any radical way. But at the same time, justified political principles may be controversial, and may fail to command actual consent. Nagel and Rawls offer interpretations of this intuition which aim to be both coherent and attractive. Their failure suggests that the underlying idea may be at bottom unstable and incoherent. There may be no middle way between actual (including implied) agreement and rational justification.

Should Political Philosophy Be Done without Metaphysics?*

Jean Hampton

Most of the points I have made in support of my argument are not such as I can confidently assert; but that the belief in the duty of inquiring after what we do not know will make us better and braver and less helpless than the notion that there is not even a possibility of discovering what we do not know, nor any duty of inquiring after it—this is a point for which I am determined to do battle, as far as I am able, both in word and deed. [PLATO, *Meno*]

In *A Theory of Justice* Rawls engaged the interest of contemporary philosophers not only with his substantive conception of justice but also with his justification of it as the conception preferred by all parties fairly placed relative to one another in an "original position." But more recently he has defended his conception of justice with an argument that uses the idea of an original position in an unfamiliar, revisionary way.[1] He does not advance this new argument out of fear that the old one failed to justify his conclusions (which is not to say that he should not have abandoned it for that reason).[2] He continues to endorse it as an argument in moral theory. But he no longer believes it offers the right kind of justification given what he now takes to be the aim of political philosophy, which is not the pursuit of the truth but the pursuit of "free agreement,

---

* This article was written while I was supported by grants from the National Endowment for the Humanities (NEH), the American Council on Learned Societies, and an NEH summer stipend for research on constitutional issues. I am very grateful for this support.

1. In this article I will refer to two of John Rawls's recent writings: "Justice as Fairness: Political not Metaphysical," *Philosophy and Public Affairs* 14 (1985): 223–51, and "The Idea of an Overlapping Consensus," *Oxford Journal of Legal Studies* 7 (1987): 1–25. Hereafter, all references will appear in the body of the text, with the articles abbreviated as "JFPM" and "IOC," respectively.

2. For examples of criticisms of the argument's validity, see John Harsanyi, "Can the Maximin Principle Serve as the Basis for Morality? A Critique of John Rawls's Theory," in his *Essays on Ethics, Social Behavior and Scientific Explanation* (Dordrecht: Reidel, 1980), pp. 37–63; and D. Clayton Hubin, "Minimizing Maximin," in *Philosophical Studies* 37 (1980): 363–72.

Ethics 99 (July 1989): 791–814

reconciliation through public reason" (JFPM, p. 230). He proposes that political philosophers in modern pluralist societies with constitutional democracies must make reference to our history and the shared experiences of our community to forge what he calls an "overlapping consensus" on a conception of justice.

In this article I want to examine Rawls's new, more community-minded, deliberately nonuniversal and nonmetaphysical justificatory method, which he calls "political." I want first to explore what this method is; second, to show that it is new and hence not the method used in *A Theory of Justice*; third, to better understand why Rawls felt compelled to adopt this kind of justification; and finally, to evaluate it. Despite my fascination with and partial endorsement of Rawls's proposal, I want to argue that we should reject his recommendation to do only political and not metaphysical theorizing about the structuring of our political institutions in constitutional democracies.

THE NEW METHOD

In *A Theory of Justice* there are many passages in which Rawls offers characterizations of his method of justification in that book; how they all hang together (if they do) is an intriguing question. Some of the passages—for example, those on reflective equilibrium—might be interpreted such that they are at least consistent with Rawls's new political method (as he himself suggests, e.g., in IOC, p. 5, n. 8). But other passages, particularly section 40 of the book, suggest a very Kantian way of understanding the contract argument; for example: "The description of the original position interprets the point of view of noumenal selves, or what it means to be a free and equal rational being. Our nature as such beings is displayed when we act from the principles we would choose when this nature is reflected in the conditions determining choice. Thus men exhibit their freedom, their independence from the contingencies of nature and society, by acting in ways they would acknowledge in the original position."[3]

The idea seems to be that in the same way Kant's moral law tests a plan of action by considering what it would be like for him if all people acted that way, the original position procedure tests conceptions of justice by forcing the deliberator who uses it to consider what society would be like for him if he were anyone in that society. The results of both tests are supposed to be authoritative and universal ("independent of the contingencies of nature and society") because they are supposed to represent the correct operation of our practical reason. The idea is that each test's endorsement constitutes the endorsement of reason.

This kind of justification has recently come under heavy attack from certain "Hegelian" critics. For example, Alasdair MacIntyre argues that

3. John Rawls, *A Theory of Justice* (Cambridge, Mass.: Harvard University Press, 1971), pp. 255–56.

a conception of justice must be rooted in "a community whose primary bond is a shared understanding both of the good for man and the good for that community,"[4] and Michael Sandel argues that Rawls's contention that justice is the first virtue of social institutions involves the dubious metaethical claim that the foundations of justice must also be independent of all social and historical contingencies (without being transcendental). Sandel contends that the original position procedure presents the self as a chooser of its ends and thus "as independent from social convention—separate and individual."[5] In contrast, Sandel characterizes Rawls's communitarian critics as proposing that the self is not independent of its aims and attachments but is always "situated" in a social life "embedded in a history which locates [it] among others, and implicates [its] good in the good of the communities whose stories [it] shares."[6] Thus Sandel sees "political discourse as proceeding within the common meanings and traditions of a political community, not appealing to a critical standpoint wholly external to those meanings."[7]

The descriptive language of this last quotation may puzzle some readers. Is Sandel saying that in fact people who are arguing over substantive issues in a political society never try to appeal to some extrasocietal critical standpoint in order to establish what position is right? Surely not, for such a descriptive claim is clearly wrong. He must therefore be saying that even when people think that they are appealing to some extrasocietal standpoint, in fact they are using the shared ideas and traditions of their community. In other words, Sandel is describing not what they intend to be doing, but what they can in fact do, based upon what he takes to be the metaethical facts. Thus, fundamental to this communitarian's position is a metaethical commitment to the community as the source of value.[8] And this commitment motivates a methodological criticism of those philosophers such as Rawls who persist in attempting to gain access to some extrasocietal source of moral truth. Such philosophers should know better, Sandel is arguing, and were they to embrace the proper metaethics, they would embrace a different methodology, one which justified political conclusions by reference to the shared beliefs and traditions of their community.

In his recent articles, Rawls is simultaneously hostile toward these critics' substantive recommendations for charting the direction of our

4. Alasdair MacIntyre, *After Virtue* (Notre Dame, Ind.: University of Notre Dame Press, 1981), pp. 232–33, quoted by Amy Gutmann, "Communitarian Critics of Liberalism," *Philosophy and Public Affairs* 14 (1985): 308.

5. Michael Sandel, "Introduction," in *Liberalism and Its Critics*, ed. M. Sandel (London: Blackwell, 1984), p. 9.

6. Ibid.

7. Ibid., p. 10.

8. But not all communitarians need share, or do share, this metaethical thesis. See, e.g., Philip Selznick, "The Idea of a Communitarian Morality," *California Law Review*, vol. 75 (1987). Michael Walzer is also prepared to endorse liberal values; see his *Spheres of Justice* (New York: Basic, 1983).

political community and sensitive to their charge that his justification of the two principles presupposes a controversial metaethics and an overly individualistic conception of persons. His response is one of partial capitulation—not substantively, and not metaethically (nowhere does Rawls suggest that he is drawn to the idea that the community is the source of all value), but *methodologically*. Although he never repudiates the Kantian style of justification used in the book, he now argues that this way of defending the two principles makes it part of a "comprehensive moral theory," and that a different, nonmoral and nonmetaphysical defense of those principles is required of him as a political philosopher.

This view leads him in his most recent papers to develop a new kind of justification for his conception of justice, which he calls "political," that makes reference only to the histories and traditions of our democratic culture—presumably in just the way that at least some of his Hegelian critics would want a conception of justice defended. However, his motivation for presenting this argument does not derive from any decision to embrace the communitarians' metaethics but, rather, from a decision to avoid metaphysics altogether when engaged in the justification of political conceptions. Indeed, Rawls makes the remarkable claim that "the aims of political philosophy depend upon the society it addresses" (IOC, p. 1), and that in a modern constitutional democracy its aim should be the development of an "overlapping consensus" on matters pertaining to justice without in any way relying on controversial metaphysics. Whereas political philosophy has traditionally been seen as a branch of moral philosophy which builds upon and applies to social structures the results of moral theorizing (in the way that, e.g., Aristotle's *Politics* builds upon his *Nicomachean Ethics*), Rawls argues that political philosophy in our time and place should be free of controversial moral assumptions and indeed of all metaphysical foundations in order that it might "provide a shared public basis of the justification of political and social institutions" that will help "ensure stability from one generation to the next" (IOC, p. 1). The political philosopher who pursues this objective is looking for and/ or striving to develop a shared fund of ideas that are latent in the culture of the community and that can be endorsed by people no matter what their metaphysical views.

Unfortunately, Rawls gives us no precise definition of what he means by 'metaphysical.' From context it doesn't seem that he can mean it in the positivists' sense as "nonsense to be dismissed" but, rather, in a more Hobbesian sense, as "doctrines for which an incontrovertible demonstration is not possible."[9] Such doctrines have the potential to arouse controversy

---

9. For Hobbes, any doctrine is part of "science" if it cannot be contested because there is a conclusive demonstration of it. Any thesis that cannot be so demonstrated is contestable and thus liable to disturb the peace of the commonwealth unless a sovereign is given authority to decide the matter. See his "Six Lessons to the Professors of Mathematics . . . in The University of Oxford" (1656), *Epistle Dedicatory*, in *English Works of Thomas Hobbes*, ed. W. Molesworth (London: John Bohn, 1840), 7:183–84, and *De Homine*, chap. 10, iv– v, pp. 41–43, in *Man and Citizen*, ed. B. Gert (New York: Humanities Press, 1972).

and provoke conflict in the community. Note that Rawls might have to count even certain theories of science, such as the thesis that species have evolved, to be part of metaphysics so understood if they have been heavily contested in the community.

But whatever else falls into this category of metaphysics, certainly normative ethics and metaethics fall into it. Many political philosophers will be alarmed by the proposal that this sort of philosophizing should be excluded from political theorizing and will regard the sanitized product as too meager, too applied, too political. Rawls replies:

> Some may think that to ensure stable social unity in a constitutional regime by looking for an overlapping consensus detaches political philosophy from philosophy and makes it into politics. Yes and no: the politician, we say, looks to the next election, the statesman to the next generation, and philosophy to the indefinite future. Philosophy sees the political world as an on-going system of cooperation over time, in perpetuity practically speaking. Political philosophy is related to politics because it must be concerned, as moral philosophy need not be, with practical possibilities. . . .
>
> Thus political philosophy is not mere politics: in addressing the public culture it takes the longest view, looks to society's permanent historical and social conditions, and tries to mediate society's deepest conflicts. It hopes to uncover, and help to articulate, a shared basis of consensus on a political conception of justice drawing upon citizens' fundamental intuitive ideas about their society and their place in it. [IOC, pp. 24–25]

So the man who is primarily responsible for breathing new life into the seemingly dead corpse of political philosophy after World War II is now challenging us to rethink what we are doing when we theorize about our political life.

Rawls does not believe this kind of theorizing is appropriate for just any time or place, but only for those societies in which the following five facts hold (all of which he takes to hold in modern democratic societies): The first fact is that the society is pluralistic. The second fact is that this pluralism is permanent, by which I take Rawls to mean that unless there were certain remarkable events or the use of extreme coercive measures, the divergence of moral and religious views in our society is highly likely to persist (IOC, p. 22; JFPM, p. 225). The third fact is that such pluralism could be overcome only by the "oppressive use of state power (which presupposes a control of the state no group possesses)." I am not quite sure of the force of the word 'oppressive' in this passage; let us take it to mean a substantial degree of coercive power over one's life which, given human nature, people find highly undesirable—and thus unacceptable. These three facts define, according to Rawls, a "common predicament" (IOC, p. 22). This predicament is worsened by the fourth fact: the existence of moderate scarcity of resources. So a workable conception of justice in any situation in which these facts hold is one that distributes scarce resources so as to "allow for a diversity of doctrines and the plurality of conflicting and incommensurable conceptions of the good affirmed by the members of existing democratic societies" (JFPM, p. 225).

The fifth fact allows for a kind of escape from the predicament: it is the existence of numerous possibilities for gain that come from well-organized social cooperation. In Rawls's discussion of this fact it is an unstated assumption that the people in this society desire to realize this cooperative gain, and that a central ingredient of a well-organized scheme of social cooperation is that it be stable. The following is a reconstructed statement of the fifth fact which renders it more precise and complete: there are numerous possibilities for gain which everyone desires to realize and which can only come about when a well-organized and, in particular, stable system of social cooperation is established.

In "Justice as Fairness: Political not Metaphysical" Rawls rests his argument on two additional "basic intuitive ideas" that he claims are latent in the political cultures of modern democratic societies. First is the idea that people should cooperate with one another in a "fair system of cooperation": "The overarching fundamental intuitive idea, within which other basic intuitive ideas are systematically connected, is that of a society as a fair system of cooperation between free and equal persons. Justice as fairness starts from this idea as one of the basic intuitive ideas which we take to be implicit in the public culture of a democratic society" (JFPM, p. 231). Second is the idea that human beings are free and equal: "Since we start within the tradition of modern democratic thought, we also think of citizens as free and equal moral persons. The basic intuitive idea is that in virtue of what we may call their moral powers, and their powers of reasoning, thought and judgement connected with those powers, we say that persons are free. And in virtue of their having these powers to the requisite degree to be fully cooperating members of society, we say that people are equal" (JFPM, p. 233). In part because these ideas are latent in our political culture, Rawls argues that in our society there is an overlapping consensus on a liberal conception of justice—in particular, on *his* conception of justice.

However, in "The Idea of an Overlapping Consensus" Rawls no longer insists that the bulk of society holds these two beliefs. Instead, the ideals of "fairness" and "equality" are taken to be instrumentally necessary to the achievement of a stable cooperative society (which, in turn, is taken to be universally desired). In particular, fairness is linked instrumentally to the achievement of cooperation and, thus, to the realization of cooperative gain.[10] And equal protection of every individual by rights that accord each one "basic liberties" is taken to be necessary for stability and harmony.[11] So in essence, fairness and equality are now

10. "When they believe that institutions or social practices are just (or fair) . . . , they are ready and willing to do their part in those arrangements provided they have reasonable assurance that others will also do their part" (IOC, p. 22).

11. He writes, "Given the fact of pluralism—the fact that necessitates a liberal regime as a *modus vivendi* in the first place—a liberal conception meets the urgent requirement

included in the fifth fact, as follows: there are numerous possibilities for gain which everyone desires to realize and which can come about only when a well-organized and, in particular, stable system of cooperation is established, and such a system can be established only if each party is treated fairly and accorded equal basic liberties.

In "The Idea of an Overlapping Consensus" Rawls goes on to argue that in any society in which these five facts hold—and that includes contemporary democracies—only a liberal conception of justice will "work" politically. Such a conception specifies certain basic rights, liberties, and opportunities; assigns a special priority to these rights; and assures to all citizens adequate means to make effective use of their basic rights, liberties, and opportunities (IOC, p. 18). By virtue of the pervasive and permanent pluralism in these societies and the need for fair and equal treatment in the distribution of scarce resources, Rawls argues that only this kind of conception will enable members to achieve the stability they need for cooperation without relying on oppressive state power. And given the fact that it makes the stable system of cooperation viable, citizens can embrace the liberal view "without being committed in other parts of their life to comprehensive moral ideals often associated with liberalism, for example the ideals of autonomy and individuality" (JFPM, p. 245). Hence, although a liberal conception of justice can be and generally is presented as a comprehensive moral doctrine (which is presumably how it is presented in *A Theory of Justice*), it can be successfully justified with an argument that is neutral between competing moral conceptions in just the way a theory must be if it is to serve as the theoretical arbiter in a pluralistic society.

Rawls believes that his two principles of justice ought to serve as that conception on which there is an overlapping consensus. However, he admits that it is "also likely that more than one political conception may be worked up from the fund of shared political ideas; indeed this is desirable, as these rival conceptions will then compete for citizens' allegiance and be gradually modified and deepened by the contest between them" (IOC, p. 3). Admitting the possibility of a contest allows Rawls to find a place in debates in political philosophy for the archrival of the

---

to fix, once and for all, the content of basic rights and liberties, and to assign them special priority. Doing this takes those guarantees off the political agenda and puts them beyond the calculus of social interests, thereby establishing clearly and firmly the terms of social cooperation on a footing of mutual respect. To regard the calculus as relevant in these matters leaves the status and content of those rights and liberties still unsettled; it subjects them to the shifting circumstances of time and place, and by greatly raising the stakes of political controversy, dangerously increases the insecurity and hostility of public life. Thus the unwillingness to take these matters off the agenda perpetuates deep divisions latent in society; it betrays a readiness to revive antagonisms in the hope of gaining a more favourable position should later circumstances prove propitious. So, by contrast, securing the basic liberties and recognizing their priority achieves the work of reconciliation and mutual acceptance on a footing of equality" (ibid., pp. 19–20).

Rawlsian theory, utilitarianism. But because utilitarianism in its purest (Benthamite) form guarantees neither political equality nor individual protection of liberties via rights, Rawls generously allows that there may be ways of "construing or revising utilitarian doctrine so that it can support a conception of justice appropriate for a constitutional regime" given the inescapable fact of pluralism in such a regime (IOC, p. 12). For reasons we shall discuss later, utilitarians may be apt to resist such generosity.

Thus far I have presented Rawls as saying that the overlapping consensus is defined either by looking at what principles are *instrumentally valuable* to the creation of a stable cooperative society, or by looking for values or principles that, as a matter of fact, everyone in the pluralist society *happens to accept,* albeit for different reasons. "The essential elements of the political conception, its principles, standards and ideals, are theorems, as it were, at which the comprehensive doctrines in the consensus intersect or converge" (IOC, p. 9). However, this process of constructing a convergence of ideas need not involve only discovery; it might be necessary for the philosopher to develop and extend, from any accepted fund of shared ideas, the principles upon which to decide new issues. But note that she would be doing so not by making reference to non-neutral moral or religious views which some members of the pluralist society do not share, but by looking for and attempting to articulate shared values and principles on which these matters can be adjudicated.

In order for this process even to be possible there must be a shared commitment to reasoned discussion. Rawls therefore argues that implicit in our public culture are shared guidelines for inquiry, and publicly recognized rules for assessing evidence. Otherwise there can be no way of interpreting, applying, or extending any conception of justice that is agreed upon. Rawls calls this part of the overlapping consensus the "conception of free public reason" (IOC, p. 8).

Finally, he proposes that there is even a shared endorsement of certain virtues by all parties in pluralist democracies, so that these too are part of the overlapping consensus. These "virtues of political cooperation" (IOC, p. 17) include such things as tolerance and reasonability in debate. Such virtues are presumably endorsed because they make possible fair social cooperation "on a footing of mutual respect" and are part of society's "political capital" (IOC, p. 17).

We can now summarize the justificatory methodology Rawls is urging political philosophers to follow whenever the five facts described above hold (e.g., in modern constitutional democracies):

> A political philosopher should justify any principle or doctrine to a pluralist community by finding or seeking to develop an "overlapping consensus," and she should do so while relying on the prevailing conception of free public reason and any shared virtues that encourage political cooperation, either by articulating the values or principles that are instrumentally necessary for the achievement of certain universally held objectives, or by looking for or else seeking

to develop theoretical overlap among the disparate groups in the society, so as to define a fund of implicitly shared ideas and principles.

Rawls calls this the "method of avoidance" (JFPM, p. 231); by using it one avoids argument on the basis of any contested premise and any controversial claim about what is true.

But where, the reader might want to know, is the original position procedure in this justification of the two principles? That procedure, according to Rawls, is a way of helping us to identify a kernel of overlapping consensus. The fact of pluralism indicates that an acceptable conception of justice for our society is one that is perceived as setting out fair terms of cooperation and one which recognizes that people are free and equal. The original position procedure is a device allowing us to pick out that conception of justice which would be fair, and which would treat people as free and equal: "The original position [is] simply a device of representation: it describes the parties, each of whom are responsible for the essential interests of a free and equal person, as fairly situated and as reaching an agreement subject to appropriate restrictions on what are to count as good reasons" (JFPM, p. 237). By representing to ourselves an agreement situation in which there is a veil of ignorance that ensures that the bargainers are free and equal, we determine which conception of justice available to us is fair, and which treats people as free and equal (JFPM, pp. 235–36). And while the veil excludes them from knowing their conceptions of the good, this does not mean that we should take it as resting on a metaphysical conception of the person in which the self is considered ontologically prior to such a conception. The veil is simply a useful means for arriving at a conception of justice which will ensure a stable cooperative society.

Finally, we should appreciate that Rawls's political justification for his two principles enables him to defend his conception of justice against Sandel's and MacIntyre's communitarian attacks with a style of argument they would have to respect insofar as it takes seriously the shared values, beliefs, and traditions of our society. And, remarkably, Rawls defends such an argument without in any way endorsing their metaethical views or their antiliberal conception of the state as a group of people bound by a shared conception of the good.[12]

RAWLS AND HOBBES

In the last section I noted how one aspect of Rawls's methodology resembles that of Hobbes. But Hobbes's way of political theorizing is still too meta-

---

12. Rawls writes, "Justice as fairness assumes, as other liberal political views do, that the values of community are not only essential but realizable, first in the various associations that carry on life within the framework for the basic structure, and second, in those associations that extend across the boundaries of nation-states, such as churches and scientific societies. Liberalism rejects the state as a community because, among other things, it leads to a systematic denial of basic liberties and to the oppressive use of the state's monopoly of legal force" (ibid., p. 10, n. 17).

physical for Rawls because it rests upon contested philosophical ideas which some members of contemporary pluralist societies could not accept.

Hobbes does not start from the fact of societal pluralism, but from an individualistic conception of human beings and what he takes to be the psychological fact that our highest goals (self-preservation and glory) are self-regarding, meaning that individuals' interests will inevitably diverge and generate conflict. Rawls does not endorse Hobbes's conception of the person, nor his facts of human nature, nor his determinism. So his reasons for insisting on defining a conception of justice that will realize a stable cooperative society are different from Hobbes's more metaphysical motivations. Rawls simply says, "Here are the circumstances which prevail in our society today; what must we do?" whereas Hobbes searches for a (universal) method for peace based upon (what we would see as contestable) theses in human psychology, philosophy of mind, and the theory of value.

Nonetheless, one might think that Rawls's political methodology is importantly Hobbesian in at least one respect: like Hobbes, he seems to be attempting to define a political modus vivendi for societies of people who are in conflict but who desire peace. It is interesting that Rawls rejects this Hobbesian characterization of his project. He does not deny that he is interested in defining a conception of justice that can serve as a modus vivendi, but he does strongly deny that the conception of justice which constitutes the overlapping consensus is *merely* a modus vivendi. A "mere" modus vivendi, according to Rawls, is one that would provide a way for conflicting factions of people to get along despite their conflict, but which would not be a way that either side would be disposed to carry on if the conflict disappeared. Only temporary social unity has been purchased by the modus vivendi: "Social unity is only apparent as its stability is contingent on circumstances remaining such as not to upset the fortunate convergence of interests" (IOC, p. 11). The parties perceive the modus vivendi as a necessary evil and not something which has any intrinsic value for them apart from its ability to secure peace in these circumstances. So if power relations changed and one party suddenly were in a position to enforce its particular viewpoint, that party would happily reject, and be correct to reject, the modus vivendi and use its power to coerce agreement from those who had previously opposed its viewpoint.

Can Rawls successfully accord his overlapping consensus the status of "right" and not merely "expedient"? I will take up this question in the next section. For now, however, I want to ask whether or not he is correct to argue that it is at least expedient (if not more than that). And the philosopher who would be most likely to be dubious about the over-lapping consensus as instrumentally valuable in the pursuit of stable, cooperative societies is Hobbes.

Hobbes is, if anything, even more concerned than Rawls about the damage to societies which contestable human doctrines can cause. But his prescription for stability in a world of potential conflict is not the creation of an overlapping consensus but the institution of an absolute sovereign. It would be, in his eyes, a hopeless task to try to find any significant overlap of views in pluralist societies such as ours, and even if such overlap were possible, he would not believe it to be permanent or extensive enough to ensure peace in the face of the inevitable generation of conflicting ideas among human beings who have differing conceptions of the good. Stability, according to Hobbes, is something that we pursue via polity and not via consensus on ideas. Only a ruler with the power to have the last word is able to forestall conflict.

Rawls never explicitly discusses polity solutions to social discord (which is odd for a political philosopher). Of course, he might argue that there must be an overlapping consensus on a particular polity in order for it to be successful in retaining power and resolving conflict. And Hobbes would agree; this is one of the ideas I interpret him as trying to get across with his contract language.[13] It is what Kurt Baier would call a "constitutional consensus."[14] But this consensus is on structure, not substance. And Hobbes would argue that even if an agreement on substance could be reached, in fact the lion's share of the work in ensuring peace would have to be done by the political structure that had the power to resolve or prevent controversies, and not by the consensus on conceptions (perhaps vaguely or ambiguously stated) which could never, by themselves, effect the peaceful resolution of conflict.

Rawls need not, and I think does not, disagree with the idea that some political adjudicators (performing as judges, or legislators, or executives) are necessary for realizing peace in a pluralist society. But I believe he would insist that history shows us that peace can also be achieved in a less costly way through reliance on an overlapping consensus. Remember Rawls's third fact, that is, that pluralism in modern societies could be ended only by the unacceptably oppressive use of state power. Hobbes's solution for conflict would strike Rawls as unacceptable because of its reliance on potentially oppressive coercion rather than consensus. Now, Hobbes thought such reliance was necessary because it was the only means to peace, but Rawls believes history has confirmed "a new social possibility: the possibility of a reasonably harmonious and stable pluralist society. Before the successful and peaceful practise of toleration in societies with liberal political institutions there was no way of knowing of that possibility" (IOC, p. 23). Once people become tolerant of disagreements in metaphysical areas and come to share agreement on a conception of justice governing their interactions with one another, peace is secured without forcing any person to give up her deeply held views. Indeed, this solution respects the beliefs of everyone. In contrast, the decision of a political ruler to resolve conflict in a situation where there

13. See my *Hobbes and the Social Contract Tradition* (Cambridge: Cambridge University Press, 1986), chap. 6.
14. See Kurt Baier, "Justice and the Aims of Political Philosophy," *Ethics*, in this issue.

is no toleration of others' views and/or where there is no consensus on a conception of justice governing their interactions will invariably result in one or more parties to the conflict losing—and losing hurts. Now, Rawls would have to admit that in a pluralist society such as our own, even if we are all perfectly tolerant of others' conceptions of the good, the overlap of shared beliefs constituting the consensus on justice can never be large or explicit enough to decide all conflicts between the parties, so that some political adjudication will always be required for peace. He observes, "We appeal to a political conception of justice to distinguish between those questions that can be reasonably removed from the political agenda and those that cannot, all the while aiming for an overlapping consensus" (IOC, p. 13). Presumably, the arbiters will have to decide those issues that cannot be removed from the political agenda and placed into the core of consensus. Nonetheless, the larger the overlapping consensus, the less society will have to rely on them, and thus, the less will any party feel its beliefs are being trampled upon or disrespected by the state.

In the end, the principle of toleration, which is the substantive heart of liberalism, turns out to be the keystone of this new, low-cost approach to political stability. Commitment to this principle is a kind of background assumption of Rawls's non-Hobbesian way of pursuing stability.

But is not this too "moral" a principle for his nonmetaphysical method of philosophizing to rely upon? Rawls need not admit that it is. Instead he can argue that the principle of toleration is really implicit in his third "fact," that only an unacceptable level of oppression could end the pluralism in our societies. If coercion designed to end discord is unacceptable, then that discord must be resolved through respect for others' differing views. And such respect is what the principle of toleration insists upon. So even if this principle can be endorsed for moral reasons, it is also necessary, according to Rawls, to endorse it for prudential reasons, because this principle (along with certain related virtues such as the willingness to listen to and not violently attack one's opponents) is what makes possible the new non-Hobbesian method for achieving peaceful cooperation in a community of people with differing conceptions of the good.

In essence Rawls is arguing that in modern constitutional democracies which reject the pursuit of peace through oppressive state power, the overlapping consensus includes the very principle which directs society to further define and expand that consensus.

MORE THAN A MODUS VIVENDI?

If this is how we are to understand the motivation behind the development of an overlapping consensus, how is that consensus more than a mere modus vivendi? Rawls argues that it is more than this when people have allegiance to it as right and not merely as instrumentally valuable (although each may have different moral, philosophical, or religious reasons for doing so): "First, the object of consensus, the political conception of justice, is itself a moral conception. And second, it is affirmed on moral grounds. . . . The fact that those who affirm the political conception start from within their own comprehensive view, and hence begin from different premises and grounds, does not make their affirmation any less religious, philosophical or moral, as the case may be" (IOC, p. 11).

But notice what Rawls has done: if this style of justification of a political conception (i.e., as part of an overlapping consensus) really makes sense, it would seem he has found a way of solving what might be called the "paradox" of liberalism.[15] On the one hand, liberalism is committed to tolerance and thus to the state's remaining impartial in its dealings with the clashing ideas of its citizens; yet on the other hand, it demands partiality with respect to itself, and thus insists on the use of coercion against anyone who would challenge the principle of tolerance. It would seem that a liberal, to be consistent, would have to tolerate even those who would challenge (and use violence to attack) that principle, so that, to paraphrase Robert Frost, the liberal could not take his own side in this argument.[16] However, Rawls's justification of a political conception as part of an overlapping consensus allows him to argue, on everyone's behalf, that the substantive conception of justice included within it is right (and worthy of enforcement through state power) even while remaining tolerant of (and impartial toward) the disparate ideas, life-styles, religions, and moral views of the citizenry. Thus we see why Rawls says that formulating a "political" conception of justice is simply applying the principle of toleration to philosophy itself (JFPM, pp. 223, 231; IOC, p. 15). His idea is that political philosophy is useful to a liberal society only if it rids itself of all metaphysical views so as to be properly tolerant of the diversity of ideas and practices in our political culture.

One may wonder whether or not this solution is too good to be true. The paradox only seems to be resolved in circumstances where there is a substantial degree of overlap between individuals' differing views and where there is no minority advocating intolerance toward beliefs other than their own. Suppose, however, that these circumstances don't hold. For example, suppose there is a group of religious fundamentalists whose premier objective is to make converts to their religion in order to achieve salvation for them, and who tolerate the views and practices of atheists and members of other religions only because they are not strong enough to use the power of the state to stamp out these heresies. Such people would see a central component of the overlapping consensus, the principle of toleration, as merely expedient in the circumstances. While it might allow them to forestall war in their dealings with the infidels, they would just as soon get rid of it if conditions allowed them to do so.

Could a political philosopher change the minds of these people if she eschewed metaphysics and used only Rawls's political method? If

---

15. This paradox is nicely introduced by Thomas Nagel in "Moral Conflict and Political Legitimacy," *Philosophy and Public Affairs* 16 (1987): 215–40.

16. Quoted in ibid., p. 215.

these fundamentalists were genuinely opposed to toleration she could not argue for it as an idea in the overlap of divergent metaphysical conceptions—because it would not be in their overlap. Perhaps she might argue that toleration was henceforth always going to be necessary to achieve a cooperative stable society, and let us go so far as to suppose that this is true. Is this style of political argument sufficient to make the religious fundamentalists accept toleration as right? No; the fundamentalists' acceptance of it on these grounds would be acceptance of it as a mere modus vivendi; if only the world could be different, they would happily jettison it.

The upshot of this argument is that the creation of an overlapping consensus in a pluralistic society cannot guarantee, even if members of this society accept toleration, that they do so because they believe it to be intrinsically right. The only argument for its acceptance that a practitioner of Rawls's method can give to one whose metaphysical beliefs do not endorse it as right is that in the circumstances it is instrumentally valuable for achieving peaceful cooperation. So either the principle of toleration is endorsed by a person's comprehensive moral conception, or it is endorsed as a mere modus vivendi. There is no political method that will allow one to argue for its endorsement as more than the latter when the person's comprehensive moral conception opposes it. In these situations, Rawls can either keep his political methodology, in which case he has allowed political philosophy in pluralist societies only the job of articulating a modus vivendi; or he can give political philosophy the role of arguing in these societies that the principle of toleration is right, in which case he has committed the philosopher to doing metaphysics. There is no intermediate "third way."

But Rawls does not disagree with any of this. And the fact that he does not enables us to get a better understanding of what he takes an overlapping consensus to be. In the situation I described, he would say that there was a modus vivendi but no overlapping consensus. This is, in fact, how he describes a similar political world: sixteenth-century Europe, where Catholics and Protestants vied for political dominance. Suppose they had decided to tolerate one another. Then, says Rawls, "we no longer have an overlapping consensus on the principle of toleration. At that time both faiths held that it was the duty of the ruler to uphold the true religion and to repress the spread of heresy and false doctrine. In this case the acceptance of the principle of toleration would indeed be a mere *modus vivendi*, because if either faith becomes dominant, the principle of toleration will no longer be followed. Stability with respect to the distribution of power no longer exists" (IOC, p. 11). If the agreement of Catholics and Protestants at that time could not count as the creation of an overlapping consensus on the principle of toleration, then Rawls essentially believes that in order for a genuine overlapping consensus to exist, the bulk of the population must endorse these ideas for a certain kind of reason, that is, a moral, religious, or philosophical reason that makes the citizens accept these ideas as right (in addition to any appreciation they may have of the instrumental value of accepting these ideas). Rawls wants this sort of reason to explain the citizenry's belief in these ideas because the stability of the community will thereby be enhanced. Indeed, that stability, he says, comes in degrees, depending upon the content of the religious, philosophical, or moral doctrines available to create the consensus (JFPM, p. 250). A consensus on the principle of toleration reached in a society in which people embrace it as Kantians, or as Millians, as Rawlsians, or as members of religions committed to it as intrinsically right, will be "far more stable than one founded on views that express skepticism and indifference to religious, philosophical or moral values, or that regard the acceptance of the principles of justice simply as a prudent *modus vivendi* given the existing balance of social forces" (JFPM, p. 250).[17]

I have three critical reactions to this Rawlsian argument. First, if that argument is right, then the primary task of a political philosopher is to find metaphysical reasons implicit in each party's belief system to support ideas as right in the consensus. If this is not possible, then either Rawls would have to say that the political philosopher must be content with stability arguments for endorsing these ideas, making them a mere modus vivendi, or he would have to hope that the philosopher could persuade people to "will to believe" in an idea's rightness (where they are not otherwise inclined to do so) for the sake of stability. The latter project, however, may be self-defeating,[18] in which case the generation of an overlapping consensus would depend upon a sixth fact, namely, that each party (or, at any rate, the vast majority) has a metaphysics that supports the ideas in the shared fund as "right" and not merely as expedient. But one may wonder whether or not any existing constitutional democracy is one in which that sixth fact holds, and thus whether or not there is any society today in which Rawls's methodology could really be practiced.

The second critical reaction is that, contra Rawls, an overlapping consensus among Millians or Rawlsians is not more stable than one among moral skeptics or persons who only accept the principle of toleration as expedient. If the pluralism in the latter society really is permanent (because the parties reject the use of the kind of state power that would destroy it), then it would seem the relative power of the parties would always be such as to support this noncoercive means to peace. Remember that Rawls's entire argument for this way of philosophizing presupposed that his five facts held. To point out that the modus vivendi would not last

---

17. In his discussions of stability, Rawls leaves out one kind of reason why one might embrace the principle of toleration and the liberal conception of justice, namely, the utilitarian reason that doing so in those situations where Rawls's five facts hold will maximize the happiness of the community. This reason for adopting these principles as right still makes them instrumentally rather than intrinsically valuable. Is this moral reason good enough, or does the utilitarian's endorsement still seem too Hobbesian to ensure stability?

18. Bernard Williams has argued that trying to do this is self-defeating. See his "Deciding to Believe," in his *Problems of the Self* (Cambridge: Cambridge University Press, 1973).

if the society became relatively homogeneous (so that the first three facts don't hold) is to change the subject; Rawls should have nothing to say to a dominant group that suddenly finds itself able to enforce its conception of the good with minimal reliance on coercion (because few would resist). His entire justification of consensus-building philosophy presupposed that this was not so.

Finally, the third and (to my mind) most important critical reaction involves the rejection of Rawls's claim that an overlapping consensus is more than a modus vivendi. Because Rawls's justification of the project of developing an overlapping consensus is instrumental, then no matter what turns out to be required for stability, his project is, and will always be, Hobbesian. To see this, suppose he is right that only when citizens embrace the elements of the overlapping consensus as right (perhaps for one of the reasons he gave in the passage just quoted) can the pluralist society remain stable. Now in this situation, each individual will not believe that the ideas he shares with his fellows constitute a mere modus vivendi, because each will believe that these ideas are correct in their own right. But what is the political philosopher's justification for his project of developing an overlapping consensus? Whatever his private metaphysical reasons, these cannot constitute the public justification of the project. It is useful to distinguish at this point between public and private philosophizing. The former is what one does when one theorizes about issues that are relevant to the construction of public institutions, especially institutions of government. The latter is what one does as an individual pursuing what one takes to be the truth about the world. Rawls is not against metaphysical speculation, theology, or moral theorizing; instead he sees them as appropriate only in the private realm. Public philosophizing, in his view, must not rely on metaphysics in constitutional democracies which accept (for reasons of stability) the principle of toleration. It endorses no contestable thesis in its justification of ideas.

So Rawls must give a public argument for the philosophical project of developing an overlapping consensus that is neutral among the citizenry's competing metaphysical conceptions. And of course he mounts just this sort of argument in "Justice as Fairness" and "The Idea of an Overlapping Consensus": he argues that this project promotes the stability of (and prevents the degeneration of) modern constitutional democracies. Any political philosopher who accepts this argument will therefore believe herself obligated to contribute to the development of an overlapping consensus for instrumental reasons. And, as any Hobbesian would point out, this means that her public justification of her project is that of constructing a modus vivendi in a permanently pluralist world. Moreover, if Rawls's stability argument is right, we can see that the modus vivendi is not so much the set of beliefs constituting that overlapping consensus as it is both that set of beliefs and the citizenry's "I-accept-them-because-they-are-right" attitude toward them. Any Hobbesian intent on peace who could be persuaded by Rawls that this way of securing peace really works would want the citizenry to adopt both these beliefs and that attitude.

The point is that even if the ideas in the overlapping consensus are believed by the citizenry to be right as opposed to merely expedient, Rawls can offer only Hobbes-style expediency arguments for the generation of the overlapping consensus itself.

But, Rawls might protest, maybe these citizens have private metaphysical views which also allow them to endorse the generation of the overlapping consensus as right. Maybe. But the only thing that they can all agree that they are doing is creating a modus vivendi. The public, neutral justification of the project is one that makes it the creation of peace and stability at the lowest political cost, and this is a Hobbesian justification.

A PLEA FOR METAPHYSICS

I am one philosopher who does not think that calling a methodology 'Hobbesian' is an argument against it. What worries me is not Rawls's kinship with the man who began modern political philosophy; rather, it is his conception of what philosophy amounts to if his prescriptions for achieving stability in our world are right.

Consider my motives if I strive to develop an overlapping consensus. I cannot be interested in showing to all the parties involved that any idea I believe they all share is true, but only that they have reason to accept it, perhaps for (moral or religious) reasons that I myself think are bad or discredited. So I am after the idea's acceptance, not a proof of its truth. Am I not behaving as a (mere) politician? Politicians, after all, only want acceptance of ideas they (for whatever reason) are pushing; philosophers are supposed to want truth.

Indeed, because it is her acceptance of it which counts (even if it is on what I take to be wrongheaded religious or philosophical grounds), why stick to logical argumentation to persuade her? Why not use rhetoric, or emotional appeals, or socialization techniques that achieve peace by changing rather than coercing people? The maxim characterizing my practice might be: "Achieve political consensus on any given tenet by taking advantage of any ideology or device that could be used to gain others' acceptance of it, no matter how boneheaded or illogical." Perhaps there is nothing wrong with members of a pluralist society engaging in this undertaking, and I can certainly see how it is a "political" undertaking. But is it in any way a philosophical one?

These questions set the stage for a discussion of the most interesting aspect of Rawls's recent work: his challenge to us to think about what political philosophers ought to be doing in our place and time. But reflections on this topic inevitably drive one back to reflections on what any sort of philosophy ought to be doing at any time. Socrates, the founder of our discipline, characterized philosophy as the pursuit of the truth, and Plato's defense of that pursuit is quoted at the start of this article. Rawls endorses what I will call "Socratic philosophizing" in fields such as ethics, or aesthetics, or philosophy of science, but he is asking us to replace it with something else when doing political philosophy in modern constitutional democracies. It is not merely that we are supposed to eschew metaphysics in this political realm; more fundamentally, we are supposed to eschew attempts at philosophical proof through argumentation that involves commitment to controversial metaphysical premises. Not truth, but noncoerced social agreement is to be our goal. And if that goal can be achieved via definitive demonstration, fine; but when it cannot, and controversy is inevitable, we are to strive for consensus rather than conversion, persuasion rather than proof.

In order to be sure we political philosophers ought to follow Rawls's advice, we need to be sure, first, that there is something about political philosophy in constitutional democracies that marks it as different both in aim and method from other kinds of philosophizing; and second, that the pursuit of consensus counts as a kind of philosophizing, even if it is not the Socratic kind. Rawls offers no explicit answer to these questions, but in order to pursue the issues they raise, let me start by offering, on his behalf, a (Socratic) argument for answering yes to them.

Consider, first, the worry that political theorizing may not be philosophy. Now, one of the central tasks of a philosophy professor is helping students to understand the logical implications of their beliefs. Accordingly, if she were to see two students arguing over some political issue and realized that they were in conflict only because one of them had drawn the wrong conclusion from his metaphysical premises, she would certainly be engaging in philosophy when she enabled the student to see this fact. Analogously, it would seem that a political philosopher who sought to show all parties involved in a social conflict how they shared political theses that followed logically from their differing metaphysical premises would be doing philosophy also.

Of course, philosophy professors correct their students so that the students' beliefs will be rationally held. A critic might worry that a political philosopher following Rawls's advice would be pursuing not this goal but the goal of consensus building, which, as I just proposed, might be better pursued with emotional or rhetorical appeals. However, whatever use these appeals may have initially, Rawls could argue that stability is best achieved and longest lasting only when the citizenry's shared beliefs are rationally, rather than irrationally, held. If this is right, then political philosophers who want successful and long-lived social cooperation must pursue an overlapping consensus of ideas using precisely the techniques of the philosophy professor, so that the ideas in this consensus are securely held by all parties in this pluralist society.

Moreover, if the philosopher were haunted by the fear (as Hobbes was) that the metaphysical theses upon which political theses rest in Socratic arguments can never be proven to be true or false, then the socially informed consensus building just described would be the only kind of political philosophizing that had any claim to being true. Although one could never say, "It is true that X is the correct conception of justice," nonetheless, one would be able to say, "It is true that if one accepts premises A, B, and C, then X is the correct conception of justice."

But Rawls is at pains to point out that his method of philosophizing does not presuppose such skepticism. Instead, the principle of toleration gives Rawls his intellectual motivation for this kind of philosophizing and provides him with an answer to the first question above, about how political philosophy differs in aim and method from other kinds of philosophizing. From Plato to the present, political philosophers have sought a remedy for social discord. But what if the Socratic practice of philosophy adds to that discord? Mustn't the political philosopher modify how she and others philosophize in order that the goal of social peace be achieved? If tolerance is the best (and most desirable) means to peace, must we not, as Rawls says, apply the principle of tolerance to the practice of political philosophy itself? Doing so means accepting a non-Socratic style of political theorizing. At one point in "Justice as Fairness," Rawls worries that liberalism, which rests on the principle of toleration, is in danger of becoming "just another sectarian doctrine" if it must be defended by arguments that rest on controversial metaphysical premises (JFPM, p. 246). Only if the philosopher applies the principle of toleration to philosophy itself as he theorizes politically does he seem properly tolerant of the diversity of ideas in his society and properly respectful of the fact that his own metaphysical beliefs may not be used to justify political coercion of others, any more than their beliefs may be used to justify political coercion of him. Such respect is demanded of him, at the very least, to ensure stability, and it may also be something that his moral or religious beliefs compel him to pay.

I find myself moved enough by these considerations to believe that, whatever else political philosophy ought to involve, it should sometimes be political. Indeed, I think we are in Rawls's debt for pointing out to us the valuable and unique intellectual role that political philosophers can play in contemporary constitutional democracies, namely, helping to create the intellectual ground rules upon which people of disparate views can peacefully interact. Such people would not even be able to present a claim for public adjudication if there were not a shared understanding of what a valid claim is, what the rules of assessing that claim are, and what "capital" the society ought to dispense in order to settle it. No matter what our religion, moral beliefs, or metaphysical commitments, if we are to work together in one system of cooperation, we have to have a "common currency" for the debating and settling of disputes or our society will be in ruins. Surely, the creation of such an intellectual common currency has been going on for years, perhaps more often in law schools than in philosophy departments (e.g., in discussions about what our constitutional tradition is). Its creation is an intellectual feat in which philosophers can usefully participate, given their training. To the extent that political philosophers engage in this enterprise, they are indeed doing something far more practical than philosophers who speculate about the truth in other fields of inquiry.

But I also want to argue, first, that this kind of practical aim is not unique to political philosophy, and second, that creating an overlapping consensus is not the only aim that political philosophy ought to have.

To make the first point, consider the fact that people who do applied ethics may also find it appropriate to refrain from advancing their own ideas about moral truth to the doctors, lawyers, or legislators who are consulting them, and to attempt instead to clarify the beliefs of their clients, draw out the conclusions implicit in these beliefs, and encourage reflection so as to enable these people to agree (and act) on a way to settle a dispute or a problem. Such "reflective consensus building" by these moral philosophers is not unlike the aim Rawls attributes to political philosophers. In general, it seems inappropriate for both moral and political philosophers to speculate about what is right when there are pressing problems that can be solved only when groups of people get philosophers' intellectual help to reach the agreement necessary to a solution.

However, I also want to argue that political philosophers must do more than simply engage in consensus building; they ought also to engage in Socratic philosophizing.

Suppose that conditions are as ripe for the practice of Rawls's method of philosophizing as they can be: the five facts prevail, everyone accepts the principle of toleration (albeit for different moral and religious reasons), the overlap of ideas is considerable enough that there is a consensus on a well-defined conception of justice and perhaps also a good (but limited) government able to decide questions on which there is no consensus. Nonetheless, there is still controversy, for example, about whether people should be accorded free health service supplied by the state or about whether a ban on pornography is a violation of freedom of speech. These are items upon which there is no consensus and which cannot be removed from the political agenda. Why not, Socrates might ask, engage in metaphysical political philosophy when publicly discussing these issues? Those who do so will not be contemptuous of their opponents' ideas, nor will they be prepared to call upon force to get the others to change their minds. Indeed, to the extent that they are committed as Socrates wishes them to be to the truth rather than to the particular belief they are presently endorsing, they ought to be prepared to argue under the assumption that they might be wrong and, thus, prepared to change their minds if their opponents offer them better arguments for the opposing view than they have for their own. Why should this spell trouble for a political community?

Rawls might argue that it spells trouble because the philosopher who insists that he is right and others wrong violates the principle of toleration, which we must all follow to insure long-lasting stability. But consider that there is a difference between tolerance of another's ideas and tolerance of another's holding of these ideas. Socrates would insist that the principle of toleration requires only the second kind of tolerance, not the first kind. Indeed, he would argue that as long as each disputant remains tolerant of and respects the fact that her opponent holds different ideas, she need not and should not be tolerant of the ideas themselves if she believes she is in possession of an argument that shows her opponents' ideas to be wrong or problematic. And if, as skeptics might claim, no such proofs are forthcoming, the disputants' discussion and speculation seem harmless enough as long as all parties respect each other as they participate in it.

Moreover, the public pursuit of the truth about these aspects of justice need not threaten the security of anyone in a pluralist society as long as there are universally shared (and enforced) guidelines for people's argumentative interaction with one another that insist, as Socrates did himself in his practice of philosophy, on respect for everyone's effort to construct his or her own belief system. Of course, people's beliefs might be threatened by the existence of an argument undermining them. But why should those who are committed to the truth sustain a tolerance of ideas when they believe they have an argument showing them to be false? Tolerance of others who hold what one takes to be false ideas is one thing; tolerance of the ideas themselves is quite another.

My point is that implicit in genuine philosophical argumentation is respect for one's opponent. One might not respect his ideas, but when one argues with him (as opposed to, say, fighting with him), one respects him and seeks to win him over to one's side not via coercion but by appeal to the truth, an appeal which might unexpectedly show one to be wrong and one's opponent to be right. A society which fostered such philosophizing would be a society which fostered such respect. Socrates himself tried to persuade the jury that eventually convicted him that philosophizing was neither a dangerous nor a divisive activity. And aren't we supposed to think that he was right that a society has nothing to fear from a group of people who are earnestly committed to working out what is true and who are respectful of one another's attempts to formulate answers— even if those answers are ones with which they disagree? Indeed, such respect seems to be what Mill argued that liberalism was all about.

Those communitarians who share MacIntyre's or Sandel's metaethics need not reject any of this. They would only want to argue that Socratic philosophizing is of necessity suffused with the shared values of the community in which the disputants participate. But even if they are right that one can search for truth only in a social framework, nonetheless, Socrates's point would be that when one engages in such a search, one is still doing metaphysics. Of course, communitarians such as Rorty would reject any enterprise characterized as the search for truth as a self-defeating search for an extrasocietal perspective that does not exist, and they would thereby reject the doing of philosophy as it has been classically understood.

But other communitarians can endorse socially informed metaphysical theorizing as worth pursuing and as different from the pursuit of mere consensus.

Perhaps one thing that scared the Athenian jury about Socrates' activity was the fact that appeals to the truth are frequently invoked to justify intolerance. Perhaps, thought the jury, Socrates' young men would believe, armed by Socrates' arguments, that they knew better than the rest of the populace what ought to happen in Athens and so foist their views upon an unwilling city.

But such is the behavior of people who are not philosophers. These people are not committed to the truth; instead, they are true believers committed to their cause.[19] True believers not only attack opposing ideas but also those who hold opposing ideas. So they fail to be tolerant in both of the ways described above. They see their intellectual opponents as "enemies," "infidels," "heretics," "fascists"—to be fought, resisted, even killed if they get in the way of building their dream, be it the kingdom of heaven, or the perfect state of anarchy, or the ideal communist state. It is their blind faith, not their metaphysics, which results in discord and even war.

I would argue that the true believer is the one enemy the philosopher has—for two reasons. First, he would block reform justified by good argument. Those who are committed to the truth act as gadflies for their society, striving not merely for stability but for stability on just terms. They will be resisted by those whose faith prevents them from hearing the better argument. Since the death of Socrates philosophers have believed that they owed it to their communities to fight such resistance and examine the theoretical foundations of society as much to overturn what is unjustifiable as to find shared bases of agreement.

Second, the true believer is the enemy of the philosopher because he will not respect his opponent's attempts to formulate and reflect on the opponent's ideas. Such respect is the foundation not only of philosophy but also of liberal society; it is that upon which we must insist if we wish to have either. One who is committed to philosophy must also be committed to remaining intolerant of others' intolerance. To attempt to reach consensus with intolerant true believers would be to betray one's belief in the respect that grounds one's very philosophizing.

Rawls himself comes very close to making this same point. In "The Idea of an Overlapping Consensus," he admits that "in affirming a political conception of justice we may eventually have to assert at least certain aspects of our own comprehensive (by no means necessarily fully comprehensive) religious or philosophical doctrine. This happens whenever someone insists, for example, that certain questions are so fundamental that to ensure their being rightly settled justifies civil strife. The religious

19. The term 'true believer' was coined by Eric Hoffer to characterize such people in his *The True Believer* (New York: New American Library, 1951).

salvation of those holding a particular religion may be thought to depend upon it. At this point we may have no alternative but to deny this, and to assert the kind of thing we had hoped to avoid" (IOC, p. 14). Rawls seems to be endorsing the assertion of our moral conception in a public, political context. And what he believes we must assert—even with force— is toleration, respect for others' ideas. Here is an idea over which he is prepared to fight. And, of course, as a philosopher he must be so prepared because philosophers are true believers also—true believers in the value of pursuing truth through philosophical argumentation that respects equally the disputants who participate in it.

It may even be that this respect is the foundation of justice. Now, insofar as Rawls's conception of justice attempts to incorporate and give voice to that respect, then if there were an overlapping consensus on it (as he believes), our society would have the foundations necessary for genuine philosophizing rather than divisive argumentative clashes among intolerant opponents. But in my view, not only is there no consensus on Rawls's conception of justice in our society, but, more disturbingly, there is no consensus on the idea that all human beings deserve equal respect. The Bill of Rights is only part of our history; the persistence of racial discrimination, sexism, and exploitation betrays a commitment by many to the second-class status of some of their fellows. Because they have that status, such people are perceived as appropriate targets of coercion by those of higher status—who need not argue with their inferiors. In contrast, a person who is committed to philosophizing with another is rejecting the idea that she has a higher status that permits her to exercise control over the other's beliefs and is instead allowing and respecting her opponent's ability to formulate and decide on his own beliefs freely. Anyone committed to philosophizing with her opponent is thus committed to respecting him as a human being. That is, she is respecting him not necessarily as a virtuous person, or as a smart person, or as a person who satisfies any particular social ideal, but as a human being who can and ought to choose how to lead his own life. Hence, a society committed to philosophizing with all human beings would also be committed to the kind of respect for one another which is the foundation of justice. If a philosopher finds herself in a society which is committed neither to justice nor to reasoned debate, then she will indeed be a divisive force in the community as she strives for reform of practices that she cannot tolerate.

And now we have come to the crux of my argument for metaphysical political philosophizing. Given that modern constitutional democracies are still not societies in which there is widespread agreement that all people should be accorded the same rights and opportunities, we have an obligation as philosophers committed to arguing with, and thus re-specting, our fellow human beings to persuade opponents of that idea and thus to change their minds. Arguing that they ought to do so because such respect promotes stability is one kind of Socratic argument (it is an argument that is supposed to assert a true causal connection). But even better in the eyes of those who have been denied such respect is an argument maintaining that disrespectful ideas and practices ought to be rejected because they are wrong.

These reflections are meant to suggest that the activity of philosophy is itself based upon substantive metaphysical beliefs about the nature of human beings. I would argue that those political philosophers who share Socrates' delight in the pursuit of knowledge with their fellow human beings should not want to give up that pursuit, or the fight for the conditions of free and equal respect that make it possible.

The priority of democracy to philosophy

Thomas Jefferson set the tone for American liberal politics when he said "it does me no injury for my neighbor to say that there are twenty Gods or no God."[1] His example helped make respectable the idea that politics can be separated from beliefs about matters of ultimate importance – that shared beliefs among citizens on such matters are not essential to a democratic society. Like many other figures of the Enlightenment, Jefferson assumed that a moral faculty common to the typical theist and the typical atheist suffices for civic virtue.

Many Enlightenment intellectuals were willing to go further and say that since religious beliefs turn out to be inessential for political cohesion, they should simply be discarded as mumbo jumbo – perhaps to be replaced (as in twentieth-century totalitarian Marxist states) with some sort of explicitly secular political faith that will form the moral consciousness of the citizen. Jefferson again set the tone when he refused to go that far. He thought it enough to privatize religion, to view it as irrelevant to social order but relevant to, and possibly essential for, individual perfection. Citizens of a Jeffersonian democracy can be as religious or irreligious as they please as long as they are not "fanatical." That is, they must abandon or modify opinions on matters of ultimate importance, the opinions that may hitherto have given sense and point to their lives, if these opinions entail public actions that cannot be justified to most of their fellow citizens.

This Jeffersonian compromise concerning the relation of spiritual perfection to public policy has two sides. Its absolutist side says that every human being, without the benefit of special revelation, has all the beliefs necessary for civic virtue. These beliefs spring from a universal human faculty, conscience – possession of which constitutes the specifically human essence of each human being. This is the faculty that gives the individual human dignity and rights. But there is also a pragmatic side. This side says that when the individual finds in her conscience beliefs that are relevant to public policy but incapable of defense on the basis of beliefs common to her fellow citizens, she must sacrifice her conscience on the altar of public expediency.

The tension between these two sides can be eliminated by a philosophical theory that identifies justifiability to humanity at large with truth. The Enlight-

---

1 Thomas Jefferson, *Notes on the State of Virginia*, Query XVII, in *The Writings of Thomas Jefferson*, ed. A. A. Lipscomb and A. E. Bergh (Washington, D.C., 1905), 2: 217.

enment idea of "reason" embodies such a theory: the theory that there is a relation between the ahistorical essence of the human soul and moral truth, a relation which ensures that free and open discussion will produce "one right answer" to moral as well as to scientific questions.[2] Such a theory guarantees that a moral belief that cannot be justified to the mass of mankind is "irrational," and thus is not really a product of our moral faculty at all. Rather, it is a "prejudice," a belief that comes from some other part of the soul than "reason." It does not share in the sanctity of conscience, for it is the product of a sort of pseudoconscience – something whose loss is no sacrifice, but a purgation.

In our century, this rationalist justification of the Enlightenment compromise has been discredited. Contemporary intellectuals have given up the Enlightenment assumption that religion, myth, and tradition can be opposed to something ahistorical, something common to all human beings qua human. Anthropologists and historians of science have blurred the distinction between innate rationality and the products of acculturation. Philosophers such as Heidegger and Gadamer have given us ways of seeing human beings as historical all the way through. Other philosophers, such as Quine and Davidson, have blurred the distinction between permanent truths of reason and temporary truths of fact. Psychoanalysis has blurred the distinction between conscience and the emotions of love, hate, and fear, and thus the distinction between morality and prudence. The result is to erase the picture of the self common to Greek metaphysics, Christian theology, and Enlightenment rationalism: the picture of an ahistorical natural center, the locus of human dignity, surrounded by an adventitious and inessential periphery.

The effect of erasing this picture is to break the link between truth and justifiability. This, in turn, breaks down the bridge between the two sides of the Enlightenment compromise. The effect is to polarize liberal social theory. If we stay on the absolutist side, we shall talk about inalienable "human rights" and about "one right answer" to moral and political dilemmas without trying to back up such talk with a theory of human nature. We shall abandon metaphysical accounts of what a right is while nevertheless insisting that everywhere, in all times and cultures, members of our species have had the same rights. But if we swing to the pragmatist side, and consider talk of "rights" an attempt to enjoy the benefits of metaphysics without assuming the appropriate responsibilities, we shall still need something to distinguish the sort of individual conscience we respect from the sort we condemn as "fanatical." This can only be something relatively local and ethnocentric – the tradition of a particular community, the consensus of a particular culture. Accord-

2 Jefferson included a statement of this familiar Scriptural claim (roughly in the form in which it had been restated by Milton in *Areopagitica*) in the preamble to the Virginia Statute for Religious Freedom: "truth is great and will prevail if left to herself, . . . she is the proper and sufficient antagonist to error, and has nothing to fear from the conflict, unless by human interposition disarmed of her natural weapons, free argument and debate, errors ceasing to be dangerous when it is permitted freely to contradict them" (ibid., 2: 302).

ing to this view, what counts as rational or as fanatical is relative to the group to which we think it necessary to justify ourselves – to the body of shared belief that determines the reference of the word "we." The Kantian identification with a central transcultural and ahistorical self is thus replaced by a quasi-Hegelian identification with our own community, thought of as a historical product. For pragmatist social theory, the question of whether justifiability to the community with which we identify entails truth is simply irrelevant.

Ronald Dworkin and others who take the notion of ahistorical human "rights" seriously serve as examples of the first, absolutist, pole. John Dewey and, as I shall shortly be arguing, John Rawls serve as examples of the second pole. But there is a third type of social theory – often dubbed "communitarianism" – which is less easy to place. Roughly speaking, the writers tagged with this label are those who reject both the individualistic rationalism of the Enlightenment and the idea of "rights," but, unlike the pragmatists, see this rejection as throwing doubt on the institutions and culture of the surviving democratic states. Such theorists include Robert Bellah, Alasdair MacIntyre, Michael Sandel, Charles Taylor, early Roberto Unger, and many others. These writers share some measure of agreement with a view found in an extreme form both in Heidegger and in Horkheimer and Adorno's *Dialectic of Enlightenment*. This is the view that liberal institutions and culture either should not or cannot survive the collapse of the philosophical justification that the Enlightenment provided for them.

There are three strands in communitarianism that need to be disentangled. First, there is the empirical prediction that no society that sets aside the idea of ahistorical moral truth in the insouciant way that Dewey recommended can survive. Horkheimer and Adorno, for example, suspect that you cannot have a moral community in a disenchanted world because toleration leads to pragmatism, and it is not clear how we can prevent, "blindly pragmatized thought" from losing "its transcending quality and its relation to truth."[3] They think that pragmatism was the inevitable outcome of Enlightenment rationalism and that pragmatism is not a strong enough philosophy to make moral community possible.[4] Second, there is the moral judgment that the sort of human being who is

3 Max Horkheimer and Theodor W. Adorno, *Dialectic of Enlightenment* (New York: Seabury Press, 1972), p. xiii.
4 "For the Enlightenment, whatever does not conform to the rule of computation and utility is suspect. So long as it can develop undisturbed by any outward repression, there is no holding it. In the process, it treats its own ideas of human rights exactly as it does the older universals . . . Enlightenment is totalitarian" (ibid., p. 6). This line of thought recurs repeatedly in communitarian accounts of the present state of the liberal democracies; see, for example, Robert Bellah, Richard Madsen, William Sullivan, Ann Swidler, and Steven Tipton, *Habits of the Heart: Individualism and Commitment in American Life* (Berkeley: University of California Press, 1985): "There is a widespread feeling that the promise of the modern era is slipping away from us. A movement of enlightenment and liberation that was to have freed us from superstition and tyranny has led in the twentieth century to a world in which ideological fanaticism and political oppression have reached extremes unknown in previous history" (p. 277).

produced by liberal institutions and culture is undesirable. MacIntyre, for example, thinks that our culture – a culture he says is dominated by "the Rich Aesthete, the Manager, and the Therapist" – is a *reductio ad absurdum* both of the philosophical views that helped create it and of those now invoked in its defense. Third, there is the claim that political institutions "presuppose" a doctrine about the nature of human beings and that such a doctrine must, unlike Enlightenment rationalism, make clear the essentially historical character of the self. So we find writers like Taylor and Sandel saying that we need a theory of the self that incorporates Hegel's and Heidegger's sense of the self's historicity.

The first claim is a straightforward empirical, sociological-historical one about the sort of glue that is required to hold a community together. The second is a straightforward moral judgment that the advantages of contemporary liberal democracy are outweighed by the disadvantages, by the ignoble and sordid character of the culture and the individual human beings that it produces. The third claim, however, is the most puzzling and complex. I shall concentrate on this third, most puzzling, claim, although toward the end I shall return briefly to the first two.

To evaluate this third claim, we need to ask two questions. The first is whether there is any sense in which liberal democracy "needs" philosophical justification at all. Those who share Dewey's pragmatism will say that although it may need philosophical articulation, it does not need philosophical backup. On this view, the philosopher of liberal democracy may wish to develop a theory of the human self that comports with the institutions he or she admires. But such a philosopher is not thereby justifying these institutions by reference to more fundamental premises, but the reverse: He or she is putting politics first and tailoring a philosophy to suit. Communitarians, by contrast, often speak as though political institutions were no better than their philosophical foundations.

The second question is one that we can ask even if we put the opposition between justification and articulation to one side. It is the question of whether a conception of the self that, as Taylor says, makes "the community constitutive of the individual"[5] does in fact comport better with liberal democracy than does the Enlightenment conception of the self. Taylor summarizes the latter as "an ideal of disengagement" that defines a "typically modern notion" of human dignity: "the ability to act on one's own, without outside interference or subordination to outside authority." On Taylor's view, as on Heidegger's, these Enlightenment notions are closely linked with characteristically modern ideas of "efficacy, power, unperturbability."[6] They are also closely linked with the contemporary form of the doctrine of the sacredness of the individual conscience – Dworkin's claim that appeals to rights "trump" all other appeals. Taylor, like Heidegger, would like to

5 Charles Taylor, *Philosophy and the Human Sciences*, vol. 2 of *Philosophical Papers* (Cambridge: Cambridge University Press, 1985), p. 8
6 Ibid., p. 5.

substitute a less individualistic conception of what it is to be properly human – one that makes less of autonomy and more of interdependence.

I can preview what is to come by saying that I shall answer "no" to the first question about the communitarians' third claim and "yes" to the second. I shall be arguing that Rawls, following up on Dewey, shows us how liberal democracy can get along without philosophical presuppositions. He has thus shown us how we can disregard the third communitarian claim. But I shall also argue that communitarians like Taylor are right in saying that a conception of the self that makes the community constitutive of the self does comport well with liberal democracy. That is, if we *want* to flesh out our self-image as citizens of such a democracy with a philosophical view of the self, Taylor gives us pretty much the right view. But this sort of philosophical fleshing-out does not have the importance that writers like Horkheimer and Adorno, or Heidegger, have attributed to it.

Without further preface, I turn now to Rawls. I shall begin by pointing out that both in *A Theory of Justice* and subsequently, he has linked his own position to the Jeffersonian ideal of religious toleration. In an article called "Justice as Fairness: Political not Metaphysical," he says that he is "going to apply the principle of toleration to philosophy itself," and goes on to say:

The essential point is this: as a practical political matter no general moral conception can provide the basis for a public conception of justice in a modern democratic society. The social and historical conditions of such a society have their origins in the Wars of Religion following the Reformation and the development of the principle of toleration, and in the growth of constitutional government and the institutions of large market economies. These conditions profoundly affect the requirements of a workable conception of political justice: such a conception must allow for a diversity of doctrines and the plurality of conflicting, and indeed incommensurable conceptions of the good affirmed by the members of existing democratic societies.[7]

We can think of Rawls as saying that just as the principle of religious toleration and the social thought of the Enlightenment proposed to bracket many standard theological topics when deliberating about public policy and constructing politi-

7 John Rawls, "Justice as Fairness: Political not Metaphysical," *Philosophy and Public Affairs* 14 (1985): 225. Religious toleration is a constantly recurring theme in Rawls's writing. Early in *A Theory of Justice* (Cambridge, Mass.: Harvard University Press, 1971), when giving examples of the sort of common opinions that a theory of justice must take into account and systematize, he cites our conviction that religious intolerance is unjust (p. 19). His example of the fact that "a well-ordered society tends to eliminate or at least to control men's inclinations to injustice" is that "warring and intolerant sects are much less likely to exist" (p. 247). Another relevant passage (which I shall discuss below) is his diagnosis of Ignatius Loyola's attempt to make the love of God the "dominant good": "Although to subordinate all our aims to one end does not strictly speaking violate the principles of rational choice . . . it still strikes us as irrational, or more likely as mad" (pp. 553–4).

cal institutions, so we need to bracket many standard topics of philosophical inquiry. For purposes of social theory, we can put aside such topics as an ahistorical human nature, the nature of selfhood, the motive of moral behavior, and the meaning of human life. We treat these as irrelevant to politics as Jefferson thought questions about the Trinity and about transubstantiation.

Insofar as he adopts this stance, Rawls disarms many of the criticisms that, in the wake of Horkheimer and Adorno, have been directed at American liberalism. Rawls can agree that Jefferson and his circle shared a lot of dubious philosophical views, views that we might now wish to reject. He can even agree with Horkheimer and Adorno, as Dewey would have, that these views contained the seeds of their own destruction. But he thinks that the remedy may be not to formulate better philosophical views on the same topics, but (for purposes of political theory) benignly to neglect these topics. As he says:

since justice as fairness is intended as a political conception of justice for a democratic society, it tries to draw solely upon basic intuitive ideas that are embedded in the political institutions of a democratic society and the public traditions of their interpretation. Justice as fairness is a political conception in part because it starts from within a certain political tradition. We hope that this political conception of justice may be at least supported by what we may call "overlapping consensus," that is, by a consensus that includes all the opposing philosophical and religious doctrines likely to persist and gain adherents in a more or less just constitutional democratic society.[8]

Rawls thinks that "philosophy as the search for truth about an independent metaphysical and moral order cannot . . . provide a workable and shared basis for a political conception of justice in a democratic society."[9] So he suggests that we confine ourselves to collecting, "such settled convictions as the belief in religious toleration and the rejection of slavery" and then "try to organize the basic intuitive ideas and principles implicit in these convictions into a coherent conception of justice."[10]

This attitude is thoroughly historicist and antiuniversalist.[11] Rawls can whole-

---

8 Rawls, "Justice as Fairness," pp. 225–6. The suggestion that there are many philosophical views that will *not* survive in such conditions is analogous to the Enlightenment suggestion that the adoption of democratic institutions will cause "superstitious" forms of religious belief gradually to die off.

9 Ibid., p. 230.

10 Ibid.

11 For Rawls's historicism see, for example, *Theory of Justice*, p. 547. There, Rawls says that the people in the original position are assumed to know "the general facts about society," including the fact that "institutions are not fixed but change over time, altered by natural circumstances and the activities and conflicts of social groups." He uses this point to rule out, as original choosers of principles of justice, those "in a feudal or a caste system," and those who are unaware of events such as the French Revolution. This is one of many passages that make clear (at least read in the light of Rawls's later work) that a great deal of knowledge that came late to the mind of Europe is present to the minds of those behind the veil of ignorance. Or, to put it another way, such passages make clear that those original choosers behind the veil exemplify a certain modern type of

heartedly agree with Hegel and Dewey against Kant and can say that the Enlightenment attempt to free oneself from tradition and history, to appeal to "Nature" or "Reason," was self-deceptive.[12] He can see such an appeal as a misguided attempt to make philosophy do what theology failed to do. Rawls's effort to, in his words, "stay on the surface, philosophically speaking" can be seen as taking Jefferson's avoidance of theology one step further.

On the Deweyan view I am attributing to Rawls, no such discipline as "philosophical anthropology" is required as a preface to politics, but only history and sociology. Further, it is misleading to think of his view as Dworkin does: as "rights-based" as opposed to "goal-based." For the notion of "basis" is not in point. It is not that we know, on antecedent philosophical grounds, that it is of the essence of human beings to have rights, and then proceed to ask how a society might preserve and protect these rights. On the question of priority, as on the question of the relativity of justice to historical situations, Rawls is closer to Walzer than to Dworkin.[13] Since Rawls does not believe that for purposes of political theory, we need think of ourselves as having an essence that precedes and antedates history, he would not agree with Sandel that for these purposes, we need

human being, not an ahistorical human nature. See also p. 548, where Rawls says, "Of course in working out what the requisite principles [of justice] are, we must rely upon current knowledge as recognized by common sense and the existing scientific consensus. We have to concede that as established beliefs change, it is possible that the principles of justice which it seems rational to choose may likewise change."

12 See Bellah et al., *Habits of the Heart*, p. 141, for a recent restatement of this "counter-Enlightenment" line of thought. For the authors' view of the problems created by persistence in Enlightenment rhetoric and by the prevalence of the conception of human dignity that Taylor identifies as "distinctively modern," see p. 21: "For most of us, it is easier to think about to get what we want than to know exactly what we should want. Thus Brian, Joe, Margaret and Wayne [some of the Americans interviewed by the authors] are each in his or her own way confused about how to define for themselves such things as the nature of success, the meaning of freedom, and the requirements of justice. Those difficulties are in an important way created by the limitations in the common tradition of moral discourse they – and we – share." Compare p. 290: "the language of individualism, the primary American language of self-understanding, limits the way in which people think."

To my mind, the authors of *Habits of the Heart* undermine their own conclusions in the passages where they point to actual moral progress being made in recent American history, notably in their discussion of the civil-rights movement. There, they say that Martin Luther King, Jr., made the struggle for freedom "a practice of commitment within a vision of America as a community of memory" and that the response King elicited "came from the reawakened recognition by many Americans that their own sense of self was rooted in companionship with others who, though not necessarily like themselves, nevertheless shared with them a common history and whose appeals to justice and solidarity made powerful claims on our loyalty" (p. 252). These descriptions of King's achievement seem exactly right, but they can be read as evidence that the rhetoric of the Enlightenment offers at least as many opportunities as it does obstacles for the renewal of a sense of community. The civil-rights movement combined, without much strain, the language of Christian fellowship and the "language of individualism," about which Bellah and his colleagues are dubious.

13 See Michael Walzer, *Spheres of Justice* (New York: Basic, 1983), pp. 312 ff.

have an account of "the nature of the moral subject," which is "in some sense necessary, non-contingent and prior to any particular experience."[14] Some of our ancestors may have required such an account, just as others of our ancestors required such an account of their relation to their putative Creator. But *we* – we heirs of the Enlightenment for whom justice has become the first virtue – need neither. As citizens and as social theorists, we can be as indifferent to philosophical disagreements about the nature of the self as Jefferson was to theological differences about the nature of God.

This last point suggests a way of sharpening up my claim that Rawls's advocacy of philosophical toleration is a plausible extension of Jefferson's advocacy of religious toleration. Both "religion" and "philosophy" are vague umbrella terms, and both are subject to persuasive redefinition. When these terms are broadly enough defined, everybody, even atheists, will be said to have a religious faith (in the Tillichian sense of a "symbol of ultimate concern"). Everybody, even those who shun metaphysics and epistemology, will be said to have "philosophical presuppositions."[15] But for purposes of interpreting Jefferson and Rawls, we must use narrower definitions. Let "religion" mean, for Jefferson's purposes, disputes about the nature and the true name of God – and even about his existence.[16] Let "philosophy" mean, for Rawls's purposes, disputes about the nature of human beings and even about whether there is such a thing as "human nature."[17] Using

14 Michael Sandel, *Liberalism and the Limits of Justice* (Cambridge: Cambridge University Press, 1982), p. 49.

15 In a recent, as yet unpublished, paper, Sandel has urged that Rawls's claim that "philosophy in the classical sense as the search for truth about a prior and independent moral order cannot provide the shared basis for a political conception of justice" presupposes the controversial metaphysical claim that there is no such order. This seems to me like saying that Jefferson was presupposing the controversial theological claim that God is not interested in the name by which he is called by human beings. Both charges are accurate, but not really to the point. Both Jefferson and Rawls would have to reply, "I have no arguments for my dubious theological-metaphysical claim, because I do not know how to discuss such issues, and do not want to. My interest is in helping to preserve and create political institutions that will foster public indifference to such issues, while putting no restrictions on private discussion of them." This reply, of course, begs the "deeper" question that Sandel wants to raise, for the question of whether we *should* determine what issues to discuss on political or on "theoretical" (for example, theological or philosophical) grounds remains unanswered.

16 Jefferson agreed with Luther that philosophers had muddied the clear waters of the gospels. See Jefferson's polemic against Plato's "foggy mind" and his claim that "the doctrines which flowed from the lips of Jesus himself are within the comprehension of a child; but thousands of volumes have not yet explained the Platonisms engrafted on them; and for this obvious reason, that nonsense can never be explained" (*Writings of Thomas Jefferson*, 14: 149).

17 I am here using the term "human nature" in the traditional philosophical sense in which Sartre denied that there was such a thing, rather than in the rather unusual one that Rawls gives it. Rawls distinguishes between a "conception of the person" and a "theory of human nature," where the former is a "moral ideal" and the latter is provided by, roughly, common sense plus the social sciences. To have a theory of human nature is to have "general facts that we take to be true, or true enough, given the state of public knowledge in our society," facts that "limit the feasibility of the ideals of person and society embedded in that framework" ("Kantian Constructivism in Moral Theory," *Journal of Philosophy* 88 [1980]: 534).

these definitions, we can say that Rawls wants views about man's nature and purpose to be detached from politics. As he says, he wants his conception of justice to "avoid . . . claims about the essential nature and identity of persons."[18] So presumably, he wants questions about the point of human existence, or the meaning of human life, to be reserved for private life. A liberal democracy will not only exempt opinions on such matters from legal coercion, but also aim at disengaging discussions of such questions from discussions of social policy. Yet it will use force against the individual conscience, just insofar as conscience leads individuals to act so as to threaten democratic institutions. Unlike Jefferson's, Rawls's argument against fanaticism is not that it threatens truth about the characteristics of an antecedent metaphysical and moral order by threatening free discussion, but *simply* that it threatens freedom, and thus threatens justice. Truth about the existence or nature of that order drops out.

The definition of "philosophy" I have just suggested is not as artificial and ad hoc as it may appear. Intellectual historians commonly treat "the nature of the human subject" as the topic that gradually replaced "God" as European culture secularized itself. This has been the central topic of metaphysics and epistemology from the seventeenth century to the present, and, for better or worse, metaphysics and epistemology have been taken to be the "core" of philosophy.[19] Insofar as one thinks that political conclusions require extrapolitical grounding – that is, insofar as one thinks Rawls's method of reflective equilibrium[20] is not good enough – one will want an account of the "authority" of those general principles.

If one feels a need for such legitimation, one will want either a religious or a philosophical preface to politics.[21] One will be likely to share Horkheimer and

18 Rawls, "Justice as Fairness," p. 223.
19 In fact, it has been for the worse. A view that made politics more central to philosophy and subjectivity less would both permit more effective defenses of democracy than those that purport to supply it with "foundations" and permit liberals to meet Marxists on their own, political, ground. Dewey's explicit attempt to make the central philosophical question "What serves democracy?" rather than "What permits us to argue for democracy?" has been, unfortunately, neglected. I try to make this point in "Philosophy as Science, as Metaphor, and as Politics" (in *Essays on Heidegger and Others*).
20 That is, give-and-take between intuitions about the desirability of particular consequences of particular actions and intuitions about general principles, with neither having the determining voice.
21 One will also, as I did on first reading Rawls, take him to be attempting to supply such legitimation by an appeal to the rationality of the choosers in the original position. Rawls warned his readers that the original position (the position of those who, behind a veil of ignorance that hides them from their life chances and their conceptions of the good, select from among alternative principles of justice) served simply "to make vivid . . . the restrictions that it seems reasonable to impose on arguments for principles of justice and therefore on those principles themselves" (*Theory of Justice*, p. 18).
    But this warning went unheeded by myself and others, in part because of an ambiguity between "reasonable" as defined by ahistorical criteria and as meaning something like "in accord with the moral sentiments characteristic of the heirs of the Enlightenment." Rawls's later work has, as I have said, helped us come down on the historicist side of this ambiguity; see, for example,

Adorno's fear that pragmatism is not strong enough to hold a free society together. But Rawls echoes Dewey in suggesting that insofar as justice becomes the first virtue of a society, the need for such legitimation may gradually cease to be felt. Such a society will become accustomed to the thought that social policy needs no more authority than successful accommodation among individuals, individuals who find themselves heir to the same historical traditions and faced with the same problems. It will be a society that encourages the "end of ideology," that takes reflective equilibrium as the only method needed in discussing social policy. When such a society deliberates, when it collects the principles and intuitions to be brought into equilibrium, it will tend to discard those drawn from philosophical accounts of the self or of rationality. For such a society will view such accounts not as the foundations of political institutions, but as, at worst, philosophical mumbo jumbo, or, at best, relevant to private searches for perfection, but not to social policy.[22]

In order to spell out the contrast between Rawls's attempt to "stay on the surface, philosophically speaking" and the traditional attempt to dig down to "philosophical foundations of democracy," I shall turn briefly to Sandel's *Liberalism and the Limits of Justice*. This clear and forceful book provides very elegant and cogent arguments against the attempt to use a certain conception of the self, a certain metaphysical view of what human beings are like, to legitimize liberal politics. Sandel attributes this attempt to Rawls. Many people, including myself, initially took Rawls's *A Theory of Justice* to be such an attempt. We read it as a continuation of the Enlightenment attempt to ground our moral intuitions on a conception of human nature (and, more specifically, as a neo-Kantian attempt to ground them

"Kantian Constructivism": "the original position is not an axiomatic (or deductive) basis from which principles are derived but a procedure for singling out principles most fitting to the conception of the person most likely to be held, at least implicitly, in a democratic society" (p. 572). It is tempting to suggest that one could eliminate all reference to the original position from *A Theory of Justice* without loss, but this is as daring a suggestion as that one might rewrite (as many have wished to do) Kant's *Critique of Pure Reason* without reference to the thing-in-itself. T. M. Scanlon has suggested that we can, at least, safely eliminate reference, in the description of the choosers in the original position, to an appeal to self-interest. ("Contractualism and Utilitarianism," in *Utilitarianism and Beyond*, ed. Bernard Williams and Amartya Sen [Cambridge: Cambridge University Press, 1982]). Since justifiability is, more evidently than self-interest, relative to historical circumstance, Scanlon's proposal seems to be more faithful to Rawls's overall philosophical program than Rawls's own formulation.

22 In particular, there will be no principles or intuitions concerning the universal features of human psychology relevant to motivation. Sandel thinks that since assumptions about motivation are part of the description of the original position, "what issues at one end in a theory of justice must issue at the other in a theory of the person, or more precisely, a theory of the moral subject" (*Liberalism and the Limits of Justice*, p. 47). I would argue that if we follow Scanlon's lead (note 21) in dropping reference to self-interest in our description of the original choosers and replacing this with reference to their desire to justify their choices to their fellows, then the only "theory of the person" we get is a sociological description of the inhabitants of contemporary liberal democracies.

on the notion of "rationality"). However, Rawls's writings subsequent to *A Theory of Justice* have helped us realize that we were misinterpreting his book, that we had overemphasized the Kantian and underemphasized the Hegelian and Deweyan elements. These writings make more explicit than did his book Rawls's metaphilosophical doctrine that "what justifies a conception of justice is not its being true to an order antecedent to and given to us, but its congruence with our deeper understanding of ourselves and our aspirations, and our realization that, *given our history and the traditions embedded in our public life,* it is the most reasonable doctrine *for us.*"[23]

When reread in the light of such passages, *A Theory of Justice* no longer seems committed to a philosophical account of the human self, but only to a historico-sociological description of the way we live now.

Sandel sees Rawls as offering us "deontology with a Humean face" – that is, a Kantian universalistic approach to social thought without the handicap of Kant's idealistic metaphysics. He thinks that this will not work, that a social theory of the sort that Rawls wants requires us to postulate the sort of self that Descartes and Kant invented to replace God – one that can be distinguished from the Kantian "empirical self" as choosing various "contingent desires, wants and ends," rather than being a mere concatenation of beliefs and desires. Since such a concatenation – what Sandel calls a "radically situated subject"[24] – is all that Hume offers us, Sandel thinks that Rawls's project is doomed.[25] On Sandel's account, Rawls's doctrine that "justice is the first virtue of social institutions" requires backup from the metaphysical claim that "teleology to the contrary, what is most essential to our personhood is not the ends we choose but our capacity to choose them. And this capacity is located in a self which must be prior to the ends it chooses."[26]

But reading *A Theory of Justice* as political rather than metaphysical, one can see that when Rawls says that "the self is prior to the ends which are affirmed by it,"[27] he need not mean that there is an entity called "the self" that is something distinct from the web of beliefs and desires that that self "has." When he says that "we should not attempt to give form to our life by first looking to the good

---

23 Rawls, "Kantian Constructivism," p. 519. Italics added.
24 Sandel, *Liberalism and the Limits of Justice,* p. 21. I have argued for the advantages of thinking of the self as just such a concatenation in chapter 2 of *Contingency, Irony, and Solidarity* (Cambridge: Cambridge University Press, 1989). When Sandel cites Robert Nozick and Daniel Bell as suggesting that Rawls "ends by dissolving the self in order to preserve it" (*Liberalism and the Limits of Justice,* p. 95), I should rejoin that it may be helpful to dissolve the metaphysical self in order to preserve the political one. Less obliquely stated: It may be helpful, for purposes of systematizing our intuitions about the priority of liberty, to treat the self as having no center, no essence, but *merely* as a concatenation of beliefs and desires.
25 "Deontology with a Humean face either fails as deontology or recreates in the original position the disembodied subject it resolves to avoid" (ibid., p. 14).
26 Ibid., p. 19.
27 Rawls, *Theory of Justice,* p. 560.

211

independently defined,"[28] he is not basing this "should" on a claim about the nature of the self. "Should" is not to be glossed by "because of the intrinsic nature of morality"[29] or "because a capacity for choice is the essence of personhood," but by something like "because *we* – we modern inheritors of the traditions of religious tolerance and constitutional government – put liberty ahead of perfection."

This willingness to invoke what *we* do raises, as I have said, the specters of ethnocentrism and of relativism. Because Sandel is convinced that Rawls shares Kant's fear of these specters, he is convinced that Rawls is looking for an " 'Archimedean point' from which to assess the basic structure of society" – a "standpoint neither compromised by its implication in the world nor dissociated and so disqualified by detachment."[30] It is just this idea that a standpoint can be "compromised by its implication in the world" that Rawls rejects in his recent writings. Philosophically inclined communitarians like Sandel are unable to envisage a middle ground between relativism and a "theory of the moral subject" – a theory that is not about, for example, religious tolerance and large market economies, but about human beings as such, viewed ahistorically. Rawls is trying to stake out just such a middle ground.[31] When he speaks of an "Archimedian

28 Ibid.

29 It is important to note that Rawls explicitly distances himself from the idea that he is analyzing the very idea of morality and from conceptual analysis as the method of social theory (ibid., p. 130). Some of his critics have suggested that Rawls is practicing "reductive logical analysis" of the sort characteristic of "analytic philosophy"; see, for example, William M. Sullivan, *Reconstructing Public Philosophy* (Berkeley: University of California Press, 1982), pp. 94ff. Sullivan says that "this ideal of reductive logical analysis lends legitimacy to the notion that moral philosophy is summed up in the task of discovering, through the analysis of moral rules, both primitive elements and governing principles that must apply to any rational moral system, *rational* here meaning 'logically coherent' " (p. 96). He goes on to grant that "Nozick and Rawls are more sensitive to the importance of history and social experience in human life than were the classic liberal thinkers" (p. 97). But this concession is too slight and is misleading. Rawls's willingness to adopt "reflective equilibrium" rather than "conceptual analysis" as a methodological watchword sets him apart from the epistemologically oriented moral philosophy that was dominant prior to the appearance of *A Theory of Justice*. Rawls represents a reaction against the Kantian idea of "morality" as having an ahistorical essence, the same sort of reaction found in Hegel and in Dewey.

30 Sandel, *Liberalism and the Limits of Justice*, p. 17.

31 ". . . liberty of conscience and freedom of thought should not be founded on philosophical or ethical skepticism, nor on indifference to religious and moral interests. The principles of justice define an appropriate path between dogmatism and intolerance on the one side, and a reductionism which regards religion and morality as mere preferences on the other" (Rawls, *Theory of Justice*, p. 243). I take it that Rawls is identifying "philosophical or ethical skepticism" with the idea that everything is just a matter of "preference," even religion, philosophy, and morals. So we should distinguish his suggestion that we "extend the principle of toleration to philosophy itself" from the suggestion that we dismiss philosophy as epiphenomenal. That is the sort of suggestion that is backed up by reductionist accounts of philosophical doctrines as "preferences" or "wish fulfillments" or "expressions of emotion" (see Rawls's criticism of Freudian reductionism in ibid., pp. 539ff.). Neither psychology nor logic nor any other theoretical discipline can supply non-question-begging reasons why philosophy should be set aside, any more than philosophy can supply such reasons why theology should be set aside. But this is compatible with saying that the general course of historical experience may lead us to neglect theological topics and bring us to the point at which, like Jefferson, we find a theological vocabulary

point," he does not mean a point outside history, but simply the kind of settled social habits that allow much latitude for further choices. He says, for example,

The upshot of these considerations is that justice as fairness is not at the mercy, so to speak, of existing wants and interests. It sets up an Archimedean point for assessing the social system without invoking a priori considerations. The long range aim of society is settled in its main lines irrespective of the particular desires and needs of its present members. . . . There is no place for the question whether men's desires to play the role of superior or inferior might not be so great that autocratic institutions should be accepted, or whether men's perception of the religious practices of others might not be so upsetting that liberty of conscience should not be allowed.[32]

To say that there is no place for the questions that Nietzsche or Loyola would raise is not to say that the views of either are unintelligible (in the sense of "logically incoherent" or "conceptually confused"). Nor is it to say that they are based on an incorrect theory of the self. Nor is it *just* to say that our preferences conflict with theirs.[33] It is to say that the conflict between these men and us is so great that "preferences" is the wrong word. It is appropriate to speak of gustatory or sexual preferences, for these do not matter to anybody but yourself and your immediate circle. But it is misleading to speak of a "preference" for liberal democracy.

Rather, we heirs of the Enlightenment think of enemies of liberal democracy like Nietzsche or Loyola as, to use Rawls's word, "mad." We do so because there is no way to see them as fellow citizens of our constitutional democracy, people whose life plans might, given ingenuity and good will, be fitted in with those of other citizens. They are not crazy because they have mistaken the ahistorical nature of human beings. They are crazy because the limits of sanity are set by

"meaningless" (or, more precisely, useless). I am suggesting that the course of historical experience since Jefferson's time has led us to a point at which we find much of the vocabulary of modern philosophy no longer useful.

32 Ibid., pp. 261–2.

33 The contrast between "mere preference" and something less "arbitrary," something more closely related to the very nature of man or of reason, is invoked by many writers who think of "human rights" as requiring a philosophical foundation of the traditional sort. Thus my colleague David Little, commenting on my "Solidarity or Objectivity?" (above), says "Rorty appears to permit criticism and pressure against those societies [the ones we do not like] *if we happen to want to* criticize and pressure them in pursuit of some interest or belief we may (at the time) have, and for whatever ethnocentric reasons we may happen to hold those interests or beliefs" ("Natural Rights and Human Rights: The International Imperative," in *National Rights and Natural Law: The Legacy of George Mason*, ed. Robert P. Davidow [Fairfax, Va.: George Mason University Press, 1986], pp. 67–122; italics in original). I would rejoin that Little's use of "happen to want to" presupposes a dubious distinction between necessary, built-in, universal convictions (convictions that it would be "irrational" to reject) and accidental, culturally determined convictions. It also presupposes the existence of such faculties as reason, will, and emotion, all of which the pragmatist tradition in American philosophy and the so-called existentialist tradition in European philosophy try to undercut. Dewey's *Human Nature and Conduct* and Heidegger's *Being and Time* both offer a moral psychology that avoids oppositions between "preference" and "reason."

what *we* can take seriously. This, in turn, is determined by our upbringing, our historical situation.[34]

If this short way of dealing with Nietzsche and Loyola seems shockingly ethnocentric, it is because the philosophical tradition has accustomed us to the idea that anybody who is willing to listen to reason – to hear out all the arguments – can be brought around to the truth. This view, which Kierkegaard called "Socratism" and contrasted with the claim that our point of departure may be simply a historical event, is intertwined with the idea that the human self has a center (a divine spark, or a truth-tracking faculty called "reason") and that argumentation will, given time and patience, penetrate to this center. For Rawls's purposes, we do not need this picture. We are free to see the self as centerless, as a historical contingency all the way through. Rawls neither needs nor wants to defend the priority of the right to the good as Kant defended it, by invoking a theory of the self that makes it more than an "empirical self," more than a "radically situated subject." He presumably thinks of Kant as, although largely right about the nature of justice, largely wrong about the nature and function of philosophy.

More specifically, he can reject Sandel's Kantian claim that there is a "distance between subject and situation which is necessary to any measure of detachment, is essential to the ineliminably *possessive* aspect of any coherent conception of the self."[35] Sandel defines this aspect by saying, "I can never fully be constituted by my attributes . . . there must always be some attributes I *have* rather than am." On the interpretation of Rawls I am offering, we do not need a categorical distinction between the self and its situation. We can dismiss the distinction between an attribute of the self and a constituent of the self, between the self's accidents and its essence, as "merely" metaphysical.[36] If we are inclined to philosophize, we shall want the vocabulary offered by Dewey, Heidegger, Davidson, and Derrida, with its built-in cautions against metaphysics, rather than that offered

---

34 "Aristotle remarks that it is a peculiarity of men that they possess a sense of the just and the unjust and that their sharing a common understanding of justice makes a polis. Analogously one might say, in view of our discussion, that a common understanding of justice as fairness makes a constitutional democracy" (Rawls, *Theory of Justice*, p. 243). In the interpretation of Rawls I am offering, it is unrealistic to expect Aristotle to have developed a conception of justice as fairness, since he simply lacked the kind of historical experience that we have accumulated since his day. More generally, it is pointless to assume (with, for example, Leo Strauss) that the Greeks had already canvassed the alternatives available for social life and institutions. When we discuss justice, we cannot agree to bracket our knowledge of recent history.

35 Sandel, *Liberalism and the Limits of Justice*, p. 20.

36 We can dismiss other distinctions that Sandel draws in the same way. Examples are the distinction between a voluntarist and a cognitive account of the original position (ibid., p. 121), that between "the identity of the subject" as the "product" rather than the "premise" of its agency (ibid., p. 152), and that between the question "Who am I?" and its rival as "the paradigmatic moral question," "What shall I choose?" (ibid., p. 153). These distinctions are all to be analyzed away as products of the "Kantian dualisms" that Rawls praises Hegel and Dewey for having overcome.

by Descartes, Hume, and Kant.[37] For if we use the former vocabulary, we shall be able to see moral progress as a history of making rather than finding, of poetic achievement by "radically situated" individuals and communities, rather than as the gradual unveiling, through the use of "reason," of "principles" or "rights" or "values."

Sandel's claim that "the concept of a subject given prior to and independent of its objects offers a foundation for the moral law that . . . powerfully completes the deontological vision" is true enough. But to suggest such a powerful completion to Rawls is to offer him a poisoned gift. It is like offering Jefferson an argument for religious tolerance based on exegesis of the Christian Scriptures.[38] Rejecting the assumption that the moral law needs a "foundation" is just what distinguishes Rawls from Jefferson. It is just this that permits him to be a Deweyan naturalist who needs neither the distinction between will and intellect nor the distinction between the self's constituents and its attributes. He does not *want* a "complete deontological vision," one that would explain *why* we should give justice priority over our conception of the good. He is filling out the consequences of the claim that it is prior, not its presuppositions.[39] Rawls is not interested in conditions for the identity of the self, but only in conditions for citizenship in a liberal society.

Suppose one grants that Rawls is not attempting a transcendental deduction of American liberalism or supplying philosophical foundations for democratic institutions, but simply trying to systematize the principles and intuitions typical of American liberals. Still, it may seem that the important questions raised by the

---

37 For some similarities between Dewey and Heidegger with respect to anti-Cartesianism, see my "Overcoming the Tradition," in Richard Rorty, *Consequences of Pragmatism* (Minneapolis: University of Minnesota Press, 1982).

38 David Levin has pointed out to me that Jefferson was not above borrowing such arguments. I take this to show that Jefferson, like Kant, found himself in an untenable halfway position between theology and Deweyan social experimentalism.

39 Sandel takes "the primacy of the subject" to be not only a way of filling out the deontological picture, but also a necessary condition of its correctness: "If the claim for the primacy of justice is to succeed, if the right is to be prior to the good in the interlocking moral and foundational sense we have distinguished, then some version of the claim for the primacy of the subject must succeed as well" (*Liberalism and the Limits of Justice*, p. 7). Sandel quotes Rawls as saying that "the essential unity of the self is already provided by the conception of the right" and takes this passage as evidence that Rawls holds a doctrine of the "priority of the self" (ibid., p. 21). But consider the context of this sentence. Rawls says: "The principles of justice and their realization in social forms define the bounds within which our deliberations take place. The essential unity of the self is already provided by the conception of right. Moreover, in a well-ordered society this unity is the same for all; everyone's conception of the good as given by his rational plan is a sub-plan of the larger comprehensive plan that regulates the community as a social union of social unions" (*Theory of Justice*, p. 563). The "essential unity of the self," which is in question here, is simply the system of moral sentiments, habits, and internalized traditions that is typical of the politically aware citizen of a constitutional democracy. This self is, once again, a historical product. It has nothing to do with the nonempirical self, which Kant had to postulate in the interests of Enlightenment universalism.

critics of liberalism have been begged. Consider the claim that we liberals can simply dismiss Nietzsche and Loyola as crazy. One imagines these two rejoining that they are quite aware that their views unfit them for citizenship in a constitutional democracy and that the typical inhabitant of such a democracy would regard them as crazy. But they take these facts as further counts against constitutional democracy. They think that the kind of person created by such a democracy is not what a human being should be.

In finding a dialectical stance to adopt toward Nietzsche or Loyola, we liberal democrats are faced with a dilemma. To refuse to argue about what human beings should be like seems to show a contempt for the spirit of accommodation and tolerance, which is essential to democracy. But it is not clear how to argue for the claim that human beings ought to be liberals rather than fanatics without being driven back on a theory of human nature, on philosophy. I think that we must grasp the first horn. We have to insist that not every argument need to be met in the terms in which it is presented. Accommodation and tolerance must stop short of a willingness to work within any vocabulary that one's interlocutor wishes to use, to take seriously any topic that he puts forward for discussion. To take this view is of a piece with dropping the idea that a single moral vocabulary and a single set of moral beliefs are appropriate for every human community everywhere, and to grant that historical developments may lead us to simply *drop* questions and the vocabulary in which those questions are posed.

Just as Jefferson refused to let the Christian Scriptures set the terms in which to discuss alternative political institutions, so we either must refuse to answer the question "What sort of human being are you hoping to produce?" or, at least, must not let our answer to this question dictate our answer to the question "Is justice primary?"[40] It is no more evident that democratic institutions are to be measured by the sort of person they create than that they are to be measured against divine commands. It is not evident that they are to be measured by anything more specific than the moral intuitions of the particular historical community that has created those institutions. The idea that moral and political controversies should always be "brought back to first principles" is reasonable if it means merely that we should seek common ground in the hope of attaining agreement. But it is misleading if it is taken as the claim that there is a natural order of premises from which moral and political conclusions are to be inferred – not to mention the claim that some particular interlocutor (for example, Nietzsche or Loyola) has already discerned that order. The liberal response to the communitarians' second claim must be, therefore, that even if the typical character types of liberal democracies *are* bland, calculating, petty, and unheroic, the prevalence of such people may be a reasonable price to pay for political freedom.

40 This is the kernel of truth in Dworkin's claim that Rawls rejects "goal-based" social theory, but this point should not lead us to think that he is thereby driven back on a "rights-based" theory.

The spirit of accommodation and tolerance certainly suggests that we should seek common ground with Nietzsche and Loyola, but there is no predicting where, or whether, such common ground will be found. The philosophical tradition has assumed that there are certain topics (for example, "What is God's will?," "What is man?," "What rights are intrinsic to the species?") on which everyone has, or should have, views and that these topics are prior in the order of justification to those at issue in political deliberation. This assumption goes along with the assumption that human beings have a natural center that philosophical inquiry can locate and illuminate. By contrast, the view that human beings are centerless networks of beliefs and desires and that their vocabularies and opinions are determined by historical circumstance allows for the possibility that there may not be enough overlap between two such networks to make possible agreement about political topics, or even profitable discussion of such topics.[41] We do not conclude that Nietzsche and Loyola are crazy because they hold unusual views on certain "fundamental" topics; rather, we conclude this only after extensive attempts at an exchange of political views have made us realize that we are not going to get anywhere.[42]

One can sum up this way of grasping the first horn of the dilemma I sketched earlier by saying that Rawls puts democratic politics first, and philosophy second. He retains the Socratic commitment to free exchange of views without the Platonic commitment to the possibility of universal agreement — a possibility underwritten by epistemological doctrines like Plato's Theory of Recollection[43] or Kant's theory of the relation between pure and empirical concepts. He disengages the question of whether we ought to be tolerant and Socratic from the question of whether this strategy will lead to truth. He is content that it should lead to whatever intersubjective reflective equilibrium may be obtainable, given the contingent make-up of the subjects in question. Truth, viewed in the Platonic

---

41 But one should not press this point so far as to raise the specter of "untranslatable languages." As Donald Davidson has remarked, we would not recognize other organisms as actual or potential language users — or, therefore, as persons — unless there were enough overlap in belief and desire to make translation possible. The point is merely that efficient and frequent communication is only a necessary, not a sufficient, condition of agreement.

42 Further, such a conclusion is *restricted* to politics. It does not cast doubt on the ability of these men to follow the rules of logic or their ability to do many other things skillfully and well. It is thus not equivalent to the traditional philosophical charge of "irrationality." That charge presupposes that inability to "see" certain truths is evidence of the lack of an organ that is essential for human functioning generally.

43 In Kierkegaard's *Philosophical Fragments*, to which I have referred earlier, we find the Platonic Theory of Recollection treated as the archetypal justification of "Socratism" and thus as the symbol of all forms (especially Hegel's) of what Bernard Williams has recently called "the rationalist theory of rationality" — the idea that one is rational only if one can appeal to universally accepted criteria, criteria whose truth and applicability all human beings can find "in their heart." This is the philosophical core of the Scriptural idea that "truth is great, and will prevail," when the idea is dissociated from the idea of "a New Being" (in the way that Kierkegaard refused to dissociate it).

way, as the grasp of what Rawls calls "an order antecedent to and given to us," is simply not relevant to democratic politics. So philosophy, as the explanation of the relation between such an order and human nature, is not relevant either. When the two come into conflict, democracy takes precedence over philosophy.

This conclusion may seem liable to an obvious objection. It may seem that I have been rejecting a concern with philosophical theories about the nature of men and women on the basis of just such a theory. But notice that although I have frequently said that Rawls *can be content* with a notion of the human self as a centerless web of historically conditioned beliefs and desires, I have not suggested that he *needs* such a theory. Such a theory does not offer liberal social theory a *basis*. If one *wants* a model of the human self, then this picture of a centerless web will fill the need. But for purposes of liberal social theory, one can do without such a model. One can get along with common sense and social science, areas of discourse in which the term "the self" rarely occurs.

If, however, one has a taste for philosophy – if one's vocation, one's private pursuit of perfection, entails constructing models of such entities as "the self," "knowledge," "language," "nature," "God," or "history," and then tinkering with them until they mesh with one another – one *will* want a picture of the self. Since my own vocation is of this sort, and the moral identity around which I wish to build such models is that of a citizen of a liberal democratic state, I commend the picture of the self as a centerless and contingent web to those with similar tastes and similar identities. But I would not commend it to those with a similar vocation but dissimilar moral identities – identities built, for example, around the love of God, Nietzschean self-overcoming, the accurate representation of reality as it is in itself, the quest for "one right answer" to moral questions, or the natural superiority of a given character type. Such persons need a more complex and interesting, less simple-minded model of the self – one that meshes in complex ways with complex models of such things as "nature" or "history." Nevertheless, such persons may, for pragmatic rather than moral reasons, be loyal citizens of a liberal democratic society. They may despise most of their fellow citizens, but be prepared to grant that the prevalence of such despicable character types is a lesser evil than the loss of political freedom. They may be ruefully grateful that their private senses of moral identity and the models of the human self that they develop to articulate this sense – the ways in which they deal with their aloneness – are not the concern of such a state. Rawls and Dewey have shown how the liberal state can ignore the difference between the moral identities of Glaucon and of Thrasymachus, just as it ignores the difference between the religious identities of a Catholic archbishop and a Mormon prophet.

There is, however, a flavor of paradox in this attitude toward theories of the self. One might be inclined to say that I have evaded one sort of self-referential paradox only by falling into another sort. For I am presupposing that one is at liberty to rig up a model of the self to suit oneself, to tailor it to one's politics, one's religion, or one's private sense of the meaning of one's life. This, in turn, presupposes that there is no "objective truth" about what the human self is *really* like. That, in turn, seems a claim that could be justified only on the basis of a metaphysico-epistemological view of the traditional sort. For surely if anything is the province of such a view, it is the question of what there is and is not a "fact of the matter" about. So my argument must ultimately come back to philosophical first principles.

Here I can only say that if there were a discoverable fact of the matter about what there is a fact of the matter about, then it would doubtless be metaphysics and epistemology that would discover that meta-fact. But I think that the very idea of a "fact of the matter" is one we would be better off without. Philosophers like Davidson and Derrida have, I think, given us good reason to think that the *physis–nomos, in se–ad nos,* and objective–subjective distinctions were steps on a ladder that we can now safely throw away. The question of whether the reasons such philosophers have given for this claim are themselves metaphysico-epistemological reasons, and if not, what sort of reasons they are, strikes me as pointless and sterile. Once again, I fall back on the holist's strategy of insisting that reflective equilibrium is all we need try for — that there is no natural order of justification of beliefs, no predestined outline for argument to trace. Getting rid of the idea of such an outline seems to me one of the many benefits of a conception of the self as a centerless web. Another benefit is that questions about whom we need justify ourselves to — questions about who counts as a fanatic and who deserves an answer — can be treated as just further matters to be sorted out in the course of attaining reflective equilibrium.

I can, however, make one point to offset the air of light-minded aestheticism I am adopting toward traditional philosophical questions. This is that there is a moral purpose behind this light-mindedness. The encouragement of light-mindedness about traditional philosophical topics serves the same purposes as does the encouragement of light-mindedness about traditional theological topics. Like the rise of large market economies, the increase in literacy, the proliferation of artistic genres, and the insouciant pluralism of contemporary culture, such philosophical superficiality and light-mindedness helps along the disenchantment of the world. It helps make the world's inhabitants more pragmatic, more tolerant, more liberal, more receptive to the appeal of instrumental rationality.

If one's moral identity consists in being a citizen of a liberal polity, then to encourage light-mindedness may serve one's moral purposes. Moral commitment, after all, does not require taking seriously all the matters that are, for moral reasons, taken seriously by one's fellow citizens. It may require just the opposite. It may require trying to josh them out of the habit of taking those topics so seriously. There may be serious reasons for so joshing them. More generally, we should not assume that the aesthetic is always the enemy of the moral. I should

219

argue that in the recent history of liberal societies, the willingness to view matters aesthetically – to be content to indulge in what Schiller called "play" and to discard what Nietzsche called "the spirit of seriousness" – has been an important vehicle of moral progress.

I have now said everything I have to say about the third of the communitarian claims that I distinguished at the outset: the claim that the social theory of the liberal state rests on false philosophical presuppositions. I hope I have given reasons for thinking that insofar as the communitarian is a critic of liberalism, he should drop this claim and should instead develop either of the first two claims: the empirical claim that democratic institutions cannot be combined with the sense of common purpose predemocratic societies enjoyed, or the moral judgment that the products of the liberal state are too high a price to pay for the elimination of the evils that preceded it. If communitarian critics of liberalism stuck to these two claims, they would avoid the sort of terminal wistfulness with which their books typically end. Heidegger, for example, tells us that "we are too late for the gods, and too early for Being." Unger ends *Knowledge and Politics* with an appeal to a *Deus absconditus*. MacIntyre ends *After Virtue* by saying that we "are waiting not for a Godot, but for another – doubtless very different – St. Benedict."[44] Sandel ends his book by saying that liberalism "forgets the possibility that when politics goes well, we can know a good in common that we cannot know alone," but he does not suggest a candidate for this common good.

Instead of thus suggesting that philosophical reflection, or a return to religion, might enable us to re-enchant the world, I think that communitarians should stick to the question of whether disenchantment has, on balance, done us more harm than good, or created more dangers than it has evaded. For Dewey, communal and public disenchantment is the price we pay for individual and private spiritual liberation, the kind of liberation that Emerson thought characteristically American. Dewey was as well aware as Weber that there is a price to be paid, but he thought it well worth paying. He assumed that no good achieved by earlier societies would be worth recapturing if the price were a diminution in our ability to leave people alone, to let them try out their private visions of perfection in peace. He admired the American habit of giving democracy priority over philosophy by asking, about any vision of the meaning of life, "Would not acting out this vision interfere with the ability of others to work out their own salvation?" Giving priority to that question is no more "natural" than giving priority to, say, MacIntyre's question "What sorts of human beings emerge in the culture of liberalism?" or Sandel's question "Can a community of those who put justice first ever be more than a community of strangers?" The

---

44 See Jeffrey Stout's discussion of the manifold ambiguities of this conclusion in "Virtue Among the Ruins: An Essay on MacIntyre," *Neue Zeitschrift für Systematische Theologie und Religionsphilosophie* 26 (1984): 256–73, especially 269.

question of which of these questions is prior to which others is, necessarily, begged by *everybody*. Nobody is being any more arbitrary than anybody else. But that is to say that nobody is being arbitrary at all. Everybody is just insisting that the beliefs and desires they hold most dear should come first in the order of discussion. That is not arbitrariness, but sincerity.

The danger of re-enchanting the world, from a Deweyan point of view, is that it might interfere with the development of what Rawls calls "a social union of social unions,"[45] some of which may be (and in Emerson's view, should be) very small indeed. For it is hard to be both enchanted with one version of the world and tolerant of all the others. I have not tried to argue the question of whether Dewey was right in this judgment of relative danger and promise. I have merely argued that such a judgment neither presupposes nor supports a theory of the self. Nor have I tried to deal with Horkheimer and Adorno's prediction that the "dissolvent rationality" of the Enlightenment will eventually cause the liberal democracies to come unstuck.

The only thing I have to say about this prediction is that the collapse of the liberal democracies would not, in itself, provide much evidence for the claim that human societies cannot survive without widely shared opinions on matters of ultimate importance – shared conceptions of our place in the universe and our mission on earth. Perhaps they cannot survive under such conditions, but the eventual collapse of the democracies would not, in itself, show that this was the

---

45 This is Rawls's description of "a well-ordered society (corresponding to justice as fairness)" (*Theory of Justice*, p. 527). Sandel finds these passages metaphorical and complains that "intersubjective and individualistic images appear in uneasy, sometimes unfelicitous combination, as if to betray the incompatible commitments contending within" (*Liberalism and the Limits of Justice*, pp. 150ff.). He concludes that "the moral vocabulary of community in the strong sense cannot in all cases be captured by a conception that [as Rawls has said his is] 'in its theoretical bases is individualistic.' " I am claiming that these commitments will look incompatible only if one attempts to define their philosophical presuppositions (which Rawls himself may occasionally have done too much of), and that this is a good reason for not making such attempts. Compare the Enlightenment view that attempts to sharpen up the theological presuppositions of social commitments had done more harm than good and that if theology cannot simply be discarded, it should at least be left as fuzzy (or, one might say, "liberal") as possible. Oakeshott has a point when he insists on the value of theoretical muddle for the health of the state.

Elsewhere Rawls has claimed that "there is no reason why a well-ordered society should encourage primarily individualistic values if this means ways of life that lead individuals to pursue their own way and to have no concern for the interest of others" ("Fairness to Goodness," *Philosophical Review* 84 [1975]: 550). Sandel's discussion of this passage says that it "suggests a deeper sense in which Rawls' conception is individualistic," but his argument that this suggestion is correct is, once again, the claim that "the Rawlsian self is not only a subject of possession, but an antecedently individuated subject" (*Liberalism and the Limits of Justice*, pp. 61 ff.). This is just the claim I have been arguing against by arguing that there is no such thing as "the Rawlsian self" and that Rawls does not want or need a "theory of the person." Sandel says (p. 62) that Rawls "takes for granted that every individual consists of one and only one system of desires," but it is hard to find evidence for this claim in the texts. At worst, Rawls simplifies his presentation by imagining each of his citizens as having only one such set, but this simplifying assumption does not seem central to his view.

case – any more than it would show that human societies require kings or an established religion, or that political community cannot exist outside of small city-states.

Both Jefferson and Dewey described America as an "experiment." If the experiment fails, our descendants may learn something important. But they will not learn a philosophical truth, any more than they will learn a religious one. They will simply get some hints about what to watch out for when setting up their next experiment. Even if nothing else survives from the age of the democratic revolutions, perhaps our descendants will remember that social institutions *can* be viewed as experiments in cooperation rather than as attempts to embody a universal and ahistorical order. It is hard to believe that this memory would not be worth having.

Liberalism and the Political Character of Political Philosophy

Paul Weithman

I

John Rawls's insistence in recent years that justice as fairness is political and not metaphysical has attracted a great deal of attention.[1] It is by now commonplace to note how many of Rawls's readers see in this insistence a retreat from what seemed the much more ambitious project of *A Theory of Justice*. In that book, readers found a theory that was "part, perhaps the most significant part, of the theory of rational choice."[2] As such, it seemed to articulate principles that could, in the spirit of Kant, be justified to all rational agents who entered the original position. Those principles were, moreover, thought universal in their application, applicable to the basic structure of societies regardless of their time or place.

By contrast, Rawls now tells us that justice as fairness is developed from the "basic intuitive ideas" of fairness, freedom, and equality latent in the public culture of democratic societies.[3] These ideas provide what Joseph Raz has called "shallow foundations," for no attempt is made to ground the basic ideas on anything deeper.[4] Explicitly disavowed is any attempt to show that the foundations of justice as fairness are true to an "independent metaphysical and moral order" like God's law or moral facts implicit in the nature of rationality;[5] indeed Rawls refrains from speaking of justice as fairness or of his principles of justice as true at all.[6]

Political philosophy, Rawls now says, proceeds by "the method of avoidance": it leaves aside controversial topics in theology, philoso-

phy of mind. epistemology, and moral philosophy.⁷ Instead, the ideas
from which justice as fairness are worked up are regarded as widely
shared by those who live in a democratic culture. And political philosophy begins from widely shared ideas because this procedure af-
fords the greatest chance of consensus on the conception of justice
that results.⁸ The justification of justice as fairness is complete, it
seems, with the achievement of what Rawls calls an "overlapping
consensus." Such a consensus obtains when adherents of diverse religious and moral conceptions accept justice as fairness on moral
grounds, even if their moral grounds for consent are very different.⁹
And justice as fairness is, Rawls now says, a conception appropriate
to the basic structures of only a limited range of societies, those with
a culture and tradition in which the basic intuitive ideas are found.

Some see a thinly veiled moral skepticism in Rawls's refusal to
assert the truth of justice as fairness. Most see in his recent essays a
de-emphasis of the Kantian elements so prominent in *A Theory of
Justice* and a move toward the realpolitik of Hobbes[10] or the pragmatism of Dewey.[11] But what elicits the strongest reaction from both those
who applaud and those who criticize Rawls's recent work is what seems
to be his politicization of political philosophy. The importance Rawls
attaches to the achievement of an overlapping consensus and the foundation of his theory in widely shared ideas have suggested to some
that what Rawls really values are political and not philosophical results—in Jean Hampton's words, "peace and stability at the lowest
political cost."[12] Moreover, Rawls seems uninterested in precisely the
sort of justification philosophers have traditionally sought. His claim
that ideas implicit in democratic culture are the appropriate starting
point for political philosophy and his refusal to justify them by dig-
ging deeper strike some as inconsistent with the claim that Rawls is
engaged in philosophy rather than practical politics.[13]

Rawls seems, in a slight paraphrase of Richard Rorty's description,
to have accorded democracy priority over philosophy. Rorty argues that
Rawls takes the moral worth of liberal democratic politics for granted. He then, Rorty says, develops a theory that "comports with the
institutions he admires. . . . He is putting politics first and tailoring a
philosophy to suit."[14] Rorty himself looks with favor on what he takes
to be Rawls's moves away from the justificatory aspirations of traditional political philosophy. He sees in them vindication of his own
animus towards metaphysics.[15] Critics, on the other hand, argue that
Rawls's current conception of political philosophy is untenable,[16] inconsistent,[17] or unable to meet its stated aims.[18] They claim that political philosophy ought to be more metaphysical and far less political

than Rawls's later essays suggest. Both Rorty and the critics operate with a sharp distinction between metaphysics and politics.[19] And all employ it to locate in Rawls's recent essays a fundamental challenge to traditional conceptions of political philosophy.

I want to use and interpret Rawls's recent work to consider the political character of political philosophy. I shall argue that Rawls is best read as dividing the labor of political philosophy into two tasks: (1) that of developing a theory of justice and (2) that of building an overlapping consensus on the conception of justice the theory presents. I shall reserve the term "political philosophy" for the enterprise that includes both of these tasks. For reasons that will become clear as we proceed, I shall call the former of the two tasks "political theory"; the latter I shall call "comprehensive public philosophy."

Corresponding to these two tasks are two very different sorts of justification. The political theorist justifies his or her conception of justice by showing that it is a reasonable conception for the society he or she addresses. The comprehensive public philosopher, on the other hand, argues not just that that conception is a reasonable one, but that those whom he or she addresses ought to accept it. He or she justifies the conception by working within one or another moral or philosophical tradition, availing himself or herself of the full range of its moral and metaphysical resources to help build consensus on the conception of justice in question.

Rawls, I shall argue, is engaged only in political theory as I have characterized it. His appeal to the shallow foundations provided by the basic intuitive ideas is meant only to provide the limited justification associated with political theory. It is meant only to show that justice as fairness is a reasonable conception of justice for the democratic and pluralistic societies to which Rawls's arguments are directed. The further arguments that Kantians, utilitarians, intuitionists, moral realists, Catholics, and Jews in those societies should accept justice as fairness all await the efforts of comprehensive public philosophy. But that is not an enterprise in which Rawls is engaged; we should not expect to find him presenting these further arguments.

Political theory and comprehensive public philosophy are tasks both political and traditionally philosophical. Distinguishing the two enterprises and analyzing the political and philosophical character of each refines our view of the relationship between politics and political philosophy generally. It also shows that Rawls's challenge to the traditional character of political philosophy has been exaggerated. Friends like Rorty and foes like Jean Hampton have overestimated the distance Rawls puts between metaphysics and political philosophy.

225

II

I want to begin by saying something more about the nature of political theory as I believe Rawls conceives it. The tasks of elaborating its nature and of arguing that Rawls is engaged in it are much facilitated by the fact that the distinction between political philosophy and political theory comports nicely with a distinction Rawls himself has drawn.

In "The Independence of Moral Theory," Rawls wrote:

> I distinguish between moral philosophy and moral theory; moral philosophy includes the latter as one of its main parts. Moral theory is the study of substantive moral conceptions, that is, the study of how the basic notions of the right, the good and moral worth may be arranged to form different moral structures. Moral theory tries to identify the chief similarities and differences between these structures and to characterize the way in which they are related to our moral sensibilities and natural attitudes.[20]

Rawls does not elucidate the notion of a moral structure but it is safe to assume, I believe, that moral theories like utilitarianism, perfectionism, and natural law theory are moral structures in his sense. So, too, is the theory in which Rawls embeds justice as fairness. That theory specifies principles of justice and a conception of justice, and connects these notions of the right with various ideas of the good and of moral worth. Thus, if moral theory is that part of moral philosophy that studies moral structures generally, political theory includes that part of moral theory that studies theories and conceptions of justice.

Rawls contributes to political theory, of course, not just by studying moral structures, but by developing the moral structure he inherited from the contract tradition of Locke, Rousseau, and Kant. Rawls's further developing of a moral structure handed down by one of the traditional schools of political thought is consistent with his remarks about the task of moral theory generally.[21] This suggests that political theory is the task in which he sees himself engaged.

But the detached, academic study and development of moral structures would not by itself advance the practical aims of Rawls's work.[22] The stated aim of *A Theory of Justice* was to develop a contractarian conception of justice that could be adopted as the moral basis for a democratic society.[23] At minimum, this practical task demands that Rawls show the conception he develops to be a workable one. And so Rawls did not merely develop and study a conception of justice in ignorance of prevailing conditions in the society he addressed. He developed a theory not premised on conditions, like limitless plenty, that do not obtain, but one that is premised on salient facts, like religious and moral pluralism, that do.

Moreover, the practical task demands that Rawls show that his conception would, if realized, be a stable one. It must be capable of generating its own moral support among citizens who live in a society well ordered by it. The political theorist, like the moral theorist, must therefore examine how his or her moral structure would influence the development of the virtues and would be related to natural human interests and motives. That is why the political theorist, like the moral theorist of Rawls's description, tries "to characterize the way in which [the moral structures he develops] are related to our moral sensibilities and natural attitudes." Rawls devotes much of the third part of *A Theory of Justice* to this task.

If Rawls's political theory is to realize the practical aims he entertains, he must develop a conception of justice that is not only a workable one but also a reasonable one for the society he addresses. That is, he must develop one that members of the society he addresses have prima facie moral reasons to adopt. That justice as fairness is reasonable in this sense is guaranteed by its foundation in basic intuitive ideas that are drawn from democratic culture and that members of democratic culture can be presumed to share. Let me elaborate.

The basic intuitive ideas of moral personality and society as a fair system of cooperation express values like freedom, equality, and fairness. These are values to which all who participate in the democratic culture from which the basic ideas are drawn are presumed to attach great importance. Freedom, equality, and fairness are, of course, moral values, which can be realized in many areas of human life. They can be taken as family values when aspired to or realized at home, or they can be taken as values aspired to and realized in a friendship. Freedom, equality, and fairness are political values when they are realized or promoted by basic social and political institutions or when citizens aspire so to order their political society that these moral values are realized by those institutions. These values are not as important in some spheres of life as in others. Freedom or autonomy might be valued far more highly in the arrangement of political institutions than in the arrangement of ecclesiastical ones, for example. It is only as political values that freedom, equality, and fairness can be presumed to be of such great importance to participants in democratic culture. It is as political values that they are expressed by the basic intuitive ideas with which Rawls begins.

But these political values and the basic intuitive ideas that express them, however important, are too abstract to provide political guidance. We cannot attempt to realize fair cooperation, for example, without knowing a great deal about fairness and how its demands are to be reconciled with those of liberty. Rawls therefore frames a conception of justice that further specifies those basic intuitive ideas and values to provide, in his words, "guidance where guidance is needed."[24] The idea of moral personality is specified to yield a conception of a citizen acting autonomously and possessing a sense of justice the content of which is given by Rawls's two principles. The idea of society as a fair cooperative scheme is specified to yield a conception of society the basic structure of which conforms to those two principles. So specified, the ideas are sufficiently concrete to serve as ideals, as objects of human aspiration. The basic intuitive ideas are thus shared resources from which Rawls develops his ideals of citizenship and of the well-ordered society. The specification of basic intuitive ideas into these ideals provides the political guidance that neither the basic intuitive ideas nor the values they express could furnish, for the ideals Rawls specifies provide detailed conceptions of a just society and of such a society's citizens.[25]

Much of the theory in which justice as fairness is located is designed to show that the well-ordered society is one in which our deeply held political values are realized. It is thus that our aspirations and desires to live in a society well ordered by justice as fairness are elicited. Consider, in this connection, the following passage from section 72 of *A Theory of Justice*:

> Best of all, a theory should present a description of an ideally just state of affairs, a conception of a well-ordered society such that the aspiration to realize this state of affairs, and to maintain it in being, answers to our good and is continuous with our natural sentiments. A perfectly just society should be part of an ideal that rational human beings could desire more than anything else once they had full knowledge and experience of what it was.[26]

Rawls's theory presents such a description of an ideally just society and elaborates it to provide us with full knowledge and experience—at least in thought—of how that well-ordered society realizes political values like freedom and equality. Rawls thinks that this knowledge will elicit in us "the aspiration to realize this state of affairs, and to maintain it in being" because we already have a strong moral interest in these political values. Description of an ideally just society, which realizes these values, therefore heightens and focuses our moral interest. Thus, arguments that show that the well-ordered society of justice as fairness realizes deeply held political values provide us with moral reasons to desire that justice as fairness regulate political society. They thereby show that justice as fairness is a reasonable conception for us.

That justice is fairness is rooted in the basic intuitive ideas of freedom, equality, and fairness found in the public culture of a democratic society is therefore crucial to its being a reasonable conception. It is the depth and prevalence of these basic ideas and the wide acceptance within democratic societies of the political values they express that gives us some reason to think that a conception of justice that specifies and combines them could gain acceptance.

How, then, do the basic ideas justify justice as fairness to Rawls's readers? Perfecting the moral structure found in the contract tradition of Locke, Rousseau, and Kant is an act of faith in the practical import of one's efforts, for it is an act of faith that members of democratic society will accept a contractarian moral structure once it is developed. It can be shown an act of reasonable faith if it can be shown that the structure itself is a reasonable one, one that members of democratic society have prima facie moral reason to adopt. Rawls's founding his conception on widely shared ideas and political values makes that faith in eventual consensus on justice as fairness a reasonable faith. Rawls's appeal to the basic intuitive ideas thus justifies or shows reasonable the act of faith in which his political theory consists. And Rawls says explicitly, in a paraphrase of Kant, that his philosophical task is that of defending reasonable faith in the possibility of a just democratic regime like the one he sketches.[27]

Once justice as fairness has been shown a reasonable conception of justice, one that members of a democratic society have prima facie moral reason to adopt, the question of what further justification it requires naturally suggests itself. For the reasonability of justice as fairness depends upon its foundation in the basic intuitive ideas and the political values they express. Acceptance of these political values gives citizens some reasons, prima facie reasons, for accepting justice as fairness. But citizens may hold other moral values and principles than those on which justice as fairness is founded, values and principles that may conflict or seem to conflict with the conception of justice Rawls outlines. To have ultima facie and not just prima facie reasons to accept that conception, citizens need to be assured that they hold no other moral values or principles that defeat it. Rawls's answer to this problem of ultima facie justification seems to challenge the traditional character of political philosophy.

Rawls explicitly denies, as I have already noted, that he tries to

demonstrate the truth of justice as fairness. Rorty infers from this
denial that Rawls thinks no further justification of the conception is
required. The priority Rorty thinks Rawls assigns to democracy implies, Rorty thinks, that showing justice as fairness a reasonable conception is showing enough. In this, Rorty sees the politicization of
political philosophy and the denial of political philosophy's traditional ambitions.

But Rawls's refusal to consider the question of truth does not have
the strong implications Rorty believes. Rawls is engaged in what I
have called "political theory," which is a part of moral theory. And it
is characteristic of moral theory generally, Rawls says, to postpone
questions about the truth of a moral structure.[28] Political theory thus
takes from moral theory the more limited ambition of laying out and
studying workable and reasonable conceptions. It does not limit its
aims because there is no moral truth or because, as Rorty believes,
"truth . . . is simply not relevant to democratic politics."[29] It does so
because the tasks of political theory are difficult enough and because
determining which conception of justice is true first requires determining which conceptions are workable and reasonable.[30] Metaphysical questions are not dismissed. They are, I will argue, left to those
working within religious and philosophical traditions.

Hampton reads Rawls's politicization of political philosophy differently than does Rorty. She focuses on the arguments she thinks the
Rawlsian political philosopher must offer to adherents of various religious and moral views if an overlapping consensus on justice as fairness is to be secured. And she focuses on the philosopher's motives
for offering those arguments. The arguments must, she says, be political and not philosophical arguments. They must be political, she
thinks, because the Rawlsian political philosopher builds consensus by
appealing only to what Rawls calls "public reason," by appealing only
to political values and principles without trying to found them on
anything deeper.[31] They will be politically motivated, since the Rawlsian political philosopher must, she thinks, give publicly acceptable
reasons for securing a consensus. The only such reason he can give,
Hampton argues, is his interest in social stability.[32]

I believe both Rorty and Hampton are mistaken in their interpretations. Rorty, as I have indicated, is mistaken in thinking that Rawls
claims no further justification is necessary beyond showing that justice as fairness is reasonable. Hampton is mistaken about the sort of
justification she thinks is available to Rawlsian political philosophers.
To show this, it is necessary to turn to the way in which Rawls thinks
an overlapping consensus on justice as fairness would be secured. The

task of securing consensus is, I suggested, a task that falls not to political theory, but to what I called "comprehensive public philosophy."

III

In an overlapping consensus, adherents of diverse philosophical and religious traditions accept justice as fairness, but for different moral reasons; each supports the conception for reasons drawn from his or her own more comprehensive moral views.[33] Thus, in an overlapping consensus, Kantians affirm justice as fairness for one set of reasons, utilitarians accept it for another, and Christians accept it for still another. Such an overlapping consensus is, of course, a political ideal. Even in societies where justice as fairness is accepted as the public conception of justice, an overlapping consensus may not obtain since some may accept it on purely prudential grounds. Even so, we can ask how an overlapping consensus could come about since it is the ideal case, Rorty and Hampton think, that reveals most about Rawls's conception of political philosophy's task.

Rawls uses consensus on the principle of toleration to illustrate the development of an overlapping consensus over time.[34] Catholics and Protestants overlap in their consensus on the principle since both accept it; their views of toleration are not congruent, however, since their moral and religious reasons for accepting the principle differ. The principle of religious tolerance, which was initially accepted to put an end to religious strife, gradually came to be accepted by Protestants and Catholics for moral reasons. An overlapping consensus on justice as fairness could, Rawls argues, develop similarly.

Rawls provides little historical detail about how consensus on the principle of toleration developed. It is, however, a history that I believe he intends us to take seriously. That history is, of course, long and complicated; I will focus only on a couple of its features that will prove useful for highlighting philosophy's role in building a consensus on justice as fairness. Careful attention to these features, which follow, shows that both Rorty and Hampton are mistaken about the way in which such a consensus is achieved.

1. The principle of toleration was known from experience to be workable even before it was accepted on moral grounds.

2. Theologians who developed, for example, Catholic arguments for the principle of toleration worked within the Catholic tradition to do so. In this, John Courtney Murray, who was largely responsible for

the Catholic church's principled acceptance of toleration, was exemplary. He drew upon all the moral and theological resources within his tradition to frame the arguments he addressed to other Catholics.[35] Those he addressed to Protestants drew on premises he thought that Catholics and Protestants shared. In neither case did he feel compelled to restrict himself to those premises that he thought would be accepted by political society at large.[36]

3. While many Catholics may long have accepted the principle on prudential grounds, Murray himself had already accepted it for moral and religious reasons when he framed his arguments. If asked by other Catholics to justify the project of constructing moral arguments for the principle he could reply that he was not simply trying to build a firmer peace with Protestants, but that he was also trying to convince his fellow Catholics of a moral principle in which he already believed.[37]

These three features of the development of consensus on religious tolerance would be mirrored in the development of an overlapping consensus on justice as fairness.

1. In the case of the principle of tolerance, experience proved the principle workable. In the case of conceptions of justice, the political theorist—Rawls—argues that the conception proposed is both workable and reasonable for the society he addresses. He does so by showing that the conception would be stable, would generate its own moral support, and is founded on that society's fundamental political ideas and values.

2. The process of building an overlapping consensus will be a long and complicated one, as was the process of building moral consensus on religious toleration. Those working to build a consensus need not address only members of their own tradition or school of thought. And arguments addressed to those outside one's own tradition need not, as Hampton claims, appeal only to a common desire for peace and stability. Instead, the basic intuitive ideas and political values on which justice as fairness is built provide moral common ground for these arguments. All in a democratic culture are presumed to share these ideas and to have at least some interest in realizing the values they express. In relying on moral common ground, these arguments will resemble those arguments for religious tolerance that Murray addressed to Protestants.

Philosophers and theologians will also address some arguments to members of the moral communities to which they belong. They will attempt to show how justice as fairness can be endorsed from within the comprehensive views of those communities, just as Murray did when he urged that Catholics should accept religious toleration on moral grounds. Like those who forged a consensus on the principle of toleration, those who argue for the moral acceptability of justice as fairness need not restrict themselves to arguments that rely on premises that would be acceptable to all. Hampton is mistaken in her suggestion that they must do so.

When Kantians, utilitarians, and moral theologians from various religions address members of their own traditions, they work within the tradition they are addressing. In doing so, they are free to draw on all its conceptual and historical resources. Thus, Kantians can, if they like, appeal to all of Kant's moral thought to show why justice as fairness should be accepted. They could do so by arguing, for instance, that Rawls's two principles really are instances of the categorical imperative and are binding on all rational beings. Catholic theologians could argue that Rawls's two principles guarantee that each individual will have the social bases of the dignity to which he or she is entitled as a creature made in God's image and likeness. Religious and philosophical arguments in favor of justice as fairness need not be deductive; indeed, it should not be expected that many moral and religious views entail justice as fairness. Instead, these arguments may show that justice as fairness would realize the political values of a given religious or philosophical tradition better than any other conceptions of justice so far developed.[38] This might require interpreting the history of a religious tradition to show that the basic intuitive ideas or the values they express have played a hitherto unappreciated role in that tradition. Or it might require, to take a different example, connecting the interpretation of political freedom provided by a philosophical view with the interpretation implicit in the ideal of the well-ordered society. These tasks will be undertaken by moral philosophers who endorse Kantianism or utilitarianism as comprehensive moral doctrines, as well as by theologians who are trying to work out the political implications of their religious views.[39]

There is no guarantee that an overlapping consensus on justice as fairness can be achieved. That is why Rawls's political theory is, as I said earlier, an act of faith. Some religions might well be without a developed tradition of political thought; it may seem unlikely, therefore that grounds for justice as fairness can be found within them. In that case, faith that adherents can participate in an overlapping consensus rests on the hope that they can accept justice as fairness because of what political beliefs they hold independent of their religion.

Other religions may initially seem hostile to liberal democracy. Rawls conjectured that long experience of social cooperation with those of other religions eroded hostility between Catholics and Protestants

and removed the barriers to moral acceptance of the principle of toleration.[40] Similarly, we might conjecture that religious and philosophical traditions that have long persisted and flourished in a democratic
culture will come to incorporate the basic intuitive ideas and political
values on which justice as fairness is founded. These basic ideas and
values might not be prominent in the traditions in question. But presentation of justice as fairness can draw attention to neglected values
like equality and fairness latent in a body of religious or philosophical thought. And it can elicit moral interest in building a liberal democracy by showing how liberal theory specifies and combines those
values in the way I discussed earlier. Political theory can therefore be
educative, teaching us about new political possibilities and about neglected aspects of our own comprehensive views.

3. When philosophers and theologians working for consensus are
called upon to justify their work, they need not appeal only to their
interest in securing peace and stability as Hampton suggests. These
may well be among their motives. But they can also claim that the
moral ideals of persons with the two moral powers and of a Rawlsian
well-ordered society realize the political values implicit in their tradition.[41] They can number among their motives the belief that their society is an unjust one that would be made far more just by its adoption
of justice as fairness. They are, they might conclude, trying to persuade other utilitarians, Kantians, or Christians of what they themselves are already convinced is right. Their position will therefore be
much like that of the theologians who built a religious consensus on
the principle of toleration because they thought intolerance morally
wrong.

To understand how an overlapping consensus on justice as fairness
or some other political conception is secured, then, it is important to
appreciate the division of labor I mentioned earlier. One task is that
of articulating a reasonable and workable conception of justice on
which members of political society will overlap in their consent. The
other task in the establishment of an overlapping consensus is that of
convincing adherents of diverse religious and philosophical views that
they should consent to justice as fairness as the appropriate moral basis
for a democratic society. I have used the term "political theory" for
the first of these tasks and "comprehensive public philosophy" to des-
ignate the second.[42]

Political theory is a limited enterprise but it is to this enterprise
that Rawls restricts himself. What further justification can be provided for justice as fairness, what further work must be done to secure
an overlapping consensus, is the task of comprehensive public philos-

ophy. The work falls here because the strong moral interest Rawls supposes we can take in the ideals of citizenship and the well-ordered society is either derivative from or must be reconciled with our interest in our comprehensive moral views. Displaying the derivation or effecting the reconciliation is the task of comprehensive public philosophy, for it requires taking as premises substantive moral claims drawn from those views. This is an important point about the development of an overlapping consensus that both Rorty and Hampton miss.

IV

I have discussed how an overlapping consensus on justice as fairness might be secured. But what will be the character of a society in which such a consensus obtains?

Philosophy and theology will not, to be sure, have a place in the public justification of the Rawlsian society's public policies—in the justification offered by judges in their opinions or by other occupants of public office in their official capacities. Policies and judicial decisions will be justified by pointing to their promotion of the political values justice as fairness articulates, including the value of conformity with Rawls's two principles. Justice as fairness itself will be publicly justified only by pointing to its reasonability for a society that is heir to the democratic tradition and accepts its fundamental political values. Public reliance on any further philosophical or religious justification would be divisive.

Rorty thinks that the prevalence of this public conception of justification will lead citizens to forswear the need for any deeper foundations, that philosophy and religion will wither under pressure from the public culture of a liberal society. A liberal society will, he says, be one that "encourages the 'end of ideology,'" one "accustomed to the thought that social policy needs no more authority than successful accommodation among individuals" and one in which "the need for [more] legitimation may gradually cease to be felt." Its citizens will inhabit what he calls a "disenchanted" world.[43]

These are sociological forecasts that resist a priori refutation. But Rawls's well-ordered society need not provide the encouragement or apply the pressure that Rorty thinks it will. To see this, consider first how the transition to a society well ordered by justice as fairness might be effected in the United States. Religion obviously looms large in American national politics. This suggests that adherents of various religious positions would demand religious or philosophical arguments for the acceptability of justice as fairness before agreeing to it as the public conception of justice for the United States. Arguments drawn from comprehensive public philosophy therefore would be necessary to move this country toward the ideal Rawlsian society. Comprehensive public philosophy would not, of course, be sufficient to effect the transition to a well-ordered society; but it would be necessary in the United States under current political conditions.

The habits of religious and philosophical thought about politics— vital and necessary during the transitional stages to a well-ordered society—could continue even after an overlapping consensus on justice as fairness has been attained. Acceptance of Rawls's principles of justice leaves open questions about what policies best implement them. And while religion and philosophy would play no role in the public justification of policies, policy questions could provide the subject matter for religious and philosophical debate even in a society well ordered by justice as fairness. The situation would then be analogous to that which now obtains with respect to religious tolerance: Catholics and Protestants overlap on the principle, but Catholic and Protestant groups engage in vigorous internal debate about what tolerance requires.

But if transition to a Rawlsian well-ordered society requires comprehensive public philosophy and if policy questions would provide comprehensive public philosophy its subject matter even in a well-ordered society, what reasons does Rorty have for thinking that it would gradually disappear? What reasons has he for thinking that the sort of justification available in the public culture would gradually come to seem justification enough?

Perhaps Rorty thinks that the felt need for the philosophical justification of public policy would be extinguished in a Rawlsian society much as he thinks the need for religious justification has already disappeared in extant liberal democracies. Indeed, there are places where he suggests as much.[44] But Rorty's empirical claims about the demise of religious belief and about religion's political marginalization are demonstrably false, at least of the United States.[45] His conjecture that the public culture of a liberal society would extinguish the metaphysical urge therefore cannot be supported by appealing to the observed impact of liberal institutions on religious belief or political vitality.

Alternatively, Rorty might suppose that religion and philosophy would die out in a truly liberal society because, good Deweyan that he is, he believes that a well-ordered society would educate its children in public schools whose curricula encouraged pragmatism and discouraged religion and metaphysics. But surely, whether schools in a well-ordered society would be public and not, for example, sectarian with the support of a voucher system, is a question of public policy. It may be that a system of secular public education would win out in policy debates. Rorty cannot assume, however, that it would and hence cannot assume that a Deweyan education would lead to "the end of ideology" in a liberal society. Of course, Rorty could assume that secular public education would win out if he could safely assume that no citizens of the well-ordered society had sufficient religious interest to care whether their children had a religious education. But since the question at issue is whether citizens of the well-ordered society would retain their philosophical and religious interests, the latter assumption is one Rorty cannot make without begging the question.

The alleged decline and political marginalization of religion do not support Rorty's claim that the public culture of Rawlsian society would eliminate comprehensive public philosophy and the metaphysical impulses that give rise to it. Neither do claims about the character of such a society's educational system. Rorty has therefore provided us no reason to think that a liberal political culture would have the impact he suggests it would.

A society in which an overlapping consensus on justice as fairness has been achieved is one in which religious and philosophical views converge on and support the conception of justice that well orders that society. Its public culture can therefore encourage citizens who want assurance that the principles by which the basic structure of their society is assessed are true to "an independent metaphysical and moral order."[46] Instead of encouraging the end of ideology, it can encourage them to seek such assurance from the comprehensive public philosophers of their tradition.

Those who retain the need for such assurance will not privately "despise most of their fellow citizens" for not sharing their moral views, as Rorty intimates. Nor will they cooperate with them only "for pragmatic, rather than moral reasons."[47] In a Rawlsian liberal society, religion and philosophy give their adherents moral and not just pragmatic reasons to be good citizens. Moreover, comprehensive moral views in a Rawlsian liberal society will overlap on basic political values and ideals. This overlap provides citizens some moral common ground, and thus some reason not to "despise" one another. The citizens of such a society will not share all moral views, but they can regard one another as cooperating in the pursuit of the same basic political values.

Rorty professes a concern with the "sort of culture [that] might lie

at the end of the road we liberal intellectuals have been travelling
since the Enlightenment."[48] That culture, he thinks, would be one
publicly disenchanted with religion, metaphysics, and ideology. It
would also be one in which the few citizens who retain the metaphysical urge suffer a powerful tension between their public and their
private lives,[49] between publicly cooperating with and privately de-
spising their fellow citizens. Rorty hails Rawls's recent work because
he thinks he finds there a sketch of the largely disenchanted culture
that lies at the journey's end. But Rorty's interpretation is, I believe,
mistaken. Rawls would lead us down another fork to a another desti-
nation. He would have us part company with Rorty, for he holds out
the possibility of ending our journey at a very different liberal culture
than Rorty envisions.

V

What, then, are we to make of Hampton's charge that Rawls has
made political philosophy into practical politics? And what are we to
make of Rorty's hope that Rawls has accorded democracy priority over
philosophy? To make anything at all of them, we must appreciate the
division of political philosophy into political theory and comprehensive public philosophy.[50]

Comprehensive public philosophy may be political in some respects.
Those who engage in it may do so for political reasons, trying to build
an overlapping consensus on justice as fairness because they think it
will make society more peaceful and stable. But the motives for engaging in comprehensive public philosophy need not be entirely political, as I have argued. A philosopher or theologian may try to
convince others in his or her tradition to accept justice as fairness
because she or he is convinced that Rawls's principles are just, given
his or her own commitment to democratic values and ideals. He or
she might believe that the society in which he or she lives would be
more just were justice as fairness widely accepted.

The comprehensive public philosopher's motives, therefore, need not
be entirely or at all political.

Neither need his or her arguments be political. The philosopher can
work within moral and religious traditions, appealing to their views
of human nature, the value of human life, human equality, the nature
of moral obligation, and the importance of justice. She or he can appeal to them by trying to find a moral basis for justice as fairness
within a tradition or by trying to bring the two into reflective equilib-

rium. If the comprehensive public philosopher is a Kantian or a utilitarian, the arguments will be straightforwardly philosophical. If he or she is a moral theologian, they may not fall squarely within the bounds of philosophical argument as it is usually conceived. But some of the theological arguments will concern philosophical problems: the purposes of political authority and the demands of distributive justice, for example. And Rorty, who shows no reluctance to assimilate theology to philosophy,[51] would reckon them philosophical, or at least "ideological," rather than political.

Now consider political theory. Political theory as Rawls practices it is a subject that combines philosophy with politics, as well as with political history and political sociology. Note first that the very decision to engage in political theory is in large part a political decision.

"The aims of political philosophy," Rawls writes in a much-noted and -quoted passage, "depend on the society it addresses."[52] A political philosopher's choice of aims depends upon his or her political judgment about the needs and shortcomings of the society for which he or she intends the work.

Some political thinkers judge their society to be primarily in need of social criticism. They write political philosophy accordingly; here utopian thought, beginning with More, comes most readily to mind. Others may judge that the greatest service a political philosopher can render is the recovery or revitalization of some aspect of the history of political thought.[53] Still others, like Locke, will judge their society in greatest need of a theory of political legitimacy and justified rebellion.

The decision to perfect the conception of justice inherited from the contract tradition is a similarly political judgment. Rawls judged that the society he addressed stood in need of "an alternative systematic account of justice that is superior . . . to the dominant utilitarianism of the tradition."[54] And, we might add, to the dominant utilitarianism of economic thought and of judicial and bureaucratic practice. He judged such an account necessary to provide a more adequate moral basis for political consensus than utilitarian or natural rights views. And he judged such a consensus necessary to overcome long-standing political controversies generated by the conflicting claims of liberty and equality.[55] Rawls's desire to achieve a morally based consensus, and thus to engage in political theory, was in part a political motive.

But Rawls's political theory is also a historical and sociological enterprise. It draws on texts, like those of Locke, Rousseau, and Kant, and ideas, like that of the social contract, central to the tradition of liberal thought. It derives its reasonability in part from its explicitly locating itself in that intellectual and political tradition. Practicing political theory demands recognition of the myriad ways in which these ideas and texts have shaped liberal political culture, the self-conceptions of citizens in liberal democracies, and the terms of political debate. Historical and sociological sensitivity is needed to isolate the basic ideas and values around which consensus can coalesce once they are further specified and combined.

Finally, Rawls says that what he calls "philosophical inclination" is an "essential" motive for doing moral theory. If moral theory is left to social theorists or psychologists, who are "not prompted by philosophical inclination to pursue moral theory," then, he says, "the inquiry will have the wrong focus."[56] What holds of moral theory generally presumably holds of political theory: political theory would have the wrong focus if not motivated in part by philosophical inclination. Political theory is, therefore, a properly philosophical task, for it requires an inclination to pursue traditionally philosophical questions. To see this, recall that one of the questions definitive of political philosophy, at least since Rousseau, is that of what a democratic regime would be like under realistically favorable circumstances.[57] Rawls, in specifying a conception of justice for such a society, provides part of the answer to Rousseau's question. His interest in providing such a conception is therefore itself a philosophical inclination.

Moreover, Rawls's attempt is focused differently than would be a social theorist's or a psychologist's attempt to provide a conception of justice. Rawls's attempt is not focused, for example, on providing a conception that would be judged most stable in light of the findings of psychology, equilibrium theory, or theories of social choice. He is interested, rather, in the question: what conception of justice is the most appropriate moral conception for a liberal democracy? Questions of psychology and social theory are taken up, but only insofar as they help to answer that question. And while the decision to develop a moral conception of justice may have been in large part a political one, that decision, once made, required Rawls to address fundamental philosophical problems about the relationship between the right and the good and about the reconciliation of liberty and equality.

Politics thus stands in a quite complicated relationship to political theory. It stands in a similarly complicated relationship to comprehensive public philosophy. The relationship between politics and political philosophy as Rawls conceives it is even more complex, for political philosophy includes both political theory and comprehensive public philosophy. The complicated nature of these relationships leads me to suggest that the question of whether Rawls has unduly politicized political philosophy is wrongly posed and should be rejected. It is a question premised on sharp but misbegotten distinctions between politics and philosophy, and between political argument and philosophical argument.

In the past two decades, historians of political thought have become increasingly suspicious of these sharp distinctions, arguing that an attempt to impose them on great political philosophers of the past is systematically misleading. Richard Ashcraft, for example, has shown how much we can learn about John Locke's political philosophy by studying its actual and foreseen political impact and by examining the political decisions Locke made in resolving to write and publish the Treatises. Detailed study of this kind shows how difficult it is to distinguish the political from the philosophical in his work. It also shows how much of Locke's thought we would misunderstand if our primary interest were in sorting his works into preconceived categories.[58]

It is similarly misleading to approach Rawls's work with such interests and categories in mind. Surely he is not just engaged in practical politics. But neither is it helpful to read him as attempting to answer timeless questions about the nature of justice. He is a philosopher whose philosophical project was shaped by political, historical, and sociological judgments about the society he addresses. His own work in political theory leaves ample room, and, indeed, assumes the subsequent metaphysical and theological arguments of others. Political theory as Rawls practices it may be done without metaphysics, but political philosophy as he conceives it need not be.

I have tried to show that Rawls has not unduly politicized political philosophy, any more than did Hobbes, Locke, and Mill; he has merely divided its labor. I have tried to show, too, that we understand better the work of individual thinkers such as Rawls and the enterprise of political philosophy generally if we attend to the intellectual and political tasks that political philosophers set for themselves.

Notes

Thanks to Elizabeth Anderson, Daniel Brudney, Barbara Herman, and Greg Kavka for comments on an early draft of this paper, and to Joshua Cohen, Neil Delaney, Alasdair MacIntyre, David O'Connor, and Richard Rorty for comments on a recent one.

1. John Rawls, "Justice as Fairness: Political Not Metaphysical," *Philosophy and Public Affairs*, 14 (1985): 223–51.

2. John Rawls, *A Theory of Justice* (Harvard University Press, 1971), 16.

3. Rawls, "Political Not Metaphysical," 225.

4. Joseph Raz, "Facing Diversity: The Case for Epistemic Abstinence," *Philosophy and Public Affairs*, 19 (1990): 8.

5. Rawls, "Political Not Metaphysical," 230.

6. Ibid., 230: "That is, [justice as fairness] presents itself not as a conception of justice that is true, but as one that can serve as a basis of informed and willing political agreement between citizens viewed as free and equal persons."

7. Ibid.

8. John Rawls, "The Idea of an Overlapping Consensus." *Oxford Journal of Legal Studies*, 7 (1987): 7–8.

9. Rawls, "The Idea of an Overlapping Consensus," 9–10.

10. Jean Hampton, "Should Political Philosophy Be Done without Metaphysics?" Ethics, 99 (1989), 791–814, 799ff. [Reprinted as the eighth essay in this collection.]

11. Richard Rorty, "The Priority of Democracy to Philosophy," in *The Virginia Statute for Religious Freedom*, eds. Peterson and Vaughan (Cambridge University Press, 1988). 260.

12. Hampton, "Should Political Philosophy Be Done without Metaphysics?," 807.

13. Patrick Neal. "Justice as Fairness: Political or Metaphysical?" *Political Theory*, 18 (1990): 46.

14. Rorty, "The Priority of Democracy to Philosophy," 260.

15. Cf. Ibid., 271ff.

16. Kurt Baier, "Justice and the Aims of Political Philosophy," *Ethics*, 99 (1989): 784.

17. Raz, "Facing Diversity: The Case for Epistemic Abstinence," 15.

18. Baier, "Justice and the Aims of Political Philosophy." 780–81; Hampton, "Should Political Philosophy Be Done without Metaphysics?," 812ff.

19. For criticism of Rorty's distinction, see Richard J. Bernstein, "One Step Forward, Two Steps Backward: Richard Rorty on Liberal Democracy and Philosophy," *Political Theory*, 15 (1987): 538–63.

20. John Rawls, "The Independence of Moral Theory," *Proceedings and Addresses of the American Philosophical Association*, 48 (1975): 5. Rawls's distinction between moral theory and moral philosophy has its origins in the division of moral philosophy Rawls found in Sidgwick. On the distinction in Sidgwick and Rawls's modifications of it, see John Rawls, "Kantian Constructivism in Moral Theory," *Journal of Philosophy*, 77 (1980): 554–56. Implicit in my argument is that Rawls's own attempts to secure but limited justification of justice as fairness and his refusal to assert its truth are natural consequences of the views expressed in "The Independence of Moral Theory." That paper was published just four years after *A Theory of Justice*. This suggests that Rawls's recent views are not the startling departure from earlier work that many have thought. I will not try, however, to substantiate this suggestion here.

21. Rawls, "The Independence of Moral Theory," 22: "All the moral conceptions in the tradition of moral philosophy must be continually renewed

. . . In this endeavor the aim of those most attracted to a particular view should not be to confute but to perfect."

22. Rawls, "Political Not Metaphysical," 226ff.

23. Rawls, *Theory*, viii.

24. Rawls, *Theory*, 20. My thoughts about political values and political guidance have been much advanced by Joshua Cohen's meticulous paper, "Democratic Equality," *Ethics*, 99 (1989): 727–51. I am grateful to Prof. Cohen for making available to me the paper's longer unpublished version.

25. Note that in "Political Not Metaphysical," 236, note 19, Rawls calls justice as fairness an "ideal-based view." I intend the discussion of moral ideals as specifications of basic ideas to help explain this remark.

26. Rawls, *Theory*, 477.

27. Rawls, "The Idea of an Overlapping Consensus," 25.

28. Rawls, "The Independence of Moral Theory," 7: "Since the history of moral philosophy shows that the notion of moral truth is problematical, we can suspend consideration of it until we have a deeper understanding of moral conceptions. But one thing is certain: people profess and appear to be influenced by moral conceptions. These conceptions themselves can be made the focus of study; so provisionally we may bracket the problem of moral truth and turn to moral theory."

29. Rorty, "The Priority of Democracy to Philosophy," 270.

30. Rawls, "The Independence of Moral Theory," 9–10.

31. Hampton, "Should Political Philosophy Be Done without Metaphysics?," 798.

32. Hampton, "Should Political Philosophy Be Done without Metaphysics?," 806-7.

33. Rawls, "The Idea of an Overlapping Consensus," 13. The term "comprehensive moral view" is used in deference to Rawls's distinction between moral views framed for a particular subject, like the basic structure of society, and those of more comprehensive scope that specify what is valuable in human life, ideals of character, etc.; see Ibid., 3, note 4.

34. Ibid., 11, 18.

35. John Courtney Murray, S.J., "The Problem of State Religion," *Theological Studies*, 12 (1952): 155–78; see 165 for a concise statement.

36. John Courtney Murray, S.J. "Freedom of Religion: I. The Ethical Problem," *Theological Studies*, 6 (1945): 229–86, 241.

37. Ibid., 239–41.

38. Rawls, "The Idea of an Overlapping Consensus," 19.

39. See, for example, Harlan Beckley, "A Christian Affirmation of Rawls' Idea of Justice as Fairness," *Journal of Religious Ethics*, 13 (1985): 210–42; 14 (1986): 229–46.

40. Rawls, "The Idea of an Overlapping Consensus," 23.

41. Consider a theological example. In their pastoral letter "Economic Justice for All" (USCC, 1986), the U.S. Roman Catholic bishops wrote that "Distributive justice requires that the allocation of income, wealth and power in society be evaluated in light of its effects on persons whose basic material

needs are unmet" (paragraph 70), and that "the investment of wealth, talent and energy should be specially directed to benefit those who are poor or economically insecure" (paragraph 92). These norms, the bishops claim, are part of Catholic moral tradition. They are said to be implicit in the Bible's injunctions to be just toward the poor (paragraph 68) and in official church documents (paragraph 70).

A society the basic structure of which conformed to the Difference Principle would, I presume, satisfy these two norms. A theologian trying to secure Catholic acceptance of justice as fairness could point this out. She could cite her commitment to the bishops' moral teaching, rather than her interest in peace and stability, as her motive for trying to build a consensus on justice as fairness.

42. Admittedly, the phrase "comprehensive public philosophy" is somewhat unfamiliar. And other terms may seem better to fit the enterprise in which, for example, utilitarian political thinkers have traditionally been engaged. The phrase does have two advantages, however. First, the adjective "comprehensive" marks the fact that those who take as theirs this second task are working within and avail themselves of the resources of comprehensive moral conceptions. Second, the phrase "public philosophy," which it modifies, resonates with the term "public theology," a label that some moral theologians have applied to the project of drawing out the political implications of their theology. This resonance serves to remind us that theologians, as well as philosophers, will have to perform the second task if an overlapping consensus on justice as fairness is to be secured. The phrase "public philosophy" was originally Walter Lippman's. See his *The Public Philosophy* (Little, Brown, 1955). For this use of the phrase "public theology", see Richard McBrien, *Caesar's Coin* (Macmillan, 1987), 238, note 34.

43. All references in this paragraph are to Rorty, "The Priority of Democracy to Philosophy," 264.

44. Richard Rorty, *Contingency, Irony and Solidarity* (Cambridge University Press, 1989), 85–87. Rorty's conjecture about the demise of philosophy under the pressure of a liberal culture is reminiscent of Thomas Jefferson's prediction about the demise of religion: "I trust there is not a young man now living in the United States who will not die a Unitarian." Jefferson made this prediction in 1822; subsequent events have, of course, shown him wrong. Jefferson's remark is quoted by Stephen Macedo in *Liberal Virtues* (Oxford University Press, 1990), 73.

45. For an accessible and convincing treatment, see Garry Wills, *Under God* (Simon and Schuster, 1990).

46. Rawls, "Political Not Metaphysical," 230.

47. Rorty, "The Priority of Democracy to Philosophy," 270.

48. Richard Rorty, "Thugs and Theorists: A Reply to Bernstein," *Political Theory*, 15 (1987): 578, note 25.

49. Rorty, *Contingency, Irony and Solidarity*, 120.

50. After completing this essay, I came upon Stephen Macedo, "The Politics of Justification," *Political Theory*, 18 (1990), 280–304. Macedo, too, notes

that Rawls divides the labor of justification (see 290ff). He criticizes Rawls's conception of justification as unrealistic, saying "[a] more realistic model of justification would allow, in effect, that participants' personal moral convictions are engaged as each feature of the political view is constructed" (290). Macedo's arguments require far more attention than I can give them here; I mention only one point in response. Successfully arguing that a conception of justification is unrealistic requires successful criticism of the moral epistemology that underlies it. Rawls's moral epistemology is Kantian. Kant thought that moral interest in the categorical imperative is best elicited by conceiving both of agents realizing their autonomy by acting from it and of the imperative as supremely regulative of a realm of autonomous citizens. Rawls thinks that moral interest in his two principles is best elicited by conceiving both of citizens whose sense of justice is informed by the principles and of the principles as supremely regulative of a well-ordered society of just citizens. But eliciting an interest in the principles in this way requires laying out the political construction as a whole rather than presenting it to citizens piece by piece. To sustain his thesis that Rawlsian justification is unrealistic, Macedo must provide some argument against Rawls's Kantian views about how best to elicit moral interest in principles of justice.

51. Rorty, "Priority of Democracy," 264.

52. Rawls, "The Idea of an Overlapping Consensus," 1.

53. Consider Quentin Skinner's work on the civic republican tradition; Richard Ashcraft's recent work on Mill is similarly motivated. For the practical import of the history of political thought, see Ashcraft. "Whose Problem? Whose Ideology? A Reply to My Critics," *Journal of Politics*, 42 (1980): 716–21, 720. For Ashcraft's work on Mill, see "Class Conflict and Constitutionalism in J. S. Mill's Thought," in *Liberalism and the Moral Life*. ed. Nancy Rosenblum (Harvard University Press, 1989), 105-26.

54. Rawls, *Theory*, 8.

55. Cf. Rawls. "Political Not Metaphysical," 226ff.

56. References in this sentence and the last are to Rawls. "The Independence of Moral Theory," 22.

57. I owe this point to John Rawls.

58. For Ashcraft's work on Locke, see his *Revolutionary Politics and Locke's "Two Treatises of Government"* (Princeton, N.J.: Princeton University Press, 1986). For his methodological arguments, see Ibid., Introduction. For his criticism of a misguided attempt to separate Locke's works into the philosophical and the nonphilosophical, see his "Political Theory and the Problem of Ideology." *Journal of Politics*, 42 (1980): 687–705. especially 693, note 23.

ON PUBLIC REASON

KENT GREENAWALT*

INTRODUCTION

Since the publication of *A Theory of Justice*[1] in 1971, John Rawls has refined, qualified, and enriched his political philosophy, responding generously and with patient analytical care to difficulties posed by critics. *Political Liberalism*[2] embodies the major developments in Rawls's thought during those two decades. Rawls continues to be a strong defender of political liberalism, but in various respects his philosophical claims are more modest than those he offered in 1971, and the political life he recommends involves more accommodation to the diverse perspectives and ways of life one expects to find in liberal democracies. In most of the chapters of the book, Rawls largely replicates what he has said in important lectures, but each chapter contains some fresh analysis and references to recent work. The most substantial addition to his previous writings is his chapter on "The Idea of Public Reason,"[3] and that is the focus of this Essay. My discussion of that topic requires some attention to another major subject, the "overlapping consensus" of views that can support a political concept of justice, but I do not say more about that subject than is needed for my discussion of public reason.

I first sketch briefly the basic problems to which Rawls's idea of public reason is an answer. I then summarize Rawls's position, drawing mainly from the chapter on public reason, but also outlining his views about overlapping consensus. After clarifying some important aspects of his position, I make some criticisms. These are largely directed at a distinction between constitutional essentials and matters of basic justice, on the one hand, and ordinary political issues, on the other, that forms a major element of Rawls's proposal about public reason. Finally, I suggest very briefly some ways to strengthen an account of the constraint of public reasons.

* University Professor, Columbia University School of Law; A.B., 1958, Swarthmore College; B. Phil., 1960, Oxford University; LL.B., 1963, Columbia. This Essay draws substantially from a book, tentatively titled PRIVATE CONSCIENCES AND PUBLIC REASONS, to be published by Oxford University Press in late 1994.
1. JOHN RAWLS, A THEORY OF JUSTICE (1971).
2. JOHN RAWLS, POLITICAL LIBERALISM (1993).
3. *Id.* at 212-54.

I. The Basic Problems

Within a liberal democracy, people will inevitably have widely differing understandings about the nature of the universe, the existence (or not) of God, and the point(s) of human life and of society. These differences are the fruit of human freedom. If these differences bore only on matters everyone agreed should be private, they would pose no threat to politics. Whether I believe in the "big bang" theory of the origin of the universe or choose to meditate in my spare time is not important for the public at large. But many of the differences have evident implications for collective social life. If, for example, I am a Roman Catholic *and* my Roman Catholicism leads me to believe that society should give "priority to the poor" and should regard a newly formed embryo as having the moral status of a full human being, these views have a clear potential import for political decisions about welfare and abortion. That creates a dilemma.

If widely variant perspectives on critical subjects dominate political life, society may suffer disunity. Citizens may not be able to depend on the application of any core principles of justice and they may find none to which they need feel loyalty. Some citizens may well find themselves coerced by the state to act on the basis of reasons with which they feel no resonance. That may be unfair and a source of great antagonism. On the other hand, if citizens are told that in politics they should not use their most fundamental beliefs about what is true, that may seem both unreasonable and a serious infringement of full liberty. This conflict is the dilemma, and it is a genuine one. Various theorists respond to it in various ways; every proposal sacrifices something of value.[4]

II. Rawls's Position

Rawls suggests that a well-ordered society will have wide agreement on principles of political justice. The agreement will be supported by an overlapping consensus of "comprehensive views." It will include a principle of public reason for public political advocacy about constitutional essentials and matters of basic justice. I need to say a little about the first two elements before focusing on the third.

According to Rawls, the fundamentals of political life should be more or less agreed upon, and set outside ordinary political wrangling. One way in which this could occur would be if everyone subscribed to

---

4. I try to show this in Greenawalt, *supra* note *.

the same religious or other comprehensive view, *and* had a similar opinion of that view's implications for politics. This route, however, is effectively blocked in liberal democracies by the inevitable plurality of comprehensive views. Nonetheless, since people with different comprehensive views might share similar ideas about political justice, a consensus on the basic political structure of society remains a possibility. It is this possibility that Rawls's theory exemplifies.

Many people read Rawls's *A Theory of Justice* as claiming a methodology for arriving at *the most rational* principles of justice.[5] In subsequent writings, Rawls has made clear that his more modest aspiration is to set out principles for liberal democracies, ones that best capture the fundamental idea of "a fair system of cooperation between free and equal persons."[6] Why should a citizen accept such principles if his comprehensive view suggests a different basis of social life *or* an unusual understanding of how the fundamental idea of fair social cooperation applies? (Imagine that a fervent religious believer thinks that theocracy may be preferable to liberal democracy or accepts Rawls's fundamental idea of fair social cooperation, but thinks that treating people as free and equal means giving all people the strongest encouragements to adopt the true faith.) Why should such a person accept principles of justice which an incomplete common reason suggests?

Rawls's response is that appropriate principles of justice are ones that are sustained, or at least could be sustained, by an overlapping consensus of comprehensive views.[7] These principles, initially developed as a "free-standing political . . . conception"[8] for the basic structure of society, fit with a wide range of comprehensive views likely to arise in a liberal democracy. A comprehensive view is "reasonable" if it acknowledges the freedom and equality of citizens on which political liberalism rests. A democratic regime can be enduring or stable only if a substantial majority of its citizens freely support it. If people understand this, they may accept principles of justice other than those their comprehensive views might initially have inclined them to favor. They may realize that efforts to create a theocracy or to provide

---

5. RAWLS, *supra* note 1. Rawls did not assert that he had arrived at *the best principles*, but he seemed to be aiming for such principles, with those he presented as the best he could do.

6. John Rawls, *Justice as Fairness: Political not Metaphysical,* 14 PHIL. & PUB. AFF. 223, 231 (1985).

7. *See* RAWLS, *supra* note 2, at 133-72.

8. *Id.* at 140-41.

strong inducements toward one set of religious beliefs would be unfair and highly disruptive.

Rawls asserts that many people in a society will accept principles of justice because these fit with their *reflective* full or partial comprehensive views;[9] others will believe the principles are appropriate without direct reference to nonpolitical aspects of their particular comprehensive views.[10] Principles of justice can be argued for as valid, or desirable, or appropriate without reliance on any particular comprehensive view, though the validity of these principles will depend largely on their capacity to fit with an overlapping consensus of comprehensive views. It is in this sense that Rawls argues that political philosophy need not be metaphysical. In a well-ordered society, a plurality of reasonable comprehensive views will support the basic political structures and ideas of justice.

One aspect of the principles of justice in a liberal democracy will be a principle of common reason. Rawls says "[t]here is no reason . . . why any citizen, or association of citizens, should have the right to use the state's police power to decide constitutional essentials or basic questions of justice as that person's, or that association's, comprehensive doctrine directs."[11] When citizens talk with all their fellows about such matters, they are to look to what is commonly shared, not to what divides them.

What precisely does Rawls imagine as the reach of the overlapping consensus of reasonable comprehensive views? In some earlier writing, it appeared that the consensus might embrace highly specific principles of justice, including such features as fair equality of opportunity and the "difference" principle, as developed by Rawls. In *Political Liberalism*, Rawls explicitly recognizes the possibility of a much weaker shared understanding, such as acceptance of basic constitutional procedures.[12] He envisions the full overlapping consensus as reaching more deeply and broadly than that. Apparently, however, it will leave room for some disagreements about important issues of justice. In the chapter on public reason, Rawls assumes that other liberal views about social justice will compete with his ideas of fair opportu-

9. A doctrine is fully comprehensive when it covers all recognized values and virtues within one rather precisely articulated scheme of thought; whereas a doctrine is only partially comprehensive when it comprises certain (but not all) nonpolitical values and virtues and is rather loosely articulated.
RAWLS, *supra* note 2, at 175.
    10. *Id.* at 155.
    11. *Id.* at 62; *see also id.* at 226.
    12. *Id.* at 158.

nity and the difference principle; and I assume that the overlapping consensus is to be capacious enough to embrace a variety of perspectives on these subjects.

I have said that my main interest in Rawls's thesis about an overlapping consensus lies in how it relates to his theory of public reason. About that relation, we can conclude preliminarily that citizens properly consult their comprehensive views to determine whether they accept political structures and principles of justice; however, in public discussions of applications of shared principles to particular circumstances, comprehensive views are to recede in favor of public reasons.

I turn now to that subject, to Rawls's account of public reason and fundamentals. Rawls talks of public reason as the reason of citizens sharing equal citizenship.[13] Justifications in terms of public reasons "appeal only to presently accepted general beliefs and forms of reasoning found in common sense, and the methods and conclusions of science when these are not controversial."[14] One employing public reasons does not appeal to comprehensive religious and philosophical doctrines, but rather "a reasonable balance of public political values."[15]

According to Rawls, the work of the Supreme Court exemplifies the use of public reason, and that is the "sole reason" it exercises;[16] for others, the requirement to use public reason is less constraining. It holds for those engaging in political advocacy in the public forum, and for candidates and elections; it does not apply to personal deliberations and reflections, or to reasoning within associations such as universities or churches, where religious, philosophical, and moral considerations of many kinds properly play a role.[17]

For citizens and legislators, "the limits imposed by public reason do not apply to all political questions but only to those involving what we may call 'constitutional essentials' and questions of basic justice."[18] Regulation of property, preserving animals, and controlling pollution are not included in this category. A liberal principle of legitimacy and a duty of civility require that on fundamental questions, principles and policies can be supported by public reason. Rawls expects that values specified by a fundamental political conception will give a reasonable

13. *Id.* at 213.
14. *Id.* at 224.
15. *Id.* at 243.
16. *Id.* at 235.
17. *Id.* at 215.
18. *Id.* at 214.

public answer to all, or nearly all, questions about constitutional essentials.

Rawls indicates what he means by constitutional essentials in the following passage:

> There is the greatest urgency for citizens to reach practical agreement in judgment about the constitutional essentials. These are of two kinds:
>
> a. fundamental principles that specify the general structure of government and the political process: the powers of the legislature, executive and the judiciary; the scope of majority rule; and
>
> b. equal basic rights and liberties of citizenship that legislative majorities are to respect: such as the right to vote and to participate in politics, liberty of conscience, freedom of thought and of association, as well as the protections of the rule of law.[19]

As far as questions of basic justice are concerned, Rawls asserts that some principle of opportunity and a social minimum providing for the basic needs of all citizens are essentials, but more stringent aspects of his own theory of justice (namely, fair equality of opportunity and the difference principle) go beyond the essentials.[20] Rawls explains that settling the constitutional essentials dealing with basic freedoms is urgent, that telling whether these essentials are realized is far easier than telling if principles governing social and economic inequalities are realized, and that gaining agreement about what the basic rights and liberties should be is also comparatively easy; "[t]hese considerations explain why freedom of movement and free choice of occupation and a social minimum covering citizens' basic needs count as constitutional essentials while the principle of fair opportunity and the difference principle do not."[21]

III. CLARIFICATIONS

The principle of self-restraint implicit in Rawls's ideal of democratic citizenship would restrict use of reasons, such as narrow claims of faith, that are not publicly accessible; but Rawls makes clear that direct reference to comprehensive views is out, even when people believe they can be arrived at by common reasoning. Rawls thus avoids the criticism that it is unfair for the holder's own belief about whether

19. *Id.* at 227.
20. *Id.* at 228-29.
21. *Id.* at 230.

common reason can establish his comprehensive view to become the standard for whether he may rely on the view.

In respect to the *precise coverage* of the requirement to limit oneself to public reasons, four points need clarification. The first concerns the range of persons and contexts for which the requirement reaches all topics. The second is the status of basic questions of justice that are not covered within constitutional essentials. The third is the importance of public reasons for situations other than those when the requirement to employ such reasons strictly applies. The fourth is the degree of constraint that compliance with a standard of public reasons involves, when the standard strictly applies.

Rawls assumes that courts should limit themselves to public reasons in all circumstances.[22] Such reasons should be the exclusive mode of justification, and of internal deliberation as well. Rawls contrasts courts with legislators and citizens, who may bring other reasons to bear on nonfundamental issues, like the treatment of animals. In this connection, Rawls does not discuss actual statutory language, or the content of reports of committees of Congress and of administrative agencies, or the language in which the executive branch formally proposes the enactment of legislation. Would he think that the justifications in such official pronouncements should be restricted to public reasons for all subject matters? The range of what such documents appropriately say is somewhat broader than the typical judicial opinion, because preambles to statutes, committee reports, etc. need not draw justifications from pre-existing law, as do most judicial opinions.[23] In a society with many reasonable comprehensive views, it is highly doubtful whether any particular comprehensive view should be presented as a major justification for new legislation, but perhaps a committee report might point out that a provision to protect animals fits with many comprehensive views that are widely held in society. Such a justification might be found in a judicial opinion, but it would be unusual.[24] If what Rawls says about courts and public reason is sound, certain other kinds of official documents are appropriately cast

22. Rawls is thinking about decisions of legal issues. I am not sure whether he thinks Supreme Court justices, or judges more generally, are limited to public reasons in *all* the functions they perform. Rawls concentrates on the Supreme Court, but he also speaks more generally of "the judiciary." *See id.* at 216.

23. *Some* judicial opinions do draw implicitly or explicitly from community morality or forms of normative evaluation that reach beyond interpretations of preexisting standards. I discuss these matters in Chapter 13 of GREENAWALT, *supra* note *, and at greater length in KENT GREENAWALT, LAW AND OBJECTIVITY 163-231 (1992).

24. Yet, in Roe v. Wade, 410 U.S. 113 (1973), for example, the Court's opinion surveys historical attitudes toward abortion.

in some (perhaps broader) form of public reason, even when they do not deal with constitutional essentials or questions of basic justice.[25]

The second question about covered topics concerns the relationship between "constitutional essentials" and "questions of basic justice." Rawls says that the requirement of public reason applies to both of these.[26] Midway in his discussion he concludes that some principle of opportunity and a social minimum providing for basic needs—certainly matters of basic justice—are among the constitutional essentials.[27] Fair equality of opportunity and the difference principle—crucial aspects of his own political conception of justice—fall outside the constitutional essentials. Do the constraints of public reason apply only to the constitutional essentials, which include *minimum* requirements of basic justice, or do the constraints *also apply* to advocacy about matters of basic justice, such as fair equality of opportunity and the difference principle, that go beyond the constitutional essentials? This is an important practical question because many political issues will turn on controversial conceptions of justice that reach beyond the minimum. Particularly since these issues will be sharply contested, it matters whether people can appropriately employ their comprehensive views in public justifications for their positions. Rawls plainly intends the constraint of public reasons to apply to advocacy about these issues of basic justice that reach beyond the constitutional essentials.[28]

The third question concerns the status of public reasons for topics when other reasons may be used. At an early point, Rawls talks as if he is beginning with the clearest illustrations of a concept of public reason and is uncertain to what extent the relevant restrictions apply to a broader range of political issues.[29] He also says that it is usually highly desirable to settle political questions by invoking the values of public reason. Later, however, he indicates that "[c]itizens and legislators may properly vote their more comprehensive views when con-

---

25. Rawls does say that the ideal of public reason "applies in official forums and so to legislators when they speak on the floor of parliament, and to the executive in its public acts and pronouncements," RAWLS, *supra* note 2, at 216, but this comment does not focus on the possible coverage of a requirement beyond constitutional essentials and matters of basic justice.

26. *Id.* at 214.

27. *Id.* at 228-29.

28. Rawls says, "[p]olitical discussions of the reasons for and against fair opportunity and the difference principle, though they are not constitutional essentials, fall under questions of basic justice and so are to be decided by the political values of public reason." *Id.* at 229 n.10. Although the reader senses that the effort to decide what falls within the constitutional essentials is important for the constraints of public reason, it turns out that that effort does not really matter when a subject falls within questions of basic justice.

29. *Id.* at 215.

stitutional essentials and basic justice are not at stake . . . ."[30] I take his comments in the following way: that the general preclusion of justifications in terms of comprehensive and other nonaccessible reasons applies for legislators and citizens only to constitutional essentials and basic questions of justice, but that, more generally, commonly accessible reasons should have a kind of priority in liberal democratic politics.

I turn now to the fourth question: what does the constraint of public reasons amount to for the topics to which it strictly applies? Here we need to consider the behavior that the constraint covers, and more particularly, the relation between grounds offered in justification and the actual grounds of decision. Some passages suggest that Rawls is concerned with public justification rather than decision. He says the limits of public reason do not apply to personal deliberations and reflections about political questions, or to reasoning within associations; the limits apply only to public political advocacy.[31] That sounds a little like people can make up their minds on various grounds, so long as they publicly discuss the issues in terms of public reasons. However, other passages make clear that this is not Rawls's full view. At numbers of places he talks about voting as covered; the ideal of public reason calls on one not to vote one's simple preferences and interests or even what one thinks is right and true by comprehensive convictions.[32] Many legislators never have to explain particular votes, and many citizens do not even reveal their votes. The constraint on voting clearly indicates that the principle extends beyond publicly stated advocacy and justification.[33] Rawls's reference to courts as exemplars of his concept of public reason strongly suggests the same conclusion. Courts, in general at least, are supposed to be guided by the reasons they state. Rawls does not imagine that judges on an appellate court have fulfilled their duty if they have self-consciously determined their decision by a comprehensive view they happen to hold in common and then have offered entirely different public reasons in a majority opinion. For judges, public reasons should guide decision as well as debate and opinion writing; Rawls holds up judicial practice as a sort of model.

30. *Id.* at 235.
31. *Id.* at 215.
32. *Id.* at 215-20.
33. I take "public advocacy" as involving an expression, that others may read or hear, of the basis of one's view. One may, instead, conceive of voting as a form of advocacy, although secret voting does not reveal even one's overall conclusion and open voting (taken alone) does not indicate the basis for one's conclusion.

Rawls's discussion leaves a bit of uncertainty on one subject that is critical to the relation between actual grounds of decision and public justification—whether the proponent of a position must himself believe in the public justification he offers. Rawls writes that the ideal of citizenship imposes a "duty of civility—to be able to explain to one another on those fundamental questions how the principles and policies they advocate . . . can be supported by the political values of public reason."[34] He says that "[w]hat public reason asks is that citizens be able to explain their vote to one another in terms of a reasonable balance of public political values . . . ."[35] Imagine the following situation: Joan believes that for possible criminalization of some late abortions, various positions can be supported as consonant with a reasonable balance of public reasons. Her comprehensive view leads her to believe that maximum criminalization is desirable. She thinks a reasonable defense of that position can be made in terms of public reasons, but her own sense of the *balance of public reasons*, taken alone, is that they support a different position. Is it appropriate for her to vote for the position that fits her comprehensive view and support the vote with an argument of public reasons in which she does not fully believe? In Rawls's language, Joan could "explain" her vote for maximum criminalization "in terms of a reasonable balance of public political values," but her explanation would not be persuasive to her. I believe that Rawls has in mind a sincere justification, one which the speaker actually credits.[36] If this is accurate, Joan is not fulfilling her responsibility to rely on public reasons if her basis for believing in maximum criminalization is the statement of a religious authority, and she offers arguments of public reason that she thinks are reasonable but finally unpersuasive. Suppose, however, religious authority leads Joan to conclude that certain arguments of public reason really are persuasive, although she does not grasp from their own terms why that is so (as a Roman Catholic might believe natural law arguments against abortion are valid, while realizing she would not reach this conclusion in the absence of the Church's position to this effect). Joan now does believe in the force of the public reasons she states. This is enough to satisfy Rawls.

---

34. RAWLS, *supra* note 2, at 217.

35. *Id.* at 243; *see also id.* at 226-27, 246.

36. This belief is based partly on correspondence with Rawls. *See also* RAWLS, *supra* note 2, at 241, which makes clear that a person must sincerely think his view is based on political values others can reasonably be expected to endorse. This passage does not quite cover the situation of conflicting values, but it supports the conclusion I have reached.

In light of the apparent need for a *sincere* justification in terms of a balance of public reasons, Rawls's comments that the limits of public reason do not apply to private reflection and associational discussion are somewhat less permissive and important than they appear at first glance. The primary way that citizens *act* to resolve political issues is by public advocacy and voting, and by urging legislators to vote. If decisions by citizens and legislators how to vote are to be determined by public reasons, just what is the significance of discerning in reflection, or in discussion with co-believers, the implications of one's comprehensive views for particular political issues? Rawls, focussing on the abolitionists and Martin Luther King, does discuss the question of whether people properly offer reasons related to their comprehensive views *as well as* public reasons. He comes down in favor of the inclusive view that such reasons may be offered, concluding that it "best encourages citizens to honor the ideal of public reason and secures its social conditions in the longer run in a well-ordered society."[37] Nevertheless, the way one reflects by oneself and discusses with co-believers will be deeply affected by a standard of public reasons for appropriate decision-making. For example, if we assumed that Supreme Court justices are supposed to decide by public reasons, we might be disconcerted to learn that three Roman Catholic Supreme Court justices were discussing with each other exactly what the implications are of Roman Catholicism for a particular constitutional issue. Thus, Rawls's limiting of the requirement of public reasons to voting and public advocacy is less significant than one might initially suppose; that requirement would infect thought and discussion of relevant issues in all settings.

IV. CRITICISMS

With these clarifications, we are ready to consider more fundamental questions about Rawls's approach. I discuss three related problems: (1) the need for, and possibility of, agreement on constitutional essentials; (2) the nature and problem of interpretation of essential principles; and (3) difficulties with crucial lines of distinction.

---

37. *Id.* at 248. However, when a society is well-ordered, with a firm overlapping consensus and an absence of deep disputes, citizens will honor the ideal of public reason by appealing to the values of the shared political conception.

A. Agreement on Essentials

Is it necessary for people in a liberal democratic society to agree on constitutional essentials? Is it desirable for them to do so? In approaching these questions, we may usefully keep in mind the present day United States. No doubt, some liberal democratic societies are so homogeneous that very wide agreement on constitutional essentials can coexist with some differences in comprehensive views—perhaps Sweden is a modern example—but Rawls mainly imagines societies much more diverse than Sweden. With its continuing substantial immigration from all parts of the world, the United States includes people of tremendously varied backgrounds and outlooks on life; it is more typical of the problem Rawls puts to himself.

In theory at least, a diverse society might manage if people agreed generally that political change should be peaceful and accomplished according to existing constitutional devices, even if they considered all substantive matters, including basic constitutional requisites, as up for argument. Professor Joseph Raz suggests that agreement on constitutional essentials is not so important to stability: "Rather, affective and symbolic elements may well be the crucial cement of society, and to these one has only to add the little power individuals have to affect societal affairs."[38] But, even if a society can be moderately stable with widespread disagreement about the wisdom of basic constitutional arrangements, Rawls is correct that *if* agreement can be achieved on basic essentials, *if* some fundamental matters are taken off the agenda, that will *contribute to stability and coherence*. Whether such agreement is *feasible* depends partly on the expansiveness of the subjects to be covered and the place of an idea of common reason.

I shall concentrate on freedom of religion and separation of church and state, but the issues I discuss are representative of those involved with most "constitutional essentials." I want initially to consider a minimal version of agreement on these two related essentials about religion and then to address a much fuller version of possible agreement. The minimal version includes agreement about what would generally be regarded as the most direct violations of religious liberty and separation of church and state: agreement, for example, that the state should not forbid people from adhering to particular

---

38. Joseph Raz, *Facing Diversity: The Case of Epistemic Abstinence*, 19 PHIL. & PUB. AFF. 1, 30 (1990).

religious beliefs or to practices of worship,[39] that no particular religion, such as Presbyterianism, will be denominated the state religion, that church officials will not by dint of their positions automatically hold important government offices, and that government officials will not automatically hold church positions. If that is what we mean by agreement on religious liberty and church-state separation, agreement in the United States is very great. Since existing agreement on these subjects is so great, it really does not matter too much whether public discussion and potential voting directly *about them* includes or excludes substantial reliance on comprehensive views.

A fuller version of religious liberty and church-state separation might include matters such as "no government promotion of religious truth," "no substantial direct aid of religious schools," and "no prayer in public schools," *and* the idea that elaboration and development of ideas of religious liberty and church-state separation will be carried forward in terms of common reason. Agreement about these matters is obviously a lot harder to attain, and certainly is not close to existing now in the United States. Many people think, for example, that the government should promote Christianity in certain ways, that the state should give substantial aid to parochial schools, that prayer should be allowed in public schools, and that decision of these issues themselves should be based substantially on reference to comprehensive views.

We might conceive of agreement as being much more abstract. People would agree that citizens should enjoy religious liberty and that church and state should be separate, but without reference to details. Agreement on such abstract ideas may exist now in the United States, but this agreement has limited significance when many people have very definite ideas on how to fill in details, and these ideas conflict powerfully with each other.

We can, thus, imagine agreement on "constitutional essentials" in liberal democracies but such agreement is likely to be limited to general abstractions and to what constitutes blatant violations. There is bound to be important *dis*agreement about a range of debated applications. Public judgments and discussion about that range of possible applications will greatly affect the political life of the society; and constraints set by public reason will matter.

---

39. State prohibitions may reach religious practices, like snake handling, that are deemed to cause some secular harm.

B. Interpreting Essentials

The problem of *interpreting* essentials can be illuminated by considering the position of someone who favors public school classroom prayer and extensive financial aid to parochial schools. Such a view might be seen as (1) *rejecting* all plausible understandings of religious liberty and church-state separation, (2) offering a genuine interpretation of these essentials but one that is out of accord with what a balance of public reasons would indicate, or (3) offering an interpretation from the perspective of a comprehensive view on questions for which public reason is indecisive.[40]

I shall explore briefly the possibility of rejection. Advocates of prayer and aid do not regard themselves as rejecting all plausible understandings of religious liberty and church-state separation; they point out that their views have enjoyed wide currency and even been dominant in long periods of the country's history. Suppose, however, that we persuade those who urge prayer and aid that their position is a move *away from* any plausible account of religious liberty or church-state separation,[41] or both. So long as they continue to believe that their approach is desirable and enjoys powerful historical support, why should they not feel they remain free to advocate it? Here we face the question why a citizen need feel loyalty to institutions and practices that are at odds with those his comprehensive view seems to recommend. The citizen facing this dilemma will need to examine how much room his comprehensive view leaves for loyalty to existing institutions when other possible social arrangements seem to fit better with his comprehensive view. To put the point a bit differently, the person will have to ask if his *reflective* comprehensive view calls for disloyalty to existing institutions in these circumstances. He may finally decide that these institutions actually do fit his comprehensive views best; or that the institutions should be accepted as a compromise necessary in the circumstances, although they are less than ideal; or that he should conform with the rules of the institutions while working to change them; or that he should feel free to decline compliance altogether, insofar as that is possible.

---

40. Of course, yet another logical possibility is that this view is the one a balance of public reasons would yield. I do not consider this position because it would eliminate (for this example) the problem I am addressing.

41. It is much more likely that a proponent of less strict separation would concede that his position deviated from a model of church-state separation than a model of religious liberty. That is, he would be more likely to concede some compromises with separation than some compromises with liberty.

Let us suppose, instead, not only that the advocate of prayer and aid offers an account of what he thinks religious liberty and church-state separation should amount to in our society, but that we agree that the account he provides is a plausible one. To give this alternative maximum persuasiveness, we might imagine that the person supports aid to parochial education primarily because of its substantial secular value, and that he supports school prayer as an accommodation to the exercise of religion of those who want to pray that interferes only minimally with those who prefer not to pray in school. We *might* conclude that public reason does not tell us how the concepts of religious liberty and separation should be interpreted in these doubtful areas, and that people must inevitably rely on comprehensive views to resolve those questions. That understanding, which I think may well prove accurate for some controversial problems about the state and religion, would increase the difficulty of defending any position that citizens should self-consciously try to limit their political justifications to public reasons.

I want to consider the possibility that more strongly favors Rawls's recommendation that citizens rely on public reasons in decision and discourse. That possibility, which I believe holds for some problems, is that public reasons, taken alone, do suggest one outcome, but that people who rely on comprehensive views to color their understanding of constitutional essentials and publicly shared principles may reasonably arrive at a different outcome. Since Rawls himself talks about failures to realize constitutional essentials as relatively easy to identify, perhaps he doubts that such situations will arise;[42] but I believe they may, so long as constitutional essentials are understood to cover more than the most gross violations of concepts like religious liberty and church-state separation.

I shall illustrate this point by reference to abortion, an issue Rawls explicitly considers. He says:

> Suppose . . . that we consider the question in terms of these three important political values: the due respect for human life, the ordered reproduction of political society over time, including the family in some form, and finally the equality of women as equal citizens. (There are, of course, other important political values besides these.) Now I believe any reasonable balance of these three values will give a woman a duly qualified right to decide whether or not to end her pregnancy during the first trimester. The reason for this is that at this early stage of pregnancy the political value of the equal-

---

42. *See* RAWLS, *supra* note 2, at 229-30.

ity of women is overriding, and this right is required to give it substance and force.[43]

Rawls suggests that public reason would, on balance, support a broadly permissive approach to abortion for at least the first trimester. I am not certain what Rawls is assuming about the status of the embryo/fetus; but suppose Joan takes the following position:

> Political values cannot tell us how much a fetus should be valued; they are either radically incomplete *on this question* or suggest that a fetus is probably of much less value than a new born baby. On either understanding, women should have substantial freedom to have early abortions. But I *know* from my comprehensive view that a fetus deserves as much moral consideration as a new born baby. On that understanding, either a woman should not have a legal right to abortion, or the appropriateness of such a right is highly debatable, and a broad right to abortion should not be considered required by constitutional essentials.

This illustration shows how comprehensive views can influence someone's sense of the application of fundamental values. In Joan's view the fundamental value of protecting "innocent human beings" against "willful killing" colors how equality for women should be regarded (or constitutes a value that here competes with full equality). Thus, someone's comprehensive view can lead her to a different understanding of the full content of a constitutional essential than she would reach if sticking to public political values alone.

A person might see some church-state issue similarly. He might, for example, suppose that if one stuck with public reasons of equality of citizenship and church-state separation, one would think they were best promoted by not having substantial aid to religious schools, despite the valuable general education those schools provide. However, thinking that religious salvation is of overarching importance for human life and that religious schools help promote that, he might decide that substantial public aid is, on balance, desirable, and represents a better understanding of religious liberty and church-state separation.

In more typical cases people will not try to figure out what political values alone would indicate; their judgments will be infused by their transcendent perspectives. Since Rawls's restrictions reach *how one votes* and *whether* one publicly advocates a particular outcome, rather than just *how* one advocates an outcome one decides to support on other grounds, his constraint to public reasons is significant, requir-

---

43. *Id.* at 243 n.32.

ing people who wish to comply with an ideal of citizenship to support positions they think are indicated by a balance of public reasons.[44]

Rawls does not deny that people may sometimes face conflicts between their own comprehensive views and public reasons, and that they must resolve these conflicts in light of their own comprehensive views. Thus, he might treat my examples as simply (somewhat complicated) conflicts of this sort. But I think their force goes beyond this; it calls into question the desirability of a standard of public reason that asks citizens to aim for justifications on particular issues that do not rely on comprehensive views.

C. Difficult Lines of Distinction

Serious technical problems arise out of difficult lines of distinction drawn by Rawls. Examination of these lines raises further doubt about the theoretical defensibility of his position and about the feasibility of its practical application.

One distinction in Rawls's schema is between what are constitutional essentials, on the one hand, and what are interpretations and applications on the other. Church-state examples can be troubling in this respect. A principle of "no government aid to religious organizations" might be considered an essential or an interpretation of the essentials of religious liberty and church-state separation. For ordinary purposes, this particular distinction is elusive, depending on the level of generality at which some basic right or fundamental principle is cast. But this distinction is important for Rawls in two ways. First, the essentials are deemed to be off the political agenda; people can argue about interpretations but they, mostly, accept the essentials. Second, if the subject does come up why existing essentials should remain as such, one is free to explain that one's own comprehensive view (part of the overlapping consensus) supports a political conception that includes such essentials. Yet, if the issue is interpretation, one must rely on public reasons (using one's comprehensive view only to provide supplementary reasons for a position). Thus, imagine someone whose religious view strongly indicates that government should give some support to religion. He may say, "I cannot accept this essential so I am not part of the overtopping consensus. There is an alternative I

---

44. Rawls apparently thinks it is all right for someone's *evaluation of public reasons* to be colored by one's comprehensive view, since he says that my notion that citizens might be required to "pluck out their religious convictions" does not represent his view. *Id.* at 244 n.33. What citizens are not to do on constitutional essentials and questions of basic justice is to go against the balance of public reasons as they see them.

could accept. Were it adopted I could embrace all the essentials." Or, he may say, "support is consistent with a proper view of the essential of church-state separation, but I must make this claim based only on public reasons." There is a kind of incongruity in saying that people may appropriately look to their comprehensive views to decide whether they support an existing political conception, including its constitutional essentials, but that comprehensive views must take a decidedly back seat when the details of the essentials are in controversy. If the proponent of aid may reject an essential based on a comprehensive view, why should he not be able to reject an unfavorable interpretation of an essential based on a comprehensive view?

An even more central distinction for Rawls is between constitutional essentials and basic issues of justice, on the one hand, and ordinary political issues, on the other. The first problem with this distinction for legislators and citizens involves discerning which issues are covered by constitutional essentials and which are not. Rawls manages fairly successfully to establish plausible criteria, but troublesome borderline cases will be inevitable. If abortion falls within the range of constitutional essentials, what of research on and implantation of fetal tissue and the enforcement of surrogate motherhood contracts? People may not always be sure whether an issue they discuss is an aspect of constitutional essentials or basic issues of justice, requiring reliance on public reasons.

A second, more serious, difficulty with this distinction concerns a frequent relation *between* constitutional essentials (and questions of basic justice) and other issues. Argument about constitutional essentials bears on the disposition of other issues. An issue, such as fetal research and implantation, may not be about constitutional essentials, but its discussion may involve some *arguments from* constitutional essentials, such as the appropriateness of abortion. Should *those arguments* rely only on public reason, although other arguments may employ comprehensive views? The permissibility of abortion and whether the fetus counts as a full human being are part of the constitutional essentials; these questions may be relevant to evaluation of fetal research and implantation because these practices may be more offensive, and their possible encouragement of future abortions is much more disturbing, if the fetus counts as a full human being and

abortion is not a protected right.[45] Should all arguments about encouraging abortions rely only on public reasons?

Rawls, I believe, has not yet faced the extent to which interpretation of constitutional essentials infects ordinary political argument. It
would be odd to say that you can use religious (and other comprehensive) perspectives to argue about constitutional essentials when the
essentials are not directly involved (the fetal research issue) but you
may not use such perspectives when the essentials are directly at stake
(the permissibility of abortion issue); but it would also be odd to say
that you can use any religious arguments for "nonessentials" *except
for* any argument that draws from constitutional essentials. This intermixture of issues presents a troublesome feature of Rawls's distinction
that resists easy resolution.

Even when the distinction among issues is clear and issues fit in
one category or another, without the perplexing intermixture problem, the idea that different sorts of considerations may be brought to
bear on different issues is troublesome. Legislators and citizens are
told that all sorts of reasons they may properly treat as relevant over a
wide range of political issues should be excised from their decision
making and public discussion concerning constitutional essentials and
basic issues of justice. Even if Rawls's underlying theory is otherwise
sound, it is not one whose force is intuitively obvious or compelling.
Most citizens and ordinary legislators in all branches of government
would probably find it strange that references to sources of truth for
most political issues were in some degree barred to them for a particular category of issues, not always *so easy* to identify. This difficulty
seriously compromises the practical usefulness of Rawls's distinction
among issues.

Finally, Rawls's approach requires that one decide what counts as
public reasons as compared with reliance on comprehensive reasons.
The problem about religious comprehensive views is relatively minor.
Rawls assumes that in genuine liberal democracies, citizens are not
going to accept *with near universality* any particular Christian view, or
Christianity in general, or Islam, Judaism, Hinduism, etc. Nor will

---

45. I do not have an opinion about the extent to which a conviction about abortion *should*
affect one's view of fetal research and implantation. Gregory Gelfand and Toby R. Levin claim
that opponents of abortion have no plausible basis to oppose fetal tissue research. *Fetal Tissue
Research: Legal Regulation of Human Fetal Tissue Transplantation*, 50 WASH. & LEE L. REV.
647, 649 (1993). I present the problem here as an example of a relation between "constitutional"
and "ordinary" problems that often exists. For an illuminating set of comments on the relation
of religion to bioethics more generally, see *Theology, Religious Traditions, and Bioethics*, HAS-
TINGS CTR. REP., July/August 1990 (Daniel Callahan & Courtney Campbell eds.).

they accept theism as opposed to nontheism. Thus, the exclusion of comprehensive views bars direct reference to Christian, Jewish, Islamic, theist, or atheist premises. Subtle questions arise about the status of religious stories and references to religious traditions as sources of general human or particular cultural understanding, but when they are carefully presented in the right way, such stories and references can fall within the domain of public reasons.

A more serious concern arises over nonreligious comprehensive views, particularly liberal nonreligious comprehensive views. When someone urges that the value of autonomy be respected, it may be virtually impossible for him and others to tell whether he is relying on a particular comprehensive perspective or the widely shared value of autonomy in our culture. Liberal nonreligious comprehensive perspectives are bound to "suffer less" from a principle of self-restraint than both religious views and nonreligious, nonliberal views. This difference may reasonably be thought to involve a kind of inequity.

D. Stability and Fairness

I have suggested some substantial problems with the principles of self-restraint that Rawls has proposed, and most especially with the line between ordinary political issues and issues that involve constitutional essentials and basic questions of justice. The basic arguments for his approach are ones of political stability and fairness.

Rawls has suggested, convincingly in my view, that diversity of comprehensive religious, philosophical, and moral doctrines is a normal condition of the public culture of democracy. If the followers of these various doctrines feel distrust and fear toward those of different views, that is a strong reason to settle on a political culture of common reason, at least for essentials. But suppose people hold widely differing comprehensive views in circumstances of mutual interest and approval; they trust and want to learn from each other. In such a culture, references back to comprehensive doctrines would not be particularly threatening. Whether such a culture could exist in a society *as* diverse, and *as* prone to hostility and violence as ours may be doubtful; but it is too early in the history of liberal democracy to write off that possibility for all liberal democracies. We should not suppose that the only means by which liberal democratic societies can unite in stability and mutual respect among citizens is by coalescing around a relatively full version of constitutional essentials and an ideal of common reason; some broader acceptance of the relevance of comprehensive views in all political dialogue is a reasonable alternative. If citizens want to be able to bring their own comprehensive views to bear on all political issues and are quite willing to accept the price that others will do so as well, there is no unfairness in comprehensive perspectives being employed to resolve the boundaries of some constitutional essentials.

CONCLUSION

Rawls's idea of public reason has some powerfully attractive features. The fundamental notion that public political dialogue will be carried forward largely in a discourse that is the shared possession of citizens bears resemblance to present understandings in the United States and has much to recommend it. The precise outlines of Rawls's proposal reflect his own acute sensitivity to the convictions of those who accept widely diverse religious and other comprehensive views, as well as to the claims of common threads of justice and reason. Were he less sensitive to one claim or the other, his resolution would be more simplistic than it is.

For reasons I have partly suggested here, I see serious problems with aspects of Rawls's account. First, I am skeptical that any single resolution is appropriate for liberal democracies in general; a principle of public reason needs to be attentive to time and place. Second, I think the demands of public reason depend to a greater degree on someone's specific place in society than Rawls acknowledges, although he helpfully recognizes some important differences, as between judges and legislators. Third, I believe much less depends on the kind of issue involved than Rawls supposes; "constitutional essentials" do not have a fundamentally different status from ordinary political issues. Fourth, I am persuaded that the distinction between grounds of judgment and public justification needs still more focused attention than Rawls gives it.[46] Although various details in Rawls's account may prove incomplete or unpersuasive, he provides strong arguments both for substantial constraints of public reason and for allowing some scope for comprehensive views in political judgment. No plausible position on these issues can afford to disregard those arguments.

---

46. I develop a position along the lines I have indicated in GREENAWALT, *supra* note *.

Contexts of the Political Role of Religion: Civil Society and Culture†

DAVID HOLLENBACH, S.J.*

In this Article I want to suggest that recent discussions of the role of religious arguments in debates about public policy sometimes rest on oversimplified presuppositions. The discussion often seems polarized between two opposing camps. On one side are those who hold that it is appropriate for citizens to appeal directly to their religious convictions in advocating positions on policy issues. On the other side are those who hold that appeal to religious beliefs is always inappropriate in a liberal democratic society. Though many of the participants in this discussion hold views that are considerably more complex than either of these two positions, I think that stating the alternatives this way can help illuminate certain aspects of the debate that I want to call into question. Formulating the matter this way points to a tendency to assume that the relation of religion and politics is governed by just two variables — religious convictions on the one hand and recommendations about policy or law on the other. It further suggests that the question of whether religion should have a public role in society is identical with the question of whether either the advocacy or the justification of public policies should be based directly on religious convictions.

I will argue that the debate needs to be framed in a different way.

---

† This Article recasts and develops ideas presented in several of my previous writings. *See generally* David Hollenbach, S.J., *Afterword: A Community of Freedom*, *in* CATHOLICISM AND LIBERALISM: CONTRIBUTIONS TO AMERICAN PUBLIC PHILOSOPHY (R. Bruce Douglass & David Hollenbach, S.J., eds., 1994); David Hollenbach, S.J., *Fundamental Theology and the Christian Moral Life*, *in* FAITHFUL WITNESS: FOUNDATIONS OF THEOLOGY FOR TODAY'S CHURCH 167-84 (Leo J. O'Donovan and T. Howland Sanks eds., 1989); David Hollenbach, S.J., *Religion and Political Life*, 52 THEOLOGICAL STUD. 87 (1991).

* Margaret O'Brien Flatley Professor of Catholic Theology, Boston College.

877

Religion is not simply a set of convictions that one should or should not invoke in political debate. It is a considerably more dynamic and multidimensional reality than the term "convictions" might suggest. And political debate is not simply argument about whether to adopt or reject certain policies. There are, of course, many ways to demarcate the sphere to which the term "political" can be applied. But if we agree that the political sphere encompasses all human activities that occur in the public life of society, then it is surely a mistake to limit it to the policy decisions reached in legislative, executive, or judicial fora. The *res publica* is much larger than the sphere of government. It includes all those communities and institutions that form the rich fabric of civil society. It also includes all those public forms of discourse, conversation, and argument that constitute a culture.

Therefore, this Article will argue that we need to frame the question of the relation of religion to public life in a way that goes beyond discussion of the direct impact of religious convictions on policy choices. Religious faiths and traditions have perhaps their most important influence on government, law, and policy-formation in an indirect way. The impact of religion on politics understood as the sphere of governmental activity is mediated through its influence on the multiple communities and institutions of civil society and on the public self-understanding of a society called culture. Parts I and II of this Article will consider these public influences of religion. Part III will then address the more specific question of how religious beliefs ought to be related to public policy in light of the discussion of the first two parts.

I. Civil Society and the Meaning of "Public"

One prominent version of the argument for insulating the political process from the influence of religious convictions harks back to the dismaying historical record of the Catholic and Protestant communities during the sixteenth and seventeenth century wars of religion. This history is seen as a precedent for what is likely to happen today if religious communities decide to press their beliefs as guides for governmental decision making or public policy. Sometimes this historical appeal is augmented by references to "moral majorities" insisting on prayer in public schools, the teaching of "creation science" in these schools, and the imposition of religious convictions about abortion on those who do not share these convictions. Occasionally, such arguments are reinforced by references to the contemporary Islamic world and to nations where attempts have been made to base both constitutional and penal law on the *Shari'ah*. These historical and contemporary examples lead to considerable fear of what are seen as the likely results of public, political activity by religious

878

communities.

At the root of these fears of a public role for religion is what John Rawls calls "the fact of pluralism."[1] The regimes of modern democratic societies evolved historically as a way of responding to the diversity of conceptions of the meaning and purpose of life. This diversity is most evident in religious disagreement. But there is also a deep pluralism in philosophical conceptions of how to live a good life. Rawls says that this religious and philosophical pluralism

> is not a mere historical condition that will soon pass away; it is, I believe, a permanent feature of the public culture of modern democracies. Under the political and social conditions secured by the basic rights and liberties historically associated with these regimes, the diversity of views will persist and may increase.[2]

Under these conditions, the "common sense political sociology of democratic societies" tells us that agreement on a single conception of the good life among all citizens is unattainable. Such agreement could be maintained "only by the oppressive use of state power."[3]

Rawls accurately points to the deep disputes that exist about the meaning of the good life in our society. But for him there is no way to resolve these disputes. Therefore he argues that the fact of pluralism demands that in politics we must deal with disagreements about the comprehensive good of human life by what he calls "the method of avoidance."[4] This method demands that in political life "we try, so far as we can, neither to assert nor to deny any religious, philosophical or moral views, or their associated philosophical accounts of truth and the status of values."[5] Avoidance of such basic questions is necessary in politics, Rawls thinks, if we are to have any chance of achieving consensus. "We simply apply the principle of toleration to philosophy itself" when debating the basic political and economic institutions that will structure social life.[6] Each man or woman must be free to hold his or her view of what the fully good life really is. But these comprehensive views of the good life must remain the private convictions of individuals. "In applying the principles of toleration to philosophy itself it is left to citizens individually to resolve for

---

1. John Rawls, *The Idea of an Overlapping Consensus*, 7 OXFORD J. LEGAL STUD. 1, 4 (1987).

2. *Id.*

3. *Id.*; *see also id.* at 4 n.7 (giving a sketch of the presuppositions of this "common sense sociology").

4. *Id.* at 12.

5. *Id.* at 12-13.

6. *Id.* at 13.

879

themselves the questions of religion, philosophy and morals in accordance with the views they freely affirm."[7] Or as Richard Rorty puts it, religious and philosophical convictions should be exempt from coercion in a liberal society under one condition: that such convictions "be reserved for private life."[8] Argument about the common good is also to be avoided in debates about more specific public policies. Liberal democracy aims at "disengaging discussions of such questions from discussions of social policy."[9] This privatization of "thick" visions of the good is not only a sociologically given fact; it is a moral constraint on political activity.

This analysis assumes that the presence of religious or comprehensive philosophical views of the good in public life inevitably leads to conflict. It further presupposes that the public sphere is identical with the domain governed by the coercive power of the state. From these presuppositions taken together, it follows that religious influence in public is identified with the coercive enforcement of the religious or philosophical convictions of whatever group is strong enough to gain control of government. Since this is clearly an unacceptable outcome, the alternative proposed is the privatization of religion.

I fully agree that the coercive imposition of religious beliefs is morally unacceptable, as do the vast majority of religious believers in the West today. The privatization of religion is not, however, the only alternative to such a coercive outcome if religion appears in public. Another approach to the question is founded on a more capacious understanding of what public life is, or at least could be. Drawing on my own Roman Catholic tradition, I want to outline such an approach. Reflection on the role played by a broader vision of the meaning of public life outside the United States may reinforce its plausibility.

For liberal thinkers like Rawls, the discussion of the role of religion in public life is framed by certain presuppositions about the institutions that structure social interaction. Their emphasis is on the state and the market as the principal domains in which social existence unfolds. At the same time, different forms of liberalism embody diverse attitudes of suspicion toward the institutions of government and the market. Libertarian liberals regard the state as the principal threat to human freedom and dignity. Consequently their aim is to keep governmental intervention minimal. Those with

---

7. *Id.* at 15.
8. Richard Rorty, *The Priority of Democracy to Philosophy, in* THE VIRGINIA STATUTE FOR RELIGIOUS FREEDOM: ITS EVOLUTION AND CONSEQUENCES IN AMERICAN HISTORY 257, 263 (Merrill D. Peterson & Robert Vaughan eds., 1988).
9. *Id.*

880

a more social democratic orientation fear that the market is the principal threat and seek to limit its impact on individuals through governmental regulation and the institutions of the modern welfare state. In both of these ways of thinking, the paradigm that shapes analysis envisions individual persons confronting the "megastructures"[10] of either government or the market economy. The relation of private and public spheres is pictured as the relation of isolated individuals to large, anonymous, and impersonal institutional structures. Public activities are those conducted within the spheres of government and/or the market. The public sphere thus becomes the area of human life ruled either by the power of government or by the constraints of the marketplace. The defense of freedom, therefore, is viewed as the effort to secure a zone of action that is protected from governmental power or market determinism. This zone is private. To use Rawls' terms, it is the domain in which individuals can live "in accordance with the views they freely affirm."

A number of recent analyses of the contemporary social problematic have raised worrisome questions about the adequacy of this bipolar disjunction of human activity into public and private spheres. For example, Alan Wolfe's important book, *Whose Keeper? Social Science and Moral Obligation*, has argued that the increasingly dense and interdependent spheres of politics and the marketplace threaten to overwhelm whatever remnants of private freedom still exist in advanced modern societies.[11] The sphere of freedom is "increasingly squeezed from two directions" — from the one side by the bureaucracy of the administrative state and from the other by powerful determinisms of markets linked together in an increasingly global network.[12] Wolfe argues that if the freedom promised by modernity is to survive under the conditions that prevail in advanced societies in the late twentieth century, we need a counterweight to this pressure from the state and the market. Solitary, private individuals cannot provide this counterweight. "We need civil society — families, communities, friendship networks, solidaristic workplace

---

10. PETER L. BERGER & RICHARD J. NEUHAUS, TO EMPOWER PEOPLE: THE ROLE OF MEDIATING STRUCTURES IN PUBLIC POLICY 2 (1977) (using the term megastructures to refer primarily to the large bureaucracies of government).
11. ALAN WOLFE, WHOSE KEEPER? SOCIAL SCIENCE AND MORAL OBLIGATION 20 (1989).
12. *Id.*

ties, voluntarism, spontaneous groups and movements — not to re-ject, but to complete the project of modernity."[13] He further main-tains that the bonds of solidarity associated with closer and more intimate relations in the realm regarded as private by liberal theory "requires that we extend the 'inward' moral rules of civil society 'outward' to the realm of nonintimate and distant social relations."[14] Wolfe does not mean to suggest that the moral framework that guides political or economic life can be based directly on the values of family life, the bonds of close friendships, or the solidarity of groups that share common religious or philosophical convictions. But he does argue that the bonds of community need to be given much greater *public* space than the sharp split of the political from the private advocated by Rawls and Rorty. The strong communal links found in the diverse groups of civil society must have greater public presence. Otherwise individuals will experience further diminishment of their freedom and power in the face of the growing complexity of distant governmental and economic megastructures. The image of human life as divided between a public sector of governments and markets and a private sector of individual autonomous freedom is unrealistic. Freedom will not flourish or perhaps even survive unless it enjoys greater presence and support in public. We need a more complex and differentiated picture of the world in which we really live.

This is not the place to rehearse the sociological arguments on which Wolfe bases his conclusions. For the purposes of this Article, I will presume that Wolfe's analysis has revealed a significant problem in the prevailing conception of the relation of the public and private realms, and ask readers to assess my argument about the role of religion in political life in light of this presupposition.

To be even clearer about presuppositions, it will be obvious why Wolfe's analysis is congenial to one who, like myself, has been shaped by the tradition of Roman Catholic social thought. Especially since the birth of modernity, the Roman Catholic tradition has been suspicious both of social theories extolling the primacy of the state and of theories granting primacy to the market. At the same time, this tradition has rejected individualistic understandings of freedom. In fact, its rejection of an individualistic understanding of the self is the source of its suspicion of both liberal contract theories of politics and laissez-faire models of economic life. Its view of the public-pri-vate relationship is not bipolar, with the megastructures of the state or the market defining the public sphere and the autonomous free-dom of the individual defining the private sphere. Rather it proposes

---

13. *Id.*
14. *Id.*

a model of social life that is richer and institutionally more pluralistic than that of standard liberal theory.

Modern Catholic teaching, to be sure, is strongly concerned about the fate of individuals. For example, Pope John XXIII stated that "[t]he cardinal point of this teaching [of the Catholic church] is that individual men are necessarily the foundation, cause, and end of all social institutions."[15] But the Pope immediately added: "We are referring to human beings, insofar as they are social by nature."[16] Human dignity and worth is never achieved in solitude, nor is the protection of this dignity simply a matter of insulating individuals from the costs (and denying them the opportunities) that attend interaction with others. Rather, the task of protecting human dignity and freedom is a task of protecting the quality of the relationships among persons in such a way that freedom and dignity can be realized. In this sense, there is no strictly private sphere. Because humans are relational beings whose identity, worth, and dignity is attained in interaction with others, human flourishing is always public or social. Thus Catholic social thought emphasizes the multiple forms of human relationship and community in which persons are formed and nurtured. Social space is not occupied only by the large institutions of government and market on the one hand and individuals on the other. This is evident in the tradition's stress on the importance of securing the well-being of "intermediary" institutions such as families and voluntary associations, and it is a key to understanding how we can envision a form of political life that is communal without being statist. It also suggests a way of envisioning the public role of religion that avoids the charge that whenever religion becomes public, religious coercion will be the result.

The distinction between the public sphere and the domain of governmental power was central to the discussion of the relation of the Catholic church to democracy that took place in the middle decades of this century and that bore fruit at the Second Vatican Council. In the 1950s, Jacques Maritain and John Courtney Murray argued for the compatibility of a public role for religion with the institutions of democracy by reaffirming the distinction between society and the state. Society is composed of a rich and overlapping set of human communities such as families, neighborhoods, churches, labor unions,

---

15. Pope John XXIII, *Mater et Magistra, in* THE GOSPEL OF PEACE AND JUSTICE: CATHOLIC SOCIAL TEACHING SINCE POPE JOHN 143, 190 ¶ 219 (Joseph Gremillion ed., 1976).
16. *Id.*

883

corporations, professional associations, credit unions, cooperatives, universities, and a host of other associations. These communities are not private but public. Especially when they are small or of intermediate size, they enable persons to come together in ways that can be vividly experienced. The bonds of communal solidarity formed in them enable persons to act together, empowering them to shape some of the contours of public life and its larger social institutions such as the state and the economy. In a democratic society, government does not rule but rather serves the social "body" animated by the activity of these intermediate communities. Pope Pius XI formulated the matter in what came to be known as the principle of subsidiarity: government "ought of its very nature to furnish help [*subsidium*] to the members of the body social, and never destroy and absorb them."[17] Or in Maritain's words, "[t]he State is inferior to the body politic as a whole, and is at the service of the body politic as a whole."[18] The body politic or civil society is the primary locus in which human solidarity is realized.

In the writings of Maritain and Murray, the society-state distinction is at the root of their affirmation both of religious freedom and of constitutional democracy. It is the basis for their firm opposition to all forms of totalitarianism, state absolutism, or religious coercion. The writ of government does not reach as far as the full scope of the public life of society. The defense of the free exercise of religion and the defense of the existence and freedom of the communities that make up civil society are directly linked to each other. Thus the right to religious freedom and the rights to public association and public expression are inseparable. As Murray concluded,

> [T]he personal or corporate free exercise of religion, as a human and civil right, is evidently cognate with other more general human and civil rights — with the freedom of corporate bodies and institutions within society, based on the principle of subsidiary function; with the general freedom of association for peaceful purposes, based on the social nature of man; with the general freedom of speech and of the press, based on the nature of political society.[19]

This argument reveals one way that a Catholic understanding of the institutions of democracy and the human rights that undergird them presents a challenge to those forms of liberalism concerned exclusively or primarily with the defense of the freedom of individuals to act as they please in a zone of privacy. The presupposition about the basis of democracy is not the sovereign autonomy of the individual. Participation in public life and the exercise of freedom in society

---

17. Pope Pius XI, *Quadragesimo Anno* ¶ 79 (National Catholic Welfare Conference, Washington, D.C., 1942).
18. JACQUES MARITAIN. MAN AND THE STATE 13 (1951).
19. JOHN C. MURRAY. THE PROBLEM OF RELIGIOUS FREEDOM 26-27 (1965).

884

depend on the strength of the communal institutions that give persons a measure of real power to shape their environment, including their political environment. As John Coleman has argued, this kind of commitment to democracy rests on "a presumptive rule about where real vitality exists in society" — in the diverse and overlapping communities that make up civil society.[20] The public and the social, therefore, are not to be identified with the sphere of government. Social practices and institutions can be truly public even though not under governmental control. Thus churches, just like all the other associations that make up civil society, must be both free from domination by the state and free to act and express themselves in public.

The importance of civil society as a public sphere that is not dominated by the state was powerfully illustrated by the way the recent collapse of communism was so rapidly brought about in Central and Eastern Europe. The power of the dissident workers and intellectuals of the "velvet revolutions" of 1989 grew out of their success in creating the solidarity of a genuine civil society, not out of direct seizure of state power or out of the barrel of a gun. What were initially extragovernmental bonds of community at Gdansk's shipyards and Prague's Magic Lantern Theater empowered men and women to effect a stunning transformation of supposedly untransformable totalitarian regimes. In the words of Bronislaw Geremek, Speaker of the Parliament in Poland, the emergence of civil society out from under the dominant apparatus of the state became possible when

> Dissidents engaged in their own peculiar type of mental resistance, which typically began with a refusal to participate in falsehood, grew into a desire to bear loud witness to one's own views and conscience, and then finally drove one to political action . . . . The idea of civil society — even one that avoids overtly political activities in favor of education, the exchange of information and opinion, or the protection of the basic interests of particular groups — has enormous antitotalitarian potential.[21]

The public role of religion in the revolutions of 1989 varied from one country to another, and the churches were surely not the sole agents of this transformation.[22] But there is no question that the commitment of the churches was crucial in sustaining the many overlapping communities that make up civil society — communities

---

20. JOHN A. COLEMAN, AN AMERICAN STRATEGIC THEOLOGY 226 (1982).
21. Bronislaw Geremek, *Civil Society and the Present Age, in* THE IDEA OF CIVIL SOCIETY 11, 11-12 (1992).
22. NEILS NEILSEN, REVOLUTIONS IN EASTERN EUROPE: THE RELIGIOUS ROOTS (1991).

that refused to submit to state domination. Adam Michnik, a Jewish intellectual and Solidarity activist, described the Catholic church's role in Poland this way several years before the revolution occurred:

> The problem faced by Polish society is that civil society doesn't exist. Society is not recognized as capable of organizing itself to defend its particular interests and points of view . . . . [T]he present totalitarian system insists that every person is State property. The Church's view is that every person is a child of God, to whom God has granted natural liberty . . . . . It follows from this that in Poland and other communist countries religion is the natural antidote to the totalitarian claims of the State authorities.[23]

In East Germany, Czechoslovakia, Hungary, as well as in Poland, the recovery of freedom, the revival of civil society, and the public presence of the churches (Catholic, Orthodox, and Protestant) were closely connected phenomena.

These recent events in Central and Eastern Europe may seem irrelevant to an effort to clarify the proper public role for religion in the United States. There is an analogy, however, between the destruction of civil society under Communist rule in the Eastern bloc and the weakening of civil society in the West that Alan Wolfe fears is occurring. To be sure, if the alternatives to present patterns of American society are communist totalitarianism, the authoritarian oligopolies that have been dominant in much of Latin American history, or the one-party states common in Africa, there can be no doubt of the superiority of the democratic institutions of the North Atlantic. But the choice we face in the politics of the United States today is not one between democracy and authoritarianism. Rather it is at least a plausible hypothesis that here the more immediate threat to a civil society capable of nurturing freedom is not an authoritarian state, but the dominance of the market and the market's instrumental rationality over increasingly large domains of social and cultural life.

If this hypothesis is correct, the liberal instinct to treat all activities that are not directly governmental as private is not only sociologically inaccurate but politically dangerous. Among the many "nongovernmental organizations" that have a crucial role to play in sustaining the vision of public life that is crucial to democracy are the churches. This is so for two reasons.

First, the assertion of the right to religious freedom was a key factor in the movement that brought about modern constitutional democracy. This right was not only "cognate" with the full range of the human rights of a democratic society, as John Courtney Murray maintained in the passage cited above. It was one of the principal causal forces, socially embodied in religious communities, that led to

---

23. Erica Blair, *Towards a Civil Society: Hopes for Polish Democracy*, TIMES LITERARY SUPPLEMENT, Feb. 19, 1988, at 199 (interview with Adam Michnik).

886

the rise of modern democracy. For this reason, the freedom of the many diverse communities of solidarity in civil society and the freedom of the churches rise or fall together. An effort to privatize religion, whether in practice or in theory, therefore, is "cognate" with an effort to privatize every human activity that is not properly part of the exercise of state power. A successful move in this direction will leave the individual human being alone and defenseless in the face of the encroaching power of the market. It will also leave the individual unable to form those bonds of solidarity that are essential if government is to be made to function in a way that keeps the market in its place. An active, public role for religion, therefore, would seem to be one of the preconditions of a vibrant democratic life.

Second, the churches possess unique resources that can contribute to the strengthening of other communities of solidarity in civil society. Ideas about love of neighbor — about commitment to the well being of other persons — are present in all religious traditions. The meaning of this love and commitment, of course, is interpreted in different ways in different religious traditions. But all these traditions possess resources that can serve as an antidote to the idea that a democratic society can be successfully constructed on self-interest or, as Rawls would have it, mutual disinterest. More than this is needed if any public realm is to thrive or even survive in the face of market pressures and the logic of instrumental market-rationality.

Further, sociologist Robert Wuthnow's empirical survey-research has shown that people's spiritual concerns translate into active efforts to respond to the needs of their neighbors only when these concerns are lived out in the context of a publicly visible and active religious community. Wuthnow's data suggest that understanding religion or spirituality as a purely private affair between an individual and his or her god, without the mediation of a religious community with a public presence in society, has little effect on believers' responses to their neighbors:

> I interpret these results to mean that religious inclinations make very little difference unless one becomes involved in some kind of organized religious community. Once you are involved in such a community, then a higher level of piety may be associated with putting yourself out to help the needy. But if you are not involved in some kind of religious organization, then a higher level of piety seems unlikely to generate charitable efforts toward the poor or disadvantaged.[24]

---

24. ROBERT WUTHNOW, ACTS OF COMPASSION: CARING FOR OTHERS AND HELPING OURSELVES 156 (1991).

The increasing privatization of religion as not only separated from the sphere of government but as a purely personal affair independent of any organized religious community thus seems to threaten to undermine any positive effects religion can have in society. Wuthnow concludes that "[i]f religious values have been an inducement for people to care for their neighbors historically, then the spread of individualism within modern religion is likely to have a dampening effect on charitable behavior."[25]

Wuthnow's conclusion on the link between religious convictions and charitable behavior is echoed in the preliminary findings of a study of political activism in the United States being conducted by my colleague Kay Schlozman in cooperation with Sidney Verba, Henry Brady, and Norman Nie. One of the conclusions of this study is that participation in church activities appears to sow seeds of political activism. "Churches are 'incubators' for tomorrow's political activists."[26] Engagement in church-related activity teaches organizational skills that are readily transferable to politics. In addition, the study has found that "contrary to political scientists' assumptions, personal gain played a minimal role in causing people to become active. The responses [of those surveyed in the study] indicate that psychological rewards, such as commitment to community and 'doing one's civic duty,' are primary motivators."[27] This suggests that an active presence of religious communities in the public life of the country can strengthen rather than threaten democracy. If one fears that public life is becoming increasingly fragile, the prescription would appear to be more church involvement in public life, not less.

II. CULTURE, PUBLIC DISCOURSE, AND THE COMMON GOOD

Such a proposal for strengthening the bonds of communal solidarity in society, of course, can be expected to be greeted with suspicion by those who fear that it will lead to coerced cohesion. This is particularly so when the proposal includes the suggestion that religious communities should play a more public role in shaping the bonds that link persons together in public. There is apprehension that this will lead churches to act simply as special interest groups, seeking power to press their own agendas through the political process. Thus the position being advocated here must respond to the legitimate question of whether any strong vision of solidarity can be pursued beyond the boundaries of small and intermediate sized communities

---

25. *Id.*
26. See the report on these preliminary findings in John Ombletts, *Activists Get Their Training at Church*, B.C. BIWEEKLY, Mar. 26, 1992, at 5.
27. *Id.*

888

without sacrificing intellectual freedom and social pluralism. Thinkers like Rawls are very skeptical that this is possible. Because he thinks the effort to achieve some consensus about the common good of the larger society is necessarily futile, he concludes that we will have to get along with a politics that is neutral on competing conceptions of the good life. Thus all talk about the "comprehensive" human good should be restricted to the private sphere.

The experience of history shows that these fears are not products of fantasy. Societies characterized by strong bonds of solidarity have sometimes been oppressive of freedom. Religious groups have sometimes used state power to stifle pluralism. And it will surely be difficult to find an alternative to the commitment to neutrality about the meaning of the human good in a nation and a world where awareness of diversity is growing.

Nevertheless, if the argument of the previous part of this Article is correct, paying exclusive attention to the dangers of closed communities and the difficulty of establishing dialogue among the subgroups in a pluralistic society also poses a serious threat to the quality of social life. We would do better, as Robin Lovin has suggested, to try to develop an understanding of the relationship of religion and politics "in terms that fit the discourse to which we aspire, rather than the distortions that we fear."[28]

Lovin points out that theories which support efforts to insulate the political domain from any religious influence are "curiously abstract" and do not describe well the role religious beliefs actually play in the lives of many people.[29] In fact, people's conceptions of how life ought to be lived — including religious conceptions — are routinely introduced into public discourse. Even those who profess to support public neutrality on the meaning of the good life find it difficult to live up to their ideal in practice. The interconnection of our lives and the common institutions we share make the demand that we be silent on the deeper issues of how we should live together itself seem like a form of repression. Is it really possible to maintain that fundamental convictions about the meaning of the good life can be regarded as private preferences rather than matters of high public importance in a society like ours? At a historical moment when persons are increasingly interdependent on each other and in which their fates are so obviously worked out in a natural environment they

---

28. Robin W. Lovin, *Perry, Naturalism, and Religion in Public*, 63 TUL. L. REV. 1517, 1539 (1989).
29. *Id.* at 1518-19.

share in common, a negative answer to this question seems almost obvious.

We also need to question whether the method proposed for securing justice in public life by those who argue for political neutrality on the full human good can actually succeed. According to Rawls and others who follow his lead, we can publicly debate about the means that will satisfy the maximum number of private preferences about the good. But they maintain that the terms of this debate must be set by "public reason." This is defined as "the shared methods of, and the public knowledge available to, common sense, and the procedures and conclusions of science when these are not controversial."[30] Rawls adopts this criterion for public morality because he thinks that no other standards of judgment are available in the face of contemporary philosophical and religious pluralism. Rorty goes further. For Rorty, the exclusion of religious and philosophical understandings of the good life from the public domain is desirable in itself, not just a necessary consequence of the fact of pluralism. It "helps along the disenchantment of the world. It helps make the world's inhabitants more pragmatic, more tolerant, more liberal, more receptive to the appeal of instrumental rationality."[31]

Common sense, uncontroversial science, and instrumental rationality are very shaky foundations for the civic unity of the nation. In fact, there is considerable evidence that the lack of more substantive discourse about the common good is a source of the alienation of many citizens from participation in political activity today. In an insightful book titled *Why Americans Hate Politics*, E. J. Dionne argues that this alienation can be attributed to the fact that current political discourse fails to address the real needs of communities. This failure is itself partly the result of the fact that interest-group politics is frequently incapable of even naming the social bonds that increasingly destine us to sharing either a common good or a "common bad."[32] Politics is perceived as a contest among interest groups with little or no concern for the wider society and its problems. Thus the "common sense" that shapes American public life today becomes increasingly governed by a cynical "I'll get mine" attitude. Neutrality about the good on the level of theory in this way becomes a self-fulfilling prophesy on the level of practice. A principled commitment to avoiding sustained discourse about the human good produces a downward spiral in which shared meaning, understanding, and community become even harder to achieve. It can lead to a politics that is little more than a quasi-market in preferences and power.

---

30. Rawls, *supra* note 1, at 8.
31. Rorty, *supra* note 8, at 271.
32. E. J. DIONNE, JR., WHY AMERICANS HATE POLITICS (1991).

890

Are there alternatives to political neutrality about the meaning of the good life that could generate greater social solidarity without stifling freedom and suppressing pluralism? A closer look at the historical record shows that memories of the role religion has played in generating political conflict and even violence, though accurate, are not the whole story. Other memories suggest ways of responding to Lovin's call to develop our thinking in ways that fit the discourse to which we aspire rather than the distortions we fear.

For example, the Catholic tradition provides some noteworthy evidence that discourse across the boundaries of diverse communities is both possible and potentially fruitful when it is pursued seriously. This tradition, in its better moments, has experienced considerable success in efforts to bridge the divisions that have separated it from other communities with other understandings of the good life. In the first and second centuries, the early Christian community moved from being a small Palestinian sect to active encounter with the Hellenistic and Roman worlds. In the fourth century, Augustine brought biblical faith into dialogue with Stoic and Neoplatonic thought. His efforts profoundly transformed both Christian and Graeco-Roman thought and practice. In the thirteenth century, Thomas Aquinas once again transformed Western Christianity by appropriating ideas from Aristotle that he had learned from Arab Muslims and from Jews. In the process he also transformed Aristotelian ways of thinking in fundamental ways. Not the least important of these transformations was his insistence that the political life of a people is not the highest realization of the good of which they are capable — an insight that lies at the root of constitutional theories of limited government.[33] And though the Church resisted the liberal discovery of modern freedoms through much of the modern period, liberalism has been transforming Catholicism once again through the last half of our own century. The memory of these events in social and intellectual history as well as the experience of the Catholic Church since the Second Vatican Council leads me to hope that communities holding different visions of the good life can get somewhere if they are willing to risk conversation and argument about these visions. Injecting such hope back into the public life of the United States would be a signal achievement. Today, it appears to be not only desirable but necessary.

---

33. For documentation and analysis of the medieval roots of constitutionalism and theories of limited government, see BRIAN TIERNEY, THE CRISIS OF CHURCH & STATE 1050-1300 (1964).

891

The spirit that is required for such discourse about the public good might be called intellectual solidarity — a willingness to take other persons seriously enough to engage them in conversation and debate about what they think makes life worth living, including what they think will make for the good of the polis. Such a spirit is partially the same but entirely different from an appeal to tolerance as the appropriate response to pluralism. Tolerance is a strategy of noninterference with the beliefs and life-styles of those who are different. It leads to what Rawls calls the "method of avoidance" as the appropriate way to deal with persons or traditions that are "other." The spirit of intellectual solidarity is similar to tolerance in that it recognizes and respects these differences. It does not seek to eliminate pluralism through coercion. But it differs radically from pure tolerance by seeking not avoidance but positive engagement with the other through both listening and speaking. It is rooted in a hope that understanding might replace incomprehension and that perhaps even agreement could result. And since it seeks an exchange that is a *mutual* listening and speaking, it can only develop in an atmosphere of genuine freedom. Also, because this exchange is mutual, the freedom in which it takes place is not the private freedom of an atomistic self. Where such conversation about the good life begins and develops, a *community* of freedom begins to exist. And this is itself a major part of the common good. Indeed it is this freedom in reciprocal dialogue that is one of the characteristics that distinguishes a community of solidarity from one marked by domination and repression.

What might such public discourse look like? First, it will concern visions of those human goods that are neither strictly political nor strictly economic. Broadly speaking, this is conversation and argument about the shape of the culture the participants either share because of their common traditions or could share in the future through the understanding of each other they seek to achieve. The forum for such discussion is not, in the first instance, the legislative chamber or the court of law. It is the university and all the other venues where thoughtful men and women undertake the tasks of retrieving, criticizing, and reconstructing understandings of the human good from the historical past and transmitting them to the future through education. It occurs as well wherever people bring their received historical traditions on the meaning of the good life into intelligent and critical encounter with understandings of this good held by other peoples with other traditions. It occurs, in short, wherever education about and serious inquiry into the meaning of the good life takes place.[34]

---

34. The similarity of this cultural endeavor with what Michael Perry calls "ecumenical politics" is evident. *See* MICHAEL J. PERRY, LOVE AND POWER: THE ROLE OF

This education and inquiry is at the heart of intellectual solidarity and the public life of society, and its presence (or absence) will have crucial political implications. As John Courtney Murray once noted, "[t]he great 'affair' of the commonwealth is, of course, education."[35] He was referring to education in the broadest sense: the organization of schools and their curricula, but even more to the level of critical cultural self-understanding among both the populace at large and among its elites. In both theory and practice today, this entire cultural and educational project of understanding, criticizing, and reconstructing visions of what it is to be authentically human (Rawls' "comprehensive understandings of the good") is often treated as a private affair. Murray's insistence that this project is not only *an* affair but *the* great affair of the commonwealth challenges this presupposition frontally. To the extent that moral and political theories seek to exclude the task of education and inquiry from the public forum by privatizing all full visions of the human good, they undermine the very foundations of public life.

David Tracy fears that this process of undermining is already far advanced. He has argued that the privatization of these cultural concerns threatens so to instrumentalize and technicize public life as to destroy it altogether.[36] In much contemporary liberal thought, both theoretical and popular, tolerance of diversity has become the premier cultural lesson to be learned. But if a community that prizes both solidarity and freedom is to be realized, engagement with the other, and not just tolerance, is required. In such engagement, a person's own deeper convictions are set forward as potential contributions to public understanding and simultaneously placed at risk of revision.

RELIGION AND MORALITY IN AMERICAN POLITICS (1991). I am not fully clear, however, about the degree to which Perry sees this dialogue about the good life (what he calls "the question of the truly, fully human") as occurring principally in the sphere of politics conceived as the domain of government and law, or whether he has a broader understanding of politics in mind, i.e., the political as all that occurs in the public life of society. If the latter, his understanding of ecumenical politics is very similar to what I am here calling cultural conversation and argument. There is also a similarity between what I am proposing and Alasdair MacIntyre's understanding of a "tradition of enquiry," though MacIntyre is virtually silent about how this understanding is related to the domain of government, law, and the political sphere narrowly conceived. *See* ALASDAIR C. MACINTYRE, WHOSE JUSTICE? WHICH RATIONALITY? 349-403 (1988).

35. JOHN C. MURRAY, WE HOLD THESE TRUTHS: CATHOLIC REFLECTIONS ON THE AMERICAN PROPOSITION 9 (1960).

36. *See* David Tracy, *Catholic Classics in American Liberal Culture, in* CATHOLICISM AND LIBERALISM: CONTRIBUTIONS TO AMERICAN PUBLIC PHILOSOPHY 196-213 (R. Bruce Douglass & David Hollenbach eds., 1994).

Seen in this light, it is no accident that the arts, the theater, and philosophy played a central role in breaking the grip of totalitarianism in Czechoslovakia.[37] Though the task of sustaining and strengthening public life in the United States today is without doubt very different than in Central Europe, the importance of genuinely public conversation and argument about what forms of human living are truly good is equally important here. As will be discussed below, such discussion occurs partly in our discourse about the institutions of political and economic life and also in discussion of more particular policies in both spheres. The quality of these political and economic debates, however, will be dependent on the depth of the larger cultural exchange. The achievement of solidarity in the political and economic domains is dependent on the strengthening of free discourse in the cultural sphere — intellectual solidarity in a cultural community of freedom.

Second, the possibility and necessity of such a truly free cultural exchange has direct implications for the role of religion in public life. We must begin to entertain the possibility of conversation about the visions of the human good held by diverse religious communities and of intellectual engagement with them. Such a suggestion will be beyond the pale if one views all religious convictions as a rigid set of beliefs held on nonrational grounds. In this view, religion is very likely to be a source of division, conflict, and even violence when it appears in public. It is inherently uncivil.

The Catholic tradition and many Protestant traditions as well, however, reject the notion that religious faith must be irrational and, therefore, uncivil. Faith and understanding go hand in hand in both the Catholic and Calvinist views of the matter. They are not adversarial but reciprocally illuminating. As Tracy puts it, Catholic social thought seeks to correlate arguments drawn from the distinctive religious symbols of Christianity with arguments based on shared public experience.[38] This effort at correlation moves back and forth on a two-way street. It rests on a conviction that the classical symbols and doctrines of Christianity can uncover meaning in personal and social existence that common sense and uncontroversial science fail to see. So it invites those outside the church to place their self-understanding at risk by what Tracy calls conversation with such "classics." At the same time, the believer's self-understanding is also placed at risk

---

37. *See* VÁCLAV HAVEL, DISTURBING THE PEACE: A CONVERSATION WITH KAREL HVIZDALA (Paul Wilson trans., 1990). Rorty has taken a dim view of the role of philosophy in the Czechoslovakian revolution, or at least of the idea that Havel and other Charter '77 leaders could take "metaphysical" claims for the basis of public morality at face value. See Rorty's review of several books by Jan Patočka, the philosopher who was the symbolic leader of Charter '77, Richard Rorty, *The Seer of Prague*, NEW REPUBLIC, July 1, 1991, at 35-40.

38. *See* Tracy, *supra* note 36.

894

because it can be challenged to development or even fundamental change by dialogue with the other — whether this be a secular agnostic, a Christian from another tradition, or a Jew, Muslim, or Buddhist.

Intellectual solidarity has religious implications. It means that in a community of freedom, religion should be represented in the discourse about the goods of public life. It equally means that religious believers must enter this discourse prepared to listen as well as to speak, to learn from what they hear, and, if necessary, to change as a result of what they have learned. The experience of the Catholic Church over the last half century has been a vivid example of such listening, learning, and changing through its encounter with liberalism. This process must and will continue as Catholics develop their self-understanding into the future. Is it too much to expect that the experience of transformation through engagement rather than tolerance could strengthen America's public philosophy in an analogous way?[39]

Serious dialogue is risky business. At least some religious believers have been willing to take this risk. The future of public life in our society could be considerably enhanced by the willingness of a considerably larger number of people to take this risk of cultural dialogue, whether they begin as fundamentalists convinced of their certitudes or agnostics convinced of their doubts. Our society needs more imagination about how to deal creatively with the problems it faces than instrumental rationality can provide. In Martha Nussbaum's words, a vision of the full human good arises from

> [M]yths and stories from many times and places, stories explaining to both friends and strangers what it is to be human rather than something else. The account is the outcome of a process of self-interpretation and self-clarification that makes use of the story-telling imagination far more than the scientific intellect.[40]

Religious traditions and communities are among the principal bearers of these imaginative sources for our understanding of the human good. They can evoke not only private self-understanding but public vision as well. Both believers and unbelievers alike have reason to risk considering what contribution religious traditions might make to our understanding of the public good. For a society to try to

---

39. *See* PERRY, *supra* note 34; *see also* Lovin, *supra* note 28, at 1517-39. Both Perry's earlier work and Lovin's theological reflection on it are discussed in my *Religion and Political Life*, 52 THEOLOGICAL STUD. 87 (1991).

40. Martha Nussbaum, *Aristotelian Social Democracy*, *in* LIBERALISM AND THE GOOD 203, 217 (R. Bruce Douglass et al. eds., 1990).

exclude religious narratives and symbols from public life simply because they are identified with religion would be to impoverish itself intellectually and culturally. This would deprive society of one of its most important resources for a more publicly shared cultural self-understanding. Religious communities make perhaps their most important contribution to public life through this contribution to the formation of culture. If they seek to make this contribution through a dialogue of mutual listening and speaking with others, it will be fully congruent with the life of a free society.

III. RELIGION AND PUBLIC POLICY, MORE NARROWLY CONSIDERED

These perspectives on the role of religion in sustaining civil society and forming culture provide a context for considering the more pointed question of the relation of religious belief to the political sphere more narrowly conceived. What role ought belief to play in the decisions of those who draft legislation, reach judicial decisions, administer the domestic and foreign affairs of the nation, or exercise the responsibilities of citizenship (minimally through the vote)? This is the question that has been central in the recent debate about the political role of religion among legal scholars and political philosophers, and it is an important and entirely legitimate one. But the perspectives outlined in this Article may shed some new light on how to go about addressing this issue.

The presupposition of those who would place stringent limits on appealing to religious belief in the formulation of law and public policy is that there is a sharp discontinuity between a community of religious believers and the larger body of public society. They see a similar discontinuity between religious reasons for particular policy choices and publicly accessible reasons for such choices. In Kent Greenawalt's analysis, religious belief is not accessible to public reason because it is deeply rooted in the personal experience of the believer. It is the experience of the believer that confirms religious truth for him or her. Thus other persons who do not share the same experiences have no way to assess the truth of the beliefs involved. Because there is "no interpersonal way in which the weight of personal experience is to be assessed," there is no interpersonal way to assess the truth of the religious beliefs grounded in such experience.[41] Though Greenawalt rejects the idea that religion is a purely private or idiosyncratic affair, the presence of subjective experience in religious belief means that, in the end, its truth cannot be publicly assessed. This Article has argued that these presuppositions ought to

---

41. Kent Greenawalt, *Religious Convictions and Political Choice: Some Further Thoughts*, 39 DEPAUL L. REV. 1019, 1031 (1990).

896

be questioned. Though religious belief is doubtless confirmed and supported by personal experience, so is the insight into the beauty of a great work of literature, music, or sculpture. In the domain of the aesthetic, judgments of value are not publicly assessable by the criteria of common sense and uncontroversial science, but that does not make them purely subjective. We can and do make judgments about the relative merits of novels, poems, and paintings. The loss of the ability to make such judgments in a particular society is a sign of decadence and decline in its culture. Religious understandings of the human good play an important role in shaping the culture of civil society. To regard religious convictions as beyond the reach of any public assessment is to deny the possibility of the kind of dialogue within a pluralistic society advocated here. Similarly, religious communities are constituent parts of civil society, and efforts to confine their activities to a zone of privacy will weaken civil society in dangerous ways.

The framework for considering the place of religious belief in the formulation of public policy thus shifts from a discussion of the role of private communities and convictions in the shaping of political life to a discussion of the proper role of the many public communities of civil society and the diverse public traditions within a culture in reaching decisions about policy in a pluralistic society. Framed this way, the proper role of religious convictions in the advocacy of particular political choices is the same as the role of convictions that are not religious. Persons or groups should not face political disability or disenfranchisement simply because their political views are rooted in religious traditions and beliefs.

At the same time, it has been argued here that it would be a serious mistake for religious communities to operate in public simply as interest groups seeking to enforce their views through state power. How is it possible to affirm that religious communities can legitimately operate in the political sphere just like nonreligious communities do, and yet to reject the idea that they can rightly function like interest groups playing the game of majoritarian politics? The answer to this question depends on clarifying the *manner in which* believers or churches move from their faith convictions to their conclusions about policy.

The issue of how churches should make this move is itself partly a religious and theological one. Certain religious traditions hold that the *Bible*, other normative scriptures, or some form of church authority can provide direct guidance for decisions about public policy.

897

In this view, for at least some areas of public life, conclusions about public policy or law are directly entailed by religious convictions with no intermediary steps in the argument. For example, some conservative evangelical or fundamentalist Christians draw policy conclusions about the rights of homosexuals or about prayer in public schools directly from the *Bible*, while Mennonites conclude that a pacifist rejection of all war is an immediate consequence of the teachings of Jesus. Some more conservative Catholics regard the legal banning of abortion as similarly entailed by the moral teachings of the pope and the Catholic bishops. From what has been said above about the need for believers to enter into dialogue with others in society as they develop their vision of the larger meaning of the social good and its consequences for policy, it is evident that I do not accept this understanding of the relation between religious belief and policy conclusions as immediate and direct. Roman Catholic thought, like much of Protestant thought as well, maintains that religious belief must be complemented by the careful use of human reasoning, both philosophical and social scientific, in the effort to reach decisions about policy that are both religiously and humanly adequate. In Tracy's terms, when Christians advocate public policies, convictions rooted in the *Bible* and Christian tradition must be brought into mutually critical correlation with understandings based on human experience and reasoned reflection on this experience. Such a stance reflects a religious and theological perspective that views faith and reason as complementary to each other, not as opposed or fundamentally bifurcated from each other.

This theological stance is not shared by all Christians. For example, some Christians hold that human reason is so corrupted by the fall that it is an unreliable guide for both religion and morality, and that culture is so distorted by sin that it should be simply opposed, not regarded as a dialogue partner. Therefore it can be asked whether the dialogic framework for the relation of religious convictions and public policy is really compatible with full participation by all religious groups in the shaping of public life. David Smolin has raised such an objection to Michael Perry's argument that religious convictions are properly admitted to the debate about policy if these convictions are open to revision through dialogue with those who do not share them, but that convictions that are taken as fixed and irreformable should be excluded from this debate. Smolin concludes that "Perry has used his own vision of good religion as the standard for admission to political and legal debate."[42] Perry's standard excludes "theologically conservative theists, including various Protestant Christians (evangelicals, fundamentalists, and pentecostals) and

---

42. David M. Smolin, *Regulating Religious and Cultural Conflict in a*

traditionalists (Roman Catholics, Anglicans, and Lutherans). Those excluded, moreover, include the religious groups most active in trying to displace the cultural hegemony of America's highly secularized elites."[43]

In his contribution to this Symposium, Perry has acknowledged the force of Smolin's complaint. He now agrees that his former argument for the inclusion of some religious convictions in the public debate and for the exclusion of others rests on theological/epistemological views that are widely contested in American society. Perry's most recent position is that because these views are contested, they ought not to be excluded from the actual public debate where this contest takes place. He proposes that his disagreement with conservative Protestants and traditionalist Catholics ought to be part of the public debate, not excluded from it. He would conduct this argument in public on properly religious and theological grounds, not exclude it from the public sphere. In an ironic way, Perry now wants to admit *all* religious-moral convictions to the public square for the same reason that Rawls and others want to exclude them: because they are controverted. Perry thus proposes that engagement with religious and philosophical difference be carried to its full conclusion — public debate should include debate that is properly theological. Perry would argue with Smolin, and in this argument try to show that Smolin's views rest on bad theology and bad epistemology.

> [I]t is one thing to say to a David Smolin, "Although your arguments, no less than mine, may serve as a (sole) basis for political choice, this is why I reject your arguments and think others should too." It is another thing to say, "I don't even have to try to meet your arguments on the merits, because, unlike mine, they may not serve as a basis for political choice."[44]

I am in fundamental agreement with the thrust of Perry's response to Smolin's critique. There should be no religious tests for entry into public debate in a democratic society. But it can be questioned whether the real differences between Perry and Smolin, which are religious and theological, are best dealt with in arguments about quite precise issues that are up for decision in the spheres of law and public policy. As Kent Greenawalt has observed, there is reason for

---

Postmodern America: A Response to Professor Perry, 76 Iowa L. Rev. 1067, 1076-77 (1991).

43. *Id.* at 1077-78.

44. Michael J. Perry, *Religious Morality and Political Choice: Further Thoughts—And Second Thoughts—On Love and Power,* 30 San Diego L. Rev. 703, 717-18 (1993).

899

skepticism about "the promise of religious perspectives being trans-formed in what is primarily political debate."[45] For example, I do not think it would be helpful for two judges, one a liberal Catholic and the other a conservative Protestant, to launch into epistemologi-cal and theological reasoning to explain why their responses to a piece of legislation regarding abortion are different. These theologi-cal and epistemological differences are better dealt with in the dis-cussions that take place in the sphere I have called cultural, not that of the political sphere conceived narrowly as the judiciary or legisla-ture. This cultural domain is fully public, and participation in it should be open to all comers. The work of the legislature and the courts, however, depends on the preexistence of some consensus in civil society and culture, and lawmakers must rely on this consensus if their activity is to be in any sense democratic. For the legislature or the courts to undertake the settlement of controverted religious or philosophical differences would border dangerously close to a form of political absolutism, even totalitarianism.

The arguments that Perry wants to have with Smolin about theol-ogy and religious epistemology should be vigorous and public. Simi-larly, serious contributions by the churches to public conversation and argument about our cultural understanding of the meaning of human life should be encouraged, not discouraged. It will be pre-cisely through the development and refinement of such understand-ing in our culture that a stronger consensus about the goods to be pursued in politics will be generated. To the extent that this larger cultural dialogue is in some measure successful, the reasons offered by believers for their more specific decisions about policy will be-come more publicly accessible in society at large.

Although the domains of government and policy-formation are not generally the appropriate ones in which to argue controverted theo-logical and philosophical issues, it is nevertheless neither possible nor desirable to construct an airtight barrier between politics and cul-ture. In general, public policy should reflect the cultural consensus about the social good that is present among the people. But at times, urgent questions of law and politics raise new questions about the cultural consensus that already exists. This was clearly the case dur-ing the civil rights movement of the 1960s. Discriminatory laws and policies were themselves the problem that had to be addressed, and religious leaders such as Martin Luther King did not hesitate to seek to overcome the racist history of American culture by advocating political and legal change directly. In the civil rights movement, ar-gument about the larger cultural vision of the human good was stim-ulated by debate about specific policies. This seems to me a fully

---

45. Greenawalt, *supra* note 41, at 1034.

legitimate example of religious engagement in the sphere of policy. Similar examples, in my view, are the United States Catholic bishops' recent pastoral letters on war and peace and on economic justice. These raised fundamental questions about the values of American society and culture in the context of addressing the more detailed questions of policy regarding nuclear strategy, unemployment, and poverty.

Thus religious contributions to policy debates need not always wait until a larger cultural consensus is achieved. Rather, public discourse between religious communities and the larger society will move back and forth between larger cultural questions of value and meaning on the one hand and more specific policy questions on the other. The more general understandings of the human good present in the culture and the more specific questions to be addressed in policy and law will mutually illuminate each other, both for religious communities and for the larger society as well. In this way, a genuine public conversation about the social good might be generated. An attempt to keep religious communities and convictions entirely separated from matters of policy will silence this conversation, especially at moments when it is most urgently needed.

Only when such conversation occurs does a free society or a community of freedom really exist. Religious arguments have a proper place in this conversation. And their presence should be governed by the conditions necessary for all genuine conversation and mutual inquiry: pursuit of the truth and respect for the other in an atmosphere of freedom. Such conditions, rather than neatly drawn lines or high walls of separation, should determine the proper role of religious belief in a pluralistic and democratic society.

901

Toward a Critical Theory of Justice

Contemporary radical criticisms of the liberal paradigm of justice carry less weight than they might because they fail to offer a positive alternative framework for reasoning about justice. Some authors do indeed offer principles of justice or images of the just society which they claim will help justify a political practice aiming to alter fundamentally the basic institutions, especially the economic institutions, of our society.[1] Such efforts, however, lack grounding in a critically oriented framework of reasoning about justice. Lacking such grounding, proposals for radical egalitarian or socialist conceptions of justice constitute little more in the way of an alternative positive theory of justice than do mere criticisms of the dominant framework.

Because his is the most comprehensive theory to date, most radical criticisms of the liberal framework focus on Rawls, although Nozick's work has received increasing attention from Marxist and socialist critics.[2] Two of the criticisms which have been leveled at Rawls's theory can provide, in my view, a start for developing an alternative framework for thinking about questions of justice. Both appear in Robert Paul Wolff's essay on Rawls's theory of justice, though others have made similar points.

Wolff's major substantive criticism of Rawls is that his theory abstracts from institutional relations of power and production. This abstraction issues in a theory, he claims, which can handle questions of justice only as questions of the distribution of social goods whose origin is neither accounted for nor justified. A better theory of justice, he suggests, would focus on the relations within which social goods arise.[3]

Wolff also levels a logical criticism at Rawls. His project of deriving substantive moral principles from formal principles of practical rationality Wolff regards as admirable, but impossible. As Rawls's theory proceeds, he must introduce an increasing number of substantive conditions into the premises. The utilization of these substantive premises makes his theory more a reflection of some contemporary moral prejudices than a validation of them.[4]

Milton Fisk makes the same general point perhaps more strongly. The contract theories claim to derive substantive principles of justice from the premises of a "state of nature" which includes only elements of the human condition independent of particular historical conditions. This poses a dilemma for the theorist. On the one hand, he or she must make the starting point full enough to generate substantive principles. On the other hand, if the theory claims universal validity and applicability for its principles, it must avoid building into the premises factors derived from a particular socio-historical configuration. Fisk argues that neither Rawls nor any other contract theorist has succeeded in avoiding this second horn of the dilemma. For that reason he claims Rawls's theory, like the liberal theories which precede it, serves primarily an analytical function as systematizing the principles of a given social order rather than the critical function of determining the rationally appropriate idea of justice.[5]

This paper explores and develops each of these criticisms of traditional frameworks for theorizing about justice more completely. I argue that formulation of questions of justice exclusively in distributive terms tends toward conceptual confusion and fails to be basic enough. I also argue that the sort of criticism of traditional theories of justice that Fisk outlines leaves us with the apparently impossible task of developing a theory which can make universalistic claims without abandoning or disguising the historical embeddedness of its origins and application.

To solve both these problems with traditional theories of justice, I offer some suggestions for an alternative framework for theorizing about justice. To outline a theory of justice, I develop certain elements of the communicative ethics which Habermas has proposed. In particular, I take up his unelaborated suggestion that the ideal speech situation, which he argues any act of speaking presupposes, expresses the ideal of justice. I argue that the ideal speech situation offers the potential foundation for a framework of theorizing about justice which focuses not primarily on distribution, but on more fundamental questions of institutional relations and domination. I argue, further, that the application of the ideal speech situation to particular social configurations constitutes a means for solving the problem of how to construct an objective and critical conception of justice which does not merely reflect actual social circumstances at the same time that it remains historically specific.

1

Since Adam Smith, almost every theory of social justice has focused primarily on questions of how social benefits should be allocated among members of the society. Insofar as it entails a theory of justice, utilitarianism is a paradigm of this distributive focus. Utilitarian methodology calls for treating all values as greater or lesser "bundles" of goods and comparing alternative distributions of bundles.

Contemporary criticisms of classical utilitarian theory as ignoring the most important questions of justice—merit, desert, rights, and so forth—may be apt. Most contemporary critics of utilitarianism, however, continue to formulate the question of justice primarily as a question of distribution. Nicholas Rescher, for example, entitles his theory simply *Distributive Justice*.[6] W. G. Runciman, to take another example, defines the problem of justice as "the problem of arriving at an ethical criterion by reference to which the distribution of social goods in societies may be assessed."[7] Rawls defines a conception of justice as "providing in the first instance a standard whereby the distributive aspects of the basic structure of society are to be assessed."[8]

The distributive paradigm of questioning about justice so dominates philosophical thinking that even critics of the traditional liberal framework continue to formulate the focus of justice in exclusively distributive terms. David Miller, for example, takes the position that liberal conceptions of justice tend to reflect the prevailing social relations, and himself argues for a more egalitarian conception of justice than traditional theories propose. Yet he defines questions of social justice exclusively as distributive questions, without examining the appropriateness of this focus.[9] Kai Nielsen, to take another example, develops a conception of radical egalitarian justice in solely distributive terms.[10] Moreover, most writers who deal with the question of a socialist conception of justice, assume that the primary difference between such a socialist conception and more traditional liberal conceptions is their mode of distributing social goods.[11]

A distributive focus on theorizing about justice is so much a part of our moral conceptualization that it does not appear possible to have any other. To find such another focus we must look back to the ancient conception of justice, in particular that enunciated in the Platonic dialogues. For the ancients, justice refers to the whole of virtue insofar as it concerns relations with others.[12] For Plato the question of justice does not concern primarily the proper distribution of social benefits and burdens. Rather, justice concerns first the organization of the community as a whole. We develop a conception of justice by constructing a vision of the organization of social positions and relations which will produce a harmonious and cooperative whole.[13]

I do not wish to adopt the Platonic conception of justice, for there is much in it that is inappropriate for us, or indeed positively pernicious. I will argue, however, that a theory of justice which takes as its primary question the structural and institutional relations of the society in its totality is better than one which focuses exclusively or primarily on questions of distribution. There are, in particular, two objections to the distributive orientation. First, formulation of many apt questions of justice in distributive terms tends to render them conceptually confused. Second, a distributive orientation tends to focus on the evaluation of the effects of given institutional forms and relations, instead of evaluating the institutional structures themselves.

Questions about the principles and procedures according to which a society ought to distribute the material benefits of social production obviously constitute crucial questions of social justice. By no means all questions most theorists would admit as questions of justice fall into that class, however. They also ask questions about the rights and liberties a society ought to protect for its members, the structure of power and decision-making, and so on. Here are some examples of such questions of justice that are not distributive in any immediate sense: Is a division between mental and manual labor just? Is it just to raise taxes without the mandate of a popular referendum? Is marriage just?

True to the utilitarian tradition, most modern theories of justice answer questions like these in terms of the relative quantity of benefits that accrue to persons. They conceptualize questions of rights, liberties, the justice of institutionalized positions, decision-making procedures, relations of authority, and so on, as questions of the proper distribution of bundles of non-material goods. Such distributively oriented treatment of questions of rights, liberties, power, and so on, however, tends to obscure the meaning of those concepts. I shall concentrate on the examples of rights and power.

Rawls, for one, takes the subject of justice to be "the way in which the major social institutions distribute fundamental rights and duties,"[14] and such a distributive understanding of rights is by no means uncommon. There is no problem in the notion of having a right to a distributive share of a certain good, and indeed many rights a conception of justice might articulate have this character. Confusion arises, however, if we talk of distributing the rights themselves.

What does it mean, for example, to "distribute" the right to free speech, or the right to trial by a jury of one's peers, or countless other rights that a liberal society takes for granted? We can conceive of a non-liberal society in which only some classes of persons are granted these rights while others are not, but this does not mean that some have a certain "amount" or "portion" of the right while others do not. Altering the situation so that everyone has these rights, moreover, does not entail that the formerly privileged group gives over some of its right of free speech or trial by jury to the rest of society's members, on analogy with a redistribution of income. In general, talk of "distributing" rights obscures their meaning as expressing rules of social and political practices, not all of which are distribution practices.

Talk of distribution of power within society is perhaps the most common way political theories wrongly construe questions of social justice in distributive terms. Democratic arrangements are frequently held to entail an equal distribution of power, while more hierarchical arrangements are defined by an unequal distribution of power. The conceptual confusion here may ultimately lie in an equivocation on the term "equality." Equality in the distribution of goods refers to sameness of quantity or value, whereas equality in relations of power and powerlessness means something like "peership."[15]

Discussion of power as some kind of "stock" which can be distributed obscures the fact that power, unlike wealth, for example, does not exist except through social relations. Having social power means standing in relation with others such that one can control their actions or the conditions of their actions. One can have a plot of land without being related to anyone else, but having the power to levy rent on it essentially entails specific relation to others and a whole supporting set of institutions. It is thus misleading to conceptualize relations of power on analogy with the distribution of an amount of goods. If the social relations of power change in such a way that a person or group gains autonomy, this does not mean that some quantity of power has been redistributed. It means, rather, that a relation of power has been eliminated.[16]

This criticism that a distributively oriented theory of justice distorts the meaning of important social and political concepts, however, does not reach to the core of the problem with distributively oriented theories. The main criticism of a distributively oriented theory of justice is that it tends to focus on patterns of distribution without even bringing into direct theoretical focus the structure of the institutional relations and the movement of social processes which bring this pattern of distribution about.

One can direct toward distributively oriented theories of justice a criticism analogous to that which Marx levels at the classical economists. Marx takes the economists to task for focusing their theorizing upon patterns and relations of distribution and largely ignoring their foundation in processes and relations of production. In Marx's view, the mode and relations of production determine the mode, process and outcome of distribution.[17]

As already noted, Wolff in a similar fashion criticizes Rawls for not taking production explicitly into account. Wolff's criticism appears rather metaphorical, however, for it is not clear what it means for a theory of justice to focus on "production." I suggest a more general understanding of those relations of the social fabric that a distributively oriented theory tends to ignore. Since a distributively oriented theory focuses on how given social goods and social positions are to be distributed among persons, it neglects to ask about the justice of the social processes and institutional relations that bring these positions and goods into being.

To illustrate this point we can take up once again the question of how a theory of justice should deal with questions of power. One might respond to the earlier argument against treating power distributively by noting that when social theorists talk about the distribution of power they really refer to the distribution of social positions that carry with them relations of power. Focusing on the distribution of positions of power among persons in the society, however, ignores the more fundamental questions of the nature and origin of those power positions. Discussion of power in distributive terms tends to focus on individual bearers and exercisers of power. While any adequate political theory must discuss the way individuals wield power, an adequate understanding of power requires as well a more structural analysis of the institutional relations which create positions that give some persons the ability to control, influence or direct the lives or actions of others. Discussion of power in distributive terms, precisely because it focuses on individual units, obscures the phenomenon of domination. Domination is a structural property of social relations considered as a system, which social actors draw upon in their exercise of power and which structures they reinforce by doing so.[18] Domination refers to the forms of social organization that make it possible for members of one group or groups systematically and repeatedly to exercise power over members of other groups, and confer privileges on some groups that others do not have. Distributively oriented theories do not have a framework comprehensive enough to gain a perspective on such basic social structures, much less evaluate their justice.

Hugo Bedau has pointed out that Rawls is nearly unique among modern theorists of justice in defining the object of justice as the basic structure of society.[19] It might be thought that for this reason Rawls ought to be excepted from my claim that modern theories of justice are distributively oriented. In the passage earlier referred to, however, Rawls explicitly says that justice concerns the way in which the basic structure, or major social institutions, "distribute fundamental rights, duties and determine the division of advantages from social cooperation."[20] Rawls intends his concern with basic structure to contrast not with a distributive orientation toward questions of justice, but with those theories that concern principles for evaluating particular actions or practices within a society. The basic structure of society refers to the most general rules to govern the overall distribution of benefits and burdens in the whole society, which he suggests may not apply to particular associations or actions.[21]

Like nearly all other modern theories of justice, then, Rawls's approach avoids asking about the justice of specific institutional structures themselves, along with the relations of power, exploitation and dependency they can produce. Several writers have argued, for example, that Rawls fails to focus on the institutional relations which underlie economic classes, and fails to justify his assumption that class inequality is inevitable.[22] In his theory Rawls implicitly assumes many institutions as given, moreover, such as competitive markets, political bureaucracies, and monogamous heterosexual families, without ever raising questions about whether the positions and relations these institutions entail are just.

It might be useful to contrast this point with an apparently similar one that Nozick makes. Nozick criticizes Rawls's theory of justice for focusing only on patterns of end-state distribution, ignoring the processes that bring about these end-states, as well as the entitlements and holdings from which persons begin.[23] Nozick here develops an appropriate criticism of distributively oriented theories, or what he calls end-state theories. But his own entitlement approach remains distributive itself insofar as it takes as the primary question of justice the rules followed in the allocation of social goods. In fact, perhaps even more than the end-state theory it criticizes, the entitlement theory ignores the questions of the justice of the institutional structures and relations within which the processes of distribution take place.

In sum, distributively oriented theories conceptualize questions of justice, whether of particular actions or practices, or of the pattern of rights and inequalities of a whole society, primarily as questions concerning the fair allocation of social goods, including non-material goods, among individuals. The approach advocated here, on the other hand, focuses on the structures of social organization that allow some individuals to have power over others, on the structure of decision making within and among institutions, and on the definition of social positions themselves. I am not arguing, of course, that questions of distribution are not important to a theory of justice, only that these questions of institutional structure should be considered first.

In section 2, I interpret Habermas's notion of the ideal speech situation as embodying a conception of justice which focuses evaluation primarily on this level of social structure and institutional relations. Section 3 shows among other things that a major reason that many theories of justice tend to ignore questions about basic forms of social organization is that they lack the historically specific focus that can bring such forms into view. I will argue in section 4 that a particular application of the ideal speech situation in a theory of justice yields such specificity.

2

One of Habermas's most central concerns has been to lay the philosophical foundation for an expanded conception of rationality that applies to normative claims as well as facts. The positivist spirit appropriately spurned traditional efforts to ground normative reason in a theological or metaphysical basis. In so doing, however, the positivist spirit we inherit abandoned entirely the project of providing the rational ground to normative discourse. Thus since norms have been judged to lack an objective basis comparable to that given to scientific reason, moral and political discourse has been reduced either to technical reason or the expressions of preference. In several works Habermas discusses the implications this dominance of technical reason over political life has for the continuance of contemporary forms of domination. He suggests that emancipatory interests can be expressed only if appeals to normative ideals regain a place in public discourse.[24] Thus the concern to give a rational foundation to normative discourse is not merely theoretical, but practical as well.

Habermas claims we can find the foundations of all rationality, both normative and non-normative, in the conditions of the possibility of communication which underlie and are presupposed by any speech act. He provides a theory of what he calls "universal pragmatics" to elaborate these conditions. I shall not summarize that theory here, but only touch enough of its outlines to indicate the place of the ideal speech situation in it.[25]

Any act of speaking which aims to be understood, according to Habermas, implicitly involves four validity claims. The speaker makes a claim to (1) comprehensibility, that the speech itself makes sense in terms of the grammar and syntax of the speakers; (2) truth, that the asserted relation to the world made by the speech is true; (3) truthfulness, that the speaker himself or herself speaks sincerely and does not deceive or hide his or her motives, feeling, interests, and so forth; (4) rightness, that in speaking the speaker acts in accordance with intersubjectively recognized norms that apply in this situation.[26]

In situations of ongoing interaction when persons understand each other and act on projects together in harmony, these four validity claims remain entirely implicit. Any one of them is, however, open to challenge, at which point they become explicit. A challenge obliges the speaker to make good on the claims. One can make good on claims to comprehensibility and truthfulness by appropriate actions. One makes good on claims to truth and rightness, on the other hand, only by entering another level of discourse which calls the claims explicitly into question and in which reasoned justification must be offered for them. The possibility of entering such argumentative discourse, Habermas claims, lies behind any act of speaking insofar as it aims to be understood. It is a condition for the possibility of such speaking.

Discourse takes place within the normative context Habermas describes as the ideal speech situation. This describes the formal conditions of a community of speakers engaged in discourse in which they have removed themselves from the immediacy of action in order to test a claim. The ideal speech situation expresses those conditions of interaction necessary for participants in such a discussion to reach a rationally motivated consensus. In a rationally motivated consensus the participants assent to a conclusion solely on the grounds that it is most reasonable.

Habermas states three conditions which must be met in the ideal speech situation:[27] (1) All those standing in the speaking situation have the same opportunity to speak and to criticize the speeches of others, and there are no limits on the content of speeches; (2) all participants must have the same opportunity to express their attitudes, feelings, intentions, interests and motives; all have the equal opportunity, that is, to require recognition of their individuality; (3) all the participants have the equal right to give commands to the others and to require others to justify themselves in terms of mutually recognized norms and rules of interaction.

Since the ideal speech situation abstracts from all contents of social interaction other than speech, and from all interests other than that of arriving at consensus in discussion, it is necessarily unrealizable.[28] As emptied of all material content and reference to material needs, it is a pure, formal ideal.

As such a formal ideal, however, it actually underlies communication as a universal condition. Insofar as any act of speaking aims at being understood and accepted, it anticipates the ideal speech situation as the condition for achieving understanding and acceptance. We would never try to achieve understanding unless we implicitly grasped the conditions required for achieving it. Thus even though the ideal speech situation is unrealizable, it has a real influence on interaction, as the motive of our attempts to achieve understanding.[29]

In this way Habermas intends to ground normative reason in the conditions of actual speaking life. Communication itself depends on the implicit understanding of a situation of interaction guided by norms that participants in discourse appeal to and abide by in order to guarantee the objectivity and freedom of their consensus.[30] These norms that define the ideal speech situation, according to Habermas, embody the universal ideals of truth, freedom and justice.

The ideal speech situation represents the idea of justice as a structure of institutionalized relations that are free from domination. The attainment of a rationally motivated consensus requires that the organization of interaction contains relations of equality, mutual recognition of the individuality of each, and reciprocity. Structures of domination create conflicts of interest that prevent commitment to consensus. These structures also prevent individuals from knowing their real interests, or expressing them even if they know them.[31] To the degree that such structural asymmetries exist, an interaction situation declines from the ideal of justice.

It is impossible to miss the similarities between the ideal speech situation and Rawls's notion of the original position. Both notions are purely hypothetical and formal, abstracting from all historical contingencies, and from all particular social circumstances. Nothing occurs in either situation except the making of proposals, and in each case a decision is reached only when there is unanimous consent. The conditions of each decision-making situation require freedom of expression, relations of equality among the participants, and the absence of coercion or the threat of coercion. Inasmuch as both Rawls and Habermas derive their respective reasoning situations from the Kantian notion of a community of ends, the similarity between the two ideas should come as no surprise.[32]

While the ideal speech situation and the original position are thus formally similar, they diverge considerably in their intent and implications, as well as the place each holds in a theory of justice. The original position and the reasoning that takes place within it are essentially individualistic, which Rawls finds to be a particular virtue of his conception.[33] He interprets the process of choosing principles as a bargaining game in which individuals all reason privately in terms of their own interests. The veil of ignorance insures that the interests of all the individuals will be the same, but the point of view from which they reason is nevertheless individual. Persons in the original position do not acknowledge the point of view of others, nor that they have a common point of view. In conformity with the bargaining game model, the process of selecting principles in the original position appears to preclude discussion or interaction among the participants. Each reasons in ignorance of what the others reason, knowing only that they all will reason in their own interests. To ensure that the individuals in the original position have as little contact as possible, Rawls even suggests that we imagine a courier mediating between them, collecting proposals, announcing them, and informing the persons when they have come to agreement.[34]

By contrast, interaction and the necessity of acknowledging the perspectives of others are paramount in the notion of the ideal speech situation. It expresses the constraints not of private reasoning but of discussion in which participants acknowledge a mutually shared aim. The norms of the ideal speech situation all refer to a reciprocal relation of recognition. All have the right to claim upon others that they take account of their needs and interests, and all have the obligation to do so for the others; no difference of power or inequality of position prevents these rights and obligations from being enacted. The ideal speech situation is more social than the original position, expressing a totalized community the individuals acknowledge among themselves without suppressing their individuality.

This difference accounts for the orientation toward questions of justice that I claim arises from each. Because of its individualistic bargaining game model, the reasoning that goes on in the original position must be distributively oriented, concerning how best to allocate social goods among the individuals. The form of the original position does not allow for a more general perspective. The primary orientation of a theory of justice based on the ideal speech situation, on the other hand, is on the structure of authority and power, the rules of decision making and control, and so on. The ideal speech situation does not merely express the conditions of reasoning about justice, but expresses an ideal of what justice itself *is,* namely, a social structure in which none exercise basic and unreciprocated power over others. Such an ideal does not concern distribution primarily, but the broad structure and content of social positions and their relations with each other. While the theory of justice Rawls articulates takes freedom from domination as an important condition for the situation in which principles are chosen, this concern does not enter the principles themselves.[35]

I have suggested, then, that the ideal speech situation can direct a theory of justice to focus its questioning on forms of social organization and relations of domination. It is important to note, however, that the ideal speech situation does not itself constitute a standard or set of principles by which actual social arrangements ought to be evaluated. The ideal speech situation expresses the ideal of justice in a purely formal way that abstracts from all particular social and historical content. As I will argue in the next section, it is not possible to have a substantive conception of justice which lacks historical specificity. Thus, as the final section will show, the ideal speech situation must be applied within concretely specified circumstances before it yields a substantive set of evaluative principles of justice.

3

Philosophers generally stipulate that a conception of justice should be held independently of particular social or historical circumstances, or practices, as a necessary condition for objectivity. In the effort to achieve this universality and objectivity, most modern philosophical accounts seek correct normative principles of social life by adopting a strategy of deriving such principles from a hypothetical starting point. Whether called the state of nature, the original position, the moral point of view, the ideal observer, and so on, this hypothetical starting point purportedly escapes the specificity of actual historical circumstances. The starting point aims to remove all natural and social contingency from human life, leaving only its formal and universal elements. Then political theorists can claim to derive the correct conception of the just social order from this universal and formal starting point.

As we have seen, however, Fisk and Wolff point out that each account smuggles into the starting point substantive premises derived more or less directly from the theorist's social circumstances. The theory of the just social order which emerges, then, merely reflects in idealized and systematized form the actual structure of the society in which the theorist dwells.

Thus many writers argue that classical liberalism makes substantive assumptions about human nature (for example, that human beings are essentially acquisitive) which reflect the particular needs of an emergent bourgeois and capitalist social order.[36]

Analogous arguments have been made about Rawls's theory to the effect that it merely reflects and legitimates the existing social system and methods of dealing with inequalities in a period of welfare state capitalism. Some of Rawls's assumptions reflect circumstances peculiar to contemporary individuals. For example, according to Wolff, the assumption that each individual has a "rational plan of life," even though he or she does not know what it is, reflects the particular perspective of the middle-class career-oriented person in advanced industrial society.[37] More generally, the principles of justice that Rawls has persons in the original position choose do seem to mirror nicely the ruling principles of the welfare state which must mitigate the inequality "naturally" generated by the capitalist economy in order to keep consumption up and to foster commitment to the legitimacy of the system.[38]

This presents us with a dilemma. If one cannot derive a substantive conception of justice from a formal starting point alone, then it appears inevitable that substantive theories must have substantive premises derived from particular social circumstances. Theories do not err in introducing substantive premises into the starting point, since this is logically necessary if they are to arrive at substantive conclusions. Rather, the error lies in presenting these substantive premises as ahistorical and thus claiming that the substantive conception applies across different social and historical circumstances.

Most contemporary social theorists conclude from this that the philosophical ideal of a rationally grounded conception of justice independent of particular social circumstances is a pipe dream, and a dangerous one at that. Many Marxists, for example, argue that the search for correct, rationally grounded, universal principles of justice is illusory. Each social formation has its own normative principles which arise from and serve to reproduce the particular social relations

of that society. Juridical forms, and the principles of justice that
govern them, are specific to modes of production. Thus Allen Wood
argues, for example, that within the slave mode of production slavery
is not unjust and within the capitalist mode of production the
appropriation of surplus value is not unjust. There is, moreover, no
transhistorical conception of justice by which these social practices
can be judged unjust. There can be no "justice in itself" independent
of the particular economic forms and social relations which engender
and embody particular conceptions and principles of justice. It
follows that any claim to have a universal and objective theory of
justice is necessarily ideological; it masks as disinterested truth what
really expresses the interests and values of the dominant class.[39]

Similarly, many contemporary non-Marxist social scientists regard
with scepticism the possibility of arriving at a normative conception
of justice that is not a mere reflection of norms actually operative in a
society. For much contemporary social science norms exist only as
facts: One can give an account of the norms people actually adhere to
and follow in a society. One can show their social origins and give a
functional account of how they contribute to the maintenance of
social integration. No basis exists, however, for saying that some
norms are right while others are not.

Given the logical problem outlined above, the traditional philosophical search for a rationally grounded theory of justice appears to
be illusory. Yet this conclusion leads to undesirable consequences.
The thesis of the impossibility of a rationally grounded conception of
justice that is more than a mere reflection of actual social
circumstances implies the impossibility of rational social criticism.
To criticize a set of social circumstances, and to judge them unjust,
one should be able to take a sufficient distance from them that they no
longer appear normal or inevitable. This seems to imply that one
needs some means of transhistorical evaluation.

Marcuse has argued that the traditional appeal to normative
universals like truth, beauty, freedom and justice serves just this
critical function. The projection of universalistic ideas of what ought
to be opens up possibilities for thinking, which otherwise would be
conditioned by what actually exists. The absence of such philosophical ideals creates the one-dimensional thinking characteristic of
contemporary culture.[40]

Yet the appeal to universals is necessarily abstract. In the classical philosophical tradition while the motive for the development of an ideal conception of justice may have been critical, the outcome more often than not has been ineffectual. Reflection on the philosophic ideal of the just society has most often served as a means of turning one's back on the real social circumstances and retreating into rarified contemplation.[41]

A theory of justice is thus presented with a dilemma. It must provide a means of distancing social criticism from the concrete social conditions under evaluation. The tradition of philosophical criticism has found such a means of distancing only in an a priori formal ideal. For a conception of justice to have any substance, however, it must be anchored in the particular social circumstances in which it exists and which it purports to evaluate, and hence be limited in application only to them. So the project of a properly critical theory of justice appears to be contradictory. It must develop a conception of justice independent of particular social circumstances, and yet at the same time derive from particular circumstances and be applicable only to them. I suggest that utilization of the ideal speech situation in what Habermas calls the "model of the suppression of generalizable interests" does just this.

4

In its crucial features the ideal speech situation is strictly formal. To arrive at it we abstract from all social circumstances and institutions, as well as particular technical economic, political and cultural circumstances. The ideal speech situation abstracts out any interests speakers might have other than an interest in discursive consensus, and assumes for the speakers that all their experience and feeling is communicable. It also abstracts from the speaking situation those real material factors that require us to cut discussions short (such as having to eat, sleep, and so forth) and to acquire the means for doing so.

Only this complete formality of the ideal speech situation permits it to have a universal character. Given the correctness of the theory of communication in which it is embedded, the ideal speech situation implicitly underlies any act of speaking which aims at understanding, as a quasi-transcendental condition for that speaking. This universality provides a theory of justice with a grounding that makes it less arbitrary than some other starting points. It also can provide a critical theory of justice with its needed capacity to distance itself from any and all actual social circumstances.

There is a price for this universalizing distance, however. Because the ideal speech situation is formal and abstract, it cannot itself serve as a standard or goal of justice. The ideal speech situation offers the vision of social relations free from domination, the ideal of pure democracy and social reciprocity. It offers this as a mere vision, however; it is no more than an unreal projection that interests thought. It is too abstract to serve as a means of evaluating particular social circumstances. Nor can principles of the evaluation of a society be derived from the ideal speech situation directly. As we have already seen, it is illegitimate to derive substantive normative principles from a purely formal beginning.

To use the ideal speech situation for developing a conception of justice applicable to the evaluation of actual societies, we must introduce material premises derived from actual social circumstances. Habermas suggests a method for the introduction of such material content into the ideal speech situation in the following question:

> How would the members of a given social system, at a given stage of the development of productive forces, have collectively and bindingly interpreted their needs (and which norms would they have accepted as justified) if they could and would have decided on the organization of social intercourse through discursive will formation, with adequate knowledge of the limiting conditions and functional imperatives of the society? [42]

As he often is, Habermas is unduly abstract in this passage. As I understand it, the method of reasoning Habermas proposes here is formally similar to that proposed by Rawls for the original position. As in Rawls, in this model we are asked to reason hypothetically about how the members of society would choose the organization of their institutions if they stood in the relations that define the ideal speech situation. The model does not, however, require the veil of ignorance which Rawls must introduce in order to assure that his self-interested individuals reasoning privately will arrive at agreement. Individuals in the original position know nothing particular about themselves or the society they live in, but know only the alleged general laws of all societies and human nature. Because the choice situation for Rawls is in this way general, the principles chosen are supposed to apply to any society, whatever its particular conditions, in which the circumstances of justice obtain. We have already seen, however, how this claim to universality tends to obscure presumptions derived from the particular circumstances of our own society.

Utilization of the ideal speech situation in accordance with the above cited question, on the other hand, entails incorporating specific knowledge of the particular society one seeks to evaluate. The participants in the discussion know at least the following things about their society: They know the basic natural constraints of their location, such as climate, topography, the character and general amount of land and material resources to which they have access, and so on. They have basic demographic knowledge such as how much relative space they have and how much food can be produced relative to the given and projected population. They know the sort of problems their technology can solve and the general level of productive capacity they have at their disposal. All the above says in concrete terms that the persons here know approximately at what point their society lies on a scale between social scarcity and social abundance. As I interpret this model, moreover, the members of the discussion also know much about the culture and traditions of their particular society. They have a notion of the tastes of their artistic and decorative tradition and a set of shared symbols and stories. They know their language, the games they play, their educational practices, and so on.

In principle, in this model of reasoning about justice, the only things abstracted from real society are those conditions of domination which prevent people in real society from pressing interests that all would agree to as legitimate if they were in a situation of equality and reciprocity. This model of reasoning must be purely hypothetical, of course, since in reality material conditions and relations of domination are inextricably linked. Imagining persons with these material constraints as standing in the ideal speech situation—even though no such persons could exist—provides a means of locating the sources of domination.

Given discussion unconstrained by domination, the model has individuals choose first the principles of social organization that best serve what they judge as their collective needs and legitimate individual interests, given the material constraints under which they operate. They choose, that is, the basic rules of interaction, authority relations, and forms of decision making within and among institutions. Among the principles and rules chosen, of course, are those relating to the distribution of the benefits of social cooperation. Such principles of distribution, however, would be dependent on prior determination of institutional forms, conditions and relations of production and authority relations, as well as on the level of material abundance of which the society is capable. For without the prior knowledge of the forms of social organization, we do not know what sorts of social benefits are to be distributed, nor what sorts of social positions and interest groups there are to decide among in distributing.

The conception and principles of justice which emerge in this way from the application of the formal conditions of the ideal speech situation to the material situation of a particular society are thus quite particular. Unlike most theories of justice, this model of reasoning about justice does not call for constructing an idea of *the* just society in general. Rather, the model allows for, even requires, a multitude of conceptions of justice, each derived from the particular conditions of the society and applicable only to them.

The model thus satisfies the condition developed in the previous section, that a theory of justice recognize the historical specificity of conceptions of justice. It grants that it is not in fact possible to articulate a substantive conception of justice that applies to the evaluation of all or many societies. There may be some social circumstances, for example, where a division between mental and manual labor is not unjust, even though there are certainly some in which it is. There may be some sorts of social circumstances in which equal distribution of certain social goods is just, to take another example, but others in which it is not.

This form of reasoning about justice in effect measures a society against itself rather than measuring the society directly against an ahistorical set of principles. It can thus be seen as a way of interpreting one Marxist understanding of the meaning of normative evaluation within capitalist society. On that account, claims about justice or injustice can be made meaningfully within capitalist society by showing how the organization of that society cannot even measure up to the standard of justice it itself generates.[43] The Habermasian model cited above differs from this strategy of measuring a society against its own standards in one respect only. Application of the ideal speech situation to the conditions of, say, this particular capitalist society does not result in the conception of justice actually held by that society with its relations of domination. Rather, it reveals the standard that would be adopted in these material and cultural conditions if those relations were absent. As Marxists point out, the conception of justice actually held within social relations of domination expresses the interests of the dominant group. The conception of justice resulting from application of the ideal speech situation to particular social conditions, on the other hand, expresses the interests of all insofar as they are compatible. It thus shows the latent possibilities of the society given its historical and material conditions with the systemic sources of its conflicts of interest removed.

This process of reasoning about justice serves two purposes. Its main function is to identify sources of domination in the social arrangements of a particular society. The thought experiment discovers relations of domination in the process of setting up its starting point of reasoning. For every social relation whose justice one wishes to examine one asks whether there are aspects of it that tend to create asymmetries in the situation of discussion. The hypothetical model abstracts from them, but not from the material conditions and constraints. The second function served by the model is to project a vision of an alternative organization of that society which is free from domination.

An example might help at this point. If feminist arguments are correct, reproductive and child care arrangements in our society are a major source of the oppression of women. The model might apply here as follows. We assume that persons must be produced in the bodies of women, that infants require human milk or a very close substitute, and that children require a prolonged period of care and education. We can also assume the general level of productivity of advanced industrial society. Evaluation of relations of reproduction and care for the young may then go as follows. Assuming the above constraints, how would we as a society construct the social relations of reproduction and child rearing if all of us—women, men and children—could discuss the question under conditions of reciprocity, equality, and the absence of domination?

We can reconstruct such a discussion in which the parties would make claims that run quite counter to present social arrangements. For example, women would be likely to urge that the biological necessity of their reproductive role not put limits on their opportunities for self-actualization and social participation. Children, to take another example, would be likely to urge that the social relations of child rearing not render them entirely powerless and economically dependent. However we might argue that this hypothetical convention would deal with such claims, there is no question that discussion of these and other issues in a situation of equality would result in a vision of the social organization of reproduction and child rearing quite different from our current practices. To the degree that our actual relations of reproduction and child rearing declines from this vision, we would have an argument that they are unjust.

To summarize, utilization of the ideal speech situation in a model of reasoning about justice that applies it to the particular material and cultural situation of a given society satisfies both the requirements for a theory of justice which have been raised in this essay. First, since the ideal speech situation focuses on relations of interaction and its application reveals the sources of domination, a theory of justice that uses it focuses primarily on forms of social organization. Thus in the above example about child care arrangements, the major questions revolve around the nature of the practices relating to children, the authority relations between adults and children, and the relation of child care institutions to other institutions. Secondly, the method of applying the ideal speech situation to particular material and cultural conditions points to a theory of justice that contains an a priori universal aspect without producing a conception of justice which claims transhistorical application.[44]

Notes

1. Evan Simpson, "Socialist Justice," *Ethics* 87 (1976): 1–17; David Schweikert, "Should Rawls Be a Socialist?" *Social Theory and Practice* 5 (1978): 1–28; Kai Nielsen, "Radical Egalitarian Justice: Justice as Equality," *Social Theory and Practice* 5 (1979): 209–26.
2. See G. A. Cohen, "Robert Nozick and Wilt Chamberlain: How Patterns Preserve Liberty," in John Arthur and William Shaw, eds., *Justice and Economic Distribution* (Englewood Cliffs, NJ: Prentice-Hall, 1978), pp. 246–62.

3. Robert Paul Wolff, *Understanding Rawls* (Princeton University Press, 1977), pp. 199–208.
4. Ibid, pp. 180–85.
5. Milton Fisk, "History and Reason in Rawls' Moral Theory," in Norman Daniels, ed., *Reading Rawls* (New York: Basic Books, 1976), pp. 53–80.
6. New York: Bobbs-Merrill, 1966.
7. Runciman, "Processes, End-States and Social Justice," *Philosophical Quarterly* 28 (1978): 37.
8. Rawls, *A Theory of Justice* (Cambridge, Mass.: Harvard University Press, 1971), p. 9.
9. David Miller, *Social Justice* (Oxford: Clarendon Press, 1976).
10. Neilsen, "Radical Egalitarian Justice."
11. See, for example, Edward Nell and Onora O'Neill, "Justice Under Socialism," in James Sterba, ed. *Justice: Alternative Political Perspectives* (Belmont, CA: Wadsworth Pub. Co., 1980), pp. 211–30.
12. Aristotle, *Nichomacean Ethics,* 1130a 1–14.
13. See *Gorgias,* especially 504d– 509c. Compare Habermas's remarks on the difference between ancient and modern views of politics in "The Classical Doctrine of Politics in Relation to Social Philosophy," *Theory and Practice* (Boston: Beacon Press, 1973), especially p. 58. See also Peter T. Manicas, "Two Concepts of Justice," *Journal of Chinese Philosophy* 4 (1977): 99–121, for a comparison of the ancient and modern conceptions of justice.
14. Rawls, *A Theory of Justice,* p. 7.
15. Elizabeth Wolgast makes this sort of point in a different context in *Equality and the Rights of Women* (Ithaca: Cornell University Press, 1979), Chap. 3.
16. For accounts of the concept of power in such relational terms, see Anthony Giddens, *Current Problems in Social Theory* (Berkeley: University of California Press, 1979), pp. 91–93; Peter T. Manicas, the *Death of the State* (New York: G. P. Putnam and Sons, 1974), pp. 10–15.
17. See Capital, III (New York: International Publishers, 1967), pp. 877–84; *Introduction to the Critique of Political Economy* (New York: International Publishers, 1970), pp. 200–204. Allen Wood develops this Marxist criticism of distribution orientation specifically with reference to theory of justice. See "The Marxian Critique of Justice," *Philosophy and Public Affairs* 1 (1972), especially p. 268.
18. See Giddens, *Current Problems in Social Theory*, pp. 88–94, for a good discussion of the concept of domination.
19. Hugo Bedau, "Social Justice and Social Institutions," *Midwest Studies in Philosophy* 3 (1978): 159–75.
20. Rawls, *Theory of Justice,* p. 9.

21. Rawls, "The Basic Structure as Subject," *American Philosophical Quarterly* 14 (1977): 159–65. Bedau points out that in *A Theory of Justice* Rawls never quite specifies what he means by the basic institutions, and that in the end it appears that they are whatever is necessary and sufficient to implement the principles of justice.

22. C. B. Macpherson, "Rawls's Models of Man and Society," *Philosophy of Social Science* 3 (1973): 341–47; and Kai Nielsen, "Class and Justice," in John Arthur and William H. Shaw, eds., *Justice and Economic Distribution* (Englewood Cliffs, N.J.: Prentice-Hall, 1978), pp. 225–45.

23. *Anarchy, State and Utopia* (New York: Basic Books, 1974), chapter 7. Eric Mack makes a similar criticism of what he calls "distributional" theories in "Distribution versus Justice," *Ethics* 86 (1976): 145–53.

24. "Technology and Science as Ideology," in *Toward a Rational Society* (Boston: Beacon Press, 1970), pp. 81–122.

25. The main outlines of that theory are most systematically developed in "What Is Universal Pragmatics," in *Communication and the Evolution of Society* (Boston: Beacon Press, 1979); see also "Wahrheitstheorien," *Wirklichkeit und Reflexion zum sechizegsten Gebuststag für Walter Shutz* (Neske: Pfelligen, 1973). I am grateful to Alan Soble for making available to me an unpublished English translation of this work. See also Thomas McCarthy, *The Critical Theory of Jürgen Habermas* (Cambridge: MIT Press, 1978), Chapter 4, for an account of Habermas's theory of communication.

26. Habermas, "Wahrheitstheorien."

27. I am roughly following the formulation given in "Toward a Theory of Communicative Competence," *Inquiry* 13 (1970): 360–75. In later works Habermas articulates four conditions. I am following the formulation in "Toward a Theory of Communicative Competence" because in that essay Habermas explicitly discusses the connection of the ideal speech situation with the idea of justice.

28. Stan Van Hooft claims that the ideal speech situation is actually realizable, but I believe he has confused its realizability with its operating as a real motive in actual speaking. See "Habermas's Communicative Ethics," *Social Praxis* 4 (1976/77): 167–74.

29. Habermas, "Toward a Theory of Communicative Competence," pp. 372–73.

30. For a different but related account of how ordinary speech is guided by implicit norms, see J. Davidson Alexander, "The Natural Standard of Speech," *Cultural Hermeneutics* 3 (1976): 267–94.

31. Habermas, "Toward a Theory of Communicative Competence," p. 372.

32. Habermas himself cites Rawls's notion as an example of the modern

tendency to take procedural legitimacy as the ultimate standard of justice, a tendency his theory of universal pragmatics and theory of social evolution attempts to account for. See "Legitimation Problems of the Modern State," *Communication and the Evolution of Society*, p. 187; Van Hooft, "Habermas' Communicative Ethics," draws some comparisons of the ideal speech situation and the original position.

33. Rawls, *A Theory of Justice*, pp. 263–65.
34. Ibid., p. 139.
35. I have developed this point in more detail in another paper. See Iris M. Young, "Self-Determination as a Principle of Justice," *The Philosophical Forum* 2 (1979): 30–45.
36. One of the most influential of these arguments is that advanced by C. B. Macpherson, in *The Political Theory of Possessive Individualism* (London: Oxford University Press, 1962).
37. Wolff, *Understanding Rawls*, p. 137.
38. In "Class and Justice" Macpherson argues that Rawls's theory presupposes the institutions of welfare state capitalism.
39. Wood, "The Marxian Critique of Justice;" see also Michael Teitelman, "On the Theory of the Practice of the Theory of Justice," *Journal of Chinese Philosophy* 5 (1978): 218–47.
40. Marcuse, *One-Dimensional Man* (Boston: Beacon Press, 1964), especially chapter 8.
41. Ibid., pp. 128–43.
42. Habermas, *Legitimation Crisis* (Boston: Beacon Press, 1975), p. 113.
43. Both Wood and Teitelman, in the articles cited, tend toward a position something like this, though they remain rather more relativistic than this position should be. The position is more solidly articulated by William McBride in "The Concept of Justice in Marx, Engels, and Others," *Ethics* 85 (1975): 204–18, and Marlene Fried, "Marxism and Justice," *Journal of Philosophy* 71 (1974): 612–3.
44. I began the research for this paper while a fellow at the University of Chicago under the National Endowment for the Humanities Fellowships in Residence for College Teachers program, 1978–79. I would like to thank J. Davidson Alexander, William McBride and Peter Manicas for helpful suggestions on earlier drafts of the paper.

Iris M. Young
Department of Humanities
Worcester Polytechnic Institute

Kantian Constructivism and Reconstructivism: Rawls and Habermas in Dialogue*

Thomas McCarthy

One regrettable consequence of the split between "analytic" and "continental" philosophy in this country has been a postponement of the encounter between two of the most highly developed and differentiated political theories of our time. For more than two decades now, John Rawls and Jürgen Habermas have been traveling different paths from their common starting point in Kant's practical philosophy. Despite the differences, they have remained close enough to make their disagreements instructive. This has not gone entirely unnoticed, either in Germany, where a discussion of the relative strengths and weaknesses of the two approaches is now underway, or here.[1] There are interesting English-language discussions by theorists who work both sides of the street, including an excellent book on the subject by Kenneth Baynes.[2] But the appearance in the fall of 1992 of Habermas's *Faktizität und Geltung*—which compares with *A Theory of Justice* in architectonic complexity—and in the spring of 1993 of Rawls's *Political*

* I would like to thank Kenneth Baynes, John Deigh, Rainer Forst, Jürgen Habermas, John Rawls, Connie Rosati, and Paul Weithman for helpful discussions and comments, though none of them will agree entirely with the final outcome.

1. See, e.g., Rainer Forst, *Kontexte der Gerechtigkeit* (Frankfurt: Suhrkamp Verlag, 1994).
2. Kenneth Baynes, *The Normative Grounds of Social Criticism* (Albany: SUNY Press, 1992). See also Seyla Benhabib, *Critique, Norm, and Utopia* (New York: Columbia University Press, 1986), chap. 8; Georgia Warnke, *Justice and Interpretation* (Cambridge, Mass.: MIT Press, 1993), chaps. 3, 5, and "Rawls, Habermas, and Real Talk: Reply to Walzer," in *Hermeneutics and Critical Theory in Ethics and Politics*, ed. Michael Kelly, (Cambridge, Mass.: MIT Press, 1990), pp. 197–203. And there are theorists who engage with both Rawls and Habermas in shaping their own approaches to democratic theory, e.g., Joshua Cohen, "Deliberation and Democratic Legitimacy," in *The Good Polity*, ed. Alan Hamlin and Philip Pettit (Oxford: Basil Blackwell, 1989), pp. 17–34; and Charles Larmone, *Patterns of Moral Complexity* (Cambridge: Cambridge University Press, 1987).

Ethics 105 (October 1994): 44–63

Liberalism makes clear that the discussion has only just begun.[3] Taking these recent works as my point of departure, I will try here to move the dialogue along a bit. Assuming the reader's familiarity with at least the broad outlines of Rawls's theory of justice, I will begin in Section I by sketching the basic features of Habermas's approach to moral and political theory. Section II will then develop a line of criticism against Rawls from a Habermasian perspective. That will be followed in Section III with a line of argument against Habermas from a Rawlsian perspective. Needless to say, this dialectical exercise is not intended to end the discussion in any respect but merely to point it in a certain direction, which is elaborated upon in Section IV.

I

Habermas shifts the focus of the critique of reason from forms of transcendental subjectivity to forms of communication. Kant, moving within the horizon of individual consciousness, understood objective validity in terms of structures of *Bewusstsein überhaupt*, consciousness as such or in general. For Habermas, validity is tied to reasoned agreement concerning defeasible claims.[4] The key to communicative rationality is the appeal to reasons or grounds—the unforced force of the better argument—to gain intersubjective recognition for such claims. Correspondingly, Habermas's idea of a "discourse ethics" can be viewed as a reconstruction of Kant's idea of practical reason in terms of communicative reason.[5] Roughly speaking, it involves a procedural reformulation of the Categorical Imperative: rather than ascribing to others as valid those maxims I can will to be universal laws, I must submit them to others for purposes of discursively testing their claim to universal validity. The emphasis shifts from what *each* can will without contradiction to what *all* can agree to in rational discourse. Validity construed as rational acceptability is not something that can be certi-

---

3. Jürgen Habermas, *Faktizität und Geltung* (Frankfurt: Suhrkamp Verlag, 1992); an English translation by William Rehg will be published by MIT Press in 1995, under the title *Between Facts and Norms*. John Rawls, *A Theory of Justice* (Cambridge, Mass.: Harvard University Press, 1971), and *Political Liberalism* (New York: Columbia University Press, 1993).

4. Habermas uses "validity" as a general term covering both the truth of assertions and the rightness of norms. It is similar in this respect to Rawls's broad use of "truth" to include "moral truth." For Habermas, the general term signals his conviction that moral claims, like truth claims, can be rationally adjudicated: the objectivity of both types of claims is tied to their rational acceptability. At the same time, choosing "validity" over a broader use of "truth" signals his desire to avoid assimilating the two types of claims: the relevant kinds of warranting reasons are importantly different.

5. Jürgen Habermas, *Moral Consciousness and Communicative Action*, trans. C. Lenhardt and S. Nicholsen (Cambridge, Mass.: MIT Press, 1990). For an excellent account of discourse ethics in the context of contemporary moral theory, see William Rehg, *Insight and Solidarity* (Berkeley: University of California Press, 1994).

fied privately; it is tied to communication processes in which claims are tested argumentatively by weighing reasons pro and con.

Like Kant, Habermas distinguishes the types of practical reasoning and corresponding types of "ought" proper to questions concerning what is pragmatically expedient, ethically prudent, or morally right.[6] Calculations of rational choice furnish recommendations relevant to the pursuit of contingent purposes in the light of given preferences. When serious questions of value arise, deliberation on who one is and wants to be yields insight concerning the good life. If issues of justice are involved, fair and impartial consideration of conflicting interests is required to judge what is right or just. And like Kant and Rawls, Habermas regards questions of the last kind, rather than specifically ethical questions, to be the proper domain of theory. This is not to deny that ethical discourse is rational, or that it exhibits general structures of its own; but the progressive "disenchantment" of the world has opened the question, How should I (or one, or we) live? to the irreducible pluralism of modern life. To suppose that the questions of the good life dealt with under the rubrics of classical ethics—happiness and virtue, character and ethos, community and tradition—could be answered in general and by philosophers is no longer plausible. Questions of self-understanding and self-realization, rooted as they are in particular life histories and cultures, do not admit of general answers; prudential deliberations on the good life within the horizons of particular lifeworlds and traditions do not yield universal prescriptions. If taking modern pluralism seriously means renouncing the idea that philosophy can single out a privileged way of life or provide an answer to the question, How should I (we) live? that is valid for everyone, it does not, in Habermas's view, preclude a general theory of a narrower sort, namely, a theory of justice. Accordingly, the aim of his discourse ethics is solely to reconstruct the moral point of view from which questions of right can be fairly and impartially adjudicated.[7] As noted above, it is geared like Kant's ethics to what everyone could rationally will to be binding on everyone alike; but it shifts the frame of reference from Kant's solitary, reflecting, moral consciousness to the community of moral subjects in dialogue; and it replaces his Categorical Imperative with a procedure of practical argumentation aimed at reaching reasoned agreement among those subject to the norms in question. Moreover, by requiring that perspective taking be general and reciprocal, discourse ethics builds a moment

6. Jürgen Habermas, *Justification and Application: Remarks on Discourse Ethics*, trans. Ciaran Cronin (Cambridge, Mass.: MIT Press, 1993), esp. chaps. 1, 2, and "Translator's Introduction."

7. Thus it would have been better named "discourse morality" or "discourse justice."

of empathy or "ideal role-taking" *into* the representation of the ideal procedure for arriving at reasoned agreement.[8]

As the trajectory of argument around Rawls's notion of reflective equilibrium illustrates, the burden of proof on moral theorists who hope to ground a conception of justice in something more universal than the considered convictions of our political culture is enormous. Because Habermas wants to do just that, the links he forges to action theory are crucial; they are meant to show that our basic moral intuitions are rooted in something deeper and more universal than particularities of our tradition. The task of moral theory, in his view, is reflectively to articulate, refine, and elaborate—that is, to "reconstruct"— the intuitive grasp of the normative presuppositions of social interaction that belongs to the repertoire of competent social actors in any society. The basic moral intuitions the theorist reconstructs are, as Aristotle noted, acquired in the process of socialization; but, Habermas argues, they include an "abstract core" that is not culture- but species-specific. Members of our species become individuals in and through being socialized into networks of reciprocal social relations, so that personal identity is from that start interwoven with relations of mutual recognition. This interdependence brings with it a reciprocal vulnerability that calls for guarantees of mutual consideration to preserve both the integrity of individual persons and the web of interpersonal relations in which their identities are formed and maintained. Both of these concerns—with the inviolability of the person and the solidarity of the community—have been at the heart of traditional moralities. In the Kantian tradition, respect for the individual is tied to the freedom of each to act on norms she can herself accept as right and concern for the general interest to the imparitality of laws that all can agree to on that basis. In Habermas's discourse ethics, which bases the justification of norms on the reasoned agreement of those subject to them, equal respect for individuals is reflected in the freedom of each participant to respond with a yes or a no to reasons offered by way of justification and concern for the common good in the requirement that each participant take into account the needs, interests, and

8. This is, of course, a difference from Rawls's favored "device of representation," the original position, which features rational egoists prudently contracting behind a veil of ignorance. Rawls represents only the "rational" directly and the "reasonable" indirectly, through the conditions of deliberation; whereas Habermas, because of the role that discourse plays in his theory, wants directly to represent the rational and reasonable deliberations of agents who have themselves adopted the moral point of view. Consequently, Habermas does not lean as heavily as Rawls does on the distinction between the rational and the reasonable, most often using them interchangeably to connote a capacity for and sensitivity to the weighing of reasons in speaking and acting. See Jürgen Habermas, *The Theory of Communicative Action*, 2 vols., trans. T. McCarthy (Boston: Beacon, 1984, 1987), vol. 1, pp. 1–141.

feelings of all others and give them equal weight to her own. Hence the actual practice of moral and political discourse depends on forms of socialization and social reproduction that can be counted upon to foster the requisite capacities and motivations.

It is, in fact, possible to read Habermas's extensive writings on politics and society as a protracted examination of the psychological, cultural, and institutional preconditions of, and barriers to, the implementation of practical discourses. Very early on, in *The Structural Transformation of the Public Sphere,* he presented a historical-sociological account of the emergence, transformation, and degeneration of the liberal public sphere in which critical public discussion of matters of general interest was to be institutionalized.[9] He noted the contradiction between its constitutive catalog of "basic rights of man" and their actual restriction to a certain class of men. And he traced the tensions this gave rise to as, with the development of capitalism, the public body expanded beyond the bourgeoisie to include groups who were systematically disadvantaged by the rising economic system and demanded state regulation and compensation. There are related discussions of the historical genesis and structural problems of the democratic public sphere in other of his writings.[10] I am not concerned here with the details of those discussions but with the proceduralist conception of deliberative democracy that serves as their normative point of reference.

That conception applies the idea of justification by appeal to generally acceptable reasons to the deliberations of free and equal citizens in a constitutional democracy.[11] The focus of what we might view as Habermas's version of the basic structure is the institutionalization of political autonomy, that is, of the public use of reason in the legal-political domain. Taking the facts of social, cultural, and ideological pluralism into account, he argues that reasoned agreements in this domain will typically involve all three types of practical reasoning mentioned above—pragmatic discourse about how best to achieve our ends, ethical discourse concerned with goods, values, and identities, and moral discourse concerning what is just, fair, or equally in the interest of all. Especially in connection with the pursuit of collective goals, the political process will also typically require negotiation and compromise which, if the agreements arrived at are to deserve to be called reasonable, will themselves have to be regulated so as to ensure a fair balancing of interests. Thus the normative conception of demo-

9. Jürgen Habermas, *The Structural Transformation of the Public Sphere,* trans. T. Burger and F. Lawrence (Cambridge, Mass.: MIT Press, 1989). See also Craig Calhoun, ed., *Habermas and the Public Sphere* (Cambridge, Mass.: MIT Press, 1992).

10. See esp. Habermas, *Faktizität und Geltung, The Theory of Communicative Action,* and Jürgen Habermas, *Legitimation Crisis,* trans. T. McCarthy (Boston: Beacon, 1975).

11. On what follows, see Habermas, *Faktizität und Geltung,* chaps. 3, 4.

cratic deliberation that Habermas proposes weaves negotiations and pragmatic deliberations together with ethical and moral discourses, under conditions that warrant a presumption that procedurally correct outcomes will be ones with which free and equal citizens could reasonably agree. He conceives of the basic principles of the democratic constitutional state primarily as a response to the question of how such conditions of rational deliberation can be implemented both in official governmental arenas and in unofficial arenas of the political public sphere.

Independent public forums, distinct from both the economic system and the state administration, having their locus rather in voluntary associations, social movements, and other networks and processes of communication in civil society—including the mass media—are for Habermas the basis of popular sovereignty. Ideally, the public use of reason in nongovernmental arenas is translated via legally institutionalized decision-making procedures—for example, electoral and legislative procedures—into the legitimate administrative power of the state. In Habermas's words, "the power available to the administration emerges from a public use of reason. . . . Public opinion worked up via democratic procedures cannot itself 'rule,' but it can point the use of administrative power in specific directions."[12] In this model of a deliberative decentering of political power, the multiple and multiform arenas for detecting, defining, and discussing society's problems, and the culturally and politically mobilized publics who use them, serve as the basis for democratic self-government and thus for political autonomy. The constitution is viewed as a "project" that is always incomplete and subject to the ongoing exercise of political autonomy, as shifting historical circumstances demand. Because the public use of reason is ineluctably open and reflexive, our understanding of the principles of justice must remain so as well. It is for this reason that Habermas limits himself to reconstructing the conditions and presuppositions of democratic deliberation and leaves all substantive questions to the public use of reason itself. His discourse theory of deliberative democracy "focuses exclusively on the procedural aspects of the public use of reason and derives the system of rights from the idea of legally institutionalizing it [i.e., the public use of reason]. It can leave more questions open because it entrusts more to the process of rational opinion- and will-formation."[13]

12. Jürgen Habermas, "Three Normative Models of Democracy" (paper presented at the Annual Conference for the Study of Political Thought, New Haven, Conn., April 1993). This appeared, together with other papers from the same conference, in the first issue of *Constellations* 1 (1994): 1–10.

13. Jürgen Habermas, "Reconciliation through the Public Use of Reason: Remarks on John Rawls's Political Liberalism" (Frankfurt, 1993, typescript), p. 24; this paper will appear in *Journal of Philosophy* as part of an exchange with Rawls. As is evident

II

In *Political Liberalism* Rawls distinguishes public from nonpublic uses of reason in a somewhat unusual way.[14] "Public" uses are connected with governmental and quasi-governmental venues and functions—for example, with parliamentary debates, administrative acts and pronouncements, and the workings of the judiciary, but also with political campaigns, party politics, and even the act of voting (pp. 215–16). "Nonpublic" reason, on the other hand, is connected with nongovernmental venues and functions—for example, with churches, universities, professional groups, and voluntary associations in civil society (pp. 213, 220)—that is, largely with the unofficial networks of private people communicating about public matters that Habermas considers to be the nervous system of the political public sphere. To be sure, in Rawls's conceptualization as well, nonpublic reason is not private reason; it is, as he says, "social" in nature and may even be concerned with the very same political issues that occupy public reason (p. 220). However, the differences between them are not merely terminological, as can be seen in Rawls's account of the limits of public reason in relation to the ideal of citizenship in a well-ordered society. At the risk of oversimplifying a complex and differentiated treatment, the key points might be summarized as follows: (1) The limits in question apply to the public—in Rawls's sense—discussion of fundamental political matters, that is, matters of "constitutional essentials" and of "basic justice" (pp. 223–24, 227–28). (2) The limits consist, roughly, in restricting debate to the ambit of the political conception of justice and the political values found in the overlapping consensus of a well-ordered society. In other words, in public discussions of fundamental issues, the reasons offered on opposing sides should be ones that all might reasonably be expected to endorse in view of their shared political conception of justice (pp. 224–25). Put negatively, they should not be reasons peculiar to a particular comprehensive moral, religious, or philosophical doctrine. (3) The limits imposed by

---

from the debates that regularly accompany both the historical births of democratic constitutions and the continuing "projects" of actualizing them, our concrete understanding of the presuppositions and conditions of democratic self-determination is itself subject to discussion in the political public sphere. Democratic discourse is reflexively open; participants may problematize the very activity in which they are engaged. Even the interpretation of such core elements of procedural impartiality as equal consideration and equal treatment are essentially contestable, as can be seen in the ongoing debates concerning the relevant respects in which citizens are to be treated as equal, e.g., which respects are to be regarded as "public" and which as "private." In this regard at least, the distinction between form (or procedure) and substance can only be one of degree and not of kind.

14. John Rawls, "The Idea of Public Reason," lecture 6 in *Political Liberalism*, pp. 212–54. Page numbers in parentheses in the text and in notes are references to this work.

public reason include restrictions on method as well as on content. Rawls characterizes these as guidelines of inquiry; they include such things as principles of reasoning, criteria of relevance, and rules of evidence. Here, too, the point is to avoid relying on what is controversial in offering public justifications regarding basic issues. Rawls elaborates: "In making these justifications, we are to appeal only to presently accepted general beliefs and forms of reasoning found in common sense, and the methods and conclusions of science when these are not controversial. . . . As far as possible, the knowledge and ways of reasoning . . . are to rest on the plain truths widely accepted or available to citizens generally. Otherwise, the political conception would not provide a *public* basis of justification" (pp. 224–25). (4) Paired with this idea of the limits of public reason is an ideal of citizenship in which, so to speak, these limits are internalized. At its core is the duty of civility, by which citizens see themselves as obligated to a public use of reason in publicly discussing fundamental issues of justice (pp. 217–18). Being thus "reasonable," in Rawls's sense of the term, they "don't appeal to the whole truth as [they] see it" (p. 218) but seek to show how their positions can be supported by political values.

The picture of public reason adumbrated in these limits and duties is likely to give pause to theorists with a more robust conception of democratic discourse. It would, in particular, be unacceptable to Habermas, who is no less interested in public criticism than in public justification. Because social-political critique often addresses basic rights, principles, and values to challenge existing understandings and to persuade citizens to view fundamental issues in a different light, it is a public use of reason that sometimes requires transgressing an established overlapping consensus. From that standpoint, Rawls's conception seems to place undue restrictions on the use of public forums to press for basic structural changes. This is reflected in problems that arise with the line he draws between public and nonpublic uses of reason. In nongovernmental venues of social life—the "background culture"—we are free, normatively speaking, to discuss basic issues of justice in light of whatever considerations we find relevant and convincing. This holds in particular for discussions within the numerous and variegated voluntary associations and movements that are characteristic of healthy democratic life. It would also hold, I suppose, for discussions of the same issues in the various public media, print and broadcast, for political liberalism surely would not place narrow restrictions on authors, editors, publicists, talk show hosts, and the like. And so our ideal society might well be teeming with public—in the usual, broader sense of the term—discussions of all kinds of issues, at all levels, and in light of all sorts of considerations. In short, it might well contain what democratic theorists would normally consider to be a healthy political public sphere. However, if this were a well-ordered society, in Rawls's sense of that term, political discussion would have to be radically transformed whenever the venue changed in relevant ways, even if the very same people were discussing the very same issues. If, for instance, the discussion figured as part of an election campaign, or were conducted in support of one, or were being carried out on the floor of Congress, only certain parts—or, to adapt one of Rawls's terms, "modules"—of the unrestricted discussions would be appropriate (pp. 252–53). The conceptual, psychological, cultural, and institutional problems this avoidance strategy raises are formidable. Can political principles and values really be separated off this way from the environments of reasons that nourish them? Particularly when we are publicly debating differences concerning basic questions of justice that are rooted in our different comprehensive views, ought we to eliminate from the debate a public examination of the very considerations that gave rise to it? Can individuals reasonably be expected to divorce their private and public beliefs and values to the extent required by an ideal of citizenship which, according to Rawls, demands that we not even vote our consciences on fundamental political issues (p. 215)? Can we even imagine a political culture in which, on the one hand, citizens form their opinions by reading, listening to, and engaging in open discussions of basic political issues but then are expected to participate in electoral campaigns and give support to legislative programs and administrative policies on different grounds?

It is clear, I think, that there is no way of erecting institutional barriers between the sea of nonofficial opinion and will formation and the islands of official and quasi-official discourse. Nor, I think, is there any way of erecting institutional filters that could screen out of the latter all controversial beliefs and values. And it is evident that no theory of political liberalism would want to do so. Rawls is clear on this point: he is not talking about institutional barriers or legal restraints on free speech but about the moral duty of civility that the ideal of citizenship entails (p. 217). In short, the weight of the art of separation falls on individuals. We have to monitor and restrain ourselves, to know when we are speaking in what Rawls calls "the public forum" and when not, and to conduct ourselves accordingly. Here we have, it seems, an ironic variation on Kant's problematic distinction between the autonomous and heteronomous self. Rawls's politically autonomous self is also constructed around self-abnegation; but now it is one's deepest convictions and the deliverances of one's conscience that must be kept in check. Whenever we are tempted to speak the whole truth, as we see it, in the public forum, we must ask ourselves, in Rawls's words: "How would our argument strike us presented in the form of a Supreme Court opinion?" (p. 254). This entails, as he notes, that the kinds of reasoning which Kant—and most other moral and political philosophers—brought to the fundamentals of justice should be excluded from the public forum of a well-ordered society. The same would hold, we might add, for some of the arguments adduced by civil rights activists (e.g., appeals to a religious tradition), feminists (e.g., appeals to controversial forms of inquiry), democratic socialists (e.g., appeals to a comprehensive view), and most other social movements agitating for basic change.[15] My point is simply that there is something intuitively wrong with these prescriptions. They clash with our considered convictions about the openness of debate in the democratic public sphere, even, and even especially when matters of grave importance are at issue.[16] If this is so, there will likely have to be adjustments made elsewhere in the theory.

I certainly will not attempt that here. But I would like to suggest that the problem is linked to Rawls's incorporation, in the course of the 1980s, of the problems of political stability into the ("second stage" of the) normative theory of justice.[17] To be sure, normative political theory has to be concerned with what he calls "the art of the possible."

15. Rawls allows that "the appropriate limits of public reason vary depending on historical and social conditions" (p. 251). This "inclusive view" permits appeal to "comprehensive"—in contrast to "public"—reasons when the society in question is not well-ordered, as was the case, in Rawls's view, with the abolitionist and civil rights movements (pp. 249–51). This contrasts with cases in which a society is "more or less" or "nearly" well-ordered, when more stringent restrictions apply (pp. 247–49). If no existing society were well-ordered, as Rawls sometimes seems to suggest, then the de facto divide between his view of what is permissible in actually existing public forums and Habermas's would not be as wide as I have suggested. But the normative-theoretical differences would remain. To bring them to a point: Who decides, and how, whether or not there are "basic injustices" that have to be protested (p. 248) or whether political struggle belongs to "the necessary historical conditions to establish political justice" (p. 251)? Habermas would argue that this must be left for participants themselves to decide, through engagement in the public sphere; and that means, in effect, that Rawls's proposed restrictions on public discourse are never warranted.

16. Rawls's discussion of the abortion debate (pp. 243–44, n. 32) is a case in point. In a well-ordered society, he writes, it would "go against the ideal of public reason" to vote or to speak in the public forum against the right to choose (at least during the first trimester), for "any reasonable balance" of the political values involved would allow that "the political value of the equality of women is overriding and that this right is required to give it substance and force." Any comprehensive doctrine that led to a different balance—e.g., one that treated the political value of "due respect for human life" as overriding and thus as precluding abortion—would be "to that extent unreasonable." In political-theoretical terms there is all the difference in the world between characterizing an argument as mistaken or inadequate and characterizing it as unreasonable and in violation of the ideal of public reason—and thus of the ideal of citizenship and the duty of civility. Rawls here makes his interpretation of the relative weights of these values the measure not only of the relative force of the competing arguments but of their very permissibility in the public forum of a well-ordered society. This clashes sharply with at least my considered convictions about the proper openness of public debate.

17. This is an important difference from Rawls's treatment of the problem in part 3 of *A Theory of Justice*. He remarks on the change in his introduction to *Political Liberalism*, pp. xv–xviii.

At the very least, it has to consider whether its ideas are "realistic" or "feasible." But there are different ways of doing that. One way, which Rawls rejects, is to treat the question of stability largely as an empirical question. The history of modern sociology is, among other things, a series of reflections on "the problem of social order."[18] What those reflections suggest is that stability is a function of myriad factors—kinship structure, childrearing practices, socialization processes, cultural values, legal practices, political institutions, bureaucratic administrations, economic interdependencies, and so forth. The point is that political stability in a democratic society does not rely solely on the sort of unity of political conception that Rawls's zeroes in on. A society might be able to afford some measure of dissensus there if it enjoyed a good measure of integration in other spheres. In short, the question of whether unity on basic political principles and values is a necessary condition of stability and if so, how much unity in which circumstances, does not admit of a general, philosophical answer.

But, of course, Rawls wants more from a consideration of stability than social science can provide. He wants to assure himself and us that the political conception of justice can be the focus of an overlapping consensus, because that would mean that it was not just a modus vivendi but could gain the (variously) reasoned support of free and equal citizens as rational and reasonable. This idea of idealized rational/reasonable acceptability is close to what Habermas means by validity.[19] So perhaps what has to be reconsidered is just the way of linking validity with stability that forms the premise for the reexamination of the theory of justice undertaken in *Political Liberalism*. I will take that into consideration in Section IV, after setting out in Section III a line of argument that Rawls might adduce against Habermas.[20]

III

The line of argument I have in mind concerns what Rawls calls the fact of reasonable pluralism. As we saw, Habermas's proceduralist

18. See, e.g., Talcott Parsons, *The Structure of Social Action* (New York: McGraw-Hill, 1937).

19. Thus Habermas could adopt as his own Rawls's statement of "the ideal expressed by the principle of legitimacy: to live politically with others in the light of reasons all might reasonably be expected to endorse" (p. 243). But Rawls means by this: "political values everyone can reasonably be expected to endorse" (p. 241), however they may disagree about the "further and often transcendental backing for those values" in their various comprehensive doctrines (p. 243). Habermas would not accept this normative-theoretical restriction on the type of warranting reasons, though, as I shall suggest in Sec. III, it might turn out in practice that public agreements in pluralistic, democratic societies can often be reached only on the basis of what Rawls calls "political reasons." But that is still a difference that makes a difference.

20. An earlier version of this line of argument appeared as chap. 7 of my *Ideals and Illusions* (Cambridge, Mass.: MIT Press, 1991). A more elaborate version will appear in the *Cardozo Law Review*, under the title "Legitimacy and Diversity."

account of deliberative democracy understands political autonomy as self-legislation through the public use of reason by free and equal citizens. It ties the legitimacy of legal norms to what all could agree to in rational public deliberation that takes the needs and interests of each equally into consideration. That deliberation is understood in turn as an interweave of different types of discourse—moral, ethical, and pragmatic—with fairly regulated bargaining processes. Ideally, the "rationally motivated consensus" that provisionally certifies a norm, policy, program, or arrangement as legitimate should comprise agreement in all these dimensions. How well does this idealized conception of democratic decision making fit with the elements of democratic politics as Habermas himself sees them? I am thinking, in particular, of his recognition of value pluralism and his acknowledgment that evaluative perspectives inevitably inform our conceptions of what is good not only for ourselves but for the communities of which we are members. On what grounds, then, could we expect free and equal citizens with different and often incompatible value orientations to be able regularly to achieve consensus on what is in the common good? That will, it seems clear, often be a matter for dissensus among citizens with different conceptions of the good. In other words, since for Habermas questions of justice have themselves to be posed in terms of what is equally *good* for all, ethical disagreements may well give rise to disagreements about what is right or just. Under conditions of value pluralism, even ideally rational discourse need not lead to rational consensus.

There are two rather different moves that Habermas is inclined to make at this point. In some places he suggests that irresolvable value conflicts should, like interest conflicts, be left to fair bargaining processes.[21] But he is also clear that, while appropriate regulations might succeed in equalizing bargaining power, they cannot neutralize it, nor can they transform the strategic interaction that is characteristic of negotiations into purely communicative interaction. So the type of "reasonable agreement" involved here cannot be said to rest on communicatively achieved consensus, though in the case of an equal balance of power, it might be said to be fair. But fair bargaining procedures are hardly the sort of rational basis for deliberative politics that Habermas, who explicitly distances himself from certain concep-

21. For instance, in Habermas, *Faktizität und Geltung*, pp. 204–5. I am focusing here on the normative-conceptual moves that Habermas makes with respect to the procedures and outcomes of deliberation. Another complementary response to phenomena of democratic disagreement comes at the institutional level, where he considers such things as legal protection, representation, majority rule, separation of powers, and the like. It is, in fact, this dual perspective on right or law, as a normative system and as a system of social action, that defines his approach in *Faktizität und Geltung*. But that is much too complicated a matter to take up here.

tions of liberalism in this regard, needs for his, let us say, more "republican" conception of democratic legitimacy.[22] The problem is further aggravated by the evident fact that individuals are often unwilling to treat values like interests and bargain with them. As contemporary disagreements concerning abortion, pornography, animal rights, capital punishment, euthanasia, and the like suggest, there is often little room for compromise on basic values. In such cases we typically resort to other procedures for settling disputes, for instance, to voting and majority rule. If those procedures are carried out in ways accepted as legitimate by all parties to the dispute, the outcomes may likewise be accepted as democratically legitimate. But then there is no more reason to characterize them as "reasonable agreements" than as "reasonable disagreements." The outcomes members accept as procedurally correct are not ipso facto rationally justified in their eyes, if that means justified solely by the force of reasons for and against. There is another force at work here as well. And while it need not be unjust, neither will it be merely the forceless force of the better argument.

The second move goes in the opposite direction, as it were— toward greater abstraction.[23] The idea is that when public discussion, rather than leading to rationally motivated consensus on general interests and shared values, instead sharpens disagreement by revealing particular interests to be ungeneralizable or particular values to be neither generally sharable nor consensually orderable, we can still reach a reasonable agreement by moving discussion to a higher level of abstraction—for example, from different preferences to freedom of choice, from opposed beliefs to liberty of conscience, from conflicting values to rights of privacy, and the like. This strategy gains some plausibility by reflecting the tendencies toward greater abstraction and generalization in modern legal and political systems. But that is not our concern at the moment. What is of interest in the present context is that this move, if pushed far enough, lands Habermas closer to Rawls. That is to say, the level of abstraction at which pluralistic societies could hope to secure general agreement amid the play of social, cultural, and ideological differences might well be similar to that of Rawls's political conception. This is an open question, to be sure, and one that cannot be answered apart from actual attempts to reach

22. In "Three Normative Models of Democracy" Habermas situates his proceduralist conception of deliberative democracy in relation to liberal and republican conceptions. While he emphasizes communicatively achieved consensus and positive liberties of political participation over the aggregation of private interests, he distances himself from communitarian versions of republicanism by his emphases on pluralism and the use of public reason to bridge social and cultural differences.

23. For instance, in Habermas, *Justification and Application*, pp. 90–91. Rawls adopts a similar view of abstraction in *Political Liberalism*, pp. 45–46.

reasoned agreements in the public spheres of actual societies.[24] But it merits close consideration.

Insofar as the moral-political significance of reasoned agreement hinges on its providing an alternative to open or latent coercion as means of social coordination, there is clearly room for alternatives to substantive consensus. If participants are themselves aware that their different interpretive and evaluative perspectives are rooted in particular traditions, practices, and experiences, and if they consider the political institutions and procedures of their society to be basically just, they may regard collective decisions in accord with those institutions and procedures as legitimate even when they disagree. That is, their underlying agreement with the operative political conception of justice may rationally motivate them (in Habermas's broader sense of the term 'rational') to consent to laws they regard as substantively unwarranted. I do not see why Habermas should want to downplay this alternative. He maintains that philosophically based moral theories can do no more than explicate the moral point of view, and he allows that this cannot exhaust the "semantic potential," as he puts it, of comprehensive doctrines. Precisely because of its highly formal nature, discourse ethics is compatible with different substantive conceptions of the meaning and value of life. Inasmuch as these differences figure in judgments regarding the common good, they will translate into differences on substantive questions of justice, that is, on whether specific laws or policies are equally in the interest of, or equally good for, all. Here, I think, Habermas has to move in the direction of Rawls. Indeed his emphasis on the conditions and procedures of democratic deliberation, rather than on its outcomes, might be seen as already pointing in that direction.[25] But even if the gap were closed, and even if Rawls

24. Habermas sees this as an empirical question: "The sphere of questions that can be answered rationally from the moral point of view shrinks in the course of development toward multiculturalism within particular societies and toward a world society at the international level. But finding a solution to these few more sharply focused questions becomes all the more critical to coexistence, and even survival, in a more populous world. It remains an empirical question how far the sphere of strictly generalizable interests extends" (*Justification and Application*, p. 91). At the same time, he has to claim some normative-theoretical distinction for the basic rights and principles that are required to institutionalize "the moral point of view" itself in procedures of rational opinion and will formation. And he does in fact argue that, understood in this way, the basic structures of justice can be justified as necessary preconditions for free and equal participation in public deliberations and, as such, can be reflexively agreed to in the very discourses they are designed to secure. See Habermas, *Faktizität und Geltung*, chap. 3.

25. In recent publications Habermas does, in fact, adopt a conception similar to Rawls's "overlapping consensus" among reasonable comprehensive doctrines. He argues, in political-sociological terms, that the growing differentiation of "political integration," centered around ideas of citizenship, from "cultural integration" more generally

loosened the link between validity and stability, there would remain significant differences in their general theoretical strategies.

IV

Reasonable persons, Rawls tells us, "desire for its own sake a social world in which they, as free and equal, can cooperate with others on terms all can accept" (p. 50). He connects this with T. M. Scanlon's principle of moral motivation, "the basic desire to be able to justify our actions to others on grounds they could not reasonably reject" (pp. 49–50). The other defining aspect of the reasonable, as Rawls understands it, is "the willingness to recognize the burdens of judgment and to accept their consequences for the use of public reason in directing the legitimate exercise of political power in a constitutional regime" (p. 54). Recognizing the burdens of judgment means understanding why reasonable disagreements among reasonable persons are not only possible but probable, that is, why they are a normal result of the free use of reason, even in the long run and all things considered. In light of the many sources or causes of such disagreement—difficulties in assessing evidence and differences in weighing it, indeterminacy of concepts and conflicts of interpretation, experiential and normative divergencies, the diversity of values and variations in selecting and ordering them (pp. 56–57)—it is unreasonable to expect that "conscientious persons with full powers of reason, even after free discussion, will all [always] arrive at the same conclusions" (p. 58). My criticism of Habermas in Section III was basically in accord with this. The argument of Section II, however, questioned Rawls's own assessment of the "consequences for the use of public reason" that flow from it. And it is to this issue that I would like briefly to return in these concluding remarks.

Stylizing somewhat, we might regard the two basic aspects of the reasonable as standing in a tension analogous to that between Kant's two standpoints. As "participants," to use Habermas's terminology, we want to justify our actions to others on grounds that all could rationally accept. As "observers," however, we note the fact of reasonable pluralism and anticipate that some of the reasons acceptable to us will be unacceptable to others. How are we to combine these two points of view on public justification? As we saw in Section II, Rawls's strategy is to discount the pluralism in advance, so to speak, by restricting public reason to the ambit of an overlapping consensus. There I argued, in

---

has made it possible for political cultures rooted in constitutional traditions to develop and coexist with wide cultural differences in other spheres. To be sure, this requires a certain degree of "concurrence" (or consonance: *Übereinstimmung*) on political fundamentals among the different subcultures. See my discussion in "Legitimacy and Diversity."

effect, that this deprives the participant's perspective of its proper weight, and I suggested that the imbalance results from the way Rawls now builds the problem of stability into his normative-theoretical approach.

The critical connections between the various strands of his approach are clearly visible in the following summary: "Justice as fairness aims at uncovering a public basis of justification on questions of political justice given the fact of reasonable pluralism. Since the justification is addressed to others, it proceeds from what is, or can be, held in common; and so we begin from shared fundamental ideas implicit in the public political culture in the hope of developing from them a political conception that can gain free and reasoned agreement in judgment, this agreement being stable in virtue of its gaining the support of an overlapping consensus of reasonable comprehensive doctrines" (pp. 100–101). The "practical aim" of attaining a public basis of justification (p. 9) motivates the strategy of beginning with implicitly shared ideas and working them up via reflective equilibrium into a political conception that can serve as the focus of an overlapping consensus and thus enhance stability. And given the "practical impossibility" of reaching agreement on the truth of comprehensive doctrines (p. 63), it seems to follow that such a conception of public reason will have to be "impartial . . . between the points of view of reasonable comprehensive doctrines" (p. xix). Thus the pursuit of a practical aim in the face of a practical impossibility dictates the strategy of *Political Liberalism*.[26] This is true not only in stage 2 when the question of stability explicitly comes to the fore, but already in stage 1 as well: it sets the very terms of the search for principles of justice. Thus, "the guidelines and procedures of public reason are seen as selected in the original position and belong to the political conception of justice" (p. 62).[27] With its "thick" veil of ignorance preventing the parties from knowing the particular comprehensive doctrines of those they represent, the original position models what we regard as appropriate restrictions on what are to count as good reasons in respect to the basic

26. Rawls's practical-political concerns are manifest in "The Domain of the Political and Overlapping Consensus," in *The Idea of Democracy*, ed. D. Copp, J. Hampton, and J. Roemer (Cambridge: Cambridge University Press, 1993), pp. 245–69, where he recommends his revised approach to the theory of justice as "more realistic," less "utopian," and not altogether impracticable "as the aim of reform and change" (p. 258). In the same volume, there are discussions of themes relevant to the points I am making here by Joshua Cohen, "Moral Pluralism and Political Consensus" (pp. 270–91); Jean Hampton, "The Moral Commitments of Liberalism" (pp. 292–313); and David Estlund, "Making Truth Safe for Democracy" (pp. 71–100).

27. And again: "The guidelines of inquiry of public reason . . . have the same basis as the substantive principles of justice. . . . The argument for [them] . . . is much the same as, and as strong as, the argument for the principles of justice themselves" (p. 225).

structure. "Beyond this, the original position also requires the parties to select (if possible) principles that may be stable, given the fact of reasonable pluralism; and hence to select principles that can be the focus of an overlapping consensus of reasonable doctrines" (p. 78). And, as Rawls indicates in the passage cited at the start of this paragraph, the concern with consensus informs the method of reflective equilibrium from the start: the political philosopher arrives at a shared public basis of justification by working out implicitly shared public ideas and principles. More emphatically yet, it is because the procedure starts from shared ideas that it can yield a conception which may be the focus of an overlapping consensus (p. 90).

In all these respects, I want to suggest, Rawls in effect cedes a certain primacy to the observer's perspective: the concern with stability in light of the fact of reasonable pluralism limits the scope of what may count as good reasons in matters of public justification. His understanding of the principle of moral motivation—a principle that could serve as the motto of Habermas's discourse ethics—supports this reading. The desire to be able to justify our actions to others on grounds they could not reasonably reject is said to entail the restrictions on public reason we examined in Section II. "Since many doctrines are seen to be reasonable, those who insist, when fundamental political questions are at stake, on what they take as true but others do not, seem to others simply to insist on their own beliefs. . . . They impose their beliefs because, they say, their beliefs are true, and not because they are their beliefs. But this is a claim all equally could make; it is also a claim that cannot be made good by anyone to citizens generally. so when we make such claims, others, who are themselves reasonable, must count us unreasonable" (p. 61), or even "sectarian" (p. 129). Rawls is specifically concerned here with the use of political power to repress comprehensive views. But the same general structure of argument underlies his restrictions on public reason: since many doctrines "are seen to be" reasonable, participants who "insist" in the public forum on what they "take as true" but others do not are being "unreasonable." The political participant's desire to act on publicly justifiable grounds is refracted through the political observer's recognition of the fact of reasonable pluralism and emerges as a desire to avoid ideological controversy on fundamental matters, that is, to avoid being "unreasonable." In political discourse, this concept of the reasonable then displaces that of moral truth (or of validity in Habermas's sense): "Within a political conception of justice, we cannot define truth as given by the beliefs that would stand up even in an idealized consensus, however far extended. . . . Once we accept the fact that reasonable pluralism is a permanent condition of public culture under free institutions, the idea of the reasonable is more suitable as part of the basis of public justification" (p. 129). By contrast, the primacy of the participant's perspective for Habermas is signaled through his tying justification to rational acceptability and the latter precisely to what could "stand up even in an idealized consensus."

Earlier I discussed the stringent restrictions that Rawls places on discourse in the public forum and now I have indicated how they are connected with the peculiar way he integrates concerns with stability and consensus into his constructivist approach. The resultant "political conception" is invoked to remove certain questions from the political agenda "once and for all," that is, to declare them not "appropriate subjects for political decision," not "suitable topic[s] for ongoing public debate and legislation" (p. 151–52). On this score, Habermas's participant-centered conception of public justification offers, I think, a considerable advantage. *It leaves the task of finding common ground to political participants themselves.* I should say, of finding, creating, expanding, contracting, shifting, challenging, and deconstructing common ground; for to suppose that the stock of shared political ideas and convictions is in some way given, there to be found and worked up, or that it could somehow be fixed by the theorists, is to hypostatize or freeze ongoing processes of public political communication whose outcomes cannot be settled in advance by political theory. This, I think, has been made abundantly evident by the ongoing, reasonable, and I would venture to guess, irresolvable controversy surrounding Rawls's own theory and practice of reflective equilibrium.[28] It is equally evident in the ongoing contestation (in which we are presently engaged) of his political conception of justice itself. Nor can these be written off as "purely theoretical" disagreements with no bearing on his practical aims. It belongs to the "full publicity condition" of a well-ordered society that "the full justification of the public conception of justice," including "everything that we would say—you and I—when we set up justice as fairness and reflect why we proceed in one way rather than another," should be publicly known or at least publicly available.[29] And so if, as appears likely, it should prove "practically impossible"

---

28. One source of controversy is obviously that the traditions of interpretation of our basic political ideas and institutions are themselves plural, contested, and continually changing. For purposes of arriving at a unified, stable, political conception, Rawls's hermeneutic turn has the disadvantage that a living tradition is, as Ricoeur and others have taught us, a conflict of interpretations—a conflict, one might add, that allows for reasonable disagreements.

29. Philosophical accounts of reason have to pass what might be called a "reflexivity test": they must be applicable to themselves without producing self-referential contradictions. On this score, I think there is a tension in *Political Liberalism* between the postfoundationalist line of argument meant to convince us, the readers, of a certain conception of public reason and the thesis that reasonable citizens may embrace it for whatever religious, metaphysical, or other comprehensive reasons they find acceptable. See Samuel Scheffler, "The Appeal of Political Liberalism," *Ethics* 105 (1994): 4–22, in this issue.

to end reasonable disagreement on such matters as are covered by the political conception, Rawls should, by the dictates of his own strategy of avoidance, apply the principle of toleration not merely to "philosophy itself" (p. 154), but to political philosophy itself.[30] This he could not sensibly do, of course, and so the line between permissible and impermissible public reasoning will simply have to be drawn somewhere—or nowhere, as in Habermas's approach. If there is no way of deciding once and for all which issues belong on or off the political agenda, the latter approach has much to recommend it.

When awareness of the burdens of judgment is incorporated into the participant's perspective, there is an obvious alternative to Rawls's opposition between unreasonable insistence on the truth of one's beliefs and reasonable avoidance of claims to truth—namely, reasonable discussion of truth or validity claims. We are not forced to choose between sectarianism and civility, in Rawls's sense; there is also the option of mutual respect and an accommodation of social, cultural, and ideological differences within democratic deliberation.[31] The virtues associated with this option have been familiar since Socrates: open-mindedness, avoidance of dogmatism, a willingness to discuss differences, to listen to others, to take their views seriously, and to change our minds, an ability to see things from the perspectives of others, to weigh judiciously the pros and cons of issues, and so on. These are just the virtues required of participants in rational discourse as Habermas conceives it. And they are the sorts of dispositions and attitudes typically singled out by proponents of unrestricted deliberation in the democratic public spheres. An ideal of mutual respect balancing commitment with openness is no less capable of accommodating reasonable pluralism and reasonable disagreement than Rawls's ideal of citizenship with its duty of civility. And it has the advantage over the

---

30. The idea that political philosophy could disengage from the "long-standing problems and controversies" of other areas of philosophy (pp. 171–72) rests in part, perhaps, on a more sanguine than warranted estimate of the powers of reflective equilibrium to resolve disputes. Heremeneutic-constructive arguments are no less open to reasonable disagreement than others. The invitation to test the political conception of justice against "our" more firm considered convictions (p. 28) is, realistically, an invitation to continue the controversy, as is unmistakably signaled by the many different assessments "we"—you and I and Rawls and Habermas and many others—have come to after taking it up.

31. The terminology of "mutual respect" and "accommodation" is taken from an essay by Amy Gutmann and Dennis Thompson, "Moral Conflict and Political Consensus," in *Liberalism and the Good,* ed. R. Douglass, G. Mara, and H. Richardson (New York: Routledge, 1990), pp. 125–47. The position they defend is not far from Habermas's. In fact, his theory of communicative action might be seen as an effort to supply the justification for the priority of mutual respect that Douglass and Mara call for in their own contribution to that volume "The Search for a Defensible Good: The Emerging Dilemma of Liberalism," pp. 253–80, esp. pp. 264–65.

latter of avoiding the sharp split between public and private reason that runs clear through Rawls's construction. Rather than obligating citizens to treat views publicly as reasonable that they regard privately, or in the background culture, "as plainly unreasonable or untrue" (p. 60), it encourages them to propose and defend publicly whatever views they think reasonable and relevant to deciding public issues.

Rawls is moved by his reflections on the historical origins of liberalism in the wars of religion and controversies over religious toleration of the sixteenth and seventeenth centuries to propose an updated model of toleration for present purposes (pp. xxiii–xxvi). In the face of deep and irresolvable conflicts between rival salvationist, credal, and expansionist religions, each claiming the certainty of faith for its transcendent conception of the good, the only alternatives were endless strife or the practice of toleration in liberal institutions acknowledging equal liberty of conscience and freedom of thought. "Political liberalism starts by taking to heart the absolute depth of that irreconcilable latent conflict" (p. xxvi). Habermas is moved by his reflections on the historical origins of the democratic public sphere in the eighteenth and nineteenth centuries to propose an updated model of deliberation for present purposes.[32] It turns on the differences, rather than the similarities, between faith and reason. Views that claim to be based on grounds that any reasonable person could rationally accept need not be privatized and tolerated. They can be publicly put to the very test they invite. This is, of course, not to deny the necessity of liberal rights and principles, separation and toleration; it is to point out that a theory of liberal democracy has to integrate them with equally strong conceptions of public opinion formation. If the fully autonomous citizens in the well-ordered society of justice as fairness can, as Rawls says, "do anything we can do" (p. 70), then they can debate fundamental questions of justice in public forums without plunging the society into doctrinal wars. Rawls clearly regards us, his interlocutors, as postfundamentalist and postfoundationalist in all important respects. There is no reason, then, why the similarly situated members of a well-ordered society should have to settle for anything less than a deliberative democracy with unrestricted public reasoning.

32. See the works cited in nn. 9, 10.

THE JOURNAL OF PHILOSOPHY

VOLUME XCII, NO. 3, MARCH 1995

RECONCILIATION THROUGH THE PUBLIC USE OF REASON:
REMARKS ON JOHN RAWLS'S POLITICAL LIBERALISM*

John Rawls's *A Theory of Justice*[1] marks a pivotal turning point in the most recent history of practical philosophy, for he restored long-suppressed moral questions to the status of serious objects of philosophical investigation. Immanuel Kant posed the fundamental question of morality in such a way that it admitted a rational answer: we ought to do what is equally good for all persons. Without espousing Kant's transcendental philosophical background assumptions, Rawls renewed this theoretical approach with particular reference to the issue of the organization of a just society. In opposition to utilitarianism and value skepticism he proposed an intersubjectivist version of Kant's principle of autonomy: we act autonomously when we obey those laws which could be accepted by all concerned on the basis of a public use of their reason. More recently, in *Political Liberalism*,[2] in which Rawls has concluded a twenty-year process of extension and revision of his theory of justice, he exploits this moral concept of autonomy as the key to explaining the political autonomy of citizens of a democratic society: "Our exercise of political power is fully proper only when it is exercised in accordance with a constitution, the essentials of which all citizens as free and equal may be reasonably expected to endorse in the light of principles and ideals acceptable to their common human reason" (PL 137). Just as previously he took a stand against utilitarian positions, now he responds

---

* [This historic interchange between Jürgen Habermas and John Rawls is the result of an initiative by Michael Kelly, Managing Editor of this JOURNAL. The Trustees and Editors wish to acknowledge their appreciation for his enterprise in this matter and his dedication in carrying it through to fulfillment.]

[1] Cambridge: Harvard, 1971; hereafter TJ.
[2] New York: Columbia, 1993; hereafter PL.

0022-362X/95/9203/109–31

primarily to contextualist positions that question the presuppositions of a reason common to all humans.

Because I admire this project, share its intentions, and regard its essential results as correct, the dissent I express here will remain within the bounds of a familial dispute. My doubts are limited to whether Rawls always brings to bear against his critics his important normative intuitions in their most compelling form. But first let me review briefly the outline of his project in its current state.

Rawls offers a justification of those principles on which a modern society must be constituted if it is to ensure the fair cooperation of its citizens as free and equal persons. His first step is to clarify the standpoint from which fictional representatives of the people could answer this question impartially. Rawls explains why the parties in the so-called original position would agree on two principles: first, on the liberal principle according to which everyone is entitled to an equal system of basic liberties, and, second, on a subordinate principle that establishes equal access to public offices and stipulates that social inequalities are acceptable only when they are also to the advantage of the least privileged. In a second step, Rawls shows that this conception of justice can expect to meet with agreement under those conditions of a pluralistic society which it itself promotes. Political liberalism, as a reasonable construction that does not raise a claim to truth, is neutral toward conflicting worldviews. In a third and final step, Rawls outlines the basic rights and principles of the constitutional state that can be derived from the two principles of justice. Taking these steps in sequence, I shall raise objections directed not so much against the project as such but against certain aspects of its execution. I fear that Rawls makes concessions to opposed philosophical positions which impair the cogency of his own project.

My critique is a constructive and immanent one. First, I doubt whether every aspect of the original position is designed to clarify and secure the standpoint of impartial judgment of deontological principles of justice (I). Further, I think that Rawls should make a sharper separation between questions of justification and questions of acceptance; he seems to want to purchase the neutrality of his conception of justice at the cost of forsaking its cognitive validity claim (II). These two theoretical decisions result in a construction of the constitutional state that accords liberal basic rights primacy over the democratic principle of legitimation. Rawls thereby fails to achieve his goal of bringing the liberties of the moderns into harmony with the liberties of the ancients (III). I conclude my remarks with a thesis on the self-understanding of political philosophy: under conditions of postmetaphysical thought, this should be modest, but not in the wrong way.

My role in the present exchange with Rawls leads me to heighten tentative reservations into objections. This intensification is justified by my intention, at once friendly and provocative, of setting the not easily surveyable arguments of a highly complex and well thought-out theory in motion in such a way that the latter can reveal its strengths.[3]

I. THE DESIGN OF THE ORIGINAL POSITION

Rawls conceives of the original position as a situation in which rationally choosing representatives of the citizens are subject to the specific constraints that guarantee an impartial judgment of practical questions. The concept of full autonomy is reserved for the citizens who already live under the institutions of a well-ordered society. For the construction of the original position, Rawls splits this concept of political autonomy into two elements: the morally neutral characteristics of parties who seek their rational advantage, on the one hand, and the morally substantive situational constraints under which those parties choose principles for a system of fair cooperation, on the other. These normative constraints permit the parties to be endowed with a minimum of properties, in particular, "the capacity for a conception of the good (and thus to be rational)."[4] Regardless of whether the parties entertain exclusively purposive-rational considerations or also address ethical questions of particular plans of life, they always reach their decisions in light of their value orientations (that is, from the perspective of the groups of citizens they represent). They need not regard matters from the moral point of view which would require them to take account of what is in the equal interest of all, for this impartiality is exacted by a situation that throws a veil of ignorance over the mutually disinterested, though free and equal parties. Because the latter do not know which positions they will occupy in the society that it is their task to order, they find themselves constrained already by their self-interest to reflect on what is equally good for all.

This construction of an original position that *frames* the freedom of choice of rational actors in a reasonable fashion is explained by Rawls's initial intention of representing the theory of justice as part of the general theory of choice. Rawls originally proceeded on the

[3] In preparing the manuscript, the following works were especially helpful: Kenneth Baynes, *The Normative Grounds of Social Criticism* (Albany: SUNY, 1992); Rainer Forst, *Kontexte der Gerechtigkeit* (Frankfurt am Main: Suhrkamp, 1994).

[4] "The Basic Liberties and Their Priority" in S. McMurrin, ed., *The Tanner Lectures on Human Values, Volume III* (Salt Lake City: Utah UP, 1982), p. 16.

assumption that the range of options open to rationally choosing parties only needed to be limited in an appropriate fashion in order to facilitate the derivation of principles of justice from their enlightened self-interest. But he soon realized that the reason of autonomous citizens cannot be reduced to rational choice conditioned by subjective preferences.[5] Yet even after the revision of the initial goal that the original position was designed to achieve, he has held to the view that the meaning of the moral point of view can be operationalized in this way. This has some unfortunate consequences, three of which I would like to address in what follows: (1) Can the parties in the original position comprehend the highest-order interests of their clients solely on the basis of rational egoism? (2) Can basic rights be assimilated to primary goods? (3) Does the veil of ignorance guarantee the impartiality of judgment?[6]

(1) Rawls cannot consistently stand by the decision that "fully" autonomous citizens are to be represented by parties who lack this autonomy. Citizens are assumed to be moral persons who possess a sense of justice and the capacity for their own conception of the good, as well as an interest in cultivating these dispositions in a rational manner. But in the case of the parties in the original position, these reasonable characteristics of moral persons are replaced by the constraints of a rational design. At the same time, however, the parties are supposed to be able to understand and take adequate account of the "highest-order interests" of the citizens that follow from these very characteristics. For example, they must take account of the fact that autonomous citizens respect the interests of others on the basis of just principles and not only from self-interest, that they can be obligated to loyalty, that they want to be convinced of the legitimacy of existing arrangements and policies through the public use of their reason, and so forth. Thus, the parties are supposed both to understand and to take seriously the implications and consequences of an autonomy that they themselves are denied. This may still be plausible for the advocacy of *self-related* interests and conceptions of the good that are not known in detail. But can the meaning of considerations of justice remain unaffected by the perspective of rational egoists? At any rate, the parties are incapable of achiev-

---

[5] "Justice as Fairness: Political Not Metaphysical," *Philosophy and Public Affairs*, XIV (Summer 1985): 223–51, p. 237 n. 20.

[6] Thomas Scanlon also criticizes the traces of a decision-theoretical orientation, though from a different standpoint, in "Contractualism and Utilitarianism," in Amartya Sen and Bernard Williams, eds., *Utilitarianism and Beyond* (New York: Cambridge, 1982), pp. 123ff.

ing, within the bounds set by their rational egoism, the reciprocal perspective taking that the citizens they represent must undertake when they orient themselves in a just manner to what is equally good for all: "in their rational deliberations the parties...recognize no standpoint external to their own point of view as rational representatives" (PL 73). But if, despite this, the parties are to understand the meaning of the deontological principles they are seeking and to take sufficient account of their clients' interests in justice, they must be equipped with cognitive competences that extend further than the capacities sufficient for rationally choosing actors who are blind to issues of justice.

Of course, it is open to Rawls to modify the design of the original position accordingly. Already in *A Theory of Justice*, he qualified the rationality of the contracting partners in various ways. On the one hand, they take no interest in one another, conducting themselves like players who "strive for as high an absolute score as possible" (TJ 144). On the other hand, they are equipped with a "purely formal" sense of justice, for they are supposed to know that they will conform to whatever principles are agreed upon in their future role as citizens living in a well-ordered society (TJ 145). This can be understood to mean that the parties in the original position are at least cognizant of the kind of binding mutuality that will characterize the life of their clients in the future, although they themselves must for the present conduct their negotiations under different premises. Such stipulations are perfectly admissible. My only question is whether, in being extended in this direction, the design loses its point by becoming too far removed from the original model. For as soon as the parties step outside the boundaries of their rational egoism and assume even a distant likeness to moral persons, the division of labor between the rationality of choice of subjects and appropriate objective constraints is destroyed, a division through which self-interested agents are nonetheless supposed to achieve morally sound decisions. This consequence may not have a great impact on the rest of the project; but it draws attention to the conceptual constraints imposed by the original (though in the meantime abandoned) intention to provide a decision-theoretical solution to Thomas Hobbes's problem. For another consequence of the rational-choice format of the original position is the introduction of basic goods, and this determination is important for the further development of the theory.

(2) For rationally choosing actors bound to the first-person perspective, normative issues of whatever kind can be represented solely

in terms of interests or values that are satisfied by goods. Goods are what we strive for—indeed, what is good for us. Correspondingly, Rawls introduces "primary goods" as generalized means that people may need in order to realize their plans of life. Although the parties know that some of these primary goods assume the form of rights for citizens of a well-ordered society, in the original position they themselves can only describe rights as one category of "goods" among others. For them, the issue of principles of justice can only arise in the guise of the question of the just distribution of primary goods. Rawls thereby adopts a concept of justice that is proper to an ethics of the good, one that is more consistent with Aristotelian or utilitarian approaches than with a theory of rights, such as his own, that proceeds from the concept of autonomy. Precisely because Rawls adheres to a conception of justice on which the autonomy of citizens is constituted through rights, the paradigm of distribution generates difficulties for him. Rights can be "enjoyed" only by being *exercised*. They cannot be assimilated to distributive goods without forfeiting their deontological meaning. An equal distribution of rights results only if those who enjoy rights recognize one another as free and equal. Of course, there exist rights *to* a fair share of goods or opportunities, but rights in the first instance regulate relations between actors: they cannot be "possessed" like things.[7] If I am correct, the conceptual constraints of the model of rational choice preclude Rawls from construing basic liberties from the outset as basic rights and compel him to interpret them as primary goods. This leads him to assimilate the deontological meaning of obligatory norms to the teleological meaning of preferred values.[8] Rawls thereby blurs certain distinctions that I shall briefly mention in order to show how this limits his options in the further development of his project.

Norms inform decisions as to what one ought to do, values inform decisions as to what conduct is most desirable. Recognized norms impose equal and exceptionless obligations on their addressees, while values express the preferability of goods that are striven for by particular groups. Whereas norms are observed in the sense of a fulfillment of generalized behavioral expectations, values or goods can be realized or acquired only by purposive action. Furthermore, norms raise a binary validity claim in virtue of which they are said to be either valid or invalid: to ought statements, as to assertoric state-

---

[7] See Iris M. Young, *Justice and the Politics of Difference* (Princeton: University Press, 1990), p. 25.

[8] This objection is not based on the thesis of the primacy of duties over rights, as in Onora O'Neill, *Constructions of Reason* (New York: Cambridge, 1989), ch. 12, pp. 206ff.

ments, we can respond only with 'yes' or 'no'—or refrain from judgment. Values, by contrast, fix relations of preference that signify that certain goods are more attractive than others: hence, we can assent to evaluative statements to a greater or lesser degree. The obligatory force of norms has the absolute meaning of an unconditional and universal duty: what one ought to do is what is equally good for all (that is, for all addressees). The attractiveness of values reflects an evaluation and a transitive ordering of goods that has become established in particular cultures or has been adopted by particular groups: important evaluative decisions or higher-order preferences express what is good for us (or for me), all things considered. Finally, different norms must not contradict each other when they claim validity for the same domain of addressees; they must stand in coherent relations to one another—in other words, they must constitute a system. Different values, by contrast, compete for priority; insofar as they meet with intersubjective recognition within a culture or group, they constitute shifting configurations fraught with tension. To sum up, norms differ from values, first, in their relation to rule-governed as opposed to purposive action; second, in a binary as opposed to a gradual coding of the respective validity claims; third, in their absolute as opposed to relative bindingness; and, last, in the criteria that systems of norms as opposed to systems of values must satisfy.

Nevertheless, Rawls wishes to do justice to the deontological intuition that finds expression in these distinctions; hence, he must compensate for the leveling of the deontological dimension which he—as a consequence of the design of the original position—initially accepts with the concept of primary goods. So he accords the first principle priority over the second. An absolute priority of equal liberties over the primary goods regulated by the second principle is, however, difficult to justify from the first-person perspective in which we orient ourselves to our own interests or values. H.L.A. Hart[9] has developed this point clearly in his critique of Rawls. Interestingly, Rawls can meet this criticism only by building a *subsequent* qualification into the primary goods which secures them a relation to basic liberties as basic rights: he acknowledges as primary goods only those which are expedient for the life plans and the development of the moral faculties of citizens *as free and equal persons.*[10] Furthermore, Rawls differentiates the primary goods that

[9] "Rawls on Liberty and Its Priority," in Norman Daniels, ed., *Reading Rawls* (New York: Basic, 1975), pp. 230ff.

[10] See Wilfried Hinsch, "Einleitung" to Rawls, *Die Idee des politischen Liberalismus* (Frankfurt am Main: Suhrkamp, 1992), pp. 38ff.

347

are constitutive of the institutional framework of the well-ordered
society in the moral sense from the remainder of the primary goods
by incorporating the guarantee of the "fair value" of liberty into the
first principle.[11]

This additional determination, however, tacitly presupposes a
deontological distinction between rights and goods which contradicts the prima facie classification of rights as goods. Since the fair
value of equal liberties requires the actual availability of equal opportunities to exercise these rights, only rights, not goods, can be qualified in this manner. Only in the case of rights can we distinguish
between legal competence and the actual opportunities to choose
and to act. Only between rights, on the one side, and actual chances
to exercise rights, on the other, can there exist a chasm that is problematic from the perspective of justice; such a rupture cannot exist
between the possession and enjoyment of goods. It would be either
redundant or meaningless to speak of the "fair value" of equally distributed goods. The distinction between legal and factual equality
has no application to "goods" for grammatical reasons, to put it in
Wittgensteinian terms. But if the notion of primary goods is subject
to correction in a second step, we may ask whether the first step—
the design of the original position that necessitates this conception—was a wise one.

(3) The foregoing reflections show that, for the parties in the original position, the capacity to make rational decisions is not sufficient
to comprehend the highest-order interests of their clients or to
understand rights (in Ronald Dworkin's[12] sense) as trumps that over-
ride collective goals. But why then are the parties deprived of practical reason in the first place and shrouded in an impenetrable veil of
ignorance? Rawls's guiding intuition is clear: the role of the categorical imperative is taken over by an intersubjectively applied procedure which is embodied in participation conditions, such as the
equality of parties, and in situational features, such as the veil of
ignorance. In my view, however, the potential gains of this turn are
dissipated precisely by the systematic deprivation of information.
This third question reveals the perspective from which I also posed
the two previous questions: I believe that Rawls could avoid the difficulties associated with the design of an original position if he operationalized the moral point of view in a different way, namely, if he
kept the procedural conception of practical reason free of substantive connotations by developing it in a strictly procedural manner.

[11] "The Basic Liberties and Their Priority," pp. 21ff. and 39ff.
[12] See, e.g., *Taking Rights Seriously* (Cambridge: Harvard, 1977).

Kant's categorical imperative already goes beyond the egocentric character of the Golden Rule: "Do not do unto others what you would not have them do unto you." Whereas this rule calls for a universalization test from the viewpoint of a given individual, the categorical imperative requires that all those possibly affected be able to will a just maxim as a general rule. But as long as we apply this more exacting test in a monological fashion, it still remains individually isolated perspectives from which each of us considers privately what all could will. This is inadequate. For only when the self-understanding of each individual reflects a transcendental consciousness, that is, a universally valid view of the world, would what from my point of view is equally good for all actually be in the equal interest of each individual. But this can no longer be assumed under conditions of social and ideological pluralism. If we wish to preserve the intuition underlying the Kantian universalization principle, we can respond to this fact of pluralism in different ways. Rawls imposes a common perspective on the parties in the original position through informational constraints and thereby neutralizes the multiplicity of particular interpretive perspectives from the outset. Discourse ethics, by contrast, views the moral point of view as embodied in an intersubjective practice of argumentation which enjoins those involved to an idealizing *enlargement* of their interpretive perspectives.

Discourse ethics rests on the intuition that the application of the principle of universalization, properly understood, calls for a joint process of "ideal role taking." It interprets this idea of G. H. Mead in terms of a pragmatic theory of argumentation.[13] Under the pragmatic presuppositions of an inclusive and noncoercive rational discourse among free and equal participants, everyone is required to take the perspective of everyone else, and thus project herself into the understandings of self and world of all others; from this interlocking of perspectives there emerges an ideally extended we-perspective from which all can test in common whether they wish to make a controversial norm the basis of their shared practice; and this should include mutual criticism of the appropriateness of the languages in terms of which situations and needs are interpreted. In the course of

[13] My *Moral Consciousness and Communicative Action*, Christian Lenhardt and Shierry Weber Nicholsen, trans. (Cambridge: MIT, 1990), and *Justification and Application: Remarks on Discourse Ethics*, Ciaran Cronin, trans. (Cambridge: MIT, 1993). On the location of discourse ethics in contemporary American discussions, see Seyla Benhabib, "In the Shadow of Aristotle and Hegel: Communicative Ethics and Current Controversies in Practical Philosophy," in Michael Kelly, ed., *Hermeneutics and Critical Theory in Ethics and Politics* (Cambridge: MIT, 1990), pp. 1–31. See also David Rasmussen, ed., *Universalism versus Communitarianism: Contemporary Debates in Ethics* (Cambridge: MIT, 1990).

successively undertaken abstractions, the core of generalizable interests can then emerge step by step.[14]

Things are different when the veil of ignorance constrains *from the
beginning* the field of vision of parties in the original position to the
basic principles on which presumptively free and equal citizens
would agree, notwithstanding their divergent understandings of self
and world. It is important to see that with this initial abstraction
Rawls accepts a *double* burden of proof. The veil of ignorance must
extend to all particular viewpoints and interests that could impair an
impartial judgment; at the same time, it may extend *only* to such normative matters as can be disqualified without further ado as candidates for the common good to be accepted by free and equal
citizens. This second condition makes a demand on the theory that
is difficult to meet, as is shown by a brief reflection. Following the
justification of the principles of justice, the veil of ignorance is gradually raised at the successive steps of framing the constitution, of legislation, and of applying law. Since the new information that thereby
flows in must harmonize with the basic principles already selected
under conditions of informational constraint, unpleasant surprises
must be avoided. If we are to ensure that no discrepancies arise, we
must construct the original position already with knowledge, and
even foresight, of all the normative contents that could potentially
nourish the shared self-understanding of free and equal citizens in
the future. In other words, the theoretician himself would have to
shoulder the burden of anticipating at least parts of the information
of which he previously relieved the parties in the original position!
The impartiality of judgment would be guaranteed in the original
position only if the basic normative concepts employed in its construction—those of the politically autonomous citizen, of fair cooperation, and of a well-ordered society, in the specific sense Rawls
attaches to these terms—could withstand revision in light of morally
significant future experiences and learning processes.

If such a heavy burden of proof is generated by the deprivation of
information imposed on the parties in the original position by the
veil of ignorance, a convenient response would be to lighten this
burden by operationalizing the moral point of view in a different
way. I have in mind the more open procedure of an argumentative
practice that proceeds under the demanding presuppositions of the
"public use of reason" and does not bracket the pluralism of convic-

---

[14] Cf. William Rehg, *Insight and Solidarity: The Discourse Ethics of Jürgen Habermas*
(Berkeley: California UP, 1993).

tions and worldviews from the outset. This procedure can be explicated without having recourse to the substantive concepts that Rawls employs in the construction of the original position.

II. THE FACT OF PLURALISM & THE IDEA OF AN OVERLAPPING CONSENSUS

Since his Dewey Lectures, "Kantian Constructivism in Moral Theory,"[15] Rawls has stressed the *political* character of justice as fairness. This shift is motivated by disquiet concerning the fact of social and, above all, ideological pluralism. In discussing the "veil of ignorance," I have already clarified the burden of proof that the theory of justice takes upon itself with its initial theoretical decisions. The decisive issue in the justification of the two highest principles of justice is less the deliberations in the original position than the intuitions and basic concepts that guide the design of the original position itself. Rawls introduces normative contents into the very procedure of justification, above all those ideas he associates with the concept of the moral person: the sense of fairness and the capacity for one's own conception of the good. Thus, the concept of the citizen as a moral person, which also underlies the concept of the fair cooperation of politically autonomous citizens, stands in need of a *prior* justification. Further, it needs to be shown that this conception is neutral toward conflicting worldviews and remains uncontroversial after the veil of ignorance has been lifted. This explains Rawls's interest in a *political,* as opposed to a *metaphysical,* conception of justice. I suspect that this terminology indicates a certain unclarity about the precise character of what is in need of justification; from this, in turn, there results an indecisiveness as to how the validity claim of the theory itself should be understood. I shall examine whether the overlapping consensus, on which the theory of justice depends, plays a cognitive or merely instrumental role: whether it primarily contributes to the further justification of the theory or whether it serves, in light of the prior justification of the theory, to explicate a necessary condition of social stability (1). Connected with this is the question of the sense in which Rawls uses the predicate 'reasonable': as a predicate for the validity of moral judgments or for the reflective attitude of enlightened tolerance (2).

(1) In order to pin down the underlying normative ideas, Rawls has recourse to the so-called method of reflective equilibrium. The philosopher arrives at the basic concept of the moral person and the adjunct concepts of the politically autonomous citizen, of fair cooperation, of the well-ordered society, and so forth, via a rational

---

[15] This JOURNAL, LXXVII, 9 (September 1980): 515–72.

reconstruction of proven intuitions, that is, intuitions actually *found* in the practices and traditions of a democratic society. Reflective equilibrium is achieved at the moment when the philosopher has attained the assurance that those involved can no longer reject with good reasons intuitions reconstructed and clarified in this manner. The procedure of rational reconstruction already fulfills Thomas Scanlon's criterion of what it is "not reasonable to reject" (*op. cit.*). Of course, Rawls does not wish to limit himself solely to the fundamental normative convictions of a *particular* political culture: even the present-day Rawls, *pace* Richard Rorty, has not become a contextualist. His aim, as before, is to reconstruct a substratum of intuitive ideas latent in the political culture of his society and its democratic traditions. But if experiences associated with an incipiently successful institutionalization of principles of justice have already become sedimented in the existing political culture—in the American, for example—such a reconstructive appropriation can accomplish more than merely the hermeneutic clarification of a contingent tradition. The concept of justice *worked out* on this basis must nonetheless be examined once again as to whether it can expect to meet with acceptance in a pluralistic society. How is this second step related to the first stage of justification of the two highest principles? Is it even properly a second step of *justification?*

Already in the final chapters of *A Theory of Justice*, Rawls addressed the issue of whether a society constituted in accordance with the principles of justice could stabilize itself: for example, whether it could generate the functionally necessary motivations from its own resources through the requisite political socialization of its citizens (TJ 496ff.). In view of the fact of social and ideological pluralism which he subsequently took more seriously, Rawls now wants to examine in a similar way whether the theoretical conception of justice falls under the "art of the possible" and hence is "practicable."[16] First of all, the central concept of the person, on which the theory ultimately rests, must be sufficiently neutral to be acceptable from the interpretive perspectives of different worldviews. Hence, it must be shown that justice as fairness can form the basis of an "overlapping consensus." So far, so good. What bothers me is Rawls's working assumption that such a test of acceptability is of the same kind as the test of consistency he previously undertook with reference to the well-ordered society's potential for self-stabilization.

---

[16] "The Domain of the Political and Overlapping Consensus," *New York University Law Review*, LXIV (1988): 223–55, p. 246.

This methodological parallel is problematic because the test cannot be undertaken in an immanent manner in the case of acceptability; it is no longer a move within the theory. The test of the neutrality of the basic normative concepts with respect to conflicting world-views now rests on different premises: it is different from a hypothetical examination of the capacity of a society already organized in accordance with principles of justice to reproduce itself. Rawls himself distinguishes in his present work between "two stages" of theory formation. The principles justified at the first stage must be exposed to public discussion at the second stage. Only when the theoretical design is completed can the fact of pluralism be brought into play and the abstractions of the original position revoked. The theory as a whole must be subjected to criticism by citizens in the forum of public reason. But this now refers not to the fictional citizens of a just society about whom statements are made within the theory but to real citizens of flesh and blood. The theory, therefore, must leave the outcome of such a test of acceptability undetermined. For Rawls has in mind real discourses whose outcome is open: "What if it turns out that the principles of justice as fairness cannot gain the support of reasonable doctrines, so that the case for stability fails?... We should have to see whether acceptable changes in the principles of justice would achieve stability" (PL 65–66). Clearly, the philosopher can at most attempt to anticipate in reflection the direction of real discourses as they would probably unfold under conditions of a pluralistic society. But such a more or less realistic simulation of real discourses cannot be incorporated into the theory in the same way as the derivation of possibilities of self-stabilization from the underlying premises of a just society. For now the citizens themselves debate about the premises developed by the parties in the original position.

The misleading parallel would be of no further consequence if it did not cast in the wrong light the "overlapping consensus" with which the principles of justice are supposed to converge. Because Rawls situates the "question of stability" in the foreground, the overlapping consensus merely expresses the functional contribution that the theory of justice can make to the peaceful institutionalization of social cooperation; but in this the intrinsic value of a *justified* theory must already be presupposed. From this functionalist perspective, the question of whether the theory can meet with public agreement—that is, from the perspective of different worldviews in the forum of the public use of reason—would lose an epistemic meaning essential to the theory itself. The overlapping consensus would then be merely an index of the utility, and no longer a confirmation of the correctness of the theory; it would no longer be of interest from the point of view of acceptability, and hence of validity, but only from that of acceptance, that is, of securing social stability. If I understand Rawls correctly, however, he does not wish to distinguish in this way between questions of justification and questions of stability. When he calls his conception of justice *political*, his intention appears to be rather to collapse the distinction between its justified acceptability and its actual acceptance: "the aim of justice as fairness as a political conception is practical, and not metaphysical or epistemological. That is, it presents itself not as a conception of justice that is true, but one that can serve as a basis of informed and willing political agreement between citizens viewed as free and equal persons."[17]

In my view, Rawls must make a sharper distinction between acceptability and acceptance. A purely instrumental understanding of the theory is already invalidated by the fact that the citizens must first be *convinced* by the proposed conception of justice before such a consensus can come about. The conception of justice must not be *political* in the wrong sense and should not merely lead to a modus vivendi. The theory itself must furnish the premises "that we and others recognize as true, or as reasonable for the purpose of reaching a working agreement on the fundamentals of political justice."[18] But if Rawls rules out a functionalist interpretation of justice as fairness, he must allow some *epistemic* relation between the validity of his theory and the prospect of its neutrality toward competing worldviews being confirmed in public discourses. The stabilizing effect of an overlapping consensus would then be explained in cognitive terms, that is, in terms of the confirmation of the assumption that justice as fairness is neutral toward "comprehensive doctrines." I do not mean to say that Rawls accepts premises that would prevent him from drawing this consequence; I mean only that he hesitates to assert it because he associates with the characterization 'political' the proviso that the theory of justice should not be burdened with an epistemic claim and that its anticipated practical effect should not be made contingent on the rational acceptability of its assertions. Thus, we have reason to ask why Rawls does not think his theory admits of truth and *in what sense* he here uses the predicate 'reasonable' in place of the predicate 'true'.

---

[17] "Justice as Fairness: Political Not Metaphysical," p. 230.
[18] "The Idea of an Overlapping Consensus," *Oxford Journal of Legal Studies*, VII (1987): 1–25, p. 6.

(2) On a weak interpretation, the claim that a theory of justice cannot be true or false has merely the unproblematic sense that normative statements do not describe an independent order of moral facts. On a strong interpretation, this thesis has the value-skeptical sense that behind the validity claim of normative statements there lurks something purely subjective: feelings, wishes, or decisions expressed in a grammatically misleading fashion. But for Rawls, both moral realism and value skepticism are equally unacceptable. He wants to secure for normative statements—and for the theory of justice as a whole—a form of rational obligatoriness founded on justified intersubjective recognition, but without according them an epistemic meaning. For this reason, he introduces the predicate 'reasonable' as a complementary concept to 'true'. The difficulty here is in specifying in what sense the one is a "complementary concept" to the other. Two alternative interpretations suggest themselves. Either we understand 'reasonable' in the sense of practical reason as synonymous with 'morally true', that is, as a validity concept analogous to truth and on the same plane as propositional truth; this reading is supported by at least one line of argumentation (a). Or we understand 'reasonable' in more or less the same sense as 'thoughtfulness' in dealing with debatable views whose truth is for the present undecided; then 'reasonable' is employed as a higher-level predicate concerned more with "reasonable disagreements," and hence with the fallibilistic consciousness and civil demeanor of persons, than with the validity of their assertions. In general, Rawls seems to favor this latter reading (b).

(a) Rawls first introduces the 'reasonable' as a property of moral persons. People count as reasonable who possess a sense of justice and thus are both willing and able to take account of fair conditions of cooperation, but who are also aware of the fallibility of knowledge and—in recognition of these "burdens of reason"—are willing to justify their conception of political justice publicly. By contrast, persons act merely "rationally" as long as they are prudently guided by their conception of the good.[19] What it means to be reasonable can indeed be explicated in terms of such qualities of moral persons. But the concept of a person itself already presupposes the concept of practical reason.

Ultimately, Rawls explains the meaning of practical reason by reference to two dimensions: on the one hand, the deontological dimension of normative validity (which I here leave to one side as

---

[19] "What rational agents lack is the particular form of moral sensibility that underlies the desire to engage in fair cooperation as such, and to do so on terms that others as equals might reasonably be expected to endorse" (PL 51).

unproblematic) and, on the other, the pragmatic dimension of a public sphere and the process of public reasoning (which is of particular interest in the present context). The public use is in a sense inscribed in reason. *Publicity* is the common perspective from which the citizens *mutually* convince one another of what is just and unjust by the force of the better argument. This perspective of the public use of reason, in which all participate, first lends moral convictions their objectivity. Rawls calls valid normative statements *objective* and he explains "objectivity" in a procedural manner with reference to a public use of reason that satisfies certain counterfactual conditions: "Political convictions (which are also, of course, moral convictions) are objective—actually founded on an order of reasons—if reasonable and rational persons, who are sufficiently intelligent and conscientious in exercising their powers of practical reason...would eventually endorse those convictions...provided that these persons know the relevant facts and have sufficiently surveyed the grounds that bear on the matter under conditions favorable to due reflection" (PL 119). Rawls does add in this passage that grounds are only specified as good grounds in the light of a recognized concept of justice; but this concept must in turn meet with agreement under the same ideal conditions (PL 137). Hence, Rawls must be understood to mean that, on his view as well, the procedure of the public use of reason remains the final court of appeal for normative statements.

In the light of this reflection, it could be said that the predicate 'reasonable' points to the discursive redemption of a validity claim. By analogy with a nonsemantic concept of truth purified of all connotations of correspondence, one could understand 'reasonable'—correctly, in my view—as a predicate for the validity of normative statements.[20] This is clearly not how Rawls himself uses this term. Otherwise, he would not say that worldviews need not be true even when they are reasonable—and vice versa. For me, the problem is not Rawls's rejection of moral realism or the consequent rejection of a semantic truth predicate for normative statements but the fact that he does attach such a truth predicate to worldviews (comprehensive doctrines). He thereby precludes the possibility of exploiting the epistemic connotations of the term 'reasonable', connotations which he must nevertheless attribute to his own conception of justice if this is to lay claim to some sort of normative binding force.

(b) On Rawls's conception, metaphysical doctrines and religious world-interpretations admit of truth and falsity. As a consequence, a

---

[20] Cf. my reflections in *Justification and Application*, pp. 25ff.

political conception of justice could only be true if it were not merely compatible with such doctrines but also *derivable* from a true doctrine. Yet from the point of view of a political philosophy that is neutral toward worldviews, we cannot determine whether and when this is the case. From this secular viewpoint, the truth claims of all reasonable worldviews have equal weight, where those worldviews count as reasonable which compete with one another in a reflexive attitude, that is, on the assumption that one's own truth claim could prevail in public discourse in the long run only through the force of better reasons. "Reasonable comprehensive doctrines" are ultimately distinguished by their recognition of the burdens of proof, which enables groups with competing ideologies to accept—for the time being—a "reasonable disagreement" as the basis of their peaceful coexistence.

Since disputes concerning metaphysical and religious truths remain unresolved under conditions of enduring pluralism, only the reasonableness of this kind of reflexive consciousness can be transferred as a validity predicate to a political conception of justice compatible with all reasonable doctrines. By way of this transference, a reasonable conception of justice preserves an oblique relation to a truth claim projected into the future. But it cannot be certain that one of the reasonable doctrines from which it is derivable is also the true one. A political conception of justice is reasonable in the sense that it can afford a kind of tolerance toward worldviews that are not unreasonable, in the sense advocated by Gottfried Lessing. What remains is an act of faith in reason: "reasonable faith in the real possibility of a just constitutional regime."[21] This view may appeal to some of our better intuitions, but how can it be harmonized with Rawls's reasons for accepting the priority of the right over the good in the first place?

Questions of justice or *moral* questions admit of justifiable answers—justifiable in the sense of rational acceptability—because they are concerned with what, from an ideally expanded perspective, is in the equal interest of all. *Ethical* questions, by contrast, do not admit of such impartial treatment because they refer to what, from the first-person perspective, is in the long run good for me or for us—even if this is not equally good for all. Now, metaphysical or religious worldviews are at the very least permeated with answers to basic ethical questions; they articulate in an exemplary fashion collective identities and guide individual plans of life. Hence, world-

---

[21] "The Idea of an Overlapping Consensus," p. 25.

views are measured more by the authenticity of the life styles they shape than by the truth of the statements they admit.[22] Because such doctrines are "comprehensive" in precisely the sense that they offer interpretations of the world as a whole, they cannot merely be understood as an ordered set of statements of fact; their contents cannot be expressed completely in sentences that admit of truth and they do not form a symbolic system that can be true or false as such. So, at least, it appears under the conditions of postmetaphysical thinking in which justice as fairness is to be justified.

But then it is impossible to make the validity of a conception of justice contingent on the truth of a worldview, however reasonable it may be. Rather, under these premises it makes sense to analyze the different validity claims that we associate, respectively, with descriptive, evaluative, and normative statements (of various kinds) independently of the characteristic complex of validity claims that are obscurely fused together in religious and metaphysical interpretations of reality.[23]

Why does Rawls nevertheless think that identity-stabilizing worldviews admit of truth? A possible motive might be the conviction that a profane, freestanding morality is untenable, that moral convictions must be embedded in metaphysical or religious doctrines. That, at any rate, would cohere with Rawls's way of posing the problem of an overlapping consensus: he takes as his model that political institutionalization of freedom of belief and conscience which brought the religious civil wars of the modern period to an end. But could the religious conflicts have been brought to an end if the principle of tolerance and freedom of belief and conscience had not been able to appeal, with good reasons, to a moral validity *independent* of religion and metaphysics?

III. PRIVATE AND PUBLIC AUTONOMY

The objections I raised in the first part against the design of the original position and in the second against the assimilation of questions of validity to those of acceptance point in the same direction. By subjecting rationally choosing parties to reasonable procedural constraints, Rawls remains dependent on substantive normative assumptions; at the same time, by tailoring a universalistic theory of justice to questions of political stability through an overlapping consensus, he compromises its epistemic status. Both strategies are pursued at the cost of a strict proceduralist program. By contrast with this

---

[22] See Forst, "Justice as Fairness: Ethical, Political, or Moral" (manuscript, 1992).
[23] My "Themes in Postmetaphysical Thinking," in *Postmetaphysical Thinking*, William Mark Hohengarten, trans. (Cambridge: MIT, 1992), pp. 28-53.

approach, Rawls could satisfy more elegantly the burdens of proof he incurs with his strong and presumptively neutral concept of the moral person if he developed his substantive concepts and assumptions out of the procedure of the public use of reason.

In my view, the moral point of view is already implicit in the socio-ontological constitution of the public practice of argumentation, comprising the complex relations of mutual recognition that participants in rational discourse "must" accept (in the sense of weak transcendental necessity). Rawls believes that a theory of justice developed in such exclusively procedural terms could not be "sufficiently structured." Since I subscribe to a division of labor between moral theory and the theory of action, I do not regard this as a serious reservation: the conceptual structuring of the contexts of interaction to which questions of political justice refer is not within the province of moral theory. Together with the content of action conflicts in need of resolution, a whole conceptual frame for normatively regulated interaction is forced upon us—a network of concepts in which persons and interpersonal relations, actors and actions, norm-conforming and deviant behavior, responsibility and autonomy, and even intersubjectively structured moral feelings all find their place. Each of these concepts deserves a prior analysis. If we then take the concept of practical reason in the procedural sense that Rawls himself intimates with his notion of the public use of reason, we could say that precisely those principles are valid which meet with uncoerced intersubjective recognition under conditions of rational discourse. It remains as a further, and primarily empirical, question whether and when such valid principles ensure political stability under conditions of pluralism. In what follows, I am interested in the consistent execution of the proceduralist program only with reference to one implication it has for the explanation of the constitutional state.

Liberals have stressed the "liberties of the moderns": liberty of belief and conscience, the protection of life, personal liberty, and property—in sum, the core of subjective private rights. Republicanism, by contrast, has defended the "liberties of the ancients": the political rights of participation and communication that make possible the citizens' exercise of self-determination. Jean-Jacques Rousseau and Kant shared the aspiration of deriving both elements from the same root, namely, from moral and political autonomy: the liberal rights may neither be merely foisted on the practice of self-determination as extrinsic constraints nor be made merely instrumental to its exercise. Rawls, too, subscribes to this intuition;

nevertheless, the two-stage character of his theory generates a priority of liberal rights which demotes the democratic process to an inferior status.

Rawls certainly proceeds from the idea of political autonomy and models it at the level of the original position: it is represented by the interplay between the rationally choosing parties and the framework conditions that guarantee impartiality of judgment. But this idea is brought to bear only selectively at the institutional level of the democratic procedure for the political will formation of free and equal citizens from which it is nonetheless borrowed. The form of political autonomy granted virtual existence in the original position, and thus on the first level of theory formation, does not fully unfold in the heart of the justly constituted society. For the higher the veil of ignorance is raised and the more Rawls's citizens themselves take on real flesh and blood, the more deeply they find themselves subject to principles and norms that have been anticipated in theory and have already become institutionalized beyond their control. In this way, the theory deprives the citizens of too many of the insights that they would have to assimilate anew in each generation. From the perspective of the theory of justice, the act of founding the democratic constitution cannot be repeated under the institutional conditions of an already constituted just society, and the process of realizing the system of basic rights cannot be assured on an ongoing basis. It is not possible for the citizens to experience this process as open and incomplete, as the shifting historical circumstances nonetheless demand. They cannot reignite the radical democratic embers of the original position in the civic life of their society, for from their perspective all of the *essential* discourses of legitimation have already taken place within the theory; and they find the results of the theory already sedimented in the constitution. Because the citizens cannot conceive of the constitution as a *project*, the public use of reason does not actually have the significance of a present exercise of political autonomy but merely promotes the nonviolent *preservation of political stability*. Granted, this reading does not reflect Rawls's intention in formulating his theory,[24] but if I am correct it uncovers one of its undesired consequences. This is shown, for example, by the rigid boundary between the political and the nonpublic identities of the citizens. According to Rawls, this boundary is set by basic liberal

---

[24] Cf. the Tanner Lectures, where he writes at the end of section VII: "The idea is to incorporate into the basic structure of society an effective political procedure which mirrors in that structure the fair representation of persons achieved by the original position" (p. 45).

rights that constrain democratic self-legislation, and with it the sphere of the political, *from the beginning*, that is, prior to all political will formation.

Rawls uses the term 'political' in a threefold sense. Thus far, we have become acquainted with the theoretical meaning: a conception of justice is political and not metaphysical when it is neutral toward conflicting worldviews. Further, Rawls uses the term 'political' in the usual sense to classify matters of public interest, so that political philosophy limits itself to the justification of the institutional framework and the basic structure of society. Both meanings are ultimately combined in an interesting way in Rawls's treatment of "political values." The 'political' in this third sense constitutes a fund both of shared convictions of citizens and of perspectives for delimiting an object domain. Rawls treats the political value sphere, which is distinguished in modern societies from other cultural value spheres, as something given, almost in the manner of a neo-Kantian like Max Weber. For only with reference to political values, whatever they may be, can he split the moral person into the public identity of a citizen and the nonpublic identity of a private person shaped by her individual conception of the good. These two identities then constitute the reference points for two domains, the one constituted by rights of political participation and communication, the other protected by basic liberal rights. The constitutional protection of the private sphere in this way enjoys priority while "the role of the political liberties is...largely instrumental in preserving the other liberties."[25] Thus, with reference to the political value sphere, a prepolitical domain of liberties is delimited which is withdrawn from the reach of democratic self-legislation.

But such an a priori boundary between private and public autonomy not only contradicts the republican intuition that popular sovereignty and human rights are nourished by the same root. It also conflicts with historical experience, above all with the fact that the historically shifting boundary between the private and public spheres has always been problematic from a normative point of view.[26] In addition, the development of the welfare state shows that the boundaries between the private and public autonomy of citizens are in flux and that such differentiations must be subjected to the political will formation of the citizens if the latter are to have the opportunity to press a legal claim to the "fair value" of their liberties.

[25] "The Basic Liberties and Their Priority," p. 13.
[26] Benhabib, "Models of Public Space," in her *Situating the Self* (New York: Routledge, 1992), pp. 89-120.

A theory of justice can take better account of this circumstance if it differentiates the "political" in accordance with the criterion of "legal regulation" (mentioned only in passing by Rawls). It is ultimately by means of positive and coercive law that the life of a political community is legitimately regulated (PL 215). The basic question then is: Which rights must free and equal persons mutually accord one another if they wish to regulate their coexistence by the legitimate means of positive and coercive law?

According to Kant's conception of legality, *coercive law* extends only to the external relations among persons and addresses the freedom of choice of subjects who are allowed to follow their own conception of the good. Hence modern law, on the one hand, constitutes the status of legal subjects in terms of actionable subjective liberties that may be exercised by each according to her own preferences. Since it must also be *possible* to obey a legal order for moral reasons, the status of private legal subjects is legitimately determined by the right to *equal* subjective liberties.[27] As *positive* or *codified law*, on the other hand, this medium calls for a political legislator, where the legitimacy of legislation is accounted for by a democratic procedure that secures the autonomy of the citizens. Citizens are politically autonomous only if they can view themselves jointly as authors of the laws to which they are subject as individual addressees.

The dialectical relation between private and public autonomy becomes clear in light of the fact that the status of such democratic citizens equipped with law-making competences can be institutionalized in turn only by means of coercive law. But because this law is directed to persons who could not even assume the status of legal subjects without subjective private rights, the private and public autonomy of citizens *mutually* presuppose each other. As we have seen, both elements are already interwoven in the concept of positive and coercive law: there can be no law at all without actionable subjective liberties that guarantee the private autonomy of individual legal subjects; and no legitimate law without democratic law making by citizens in common who, as free and equal, are entitled to participate in this process. Once the concept of law has been clarified in this way, it becomes clear that the normative substance of basic liberal rights is already contained in the indispensable medium for the legal institutionalization of the public use of reason of sovereign citizens. The main objects of further analysis are then the communicative presuppositions and the procedures of a discursive process of opinion and will formation in which the public use of reason is man-

[27] This principle of Kantian legal theory is taken up in Rawls's first principle.

ifested. I cannot discuss this alternative in greater detail in the present context.[28]

Such a procedural moral and legal theory is at the same time more and less modest than Rawls's theory. It is more modest because it focuses exclusively on the procedural aspects of the public use of reason and derives the system of rights from the idea of its legal institutionalization. It can leave more questions open because it entrusts more to the *process* of rational opinion and will formation. Philosophy shoulders different theoretical burdens when, as on Rawls's conception, it claims to elaborate the idea of a just society, while the citizens then use this idea as a platform from which to judge existing arrangements and policies. By contrast, I propose that philosophy limit itself to the clarification of the moral point of view and the procedure of democratic legitimation, to the analysis of the conditions of rational discourses and negotiations. In this more modest role, philosophy need not proceed in a constructive, but only in a *reconstructive* fashion. It leaves substantial questions that must be answered here and now to the more or less enlightened engagement of participants, which does not mean that philosophers may not also participate in the public debate, though in the role of intellectuals, not of experts.

Rawls insists on a modesty of a different kind. He wants to extend the "method of avoidance," which is intended to lead to an overlapping consensus on questions of political justice, to the philosophical enterprise. He hopes to develop political philosophy into a sharply focused discipline and thereby to avoid most of the controversial questions of a more general nature. This avoidance strategy can lead to an impressively self-contained theory, as we can see from the wonderful example before us. But even Rawls cannot develop his theory in as freestanding a fashion as he would like. As we have seen, his "political constructivism" draws him willy-nilly into the dispute concerning concepts of rationality and truth. His concept of the person also oversteps the boundaries of political philosophy. These and other preliminary theoretical decisions involve him in as many long-running and still unresolved debates. The subject matter itself, it seems to me, makes a presumptuous encroachment on neighboring fields often unavoidable and at times even fruitful.

JÜRGEN HABERMAS

Johann Wolfgang Goethe-Universität
translated by Ciaran Cronin

[28] Cf. my *Faktizität und Geltung* (Frankfurt: Suhrkamp, 1992), chs. III and IV. English translation, *Between Facts and Norms*, Rehg, trans. (Cambridge: MIT, forthcoming).

Acknowledgments

Raz, Joseph. "Liberalism, Autonomy, and the Politics of Neutral Concern," *Social and Political Philosophy, Midwest Studies in Philosophy* 7, edited by Peter A. French, Theodore E. Uehling, Jr., and Howard K. Wettstein (1982): 89–120. Reprinted with the permission of the University of Minnesota Press. Copyright 1982.

Kymlicka, Will. "Liberal Individualism and Liberal Neutrality," *Ethics* 99 (1989): 883–905. Reprinted with the permission of the University of Chicago Press.

Cohen, Joshua. "Moral Pluralism and Political Consensus." In *The Idea of Democracy*, edited by David Copp, Jean Hampton, and John E. Roemer (New York: Cambridge University Press, 1993): 270–91. Reprinted with the permission of Cambridge University Press.

Waldron, Jeremy. "Disagreements about Justice," *Pacific Philosophical Quarterly* 75 (1994): 372–87. Reprinted with the permission of Basil Blackwell.

Scheffler, Samuel. "The Appeal of Political Liberalism," *Ethics* 105 (1994): 4–22. Reprinted with the permission of the University of Chicago Press.

Baier, Kurt. "Justice and the Aims of Political Philosophy," *Ethics* 99 (1989): 771–90. Reprinted with the permission of the University of Chicago Press.

Raz, Joseph. "Facing Diversity: The Case of Epistemic Abstinence," *Philosophy and Public Affairs* 19 (1990): 3–46. Copyright 1990 by Princeton University Press. Reprinted by permission of Princeton University Press.

Hampton, Jean. "Should Political Philosophy Be Done Without Metaphysics?" *Ethics* 99 (1989): 791–814. Reprinted with the permission of the University of Chicago Press.

Rorty, Richard. "The Priority of Democracy to Philosophy." In *Objectivity, Relativity and Truth* (New York: Cambridge University Press, 1991): 175–96. Reprinted with the permission of Cambridge University Press.

Weithman, Paul. "Liberalism and the Political Character of Political Philosophy." In *The Liberalism-Communitarianism Debate: Liberty and Community Values*, edited by C.F. Delaney (Maryland: Rowman and Littlefield, 1994): 189–211. Reprinted with the permission of Rowman and Littlefield Publishers Inc.

Greenawalt, Kent. "On Public Reason," *Chicago-Kent Law Review* 69 (1994): 669–89. Reprinted with the permission of the Chicago-Kent College of Law. This article is drawn from a chapter in his book *Private Consciences and Public Reasons* (Oxford University Press, 1995).

Hollenbach, David. "Contexts of the Political Role of Religion: Civil Society and Culture," *San Diego Law Review* 30 (1993): 877–901. Reprinted with the permission of the *San Diego Law Review*.

Young, Iris M. "Toward a Critical Theory of Justice," *Social Theory and Practice* 7 (1981): 279–302. Reprinted with the permission of *Social Theory and Practice*. Copyright 1981.

McCarthy, Thomas. "Kantian Constructivism and Reconstructivism: Rawls and Habermas in Dialogue," *Ethics* 105 (1994): 44–63. Reprinted with the permission of the University of Chicago Press.

Habermas, Jürgen. "Reconciliation Through the Public Use of Reason: Remarks on John Rawls's Political Liberalism," *Journal of Philosophy* 92 (1995): 109–31. Reprinted with the permission of the Journal of Philosophy, Inc., Columbia University, and the author.